Praise for *Older Jews and the Holocaust*

"An essential and original work that broadens the scope of Holocaust scholarship. By foregrounding age as a crucial category of analysis, the editors and contributors illuminate new dimensions of persecution, survival, fate, and memory."

—Michael Newman, chief executive, Association of Jewish Refugees

"This original and richly varied collection of essays makes important contributions both to Holocaust studies and the historiography of old age. It ranges from pre-Holocaust and postwar care institutions to wartime experiences of survivors and previously under-appreciated stories of older refugees and displaced persons scattered across the globe."

—David G. Troyansky, professor of history,
Brooklyn College and the Graduate Center, CUNY

"What did it mean to be old in the Holocaust? In offering answers to this question, this volume offers a plethora of surprising, unsentimental, and innovative insights into the history of the Shoah. The authors reveal our preconceptions, invite us to think inclusively, and present bold new visions of victims' agency and powerlessness as well as global dimensions of the genocide."

—Anna Hájková, author of *The Last Ghetto: An Everyday History of Theresienstadt*

"This is a groundbreaking volume, wholly original, thoughtfully conceived, and brilliantly executed. The editors' elegant introduction frames the contributions by top-notch scholars whose chapters engage key aspects of the history of older Jews during and after the Holocaust. Each offers a fresh lens on this many-faceted experience, opening doors no one even knew were there."

—Debórah Dwork, author of *Saints and Liars: The Story of Americans Who Saved Refugees from the Nazis*

Older Jews and the Holocaust

OLDER JEWS *and the* HOLOCAUST

Persecution, Displacement, and Survival

EDITED BY
CHRISTINE SCHMIDT,
ELIZABETH ANTHONY,
AND JOANNA SLIWA

Wayne State University Press
Detroit

ISBN 9780814352052 (paperback)
ISBN 9780814352045 (hardcover)
ISBN 9780814352069 (ebook)

Library of Congress Control Number: 2025947128

On cover: Close-up portrait of an elderly Jewish survivor in France [perhaps taken in an OSE home]. United States Holocaust Memorial Museum, courtesy of Andre Limot, ca. 1946–48. Cover design by Ashley Muehlbauer.

Published in association with the United States Holocaust Memorial Museum

This book is published in association with the United States Holocaust Memorial Museum's Jack, Joseph and Morton Mandel Center, whose mission is to ensure the long-term growth and vitality of Holocaust Studies. The opinions expressed in this publication represent those of the author, and are not endorsed by the Museum or the Mandel Center.

With assistance from the Conference on Jewish Material Claims Against Germany

Supported by the German Federal Ministry of Finance

Funded by:

Wayne State University Press rests on Waawiyaataanong, also referred to as Detroit, the ancestral and contemporary homeland of the Three Fires Confederacy. These sovereign lands were granted by the Ojibwe, Odawa, Potawatomi, and Wyandot Nations, in 1807, through the Treaty of Detroit. Wayne State University Press affirms Indigenous sovereignty and honors all tribes with a connection to Detroit. With our Native neighbors, the press works to advance educational equity and promote a better future for the earth and all people.

Wayne State University Press
Leonard N. Simons Building
4809 Woodward Avenue
Detroit, Michigan 48201-1309

Visit us online at wsupress.wayne.edu.

CONTENTS

ACKNOWLEDGMENTS

This volume represents several years of collaborative work, and the editors are deeply grateful to all of the contributors for their painstaking research and commitment to the project, as well as their ongoing dialogue and cooperation throughout the lengthy review process. Our thanks go to Sandra Korn and their colleagues at Wayne State University Press, including Stephanie Williams, Traci Cothran, Kelsey Giffin, Emily Gauronskas, and Carrie Teefey, for their enthusiastic support of this project. We are grateful, too, to Amy Pattullo for her careful copyediting, and Daniela Blei for supporting us with indexing, as well as Maciek Zabierowski and Academic Language Experts for their translation services. We are indebted to Debórah Dwork for her enduring friendship, for championing the book from its inception, as well as the editors' cooperation, which saw a happy reunion of "Clarkies" across time and space. We are also grateful to Atina Grossmann, Anna Hájková, and Marion Kaplan for their feedback and support when we first discussed the idea for the book with them. The editors thank Laura Foster, Annie Martin, Nancy Hartman, and Lisa Leff at the United States Holocaust Memorial Museum and Wesley Fisher and Hannah Rosenbaum from the Conference on Jewish Material Claims Against Germany (Claims Conference) for their guidance and encouragement, as well as Wiener Holocaust Library colleagues Toby Simpson, Barbara Warnock, and Jenny Rofe-Radcliffe for their commitment to this project. We also thank the anonymous reviewers who helped improve the manuscript. We are grateful to the archives, libraries, private donors, and other repositories—and the archivists, librarians, and other custodians who care for the collections—that have made the research presented in this volume possible through countless hours of preserving, cataloging, and making collections accessible. Finally, we gratefully acknowledge the generous support of the Claims Conference; the Wiener Holocaust Library; the US Holocaust Memorial Museum; the Ernest Hecht Charitable Foundation;

the Remembrance, Responsibility, and Future Foundation, or EVZ; and the German Federal Ministry of Finance.

We are grateful for opportunities to share our and the volume contributors' ongoing research and findings at the *Older Jews and the Holocaust* symposium held at the US Holocaust Memorial Museum (September 2024), the Lessons and Legacies International Conference on the Holocaust at Claremont McKenna College and the University of Southern California (November 2024), and the American Historical Association Conference (January 2025), among other events. The work on this volume inspired a workshop on the topic for doctoral candidates and early career researchers at the Wiener Holocaust Library in December 2024, hosted by the Holocaust and Genocide Research Partnership (an initiative of the Wiener Holocaust Library and the Holocaust Research Institute, Royal Holloway, University of London).

Throughout the work on this volume, we were cheered on by our family members and friends. Christine thanks especially Henry (Hank) Greenspan and participants in his testimony interpretation workshop, as well as Ben Barkow, Leah Sidebotham, Dan Stone, and Madeline White for their encouragement and feedback—and Gábor Kádár and Nora Kádár, for their continued support and enthusiasm. Betsy is grateful to her colleagues Jocelyn Barrett-Gonzales, Jenna Galberg, and Leah Wolfson for their thoughtful engagement and invaluable contributions across so many aspects of this project. She also appreciates Maya Falb for her dedicated research assistance and Roland Engel for his unflagging confidence and encouragement. A conversation with her Claims Conference colleague Chen Yurista inspired Joanna to pursue this project. She is grateful to Lukasz Sliwa and Betsy Anthony for commenting on her text when she first started working on the topic in 2019, and to Karol Maźnicki for his unwavering support.

INTRODUCTION

Christine Schmidt, Elizabeth Anthony, and Joanna Sliwa

In a photograph held by the United States Holocaust Memorial Museum (USHMM), an older woman with spectacles and white hair reclines calmly against a lace-adorned pillow, chin in delicately age-lined hand, looking off camera as light floods her room from above.[1] This empathetic portrait of a Jewish survivor, dated between 1946 and 1948, was taken by Walter Limot (né Lichtenstein), an accomplished still photographer in Germany's film industry who was forced to flee the Nazis. The Jewish international aid organization, Oeuvre de Secours aux Enfants (OSE), hired Limot after the war to photograph its residences, among other subjects. This image of an unnamed older woman, likely taken in France, is among a collection of Limot's work donated to the USHMM by his son, Andre, in 2005.[2] Most of the Photo Limot studio's images, particularly in OSE homes, feature children and their caregivers, but this evocative portrait, found on the cover of this volume, is one of the few images singularly focused on a visibly older person in the collection. The subject is described as "an elderly Jewish survivor in France," sparse archival shorthand based on the donor's identification that suggests we know nothing else about her. Who was she? What was she thinking and doing when this photograph was taken? How did she survive? What did her future hold? And how and why did Limot photograph her? If the children photographed likely represented hope for the rebirth of a future Jewish world in the aftermath of the destruction of the Holocaust, what did rare images of elderly Jewish survivors represent? These kinds of questions—and the imperfect evidence from which they arise—drive the present volume.

Older Jews and the Holocaust aims, for the first time in a single volume, to center the marginalized experiences of older Jews before, during, and after the Holocaust. While many of the patterns of persecution of older Jews mirror those of Jews of all ages, there were important differences and particularities that affected their experiences and fates because of their age, and their age often impacted their actions. Understanding the choices and processes that shaped the lives of older Jews offers a new lens onto daily life during the Holocaust and genocide more broadly. We often hear that during the Holocaust, children and the elderly were among the most vulnerable populations specifically targeted for murder by the Nazis and their collaborators. Yet while there is a thriving scholarship, along with literature, film, exhibitions, and other representations of children in Holocaust studies, albeit only since the 1990s, there is still little focused attention on elderly Jewish women and men, beyond noting their vulnerability and murder.[3] Hope, which often undergirds a focus on children, seems a more durable concept in the historiography and public memory of the Holocaust than devastation and despair, commonly associated with the fate of the elderly.

This volume reaches beyond this standard narrative to recover the experiences and responses of older Jewish people as complex, multifaceted human beings. Rather than a comprehensive monograph, the volume takes a pulse on new avenues of research in diverse time periods, geographies, and contexts. It shines a light on underused archival evidence to bring fresh perspectives on age and aging during the Holocaust period, extending the boundaries of our understanding of the Holocaust—both beyond Europe and beyond the period between 1933 and 1945. Taking age as a starting point, the authors help us understand continuities and discontinuities with older Jews' prewar lives, their oppression before the war and choice to flee or stay, their migration to points beyond Europe, their murder under the Nazis and accomplices, and their struggles into the postwar period, if they survived. As this volume shows, age intersected with a host of other factors, such as gender, sexuality, culture, social class, and ethnicity, illuminating a complex, rich picture of older Jews' lives and highlighting their self-perceptions, responses, identity, and agency as historical actors. Because they were the primary population targeted for genocide by the Nazis, Jews are the focus of this volume, yet because others were also targeted—political opponents, Roma and Sinti, people with disabilities, and those deemed "asocial" or "racially inferior"—the questions explored in these chapters usefully apply to older people in other victimized groups of the period as well as to other cases of genocide.

A key issue each chapter discusses is how to define "the elderly" or "older": What age is considered elderly? As scholar Xin Tong, a contributor to this volume, notes, "the World Health Organization defines individuals aged sixty and above as older adults. However, different periods, countries, and cultural contexts have varied understandings of what constitutes an elderly person, distinguishing between birth age, biological age, psychological age, and social age. In the twentieth century, various factors influenced life expectancy. In 1930, the life expectancy at birth for American men was fifty-eight years and for women sixty-two years. At that time, the average life expectancy in China was less than forty years. When the Nazis came to power, the life expectancy for German men in 1934 was 59.9 years. Therefore, there is no strict, uniform, and unequivocal definition" of what constitutes "elderly."[4] While most chapters deal with Jews aged at least fifty, *Older Jews and the Holocaust* tackles age as a multilayered category of analysis that includes not only strict chronology but also self-understanding and contemporary social constructs on age, aging, and older people, which were and are in flux. These included the imposition by the Nazis of a differential standard of care for aging populations, distinguishing between so-called Aryans and Jews, the latter deemed expendable, and which, in different carceral contexts, distinguished those who were and were not to be forced into labor duties.[5] While fifty or even forty-five years of age is quite far from today's understanding of what constitutes old age, age is defined in these chapters through relational and contextual factors, such as state pension eligibility and retirement age; marital relationships and widowhood; child-bearing, child-rearing, and the age of one's children; as well as subjective notions of appearance and physical ability, which varied according to the context.[6] Moreover, Jewish persecutees did not age alone, and the chapters analyze how concepts of aging were defined in relation to how others—spouses, families, relief workers, civil servants, and organizations and institutions—responded to aging and deaths of older people. The malleability of the concept of age relates to decisions we have made about appropriate terminology, particularly as the authors in this volume have problematized the application of modern terms to the past. Thus we use terms like "old," "older people," and "elderly" interchangeably, but with a clear assumption of the variable, constructed nature of the concept of age in different and changing contexts before and immediately after the war.[7]

Centering a marginalized group such as older people within the largely silent scholarship is an act of recovery, and not an easy one at that. As we, the editors, began to solicit chapters for the volume, we were met with undeniable interest but some doubtful or hesitant responses, particularly as the bedrock of historical research—sources—seemed too scant for some prospective authors to write much on older Jews within their areas of specialty. Their particular vulnerability make the elderly difficult to find in the archival record.[8] The lack of sources is a challenge noted by most contributors to this volume, but the authors have retrieved the voices, perspectives, and experiences of older Jews in oblique ways, reading against the grain and borrowing anthropological and cultural history concepts and methods practiced by those who have come before us in feminist, indigenous, Black, postcolonial, and queer studies.[9] Notwithstanding a lack of nuanced representation of older people in Holocaust historiography, it would be a disservice to ignore the recent pathbreaking contributions to scholarship in Holocaust studies that have begun to reorient our focus to the nuances of elderly Jews' experiences, including significant contributions by Bettina Brandt, Anna Hájková, Wolf Gruner, Elizabeth Strauss, Dan Stone, Melissa Jane Taylor, as well as a recent two-volume special issue of *Yad Vashem Studies*.[10] The chapters in this volume, therefore, join an emerging, critical historical dialogue on age and aging and the Holocaust, building on these foundational layers with new research and the reconsideration of existing sources.

It is worth dwelling a bit longer on why we have had, until recently, significant gaps in our knowledge about older Jews during the Holocaust period. Although there is a tremendous amount of literature focused on the impact of the Holocaust on the aging process of survivors, particularly within the fields of medicine, gerontology, and psychology, older Jews have been largely ignored in the historiography beyond references to their decimation.[11] This has been dictated in part by their mortality rate: like children, only a small number of elderly survived. At the end of World War II, most survivors were indeed young, since the chances for older Jews of surviving the physical and psychological onslaught of the Holocaust were slim. Older Jewish relatives were in many cases left behind when younger family members managed to flee, either due to their ill health or because they could not conceive of starting their lives over elsewhere in advanced age. (At the same time, chapters in this volume [for example, Schmidt, Tong, Hanrahan] that focus on elderly refugees challenge this notion and encourage further study on the challenges of adaptation to new countries, especially in comparison to younger refugees.) Moreover, older Jews were less likely to survive the physical strains of deportation, ghettoization, the so-called death marches toward the end of the war, and the extreme conditions that produced rampant starvation, disease, ill-treatment, and sheer brutality. Due to National Socialist ideas about the victims' "usefulness," they were the focus of targeted campaigns to cull the populations of camps and ghettos, with both the children and elderly selected first for deportation and death over those physically able to work, or the elderly deprived of food rations so that their younger family members could survive.[12]

The fates of elderly Jews during the Holocaust are woven to some extent into narratives of survival strategies. Although more recent studies have complicated the pictures drawn by early chroniclers of the Holocaust, some survivor historians, such as H. G. Adler and Rachel Auerbach, did provide space in their work to describe the struggles and experiences of older Jews in Theresienstadt and Warsaw, respectively.[13] Holocaust scholar Nechama Tec examined a Jewish partisan unit in what is today Belarus that, along with young men, accepted and accommodated children, women, and older people, and resulted in the survival of more than a thousand Jews.[14] Historian Eliyana Adler has engaged with the history of more than two hundred thousand Polish Jews, some of them elderly, who fled the Nazis to the Soviet interior. The survivors of this group comprised approximately 70 percent of those who returned to Poland.[15] Historian Michael Geheran (also a contributor to this volume) has analyzed elderly Austrian and German Jewish veterans of World War I and the preferential treatment, if temporary, they received under the Nazis, or how they otherwise managed to survive due to their status.[16] Older people also emerge in multifaceted ways in scholarship focused on certain types of source evidence, such as in historian Alexandra Garbarini's work on diaries, which sensitively grapples with the writing of older adults.[17]

The scholarship has pointed to intersections between age and gender as well as ethnicity and culture to better illuminate the particular circumstances that impacted older Jews and their responses. Older people, in some contexts, and especially men, were the least likely to survive the Holocaust. Nazi race policies designated Jews above a certain age as useless for the purposes of performing forced labor. For example, in fall 1939, sixty was the cutoff age for forced laborers in the General Government (the part of central Poland occupied by but not incorporated into Germany). Similarly, the German authorities considered older people in ghettos to be disposable, and Jewish leadership often reacted to this with the sacrifice of elderly inmates for the sake of protecting younger ghetto residents. In the ghetto in Łódź, a Polish city annexed to Germany, the Jewish elder of the ghetto (here, the use of "elder" in his title reflected status in addition to age) urged the ghetto population in September 1942 to deliver children and older people for deportation so that the working Jews could continue to prove their usefulness to the German authorities and thus possibly survive. During actions in ghettos, Jews who looked older or belonged to the group targeted for immediate death or shipment to a killing center were singled out. Contrary to an idealized view of social deference, the elderly did not constitute a protected group even within the Jewish ghetto society, as historian Anna Hájková has illuminated.[18] Age affected communal relations, particularly in extremis, but also exerted influence on the decisions of family members. In a now-classic study, historian Marion A. Kaplan has examined how both gender and age affected Jews' decisions to emigrate from Germany in the early years of Nazi rule.[19]

Although a focus on the postwar period is relatively recent in Holocaust studies, analyses of Jewish survivors who returned to their home countries, as well as those focused on Jews who languished in displaced persons' (DP) camps before their emigration, present other avenues to glean information about the perspectives, wishes, and experiences of the exceptional older Jews who survived. Historian Michael Brenner has discussed examples of elderly survivors among returnees and DPs in postwar Germany, as well as the creation of Jewish nursing homes, giving some useful age distribution statistics.[20] Historian Atina Grossmann has noted the prevalence of elderly among Jews left alive in Germany after the war, a demographic diametrically opposite to that seen in DP camps.[21] Historian Elizabeth Anthony has also provided an in-depth study of a Jewish nursing home in postwar Vienna, which also informs part of her contribution to this volume.[22] To date, however, no comprehensive monograph on the experiences of elderly survivors has been published.[23]

What is revealed by examining the lives and fates of older Jewish persecutees? How does this volume not only recover their experiences and perspectives but move the field forward? What do these chapters tell us about experiences of age in relation to genocidal violence? The chapters in this book make clear a vast diversity of circumstance and experience, which underscores the need to conduct further research on this neglected group, during the Holocaust and in the history of genocide more generally. The volume shows that intergenerational relations were incredibly important; older Jews did not live in a bubble but were intrinsically linked to other age groups, such as children, and their fates were often linked. This volume makes an important case for future research that incorporates deeper engagement with the relational aspects of age as a category of analysis concerning older and younger Jewish victims, as well as with regard to Nazi policy and Jewish responses to the onslaught. The chapters also shed new light on enduring notions of care and rehabilitation for vulnerable populations, of urgent concern in contemporary situations of humanitarian crisis, mass atrocity, and genocide, and relate to new research on divisive concepts of rejuvenation and the politics of aging.[24] The volume provides a foundation for establishing age and its relational aspects as a necessary and important category of analysis within Holocaust and genocide studies and aims to foster sensitivity with and inclusion of the concept of age, so that it will become a matter of course to include it in the academic study of *any* mass atrocity or genocide. And it does so with a view to bringing this growing body of work to wider attention.

Each chapter of *Older Jews and the Holocaust* speaks from a different scholarly perspective on the experiences of elderly Jews and the individuals and institutions around them before, during, and after the Holocaust. Dan Stone's broadly cast chapter sets the stage for the volume by examining pre–World War II continuities of perspective, emphasizing that the Holocaust subverted twentieth-century notions of progress and modernity. Stone argues that the brutal treatment of the elderly exemplifies Nazi ideology's attack on the Jews per se, since its attitude to the weakest in society goes to the heart of what Nazism was all about. Drawing on the work of philosopher Theodor Adorno, his chapter argues that the murder of the elderly signified a key point in overturning nineteenth-century notions of progress and legal freedoms and offers a chilling reminder of the legacies of genocide where the most vulnerable are targeted.

To better understand the interwar period and the social and political factors that shaped the experiences of older Jews during the war, Marek

Tuszewicki's chapter examines the operation of Jewish nursing homes in interwar Poland. He unveils the intricate entanglements between local governments and Jewish religious communities in relation to the development of the pension system in the Second Republic, which had not fully been established before 1939. His findings reveal the Jewish minority's vulnerability in terms of civil rights, but his study orients us to look closely at the agency of older Jews: he examines how Jewish actors fought to change the circumstances and to provide social security for elderly Jews in their communities.

Age is a key determinant in analyzing forced migration during the Holocaust period, and some older Jews found refuge outside of Europe. Niamh Hanrahan's chapter analyzes the circumstances of flight for two older Jewish women. Based on scant evidence that documented their journey, her chapter considers the trajectories available to older German Jews through the case of mother and daughter Antonia Jacoby and Fanny Behrendt, who fled from Germany to Japan. Hanrahan's chapter examines the relationship of gender and class to age and how these frames impacted the women's transnational migration and their perceptions of their flight and exile. Building on the theme of global perspectives on the experiences of the elderly, Xin Tong's chapter examines case studies of culturally elite older German Jewish refugees in China who sometimes fled with their families. Using both Western and Chinese sources, Tong reconsiders the historiography and memory of Jewish exile in China through the prism of age. Her chapter reveals that the study and public memory of Jewish exile in Shanghai has evolved into a shared memory between East and West, both global and local, and has achieved a remarkable dialogue that has crossed cultures, ethnic groups, and social groups to advance an understanding of common humanity. Both chapters reinforce that the forced migration and exile of older Jewish refugees cannot be studied in a vacuum since they involved a multitude of forces and actors that shaped migrants' experiences.

Furthering the themes of flight, documentation, and self-perception, Christine Schmidt's chapter on Nelly Wolffheim, a feminist specialist in Freudian-based psychoanalytic pedagogy who fled Nazi Germany for Britain in 1939 at the age of sixty, examines how an older Jewish refugee woman worked as an early chronicler and advocate in exile for recording and understanding the experiences of older people during and immediately after the war. Wolffheim recorded twenty-two interviews for the Wiener

Library in London in the 1950s, in which she studied and amplified the experiences of middle-class Jewish refugees and survivors—in particular the voices of older women. Wolffheim thus subverted the notion that elderly persecutees of Nazism faded into anonymity and uselessness. The theme of gender is further analyzed in Michael Geheran's chapter, which examines German Jewish war veterans in Theresienstadt, and how their experience in the Kaiser's military shaped their self-perceptions and those of fellow ghetto inhabitants. Using veterans' own writing and testimony, Geheran's chapter emphasizes the intersection of gender and cultural values to understand how older German Jewish veteran men coped with their experiences of confinement, loss, brutality, and other hardships in the Theresienstadt ghetto. He shows how older Jewish men adapted to their circumstances. Both Schmidt's and Geheran's chapters restore agency and voice to historical actors who have not been treated in the literature.

The authors necessarily draw on interdisciplinary, mixed methods to shed light on the experiences of older Jews. Shifting focus from German Jewish experiences and drawing on anthropology and psychology to illuminate the history of emotions, Maria Ferenc and Katarzyna Person's chapter takes a microhistorical approach to the fate of older survivors of the first liquidation action of the Warsaw ghetto in the summer of 1942 and examines age-related "survivors' guilt" expressed after the war. The authors analyze how the surviving group felt, and how their pervasive sense of burden while in hiding contributed to their impressions of the chances for survival of their families. Ferenc and Person demonstrate how these anxieties were strengthened by social definitions—and expectations—of the elderly and the perceived hierarchies of survivors after the war.

Lidia Zessin-Jurek and Katharina Friedla's chapter examines the demographic changes to and experiences of a group of older Polish Jewish survivors who fled to and were displaced during the war in the Soviet Union. Building on quantitative framing, the chapter analyzes their forced migration and deportation within the Gulag system and how the elderly of this migrant population fared under such brutal circumstances. Zessin-Jurek and Friedla analyze the Soviet experience of elderly Polish Jews through accounts mainly by their younger relatives who accompanied them, and which were recorded immediately after the war and years later.

The volume not only examines prewar and wartime continuities and breaks, but also adds to the growing literature on the immediate postwar period, particularly regarding the neglect and care of older survivors and the agency of those who experienced humanitarian interventions. Roxy Moore's chapter homes in on postwar humanitarian photography, where we see represented starkly the exceptional survival of elderly Jews. The images were taken for the Jewish Committee for Relief Abroad (JCRA), also known by the name of its operational arm, the Jewish Relief Unit (JRU), an Anglo-Jewish aid organization founded in 1943 to offer aid to DPs. Moore's chapter uses photography as a lens through which to explore both the complexities of life for older Jews in the aftermath of World War II and the diversity of Anglo-Jewish care and support delivered to them in the British occupation zone of postwar Germany. Moore argues that, although the JRU drew on both traditional Jewish cultural conceptions of elder care and theories of modern humanitarianism, representations of its work were often driven by conflicting fundraising considerations. Kierra Crago-Schneider's chapter shifts the focus on older DPs to the US-occupied zone of Germany. Extricating vulnerable older Jewish DPs from the challenging category of the "hardcore," where they were most often lumped (and largely forgotten), her chapter examines older survivors who had been displaced in Germany and China and who ended up in the US-occupied zone, as well as those who had migrated to Mandate Palestine and returned to Germany. She argues that the policies in the US zone impacted survivors and the choices they made and reveals how the "hardcore" advocated for their futures.

Early forms of organizational care for older Jewish survivors after the Holocaust have helped shape the work of advocacy and assistance for older adults ever since. Joanna Sliwa's chapter analyzes the early initiatives of the Conference on Jewish Material Claims Against Germany (Claims Conference), which was created in 1951, and its member organization, the American Jewish Joint Distribution Committee (JDC), to develop programs for elderly survivors from 1954 to 1960. She traces the shifts in care for older survivors as they were influenced by the medical needs of elderly Jews, political and social changes, economic factors, population movements, and reparation and compensation programs in Belgium, the Netherlands, Italy, and Yugoslavia. Similarly, Anat Kutner's chapter examines the circumstances for older Jewish survivors in the young State of Israel, particularly after it relaxed immigration restrictions that had previously barred older Jews and other vulnerable people under the British Mandate.

The new immigration rules therefore included many elderly Holocaust survivors, who carried the psychological and physical scars of their experiences during World War II. She traces how JDC responded to these needs and how the changing circumstances for older survivors in Israel, in turn, reshaped the work of JDC for years to follow.

Through an analytical lens focused on the postwar lives of survivors, we can glean a deeper understanding of the continuities and breaks to previous social structures and hierarchies during the Holocaust. Elizabeth Anthony's chapter examines the particularities that enabled many older Viennese Jews to survive and to return to postwar Vienna. The postwar Jewish community in Vienna was disproportionately older and included a surprising number of elderly concentration camp survivors. Her chapter examines the postwar lives of those who had managed to remain alive in Vienna, sometimes in hiding, as well as returnees, and how their protected circumstances and a confluence of a variety of factors, including the destination of their deportation, enabled them to survive. Anthony points to the extremely difficult wartime work of the Israelitische Kultusgemeinde Wien (IKG, or Viennese Jewish Community), which, stripped of resources itself, aimed to support the emigration of younger Jews and ameliorate the impoverishment of the older Viennese Jewish population, as well as their postwar efforts to set up *KZ Rückkehrerheime* (homes for concentration camp returnees). Finally, Borbála Klacsmann's chapter uses postwar compensation files to analyze the experiences of older Hungarian Jews during and after the war. Recovering a demographic that appears only sporadically in the literature on the Holocaust in Hungary, Klacsmann examines the indemnification, as well as the wartime and postwar experiences of elderly survivors in three time periods: the immediate postwar years, early socialism, and the 1960s–70s. She demonstrates how Hungarian Jewish survivors negotiated their postwar lives over time, including restitution, amid government-imposed challenges. Her study demonstrates the precariousness of older and aging survivors, particularly as they were compensated unevenly or not at all, under changing political circumstances.

In conclusion, the chapters in this volume add texture and complicate our understanding of the experiences of older people targeted as Jews for persecution and murder by the Nazis and their allies during the Holocaust period. As we, the editors, solicited the contributions, we were emerging into a postpandemic society, where the elderly were often figured as expendable in the changing global Covid-related discourse and protective measures enacted around the world. And as we put the final touches on the manuscript, debates about the viability (or not) of US presidential candidates due to their age were raging. This book and the complexities presented by each chapter offer a counterargument to subtle and overt ageism, which may have also contributed to neglect of this demographic in Holocaust historiography and public memory thus far. Rather than presenting an idealized portrait of "the elderly" as a homogenous group worthy of unquestioning reverence, the book examines their perceptions, identities, and choices in nuanced ways. It recovers and centers the voices and perspectives of the aged. The volume prompts additional questions not yet covered in the chapters, and which are ripe for further analysis: for example, what is the relationship of age to Jews who took part in resistance, joined partisan movements, went into hiding, or escaped ghettos and camps? How did age influence the decision-making processes of members of the Nazi-appointed Jewish councils? How did age dynamics influence postwar Jewish communities and their leadership, as well as the political decision-making of the surviving remnant in DP camps? Drawing upon a wealth of archival records, much of which has now been digitized (such as the JDC Archives), scholars are better equipped to tackle the question of numbers of older Jewish survivors in various countries. This is therefore not the definitive publication of research on older people—rather, it should serve as an important catalyst for future research, education, and memory on the fates of older people during the Holocaust and during genocides past and present.[25]

Notes

1 "Close-up portrait of an elderly Jewish survivor in France [perhaps taken in an OSE home]," United States Holocaust Memorial Museum (USHMM), courtesy of Andre Limot, ca. 1946–48, photograph 05248. The image is also held in the JDC Archives, but there is a discrepancy: here, the image is located in Czechoslovakia, ca. 1947: "Elderly woman resident of Jewish home for the aged supported by JDC," NY_07449. Based on the provenance of the Limot collection held by the USHMM, the USHMM's description seems to be more accurate.

2 Andre Limot OSE Home Collection, USHMM 2005.396.

3 The turn in Holocaust studies to examine Jewish children's experiences began in earnest in the 1990s. It stemmed from the efforts of child survivors and scholars, among others. The first Hidden Child Conference, in New York City in 1991, allowed child survivors and their Holocaust experiences to be recognized internationally. And historian Debórah Dwork's trailblazing study, *Children with a Star: Jewish Youth in Nazi Europe* (Yale University Press, 1991), offered a comprehensive view of how Jewish children lived and died during the Holocaust and established oral histories of child survivors as a legitimate source of historical research.

4 See chapter 4.

5 See, for example, Dan Stone, "'Somehow the Pathetic Dumb Suffering of These Elderly People Moves Me More Than Anything': Caring for Elderly Holocaust Survivors in the Immediate Postwar Years," *Holocaust and Genocide Studies* 32, no. 3 (Winter 2018): 384–403, here 386; and Anna Hájková, "Speculations About German Jews: Elderly People from Germany in the Theresienstadt Ghetto," *Yad Vashem Studies* 50, no. 2 (2022): 55–84, who discusses the upper age range limit for forced labor in Theresienstadt and its relationship to defining old age. Originally published as "Mutmaßungen über deutsche Juden: Alte Menschen aus Deutschland im Theresienstädter Ghetto," in *Alltag im Holocaust: Jüdisches Leben im Großdeutschen Reich 1941–1945*, ed. Andrea Löw, Doris L. Bergen, and Anna Hájková (Oldenbourg, 2013), 179–98.

6 The World Health Organization today defines those aged sixty and above as older adults: World Health Organization, accessed Aug. 24, 2024, www.who.int/health-topics/ageing#tab=tab_1.

7 The volume follows Elizabeth Strauss's exhortation to move beyond "precise, universal definitions" that are sometimes implicitly inflected with National Socialist ideology that classified Jewish victims as "useful" or "useless." See Elizabeth C. Strauss, "'This Rug, Handmade by a Resident of the Old Age Home, Should Serve as Evidence of the Willingness and Ability of Elderly People to Work': Elderly Survival Strategies in the Łódź Ghetto," *Holocaust and Genocide Studies* 35, no. 3 (Winter 2021): 424–44 (426).

8 The notion of vulnerability is contested but for a productive engagement of "vulnerability" in the archive that engages with Judith Butler's work, see Malin Thor Tureby, "'No, I Never Thought We Were Different': Vulnerability, Descriptive Discourses and Agency in the Archive," in *From Dust*

to Dawn: Archival Studies After the Archival Turn, ed. Ann Öhrberg et al. (Uppsala Rhetorical Studies, 2022), 333–58.

9 Select references to methodological inspirations include E. P. Thompson, *The Making of the English Working Class* (Gollancz, 1963, 1968); Michel-Rolph Trouillot, *Silencing the Past: Power and the Production of History* (Beacon Press, 1995); and Caroline Dodds Pennock, *On Savage Shores: How Indigenous Americans Discovered Europe* (Orion: 2023).

10 See, *inter alia*, Bettina Brandt, "Nelly and Trudie: Deciphering a Transatlantic Family Holocaust Correspondence" in *On Being Adjacent to Historical Violence*, ed. Irene Kacandes (Walter de Gruyter GmbH, 2021), 315–22; Elizabeth C. Strauss, "'Everything Is Old': National Socialism and the Weathering of the Jews of Łódź," *Genealogy* 8 (2024): 1–13 and Strauss, "'This Rug'"; Melissa Jane Taylor, "Family Matters: The Emigration of Elderly Jews from Vienna to the United States, 1938–1941," *Journal of Social History* 45, no. 1 (2011): 238–60; Stone, "Caring for Elderly Holocaust Survivors"; Wolf Gruner, "'It Cries to Heaven!' Elderly Jews and Their Individual Resistance to Nazi Persecution in Germany," *Yad Vashem Studies* 50, no. 2 (2022); Anna Hájková, "Speculations About German Jews," *Yad Vashem Studies* 50, no. 2 (2022). The special issue, *Yad Vashem Studies* 50, nos. 1–2, focused on elderly Jews during the Holocaust and includes essays by Michael A Meyer, Emmanuelle Moscovitz, Beth B. Cohen, Beate Kosmala, and Michaela Raggam-Blesch. Pat Thane's "Social Histories of Old Age and Aging," *Journal of Social History* 37, no. 1 (2003): 93–11 provides a useful broader understanding of historical research using age as a category of analysis.

11 Studies focused on aging and survivors is too vast to cover here. But see, for example, Yoram Barak and Henry Szor, "Lifelong Posttraumatic Stress Disorder: Evidence from Aging Holocaust Survivors," *Dialogues in Clinical Neuroscience* 2, no. 1 (2000): 57–62; Jochanan Stressman et al., "Holocaust Survivors: Health and Longevity 70 Years Later," *Journal of the American Geriatrics Society* 71, no. 10 (2023): 3199–3207; and Paula David, "Aging Holocaust Survivors: An Evolution of Understanding," *Kavod: A Journal for Caregivers and Families* 1 (Winter 2011), kavod.claimscon.org/2010/09/aging-holocaust-survivors-an-evolution-of-understanding/, for a useful survey of relevant studies in medicine, social work, and gerontology.

12 Strauss, "'This Rug,'" 425; Hájková, "Speculations About German Jews," 57.

13 See, for example, H. G. Adler, *Theresienstadt 1941–1945: Das Antlitz einer Zwangsgemeinschaft* (Mohr Siebebeck, 1955); Rachel Auerbach, "Yizkor,

1943," in *The Literature of Destruction: Jewish Responses to Catastrophe*, ed. David G. Roskies (Jewish Publication Society of America, 1989), 459–64; and Rachel Auerbach, "The Librarians," trans. Seymour Levitan, *Pakn-Treger: Magazine of the Yiddish Book Center*, (Summer 2017/5777), www.yiddishbookcenter.org/language-literature-culture/pakn-treger/2017-pakn-treger-translation-issue/librarians.

14 Nechama Tec, *Defiance: The Bielski Partisans: The Story of the Largest Armed Rescue of Jews During World War II* (Oxford University Press, 1993).

15 Eliyana Adler, *Survival on the Margins: Polish Jewish Refugees in the Wartime Soviet Union* (Harvard University Press, 2020).

16 Michael Geheran, *Comrades Betrayed: Jewish World War I Veterans Under Hitler* (Cornell University Press, 2020).

17 Alexandra Garbarini, *Numbered Days: Diaries and the Holocaust* (Yale University Press, 2006).

18 Anna Hájková, *The Last Ghetto: An Everyday History of Theresienstadt* (Oxford University Press, 2020).

19 Marion A. Kaplan, *Between Dignity and Despair: Jewish Life in Nazi Germany* (Oxford University Press, 1998).

20 Michael Brenner, *After the Holocaust: Rebuilding Jewish Lives in Postwar Germany*, trans. Barbara Harshav (Princeton University Press, 1997).

21 Atina Grossmann, *Jews, Germans, and Allies: Close Encounters in Occupied Germany* (Princeton University Press, 2007).

22 Elizabeth Anthony, *The Compromise of Return: Viennese Jews After the Holocaust* (Wayne State University Press, 2021).

23 Research on the topic includes Elizabeth C. Strauss, "'Cast Me Not Off in My Time of Old Age . . .': The Aged and Aging in the Łódź Ghetto, 1939–1944" (PhD diss., University of Notre Dame, 2013) and Janika Raisch, "Agency in the Warsaw Ghetto: An Intersectional Analysis of Daily Life, Survival, and Death of Elderly Jews" (master's thesis, Uppsala University, 2022).

24 See, for example, Mischa Honeck, *No Country for Old Age: America's War on Aging from Valley Forge to Silicon Valley* (University of North Carolina Press, 2025) and James Chappell, *Golden Years: How Americans Invented and Reinvented Old Age* (Basic Books, 2024).

25 A temporary exhibition, Older Jews and the Holocaust, is planned for the Wiener Holocaust Library in autumn 2025–spring 2026.

1

WHEN THE NINETEENTH CENTURY ENDED FOR JEWS

The Elderly and the Holocaust

Dan Stone

> While indeed progress from the slingshot to the megaton bomb may well amount to satanic laughter, in the age of the bomb a condition can be envisaged for the first time in which violence might vanish altogether.
>
> —T. W. Adorno[1]

Introduction

In his remarkable book *The Black Seasons*, Michał Głowiński refers at one point to his maternal grandparents' unlikely survival as "one of the miracles of the occupation years." He goes on to offer what he calls a "digression about the fate of the elderly, who had no chance of survival during the Holocaust":

> For years I've thought of the Holocaust as a slaughter carried out against those born in the nineteenth century, an enormous mass of people shaped in that century, living by the imaginations and ideas they absorbed in that era. A slaughter of those for whom the idea of murder by industrial methods was beyond comprehension for the simple reason that it transcended the boundaries of their technological imagination. Sometimes I ask myself when the nineteenth century ended for Jews, and I think it was not at the moment it did for others, when the First World War began, but rather at

> the moment when the crematoria in Treblinka, Auschwitz, and other such places designated for genocide were set in motion.[2]

In the same way that A. J. P. Taylor famously argued that the First World War was the "unexpected climax to the railway age," so Głowiński here suggests that the killing centers were the unexpected climax to the age of technological progress.[3] If one takes Stefan Zweig's famous memoir as representative of his generation's experience, then Głowiński's argument makes sense. In a long, elegiac reflection on the achievements of the nineteenth century, Zweig writes: "People no more believed in the possibility of barbaric relapses, such as wars between the nations of Europe, than they believed in ghosts and witches; our fathers were doggedly convinced of the infallibly binding power of tolerance and conciliation. They honestly thought that divergences between nations and religious faiths would gradually flow into a sense of common humanity, so that peace and security, the greatest of goods, would come to all mankind."[4] When Zweig here talks about "people," he is of course referring primarily to the middle-class Jews of Vienna. Similarly, in his novel about the Pisan Jewish community leader Giuseppe Pardo, Silvano Arieti writes of the mostly elderly people who chose to remain in Pardo's house on the north side of the River Arno after the Germans occupied that part of the town. Following Pardo's attempt to persuade them to leave, Arieti writes of Pardo's guests:

> One by one they answered, as they had already done on many occasions. They had not noticed Pardo's special alarm. So this time they answered in their customary manner, rather slowly, and with an abundance of words—a habit that a certain class of people had retained from the period of the end of the nineteenth century and were zealously sticking to as an emblem of the glorious past. These people retained a special kind of formality not just in their manner but in particular words they chose to speak. Contrary to the way such speech would be interpreted today, this was a sign not of distance but precisely of friendship and closeness, the identification card of a group of people who wished to preserve the niceties of life.[5]

The shattering of these dreams of "the niceties of life," not to mention of unfettered and unstoppable progress began, for the Central European Jews, with the experience of World War I, which was a cataclysm shared with the general population. But the Nazi killing centers were the places where Jews' dreams of and belief in equality before the law, common citizenship, and unmolested freedom in multifaith liberal states finally came to a brutal and unequivocal end.

This chapter combines theoretical reflections on the Holocaust as "industrial genocide" and as a marker of the end of the nineteenth century.[6] A great deal has been written about World War I signaling the birth of modern warfare but, following Głowiński and Zweig, there are good reasons for arguing that for the Jews, especially the Jews of Central and Eastern Europe, the Holocaust definitively closed that era, when notions of emancipation, religious tolerance, Jewish social and political progress, and civic acceptance came crashing to an end. Using sources from before, during, and after the war by elderly Jews, postwar survivors' accounts, as well as documents from aid agencies, especially the London-based Jewish Committee for Relief Abroad, which assisted the small number of elderly survivors in the British zone of occupied Germany, I will argue that for the Nazis, the genocide of the Jews marked a revolt against the nineteenth century, understood as an age of progress.

Although the thesis of the dialectic of Enlightenment, which states (in Walter Benjamin's formulation) that there is no document of civilization which is not at the same time a document of barbarism, is well known, for the victims of the Holocaust it was a huge, traumatic shock to realize that "progress" had also contained the seeds of its own destruction. Nazism was not simply an anti-Enlightenment revolt, it was a symptom of modernity, a vision of modernity that only makes sense in the context of prevailing notions of progress and civilization.[7] Using the example of the elderly victims of the Holocaust, I show that Nazism's vision of destruction was total: in order to bring about the "Aryan" race's victory over the forces of the "international Jew," there could be no compassion even for the weakest and most vulnerable. Indeed, precisely the annihilation of the weakest constitutes the heart of Nazi thinking. This chapter offers a way of understanding the elderly victims that shows both how the elderly and those who cared for them understood what was happening as well as analyzing the perpetrators' motivations for targeting them. Above all, it argues that the annihilation of the elderly, though it has largely been overlooked given that so few old people survived, was crucial to the Nazis' project to rid Europe of its Jews, for the elderly embodied precisely those values that Nazism wanted to overturn: a sense of community, continuity, wisdom, and protection of vulnerable, revered elders; above all the Nazis regarded them as representatives of a different, soon-to-be superannuated age. Nazism was not, in Zweig's terms, a "barbaric relapse"; rather, it was one expression of modernity's ability to incubate and then to channel forms of fantasy thinking, especially at moments of major international crisis. Thus, the article does not subscribe to a simplistic rejection of "progress"; rather, following Adorno, I work on the assumption that Benjamin's slogan is "not entirely without hope," that a situation can be envisaged in which "progress would transform itself into the resistance to perpetual danger of relapse." But this would be quite different from the nineteenth-century notion of progress which instated itself, fetish-like, as totality.[8]

The Elderly in the Holocaust

The starting point for this chapter is the murder of the elderly during the Holocaust. This is something often discussed in passing, since in accounts by survivors the focus is, by necessity, on the young and fit. But the majority experience during the Holocaust was not survival but death, and in the case of the elderly an overwhelming majority were killed. As historian Sarah Abrevaya Stein notes of Aron Hasson, not just one of the few survivors of the Holocaust in Salonica but a sixty-five-year-old: "In the context of the survivor community of postwar Salonica, to be sixty-five was to be ancient, a relic of a lost world."[9] The Nazis' rage against the Jews left no room to spare the weakest; quite the contrary. Elderly Jews were often at a loss to explain what was happening to them, even the best equipped to do so. Caesar Seligmann, for example, born in 1860 and the president of the Vereinigung für das liberale Judentum in Deutschland (Union for Liberal Judaism in Germany) from 1912 to 1937, completed a memoir of his life in 1941 after emigrating for Britain in 1939. He noted that his life had been turned upside down: he was too old to learn English and was moving around the country, from Aberdare in South Wales to Cheltenham, Cambridge, and London, to escape the German bombs. When he and his wife moved to Oxford in March 1941, it was their fourteenth move in two years. He was unable as yet to make sense of it all:

> As for my inner life, I hardly dare to portray it, because we have not yet reached and likely will hardly be able to reach the state of inner tranquil calm that is the prerequisite for objective reflection. We live in memories and hopes, that is to say in the past and the future, and not in the present. The present is like an incalculably large sea, in the middle of which we are being hurled around by all the waves, without being able to see a shore.[10]

Even before the killing process began, the Nazis targeted the elderly in ways that paved the way for further persecution. Numerous accounts testify to the mistreatment of elderly men in Buchenwald, Dachau, and Sachsenhausen in the wake of the November Pogrom (*Kristallnacht*); their experiences and the experience of other Jewish men seeing them made it clear that the Nazis would not shrink from attacking the most vulnerable, and worked to "persuade" the German Jews that they needed to take emigration seriously—although ironically, it would most often be the elderly who were least able to leave the country. With the German-Jewish emigrants tending to be from younger age groups, the result was that "The group aged 51 and over, which constituted less than one sixth of the refugees who settled in Palestine, formed a ratio almost three times as great within the population which remained at home," as a report of 1944 explained.[11]

Aged German Jews were subjected to measures that distinguished them from the elderly elsewhere, perhaps as a way of signaling to them, to their families, and to the wider "Aryan" community that they would be treated according to civilized standards. As historian Jonathan Zatlin has shown, the elderly German Jews were tricked out of their savings, as the Nazis used the deception of "old age care" before deporting them to Theresienstadt. They were forced to buy "retirement home contracts" (*Heimeinkaufsverträge*), thus ensuring that the Nazi regime stole most of their life savings while creating the impression that they were to be cared for properly. In other words, "The treatment of the elderly was thus essential to the success of the genocide," because it suggested to the elderly and the young, to Jewish and non-Jewish Germans, that the regime's intentions toward elderly Jews were honorable.[12]

Not all were convinced. Indeed, once the "retirements" began, the suicide rate among Jews in Berlin shot up. In the third quarter of 1942, 481 out of a total of 669 suicides in Berlin (75 percent) were Jews, the majority of them women aged over sixty.[13] Perhaps that should not surprise us, given the nature of the roundups; as Victor Klemperer recorded in his diary on July 2, 1942: "The removal of the old people's home to Theresienstadt brutal. Lorry with benches, crowded together, only the tiniest bundle could be taken, cuffs and blows."[14] That did not prevent the regime from carrying out theft on a grand scale; as Zatlin notes, "Between June and December 1942, the Gestapo extorted at least 43 million Reichsmark from the elderly. By June 1944, when most of the elderly had 'retired', the scheme had raised some 109 million marks."[15]

Far from being cared for in Theresienstadt, the elderly suffered from hunger and overcrowding, and were among the first to be deported to Auschwitz. The number of elderly who died in the camp rose rapidly, from an average of five a day in May 1942 (before the so-called *Alterstransporte* [elderly transports] started) to thirty-two a day in July, seventy-five in August, and 131 deaths every day in September. "As the survivor and historian Josef Polák put it, the elderly died 'often on the bare floor and had no mattress or blanket, much less medical care.'"[16]

Zatlin notes that "in the end, 13.4 percent of German Jews sent to Theresienstadt survived, but only 5 percent of the elderly." And he concludes that the contracts "helped reinforce the illusion that Theresienstadt was a retirement community, an illusion that was integral to the Gestapo's plans to murder German Jews over the age of sixty-five, which itself served to facilitate the murder of the rest of German Jewry."[17] In other words, with the Theresienstadt deception in which the German Jews were robbed of their savings and given to believe that they would be cared for in comfort for the rest of their days, we see the significance of the elderly to the Holocaust as such.

At Auschwitz, one of the most feared SS guards was Otto Moll, known for his sadism. Shlomo Dragon, one of the surviving members of the Sonderkommando in Birkenau, recalled in an interview that:

> No one dared to resist him, even in the slightest way, since we knew that we'd all be killed. Mere mention of the name Moll was enough to make everyone quake. Moll had another job: to take all the old and sick people who'd come in the trucks to a place behind Crematorium IV. There, in one of the pits, a fire was burning. He gave an order to throw the people into the fire and burn them alive. He was just a sadist.[18]

After citing this passage, Lawrence Langer observes that "If we are left aghast by such testimony, it may be because it leads to no meaning or sense but remains a succinct expression of the historical disbelief that lies—in these instances quite literally—at the searing core of the Holocaust experience."[19] Langer is talking about the brutality of the murders in general, but Dragon's specific reference to the elderly reminds us that the SS guards at Birkenau often did not even regard them as worth sending to the gas chamber; instead they were burned alive in pits. This is with reference to people who are supposedly revered in all societies as elders, as people who need valuing and protecting.

Surviving documentation contains numerous examples of old people being murdered, almost in passing, as if it had become so predictable and normal in the context of the assault on the Jews all across Europe that it barely merited a comment. Historian Wendy Lower describes a killing outside Miropol, in Ukraine, on October 12, 1941:

> When they arrived at a clearing, the Germans began to shout: "Dig! You Russian pigs, *Kaputt*!" They sneered at the girls and began to pass the time. After the girls finished digging out a layer a few feet deep in a circular area "about the size of a room," the Germans ordered elderly Jewish men to the site.
>
> The Jewish men completed the pit and were killed on the spot.[20]

Whether in the context of the "Holocaust by bullets," that is to say, the period of the face-to-face shootings of Jews in the western Soviet Union by the Einsatzgruppen of the Reich Security Main Office and their collaborators (mostly Order Police and local auxiliaries), or in that of the deportations by train from ghettos or transit camps to the killing centers, the elderly are often mentioned in ways that suggest that, given what was happening to them, no one could expect anything but brutal radicalism and total disdain on the Nazis' part.

The examples are easily multiplied. In his report on Treblinka, one of the camp's few survivors, Abraham Krzepicki, noted: "Already we could see elderly people stretched out on the floor of the first car, half unconscious. We didn't like the looks of this."[21] At the other end of Europe, at the transit camp of Westerbork, from where Dutch Jews were shipped to the killing centers, the following occurred in July 1942:

> There now began the sort of spectacle that would be repeated hundreds of times with ever-increasing horror: "One of those selected was a young man, who was to be separated from his aged father. The old man, a Polish Jew with a long beard, came to plead with them. We did not know, then, what sadists the Germans really were. 'So you want to stay with your son? All right then, you can go along with him tomorrow.' That was all he got out of them."[22]

And the same is true whether one looks at the ghettos or the camps. In Łódź, Chaim Rumkowski is remembered for his infamous "give me your children" speech; less well remembered is the fact that in the same speech, Rumkowski explained that he was being asked by the Germans "to give up the best we possess—the children and the elderly." He said almost nothing further about the elderly, however, leaving one to assume that as he put it in an earlier speech, he had nothing to say about them other than: "As far as older people are concerned, working people's parents who are unable to work, I trust that God will not forsake them."[23] The result is not hard to imagine: the elderly were, along with small children and the sick, the first to be deported. Nor were they treated with any special care: "Because the operation proceeded so rapidly," wrote one of the chroniclers of the Łódź ghetto, "the authorities gave no thought to the motives or causes of any particular act. At 38 Zgierska Street, an elderly woman from Sieradz did not understand if she had been ordered to go to the left or the right and, instead of going to a wagon, she walked over to a group of 'remainers.' This the authorities interpreted as an escape attempt. The woman was shot to death on the spot."[24] The chroniclers also recorded many cases of suicide among the elderly in the ghetto, as well as many elderly who voluntarily reported for deportation, believing that whatever awaited them could not be worse than what they were already experiencing.[25] The deportation of the elderly from the ghetto affected every family; it also had a devastating impact on religious observance in the ghetto, as most of the rabbis, being elderly, were deported to Chełmno, following which Rumkowski abolished the Committee of Rabbis.[26]

The same assault on the elderly took place in the other ghettos. A report on the Lublin ghetto that forms part of the Warsaw ghetto's Oneg Shabbat archive, noted that on the same day that the Germans emptied the orphanage and shot the children outside of the town (March 24, 1942), "the Germans liquidated the old people's home—70 residents were shot in the courtyard—as well as the provisional hospital."[27] In Przemyśl, the children's shelter and old age home were in the same building. "Twenty-five children and all 40 old people were taken during the August [1942] *Aktion*. On the orders of the Gestapo, we led both the children and the old folk straight out onto the square."[28] Nor were things different in the Warsaw ghetto. Once one stops thinking in terms of "industrial genocide" and focuses on what happened on the ground, the real horror of the murders begins to sink in. As Henry Shoskes wrote in one of the first postwar studies of the ghetto:

> Even these horrible hours in the ghetto gave birth to jokes. Strange jokes which made you shiver, jokes which gave proof of the superiority of the victim over the murderer—such as this one: An SS man was told to make order in a home for aged and infirm Jews in the ghetto in Warsaw. There were sixty persons living in a space where hardly thirty should have been. Therefore he was to kill half of them. He came to the room where the old people slept and, walking down the rows of the beds, shot every second one. Then he had the dead bodies carried out. He remained in the door to count them. He counted: "Twenty-eight, twenty-nine, thirty . . . thirty-one." Suddenly he began to sob. "What have I done?" he cried out. "I have killed an innocent person!"[29]

Nor is the story different if one looks at escape attempts, as Françoise Frenkel described in her memoir, *No Place to Lay One's Head*:

> A septuagenarian lived there who had succeeded in crossing the demarcation line in the most dramatic manner. He had set out with his son, but just as they had arrived in the Free Zone, the two men found themselves separated. When the older man learned that his son had been recaptured and sent to the Drancy concentration camp, he fell into a profound depression. His neighbours in the hotel arranged between them to take it in turns distracting him: some took him out on the Promenade, others would pay him a visit to cheer up. But Monsieur Samuel Mendelsohn knew how to evade the well-meaning watchfulness of his circle of friends and, one night, he hanged himself from the window of his room. The door was sealed and, from then on, one hurried past on that floor. One neighbour's tragic end resonated with us as too brutal an example of the possible fate lying in store for each of us.[30]

Frenkel gives another example of three elderly women who had attempted to cross over to Switzerland:

> Three elderly ladies with startlingly bright white hair appeared before the court at the same time, defended by the same lawyer. The youngest of them was . . . sixty-two years old, the eldest seventy-two. The tallest woman stood between the other two, who were slighter, almost fragile. They appeared together, all for the same offences: travel without a permit, forged papers, attempted flight.
>
> One of them had a married daughter in Zurich; the other, deprived of her son, who had been deported by the Germans, had wanted to accompany her friend. The third had been forced to leave the Jewish community's retirement home in Toulouse, which had been closed by order of the Vichy government, and she had quite simply found herself without a roof over her head. She had set off for Switzerland, a country she had been assured would be a safe haven for such unfortunate souls.
>
> Looking at those three old women, I wondered how they had imagined being able to cross the barbed wire! Had they considered the difficulties they would encounter? Or were they simply unaware of them? Or did they think that, since the Red Sea had parted to allow the children of Israel to pass, the strands of barbed wire would also separate to allow passage for the likes of such poor old women seeking their freedom? Did they still believe in the miracles that featured so prominently in their ancestors' stories? Had they forgotten that, since those long-gone times, their God, the Eternal, God of lightning and vengeance, appeared to have well and truly abandoned his chosen people?[31]

The elderly tried to cling to their familiar world as long as they could. Rudolf Mrázek gives the example of Alice Bloemendahl, a Dutch Jewish woman in Theresienstadt, who

> had been approached by a Jewish official from the Council of Elders: "Would you like to go to the *Altersheim* to be a woman-reader?" Mrs Bloemendahl did, and she recalled after the war: "My listeners (they were often seriously ill) lay deep in their pillows. . . . The listeners in one room varied between seven and twenty, but sometimes there were forty and more. . . . I began with *Erinnerungen an Frauen*. Two novels, one

> by Ernst Penzoldt and the other by Theodor Fontane, followed." Then she read Heinrich Heine's "Rabbi of Bacharach" from the *Book of Songs*. "By demand," Mrs Bloemendahl recalled, "I have also read *Geschichte Napoleons*."[32]

Here the nineteenth century truly invaded Theresienstadt; Bloemendahl's description makes the ghetto sound like a Habsburg convalescent home. Soon after, for the Jews of Europe, the nineteenth century ended. It ended for them not because the Holocaust, *pace* Głowiński, "transcended the boundaries of their technological imagination," although this was also probably true for many. Rather, the nineteenth century ended for Jews with the Holocaust because of the Nazi mania for a "transvaluation of all values" which those brought up in the late 1800s had been taught to regard as immutable.

After "Liberation"

On encountering Belsen, one Canadian soldier observed that: "The thing that stuck in my mind was the age, all the elderly people had apparently died, and so the average age of those people there was probably in their 30s or 40s, as an average age. But there was no people there over 60, or 65, very little of those, I think, they had all been . . . terminated and buried, before we got there."[33]

"Liberation" needs to be written in quotation marks for the simple reason that even though they had outlived the Nazi regime, for the majority of survivors the prospect of rebuilding their lives in the absence of their families, communities, and hometowns, without support networks and usually in a state of mental and physical distress, meant the beginning of a whole new set of troubles.[34] This situation was still the case several years after the war; indeed, by the late 1940s it had become more noticeable given the existence of the so-called "hard core" displaced persons, who could not or would not leave Germany, mostly because they were too old and sick. Their position was clearly set out by a JDC (American Jewish Joint Distribution Committee) report of October 11, 1949; beginning with the observation that of the 150,000 Jewish displaced persons (DPs), only a fifth remained, the report then explained:

> What remains is the pitiful rest of the survivors—the sick and the infirm. For them the Liberation was no liberation, but only opened the way to the sick-bed. They could once be counted in thousands, but now their ranks have been depleted by their own inability to stand up to the impact of normal life and by their dwindling powers of resistance.[35]

Referring to the "hard core" DPs as "the survivors of the survivors," the report made recommendations for the physically and mentally ill, those with tuberculosis, and "invalids," that is, those who had lost limbs or other body parts as a result of fighting against the Germans or being victims of medical experiments in Nazi camps. Finally, it devoted a short section to the "aged." It noted that the mass health examination that ended in December 1948 revealed that the elderly constituted "the abnormally low percentage of 1.5%"; this shockingly low figure, it argued, "was the direct result of the organized destruction of European Jewry, to which children and elderly people were most exposed."[36] The report concluded that there were about one hundred "unaccompanied aged persons living in camps and installations who will need custodial care," and it recommended that, in view of the wish of most of the remaining DPs not to remain in Germany, an old age home be established for them in Israel to which they could be transferred by April 1, 1950, three months before the cessation of the IRO (International Refugee Organization).

Of course, by the end of 1949, the majority of Jewish DPs had left Germany. Nevertheless, the statistic of one hundred elderly survivors (plus another hundred elderly German Jews living in old age homes in Munich and Frankfurt who did not fall into this report's purview) is startlingly low, even without knowing precisely what the report means by "aged" (no age range is given) and even though the report covers the American zone—where the majority of Jewish DPs were based. It is corroborated by an IRO report from January 1950, which provided statistics on all DPs (not just Jews), and indicated that there were ninety "unattached" elderly Jews (aged over sixty) and twenty-two Jewish couples in which one or both were aged over seventy, who required institutional care (i.e., were classified as "hard core").[37] The report is therefore testament to the almost total obliteration of the elderly Jews during the Holocaust.

Long before this JDC report was written, it and other charities had been caring for elderly survivors since the end of the war.[38] In the British zone, the Jewish Relief Unit (JRU), created by the London-based Jewish Committee for Relief Abroad, was the foremost charity. Although it lacked the resources disposed of by the JDC, it nevertheless did what it could—military authorities and finances permitting—to aid the survivors. Among its papers are numerous examples of the work it did with the elderly, in DP camps—primarily Hohne (Belsen)—and in the Jewish *Gemeinden* (communities) that struggled to re-establish themselves after the war. In Hamburg, for example, whose Jewish community ran twelve old age homes before the war, the community's representatives appealed to the JRU for help with the few elderly survivors who had found their way back to the city. In their letter of June 1946, two of the city's Jewish representatives noted that the majority of the elderly had been killed "in the concentration camps" and that for the few who survived (forty to fifty Jewish men and women aged sixty-five to eighty-five), the community was running just one old age home, on the Rothenbaumchaussee, and that this

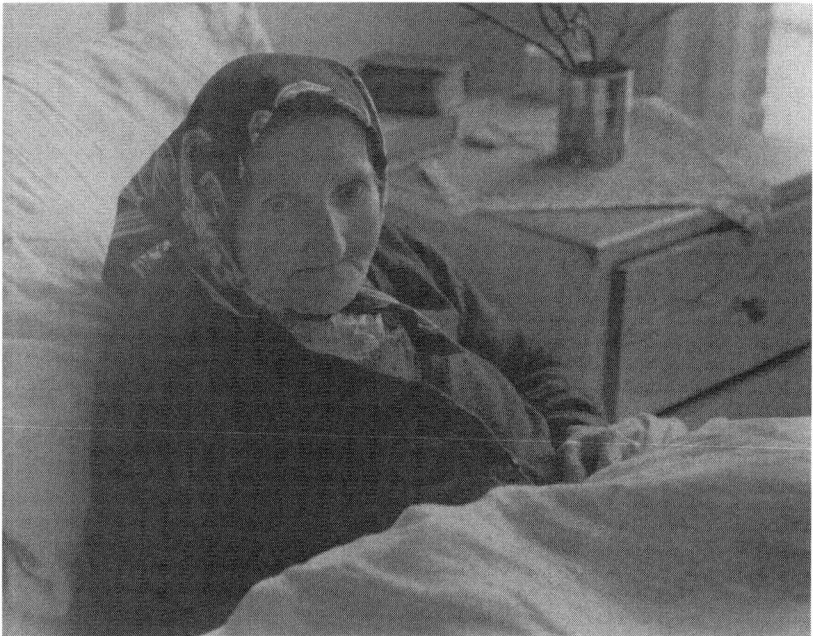

FIGURE 1.1. "An Aged Woman in Belsen Hospital," December 31, 1946, WHL 35/6/3/205. The image appeared in the Central British Fund pamphlet *Hear O Israel, the Story Is Told* (ca. 1947), RHP, HA1-3/29, Wiener Holocaust Library.

building was under threat of being requisitioned by the British army. They stressed that it was only natural that "after the terrible years of persecution and concentration camps, our elderly should be able to end their lives in peace in the place where, following their return to Hamburg, they have found accommodation."[39] Given this threat, they asked for help with obtaining the return of another former Jewish old age home, on the Sedanstrasse. The correspondence over this matter carried on for several months until in October the JRU received notice from Norfolk House—the London headquarters of the Control Office for Germany and Austria—that the house would not be evacuated. In the meantime, the community feared that its elderly would become homeless; the JRU had to undertake considerable activity to obtain this result—that is to say, simply to ensure that the status quo would remain in place.[40]

The JRU documents also include some affecting photographs, such as one of an old woman in the hospital at Belsen DP Camp, taken at the end of 1946 (fig. 1.1). Knowing nothing about who this woman is, it is hard to say anything with certitude. But the photographer captured an image meant to suggest loneliness, bewilderment, and helplessness, and captioned the photograph "An aged woman in Belsen hospital—completely alone in the world. She has not a single known relative, and will remain in the camp hospital until she dies." And yet somehow she survived. In her diary from Bergen-Belsen, the young Yugoslav communist Hanna Lévy-Hass wrote about what she witnessed in the barracks for older women in February 1945: "These sick old women lie down, slowly dying; they rot alive. I don't know how else to say it. And yet, they show such a will to live, it's unbelievable."[41] We do not know the circumstances of this woman's survival but the photograph and its caption make it clear that, having survived, the woman is alone.

This reading would certainly fit with what we know of elderly survivors, who only rarely were accompanied by family members. In June 1948, Jacob Marx, who ran the Jewish old age home in Cologne, wrote to E. G. Lowenthal, the JRU's German-born Field Director for Germany, with short biographies of the home's inhabitants. Analie Fromm, born in 1868 and widowed in 1931, spent three years in Theresienstadt; she lost a son and a daughter in the Holocaust. Wilhelmine Israel, born in 1859 and thus nearly ninety years old at the time of this correspondence, had also spent the years 1942–45 in Theresienstadt and she too had lost two of her five children to the Nazis. She was now living in the old age home, sharing a small room with her daughter, Emma Oppenheimer. The latter was born in 1891; her husband was murdered by the Nazis in 1944, and she had a daughter living in Sweden, who she was trying to find a way to visit. Almost all of the inhabitants of the Cologne old age home were Theresienstadt survivors, the majority of them women. Marx rarely made any comments about them other than strictly biographical. But occasionally one gets a glimpse; with respect to Helene Zirker (born 1866), for example, who was widowed in 1944 and whose only son lived in Africa, he wrote: "She is an old, frail, grandma." Of Samuel Unger (born 1873), whose two daughters were killed in Riga, and who was living in the old age home with his wife Flora (born 1874 and in good health), Marx noted that he was "a suffering old man." And of Lina Oppenheimer (born 1891), whose two children were murdered by the Nazis and whose husband was "100% war damaged" and had to be "cared for like a small child," Marx observed that "her lot is exceptionally hard."[42]

It is thus hardly surprising that when Lowenthal wrote (some time earlier) to the Law and Security Office of the Cologne Housing Department asking for further assistance, he emphasized that many of the inhabitants of the old age home were "former racial persecutees, whose lives should be made as bearable as possible under the current circumstances."[43] Yet six years later, in addition to the Jews living in the old age homes belonging to the *Gemeinden*, there were still elderly residents among the last group of two thousand remaining DPs in Föhrenwald. When David Rosenstein, president of the (American) National Federation of Settlements and Neighborhood Centers, visited the camp with his wife in 1953, he was shocked not at the living conditions of Föhrenwald's inhabitants, who were well provided for, but at "the hearts and minds of this community, which, 8 years after the war, is still living almost entirely on relief—vegetating, without constructive plans for the future." Among them were "those in the old-age group—men and women over 60." Rosenstein described them as "tired and despondent people, who look back on a life of misery and hardship" for whom "resettlement planning is extremely difficult, if not impossible."[44] He proposed attempting to persuade the Föhrenwalders—about half of whom were returnees to Germany from Israel and elsewhere—to move to Israel. But having already said that resettling the elderly was next to impossible, he said nothing more specifically about them. The elderly, as was often the case, were not abandoned but nor were they a high priority, since, presumably, how they were going to make the rest of their lives productive was not a pressing issue for the JDC and other charities.

What we see in the postwar "relief" for the elderly is thus confirmation of Adorno's notion of progress: on the one hand, an attempt to revisit and revive nineteenth-century values of respect for community and care for the weak; on the other, a sense that such action was really a sad but committed desire to help the surviving remnant of the elderly live out their remaining days in as much comfort as could be provided under the straitened postwar circumstances. Requests for apple puree, floor polish, and books bespeak a desire to grant the elderly inhabitants a basic, acceptable standard of living, not a commitment to reviving grand nineteenth-century speculative philosophies of history leading to "perpetual peace" or the "unfolding of *Geist*."[45] This was thus not a return to progress understood as unfettered, something to be taken for granted and celebrated. It was rather a dedication to a kind of humanitarian care and a belief that, in these circumstances, progress meant resistance to the perpetual danger of relapse. As both Adorno's thought and the empirical reality of "liberation" indicate, "redemption must take the form of its unceasing refusal."[46]

The End of the Nineteenth Century

In his famous essay, "Useless Violence," Primo Levi tried to understand what he calls "orthodox Nazi" logic. It is clear, he says, that for the orthodox Nazi, all Jews must be killed, including of course children and pregnant women, "so that no future enemies should be born." But he is confounded by the Nazis' decision, during the "furious roundups" across Europe, to "violate the houses of the dying," that is to say, old age homes:

> Why go to the trouble of dragging them on to their trains, take them to die far away, after a senseless journey, die in Poland on the threshold of the gas chambers? In my convoy there were two dying ninety-year-old women, taken out of the Fossoli infirmary: one of them died en route, nursed in vain by her daughters. Would it not have been simpler, more "economical," to let them die, or perhaps kill them in their beds, instead of adding their agony to the collective agony of the transport? One is truly led to think

> that, in the Third Reich, the best choice, the choice imposed from above, was the one that entailed the greatest amount of affliction, the greatest amount of waste, of physical and moral suffering. The "enemy" must not only die, but must die in torment.[47]

Levi understood but did not want to understand: it was indeed precisely the Nazis' intention that the "enemy" should feel the weight of their power, that the victims' suffering should be maximized. And in his example of the two ninety-year-olds we see Nazi logic distilled: in order to save the Aryan race, all Jews must be killed. As Adorno put it, "One of the Nazis' symbolic outrages is the killing of the very old."[48] For these two women, born in the middle of the nineteenth century, teenagers at the unification of Italy and already approaching old age at the start of World War I, the deportation train to Auschwitz led not only to their murder. Their story also represents the murder of an age and its dream of progress. Adorno wrote in one of the bleakest of post-Holocaust works of philosophy, *Negative Dialectics* (1966), that "since Auschwitz, fearing death means fearing worse than death." "What death does to the socially condemned can be anticipated biologically on old people we love; not only their bodies but their egos, all the things that justified their definition as human, crumble without illness, without violence from outside."[49]

And yet in Levi's example of the two old women placed on the train to Auschwitz, we encounter people who are experiencing the natural end of their bodies and minds and being forced into the category of the socially condemned: a kind of double dying. Having come to maturity in the "age of progress," they were committed to die in the age of its dialectical antithesis. The havoc that the memory of fascism continues to play on the world stage indicates that apocalyptic fantasies continue to attract, especially at moments of crisis, and that belief in unidirectional social, political, or technological progress is not only naïve but dangerous.

Notes

1 Theodor W. Adorno, "Progress," in *Critical Models: Interventions and Catchwords*, trans. Henry W. Pickford (Columbia University Press, 1998), 153.

2 Michał Głowiński, *The Black Seasons*, trans. Marci Shore (Northwestern University Press, 2005), 53.

3 A. J. P. Taylor, *The First World War* (Hamilton, 1963), 20.

4 Stefan Zweig, *The World of Yesterday*, trans. Anthea Bell (Pushkin Press, 2009), 26.

5 Silvano Arieti, *The Parnas: A Scene from the Holocaust* (Paul Dry Books, 2000), 36–37.

6 "Industrial genocide" is a concept that obscures as much as it reveals.

7 For the best-known version of this argument, see Zygmunt Bauman, *Modernity and the Holocaust* (Polity Press, 1989). For reasons why caution is recommended with Bauman's thesis, see my *Histories of the Holocaust* (Oxford University Press, 2010) and Jack Palmer and Dariusz Brzeziński, eds., *Revisiting Modernity and the Holocaust: Heritage, Dilemmas, Extensions* (Routledge, 2022).

8 Adorno, "Progress," 154, 160.

9 Sarah Abrevaya Stein, *Family Papers: A Sephardic Journey Through the Twentieth Century* (Picador, 2021), 210.

10 Caesar Seligmann, "Mein Leben: Erinnerungen eines Grossvaters" (unpublished typescript, 1941), 139, Leo Baeck Institute, ME 595, Center for Jewish History, https://digipres.cjh.org/delivery/DeliveryManagerServlet?dps_pid=IE8876051.

11 Arieh Tartakower and Kurt R. Grossmann, *The Jewish Refugee* (Institute of Jewish Affairs of the American Jewish Congress and World Jewish Congress, 1944), 352. See also Melissa Jane Taylor, "Family Matters: The Emigration of Elderly Jews from Vienna to the United States, 1938–1941," *Journal of Social History* 45, no.1 (2011), 238–60.

12 See Jonathan R. Zatlin, "The Ruse of Retirement: Eichmann, the *Heimeinkaufsverträge*, and the Dispossession of the Elderly," in *Dispossession: Plundering German Jewry, 1933–1953*, ed. Christoph Kreutzmüller and Jonathan R. Zatlin (University of Michigan Press, 2020), 171.

13 See Zatlin, "Ruse of Retirement," 172, citing Christian Goeschel, *Suicide in Nazi Germany* (Oxford University Press, 2009), 109.

14 *To the Bitter End: The Diaries of Victor Klemperer, 1942–45*, trans. Martin Chalmers (Phoenix, 2000), 111.

15 Zatlin, "Ruse of Retirement," 179. See also Martin Dean, *Robbing the Jews: The Confiscation of Jewish Property in the Holocaust, 1933–1945* (Cambridge University Press, 2008), 250–51. Dean calculates that nine thousand

"home purchase contracts" were issued between June 1942 and July 1943, with a value of 125 million DM.

16 Zatlin, "Ruse of Retirement," 181.

17 Zatlin, "Ruse of Retirement," 181–82.

18 Gideon Greif, *We Wept Without Tears: Testimonies from the Jewish Sonderkommando from Auschwitz* (Yale University Press, 2005), 160.

19 Lawrence L. Langer, *The Afterdeath of the Holocaust* (Palgrave Macmillan, 2021), 76.

20 Wendy Lower, *The Ravine: A Family, a Photograph, a Holocaust Massacre Revealed* (Head of Zeus, 2021), 52.

21 Abraham Krzepicki, "Eighteen Days in Treblinka," in *The Death Camp Treblinka: A Documentary*, ed. Alexander Donat (Holocaust Library, 1979), 79.

22 Jacob Presser, *Ashes in the Wind: The Destruction of Dutch Jewry* (Souvenir Press, 2010), 409.

23 Chaim Rumkowski, "'Give Me Your Children!', 4 September 1942"; and "'Work Protects Us from Annihilation', 2 March 1942," both in *Łódź Ghetto: Inside a Community Under Siege*, ed. Alan Adelson and Robert Lapides (Viking, 1989), 233, 328.

24 Lucjan Dobroszycki, ed., *The Chronicle of the Łódź Ghetto, 1941–1944* (Yale University Press, 1984), 252, entry for Sept. 14, 1942.

25 See Elizabeth C. Strauss, "'Cast Me Not Off in My Time of Old Age . . .': The Aged and Aging in the Łódź Ghetto, 1939–1944" (PhD diss., University of Notre Dame, 2013), 173.

26 Strauss, "'Cast Me Not Off,'" 212, citing Isaiah Trunk, *Judenrat: The Jewish Councils in Eastern Europe Under Nazi Occupation* (University of Nebraska Press, 1996 [1972]), 193. Trunk notes that following the deportation of most of the rabbis, "Rumkowski then abolished the 'Committee of Rabbis' and personally took over the function of performing marriage rites."

27 "12 April 1942, Warsaw Ghetto, Oyneg Shabes Bulletin Containing Information About the Situation of Jews in Various Localities in the Territory of the Republic of Poland in the Period July 1942 to March 1942," in *The Ringelblum Archive: Underground Archive of the Warsaw Ghetto*, vol. 3, *Oyneg Shabes: People and Works*, ed. Aleksandra Bańkowska and Tadeusz Epsztein (Jewish Historical Institute, 2020), 227–28.

28 Statement of Anna Maas, Central Jewish Historical Commission (Poland) statement no. 690, in *The Children Accuse*, ed. Maria Hochberg-Mariańska and Noe Gruss, trans. Bill Johnston (Vallentine Mitchell, 1996), 268.
29 Henry Shoskes, *No Traveler Returns: The Story of Hitler's Greatest Crime* (Doubleday, Doran, 1945), 79.
30 Françoise Frenkel, *No Place to Lay One's Head*, trans. Stephanie Smee (Pushkin Press, 2018), 114–15.
31 Frenkel, *No Place to Lay One's Head*, 228–29.
32 Rudolf Mrázek, *The Complete Lives of Camp People: Colonialism, Fascism, Concentrated Modernity* (Duke University Press, 2020), 179.
33 Mervin Mirsky, cited in Mark Celinscak, *Kingdom of Night: Witnesses to the Holocaust* (University of Toronto Press, 2022), 55–56.
34 See Dan Stone, *The Liberation of the Camps: The End of the Holocaust and Its Aftermath* (Yale University Press, 2015).
35 JDC Health Dept., Germany, *Report on Hard Core Problem*, October 11, 1949, JDC Archives, NY_AR45-54_00036_01005, item 676508, search.archives.jdc.org/multimedia/Documents/NY_AR_45-54/NY_AR45-54_Count/NY_AR45-54_00036/NY_AR45-54_00036_01005.pdf#search=. These issues did not apply only to Jewish "hard core" DPs; see Mark Wyman, *DPs: Europe's Displaced Persons, 1945–1951* (Cornell University Press, 1998), 203–4.
36 JDC Health Dept., Germany, *Report on Hard Core Problem*, 16. For the broader context of Jewish DP demography, see Avinoam J. Patt, *Finding Home and Homeland: Jewish Youth and Zionism in the Aftermath of the Holocaust* (Wayne State University Press, 2009), 210–11, 269–70.
37 International Refugee Organization, "Refugees Receiving IRO Care and Maintenance Who Require Institutional Care (Hard Core)," January 31, 1950, annex 8: Diagnosis, Religion, Austria, Germany and Italy, Lady Rose Henriques Papers (henceforth RHP), HA20-4/7/8, Wiener Holocaust Library, London (henceforth WHL).
38 See Dan Stone, "'Somehow the Pathetic Dumb Suffering of These Elderly People Moves Me More Than Anything': Caring for Elderly Holocaust Survivors in the Immediate Postwar Years," *Holocaust and Genocide Studies* 32, no. 3 (2018), 545–64.
39 H. Goldstein and Dr L. Loeffler (Jewish Community, Hamburg) to Dr G. Weis, Legal Advisor, Jewish Relief Unit, Eilshausen near Herford,

June 14, 1946, RHP, HA10-IV/B7-1 and B7-2, WHL. There is an English translation of the letter at B7-3-4 but it is clunky.

40 Louis Smith, General Department, Control Office for Germany and Austria, to Mrs. R. L. Henriques, Jewish Committee for Relief Abroad, October 18, 1946, RHP, HA10-IV/B7-19, WHL.

41 Hanna Lévy-Hass, *Diary of Bergen-Belsen, 1944–1945*, trans. Sophie Hand (Haymarket Books, 2009), 106.

42 Jacob Marx to E. G. Lowenthal, June 23, 1948, RHP, HA7/5-10/66/F—HA7/5-10/89/F, WHL.

43 E. G. Lowenthal to Dr Schlochauer, October 31, 1947, RHP, HA7/5-10/28/B, WHL: "ehemals rassisch Verfolgte sind, denen man unter den gegebenen Umständen das Leben so erträglich wie möglich gestalten sollte."

44 David Rosenstein, "Our Unfinished Job in Germany" (December 8, 1953), 83 Cong. Rec. 2 (1954) JDC Archives, item 2639404, search.archives.jdc.org/multimedia/Documents/Geneva45-54/G45-54_Count/USHMM-GENEVA_00007/USHMM-GENEVA_00007_00308.pdf#search=.

45 See for example the documents in RHP, HA7/1-21, WHL, concerning the old age home Rosenau near Düsseldorf, in which requests for these items can be found.

46 Josh Cohen, *Interrupting Auschwitz: Art, Religion, Philosophy* (Continuum, 2003), 25.

47 Primo Levi, "Useless Violence," in *The Drowned and the Saved*, trans. Raymond Rosenthal (Abacus, 1989), 96.

48 Theodor Adorno, *Minima Moralia: Reflections from Damaged Life*, trans. E. F. N. Jephcott (Verso, 1989), 22.

49 Theodor W. Adorno, *Negative Dialectics*, trans. E. B. Ashton (Routledge, 1990), 371.

2

JEWISH HOMES FOR THE AGED AT THE CENTER OF INTERWAR POLISH POLITICS

Marek Tuszewicki

After the end of World War I, the Polish state's universal pension system only applied in the area formerly within the borders of the German Empire, where social welfare regulations introduced by Otto von Bismarck in the 1890s were in operation. Entitlements to financial support for the aged were also available to civil servants who acquired them in Galicia under Austrian rule (before 1918), as well as to a small group of miners. The newly reborn republic continued these obligations. In addition, over the course of the 1920s, the pensions of white-collar workers, civil servants, and professional military personnel, among others, were regulated in Poland. Finally, in 1933–34, a relatively broad, nationwide pension insurance law was introduced for workers and white-collar employees. The so-called Consolidation Bill set the age of eligibility at sixty-five, regardless of gender (sixty for some professions). Nevertheless, in 1938, only about half a million citizens (at most one-fifth of all Polish residents over the age of sixty) enjoyed disability or old-age pensions, with the majority of these benefits actually being disability and widow's benefits.[1]

In addition to the pension law, further provisions for the elderly were established and regulated in Poland over the course of the 1920s. In August 1923, the legislature (*Sejm*) passed the Social Welfare Law establishing in most of the territory a system of transferring public funds for, among other things, the care of senior citizens.[2] Municipalities were responsible for providing social welfare services, which in the case of Jewish communities were primarily larger cities. The practical dimension of care might be carried out by private or religious institutions, but its costs were nevertheless assumed by local governments. Each year, city councils discussed the distribution of subsidies to welfare associations as part of the preparation of their budgets. Jewish politicians took an active part in the work of the municipal authorities, as a result of which subsidies were given to various associations supporting the elderly in their own homes (e.g., by providing fuel for the winter), as well as to nursing homes statutorily dedicated to caring for the oldest members of the Jewish community. In the democratic system that Poland adopted after regaining independence, politics at the local level remained an important factor influencing the shape of social life. Although in the 1930s the number of residents (regardless of religion) placed in institutions was estimated at only about fifteen thousand,[3] these were usually people unable to undertake independent gainful employment, and thus the institutions themselves were seen as fulfilling extremely important social purposes.

In this article, I will trace the circumstances of the operation of Jewish nursing homes for the elderly in interwar Poland. I am particularly interested in their entanglement with national political realities, local governments, and religious communities. To give a broader picture of the dilemmas faced by these facilities, I will turn my attention to the development of the pension system in the Second Republic. It emerged with difficulty and had not managed to fully develop before 1939, yet the debates surrounding it reveal both how the Jewish minority was handicapped in their bid for a pension as well as the readiness of its representatives to actively fight to change this state of affairs.

The Problem of Pensions

The Jewish community monitored the legislative work on the Polish pension law with interest. It saw in the state pensions an opportunity to order social relations in the spirit of justice, and it accepted a budgetary expenditure of this kind despite the disproportionate tax obligations it was incurring.[4] An interesting expression of the community's hopes was the April 1929 memorandum of the Agudat ha-Shochtim (Union of ritual butchers), calling on the interior minister to provide state pension benefits to all *shochtim*.[5] In the years leading up to the implementation of the consolidation bill on social welfare, the regulations were discussed, as reported in the Polish-language Jewish press,[6] as well as in the popular Yiddish press.[7] Also, the bill's swift passage through the *Sejm* in 1933 expanded eligibility for benefits to include blue-collar workers.[8] At the same time, Jews may have feared that the lack of comprehensive solutions in this matter would embolden those in power to seek ad hoc ways to assist the needy at the expense of artisans and small merchants. As early as 1921 the *Sejm* debated a bill to revise retail tobacco and innkeeping licenses, about 40 percent of which were held by Jews. The concessions were to be taken away from the current holders and given to war invalids, widows, and orphans of the fallen, as well as state pensioners. After several years of political tug-of-war, the law to revise the licensure went into effect against the protests of Jewish members of parliament (MPs). In practice, its effects proved limited due to the widespread practice of subletting concessions.[9]

Statistical data on the beneficiaries of the pension system does not tell us how many of them were Jews.[10] The Consolidation Bill primarily met the needs of Christian society. A clear majority of the Jewish population in 1931 (55.5 percent) were self-employed, had few or no employees, and were recruited from the small- and medium-sized industrial and commercial sectors. Laborers and white-collar workers, to whom the law's provisions mostly were directed, were noticeably smaller subgroups of the Jewish working population—about 30 percent—while the number among Christians reached almost 75 percent.[11] Among the remaining categories of pensioners were a small number of Jews who had been soldiers in the Polish military and veterans of nineteenth-century independence uprisings. In the early 1920s, the number of Jewish pensioners in the post-German system decreased because some beneficiaries moved to the Weimar Republic. Nevertheless, certain groups of recipients of so-called partition pensions still lived within Poland's borders. Among those covered by pension insurance from the beginning of the republic were former Austrian military officers and public officials. However, many complained about a lack of benefits, including several hundred Jewish families, which gave rise to parliamentary interventions. In the *Sejm*, Jewish MPs Hersz Heller and Henryk Rosmarin, among others, spoke on the issue, demanding the most urgent ratification of the Vienna Convention of November 30, 1923.[12] The Polish-Jewish press from the area of former Galicia also took a keen interest in the issue.[13] As it seems, the ratification of the convention at the end of 1928 did not close the matter, which recurred both in the pages of the press[14] and during parliamentary discussions on the budget.[15]

In the interwar period, Jewish community officials could count on pensions paid from community funds. They were provided primarily to rabbis, distinguished officials, teachers, and *shochtim*, as well as to their widows and orphans. This was based on both the communities' regulations and acts of Polish law.[16] At the same time, even a small group of pensioners represented a very serious burden on the community's budget. The then-existing pension system received criticism for its effect on the individual worker. Opinions expressed in *Nowy Dziennik* (the Jewish daily published in Kraków), among others, pointed to the need to lower the retirement age or to ease the restrictions on the period of unemployment for white-collar workers.[17] Sometimes these criticisms included observations that pension laws were applied to Jews in an unfair manner. In the late 1930s, when antisemitism in Poland increased significantly, critics also pointed out that access to pensions served the competitiveness of Christian small trade and actually constituted an indirect support of it.[18]

Toward the First Old People's Homes

In the period leading up to the outbreak of World War I, Jewish society's initiatives to build old people's homes usually met with a positive response from state and local authorities. Sometimes Christian officials directly participated in the organization of such institutions, although on a limited scale by, for example, contributing to the upkeep of some of the residents or renovations, as was done in Wilno.[19] Investment in a nursing home was an opportunity for wealthy founders to emphasize their social standing. It is no coincidence that establishments in Drohobycz (1888), Lwów (1898), and Kraków (1898), among others, began construction or were opened on the occasion of imperial anniversaries. The presence of representatives of the secular authorities was noted at most cornerstone-laying ceremonies and facility inaugurations. Above all, however, before the outbreak of the Great War, city and state leaders were interested in the development of Jewish hospitals and care facilities such as orphanages or homes for the elderly, which contributed to improving sanitary conditions and residents' health. In addition to their humanitarian aim, the operation of institutions for the elderly was expected to contribute to a reduction in begging, various types of crime, and cases of death in loneliness. In short, the Christian authorities favored the establishment of homes for the Jewish elderly for utilitarian reasons. It also seems not insignificant that they were erected by funders and maintained liquidity based on wealthy trust funds. The denominational distinctiveness of these establishments was not a subject of discussion.

This does not mean that at their origins these initiatives were not accompanied by frictions of a political nature, particularly within the Jewish community itself. At the turn of the twentieth century, the ability to bridge differences in worldview supported the realization of a modern institution for the elderly. The philanthropists funding Jewish care facilities owed their wealth to their openness to the non-Jewish world, sometimes even promoting assimilationist trends. However, the challenges of everyday life forced even very wealthy donors to act in a spirit of broad social understanding. This was due to the scale of the undertaking: the large costs of purchasing property, constructing or renovating a building, and then contributing to the upkeep of the residents. The choice of a path of consensus based on Jewish values was facilitated by the charitable nature of the institution, focused on helping those in need regardless of their degree of religiosity. The internal organization of the institutions also largely reflected the ideal of old age prevalent in Jewish culture. Old men and old women (in their respective ways) were expected to spend the last years of their lives in reverie, study, and prayer to prepare themselves for the best possible crossing over the threshold of death. It was inevitable that there would be a large group of men and women associated with traditionalist circles actively working on behalf of the charitable foundations or their residents. Supportive though this may have been, it caused tensions that sometimes turned into open conflict.[20]

Discord of this kind became evident in the case of the Warsaw Moshav Zkenim Society and weighed on the fate of the institution until the mid-1930s. In addition to representatives of the conservative Nalewki Street bourgeoisie, among the founding members of the society in 1911 were individuals from assimilated circles, including Prof. Adolf Peretz and Dr. Henryk Nussbaum. Friction between these groups took place even during meetings preceding the opening of the nursing home.[21] The interwar period did not diminish the intensity of the dispute. In the mid-1920s, the old people's home on Górczewska Street became divided into a shelter, with about a hundred residents, mainly from the poorer strata of Jewish society, and the smaller Hearth for Elder Intellectuals (Ognisko dla Starców Inteligentów), which could house about 70 people. The dominant language of the shelter was Yiddish, while at the Hearth, located in a separate building, Polish was most prevalent. The bulletin issued on the occasion of President of the Republic of Poland Ignacy Mościcki's visit to the Hearth on November 21, 1928, was prepared entirely in Polish, and the Jewishness of the institution was marginalized in its content and graphic design.[22] In 1929, the Yiddish paper *Unzer Ekspres* even reported that a condition for admission to the new pavilion was that prospective residents pass an exam in Polish.[23] A year later, the society's general meeting was attended by only twenty people out of more than one thousand members. Although this was happening at the apogee of the economic crisis, the author of a critique published in the pages of *Der Moment* reasoned that the low attendance was primarily related to assimilation.[24]

Despite this controversy, the Moshav Zkenim Society in Warsaw functioned efficiently. In the 1930s, the two houses on Górczewska Street became the most important institutions for helping the elderly in the Polish capital. Their position was not threatened by either the Great Depression or the rise of antisemitism during the late Sanation (Sanacja) government.

In the New Poland

In the first decades of the twentieth century, the conditions for the operation of Jewish nursing homes in Eastern Europe completely changed. To some extent, this was a consequence of migration processes that deprived a significant number of adult community members of the support of their closest relatives. As the years progressed, these people became older and increasingly dependent on outside assistance. The crises accompanying the outbreak of the Great War and the border-shaping conflicts in Eastern Europe of 1919–20 exacerbated the situation of the elderly. They brought humanitarian catastrophe to urban residents, depriving many of property, a workplace, or a roof over their heads. Some of those affected hoped to find refuge in welfare institutions and were ready to entrust the rest of

FIGURE 2.1. President of Poland Ignacy Mościcki (center, foreground) during a visit to a Jewish nursing home in Warsaw (Hearth for Elder Intellectuals), November 21, 1928. Source: Narodowe Archiwum Cyfrowe.

their salvaged property to them. However, the crises also hit the financial foundations of nursing homes. Some of them irretrievably lost the funds accumulated in bank accounts and the support of wealthy patrons. Others could no longer count on regular contributions from association members, subsidies from the communal kosher meat tax (*korobka*), and in a few cases (e.g., Radom) they were temporarily deprived of their own buildings.[25]

The systemic differences inherited from the social welfare systems of Germany, Austria-Hungary, and Russia affected the functioning of welfare institutions in the new reality. The process of adapting their forms of organization to postwar conditions continued in the 1920s. The state administration had to urge the slow-moving associations to change the statutes that were previously approved by the partition authorities.[26] Jewish old-age homes in the area formerly belonging to the German Reich were hit by the period of transition the hardest. Due to the emigration of Jews to the Weimar Republic, these areas lost most of their established population as well as potential future residents. Therefore, the Beniamin Salomon Latz Shelter for the Aged and Infirm (Schronisko dla Starców i Zniedołężniałych) in Poznań took care of a small group of old people and used the synagogue hall for a library of Judaica rescued from the Torah study halls (*beit midrash*) in Greater Poland.[27] On the other hand, the shelter in Bojanowo near Poznań, built as a countryside palace, practically ceased providing care to the elderly.[28]

The most important change that affected old people's homes in interwar Poland reached beyond partisan organizational arrangements. It concerned how the income of the institutions was determined. The adoption of the Social Welfare Act established that the fate of old people's homes would be tied to subsidies from municipal budgets. Decisions on this issue were to be made in the course of discussions by representatives of political parties and representatives of various interest groups at local councils. Oversight of budget decisions was exercised by government administrative bodies, primarily county departments, which, on the one hand, were supposed to watch over the local government's fulfillment of its obligations under the law, while, on the other hand, they did not hesitate to cut funds at the expense of charitable institutions.

Although before the outbreak of World War I a significant number of Jewish old-age homes had independent sources of income or were run by religious communities, in the interwar period their operation depended on receiving subsidies from municipal funds. These sums typically formed the largest portion of the budget for the societies operating the facilities and provided a relatively secure source of income, in contrast to the less predictable donations or aid from abroad. Jewish community leaders at the national and local levels were well aware of this. The pressure that public opinion placed on them in this regard emerges in the press. At the same time, the denominational character of old people's homes was maintained throughout interwar Poland. Apart from the lower-level staff, most of the employees and the management were Jewish. The reasons for the distinctiveness of the Jewish institutions also remained the same: to create a space that was friendly to aging Jews, where they would be assured not only of care but of the freedom of religious and dietary observance, and also of continuing contact with their own ethnic-religious environment. Christian institutions, even those that were formally secular, in many cases depended on the work of clergy and were not prepared to meet Jewish ritual norms.

The system of subsidies confirmed by the welfare law was a solution regulated by the democratic process and theoretically free from discrimination on the basis of nationality or religion. During the interwar period, cities overwhelmingly fulfilled their obligation to contribute to Jewish homes for the elderly, and the amount of budget expenditures was subject to adoption by popularly elected bodies (city boards and councils with Jewish representatives). Moreover, institutions that cared for the elderly could count on local government subsidies even during periods of economic crisis and were among the last to be denied support. When schools, libraries, and nationwide Jewish community projects fell victim to austerity (e.g., the Institute for Jewish Research in Wilno), old people's homes usually continued to feature among planned municipal expenditures. Support was not universal: National Democrats (Endecja) took a consistent stance against any participation of city or state budgets in financing Jewish institutions—including old people's homes. But the Christian majority in the Second Republic did not share this attitude. As it seems, it viewed old people's homes or orphanages primarily through the prism of their humanitarian role. And yet cities overwhelmingly chose the route of only partially financing Jewish old-age homes from municipal budgets. The remaining funds had to come from such sources as societies' membership fees, occasional donations, money and items sent from abroad, and subsidies from the religious community.

In the first half of the 1920s, the Jewish press raised alarms about attempts by the National Democratic majorities on the city councils to limit Jewish participation in the distribution of subsidies. At a budget meeting of the Wilno council in July 1922, the Polish parties (with the exception of the Socialists) decided not to vote at all on subsidizing institutions owned by Jews. The author describing the issue in *Der Moment* regretfully stated that the vote passed without a protest, not only among the Polish but even among the Jewish public.[29] In Łódź, on the other hand, during a budget debate in 1926, Jewish councilors criticized the Polish majority for failing to finance a Jewish home for the elderly although Jews contributed about 40 percent of the city's tax revenue (meanwhile the Christian Charity Society had received a sizable subsidy).[30] At its inception, the Sanation rejected antisemitism, which could have given hope that local government policies would also change after the 1926 coup in Poland. These expectations were fulfilled to a limited extent.

For example, in 1929 the socialist *Lodzer Veker* compared the expenditures of the "red" coalition of the Łódź city council with those of the "black" coalition (of the Polish Right), proving their indisputable increase and showing the significant share of Jewish institutions' contributions to the subsidies allocated.[31] In many cities, however, disappointment was mainly expressed at the lack of fairness toward the needs of minorities. In 1928, the Lublin press reported that the magistrate was still treating Jews as "stepchildren," allocating to their institutions a fraction of what it did for Christian charities. The magistrate was not only expected to continue the process of reducing Jewish subsidies, but even to be more effective in doing so than the one dominated by its nationalist predecessors.[32] A similar situation occurred that same year in Siedlce. There, the city council, dominated by Polish Socialists (PPS), decided to maintain the previous pattern of funding for Jewish institutions, that is, a tripartite division of support for the magistrate, the Jewish religious community, and the Jewish public (separate from the Jewish community [*kehillah*]). A new argument in favor of such a solution was the alleged impossibility of verifying how many aid recipients were actually Siedlce residents.[33]

The economic perturbations of the 1920s did not yet foreshadow the tragedy that befell Poland during the Great Depression. The economic collapse affected broad masses of society, particularly hitting the trade and clothing crafts, which employed a significant percentage of Polish Jews.

Welfare institutions became unwitting victims of the deteriorating economic situation of their social base. Income from membership fees and annual charitable giving declined dramatically, and the impassioned exhortations of social activists and religious authorities did little to help. In the face of the crisis, the struggle for municipal subsidies was simultaneously becoming a fight for survival. Meanwhile, financial problems in earlier years had pushed local governments to seek savings in the social welfare sphere, and the Great Depression deprived welfare institutions of any sense of security for several years. City budgets, depleted by falling tax revenues, were undergoing far-reaching revision. Under the new conditions, the radical slogans of the National Democrats resounded particularly loudly, calling for the complete elimination of subsidies to Jewish institutions and shifting the responsibility for their upkeep onto the shoulders of Jewish religious communities. For example, in 1935 the National Democrats in the Przemyśl City Council spoke out against financing Jewish institutions with non-Jewish funds. Their stance won praise from the right-wing press reporting on the "outrageously high" amounts estimated in the following year's budget:

> The Non-partisan Bloc [Sanation] remained deaf to these arguments. Not a single (!) Jewish item was deleted. Thus, among other things, a 250 złoty subsidy was passed for a Hebrew school, a 1,000 złoty subsidy for a secondary school, a 100 złoty subsidy for dormitories, a 2,000 złoty subsidy for a hospital, and a 1,000 złoty subsidy for an orphanage. The scandal was the passing of a subsidy of 6,000 złoty for the Jewish old people's home, which should be maintained by the Jewish community and whose management, despite abundant subsidies, does not allow the magistrate to inspect.[34]

Obtaining the sum of 6,000 złoty for the needs of the Przemyśl old people's home in 1935 may seem like a success, but this is not how it was perceived by the Jewish community. The local government, which should have provided substantial help to the elderly, declared that it would grant the institution an amount representing about half of the total funds required for the operation. The rest of the income came from the subsidy of the *kehillah*, the Landsmannschaften from America, and voluntary donations.[35] Such a trimmed budget made it possible for the home to survive to care for a group of about twenty-six people, but made it very difficult to undertake other types of activities. It does not take advanced calculations to see that maintaining a relatively small group of wards with an absolutely minimal daily food allowance of a half złoty per person would bring the cost of food alone to about 4,750 złoty per year. Preparing holiday meals; renovating the infrastructure; paying the administrator, kitchen staff, and nurse also added to this burden. Expanding the institution in such circumstances could not even be considered.

Not only did local government attempts to reduce subsidies become more frequent in the 1930s, but so did interventions by city budget supervisors. For example, in 1932 the mayor of Biała Podlaska reduced the subsidy of a Jewish old-age home from 9,000 złoty to 7,500 złoty, based on an instruction from the county department.[36] In the second half of the 1930s, cuts made directly by the county department reduced the subsidy of the Baranowicze institution from 3,000 to just 1,000 złoty. The fact that the original, very low amount was the result of a laboriously negotiated "settlement" between Jewish circles and Sanation councilors added a special flavor to the event.[37] In addition, much more often than in the previous decade, Jewish activists faced cases of magistrates paying only part of the promised subsidies or, at best, delaying payments.[38] Faced with the economic arguments raised by the Christian side, Jewish politicians proposed temporary solutions to the institution's problems by, among other things, taking out bank loans or issuing promissory notes. Such solutions—including those in Brześć,[39] Międzyrzec Podlaski,[40] and Baranowicze[41]—were sometimes put into effect, but were occasionally thwarted by authorities strictly enforcing the rigors of public finance. In the absence of any hope of changing the trend in the city councils, those in charge of the old-age homes, together with Jewish politicians, sought support directly from the state authorities. During the governor's visit to Baranowicze in 1935, representatives of various unions and associations submitted petitions to him. Representatives of the Moshav Zkenim society also complained that the city was not paying the institutions the promised funds. The governor stated categorically that monies for orphans and the elderly must be found and within a few weeks, before the close of the fiscal year.[42] The intervention apparently helped, however, and the following year a representative of the old people's home again visited the Nowogródek provincial office. He was received by the head of the social welfare department, who hid behind formal considerations (i.e., that providing permanent financial assistance was the city's responsibility), but promised to consider one-time support.[43]

Over time, the Jewish community became convinced that the Christian majority was losing interest in maintaining a viable level of subsidies for Jewish institutions. As early as the 1930s, the press began to feature voices expressing fatigue over the relentless annual battle to secure the necessary support for facilities like old people's homes, among other things. An author from Brześć Litewski called on the boards of charitable societies not to stop at the "scraps" thrown to them by magistrates, but to demand full funding from municipal budgets. In doing so, he raised the argument about the double taxation of Jews and the constitutionally guaranteed ritual-religious distinctiveness.[44] Proposals of this kind, however, were rare. It seems that Jewish circles perceived them as unrealistic in the political conditions of the Second Republic, especially after the catastrophe of the Great Depression. Nor can it be ruled out that they feared (which resounds even in the voice from Brześć) the loss of influence over the institutions they ran, perceiving such a solution as tantamount to the threat of their liquidation.

The Main Jewish Shelter Home in Warsaw

The only exception to the rule that old people's homes remain under the full control of the Jewish community was the Main Shelter Home for Orphans and Old People (Główny Dom Schronienia Sierot i Starców Starozakonnych) in Warsaw. It was established in the early 1840s as a foundation of a wealthy Jewish philanthropist. After the fiasco of the 1863 uprising, the Russian authorities limited the legal autonomy of charitable institutions and effectively took over the facility. Efforts by the Jewish community to reclaim it were unsuccessful, but in 1874 the well-known social activist Hilary Nussbaum was appointed superintendent of the institution.[45] From then on, until September 1939, the Main Shelter Home remained under the control of a peculiar duumvirate: its management lay with the non-Jewish authorities, but curatorial care was exercised by a widely respected representative of the Jewish community. As of 1907, the Warsaw magistrate took control of the institution.[46] The Jewish community, represented by its chairman, Michał Bergson (who was also the house's curator, overseeing the institution on behalf of the municipality), handed over management of the foundation to the city, stipulating the condition of retaining the institution's existing name and character. The transfer of management, interpreted as the transfer of the property between Leszno and Wolska Streets to the city municipality, was confirmed by a communiqué in 1921 by a special committee appointed by the city council. According to historian Hanna Kozińska-Witt, this created a unique situation in Eastern Europe, when several important Jewish institutions (and not just the Shelter Home) became the property of the city.[47]

In the early 1930s, the Warsaw authorities began a process of reforming the city's relief institutions by relocating them to the provinces. The first to be transformed were institutions for combating begging, whose residents were primarily Christian. However, in December 1933, a move was announced with little notice to move the elderly from the Main Shelter Home to a leased palace in Broszków near Siedlce. The change was seen as scandalous. Jewish public opinion interpreted the actions of the municipal authorities, actually recruited from the nationalist Camp of Great Poland (Obóz Wielkiej Polski), as an attack on a Jewish charity that had been in existence for almost a century.[48] The belated action taken by the home's curator, representatives of the religious community, and city councilors proved to be of little effect. Apart from public protests, nothing was done to halt the transfer, and the first practical effects of their efforts—including those aimed at giving the elderly from the province a ritual burial—did not appear until several weeks later.

Already in the spring of the following year, the city's administration resigned over controversy surrounding the city's budget. The new mayor of Warsaw was a politician of the Sanation camp. He set about arranging the affairs of the capital in the spirit of "cleaning up the mess" left by his predecessors, and one of the problems he took up at the time was resolving the crisis surrounding Broszków. The Yiddish press did not hide its satisfaction at the news that engineer Maurycy Rotmil had been summoned to the mayor's office and entrusted with the position of director of the home "in exile." Rotmil was a very experienced social activist. He held numerous positions in welfare institutions, including overseeing the operation of the Jewish hospital and the welfare station on behalf of the magistrate. In July 1931, he had been removed from city service for a number of offenses committed in his official capacity. The Jewish press was critical in its assessments of the charges against him. It interpreted the official's conduct positively, proving his impeccable integrity and many years of success in high positions. Antisemitism was thought to play a role. Rotmil's return to favor in April 1934 was seen as a symbolic victory over the discredited nationalists.[49]

The new Warsaw authorities were not willing to reverse their decision to reorganize social welfare, which was bringing tangible savings. Instead, the mission in Broszków was to "clean up" the situation on the ground. As it seems, the corrective regime put in place by Rotmil bore fruit, although he was dismissed in 1935 over a conflict with his staff. His position was subsequently filled by other Jewish officials. At the same time, the Shelter Home building, contrary to the concerns of the Jewish public, did not change its purpose. The new municipal authorities placed in it the youngest orphans from the House for Jewish Foundlings located on Płocka Street (which was turned into a hospital). The buildings on Leszno and Wolska Streets operated continuously under the aegis of the institution founded almost a century prior, but served almost exclusively to care for infants and orphaned children. In Broszków, on the other hand, until the end of the interwar period there was a Shelter for Jews Unfit for Work (Schronisko dla Niezdolnych do Pracy Żydów), maintained by the Warsaw authorities, but managed by Jewish officials.[50]

Within the Jewish Community

Voices calling on religious Jewish communities to assume responsibility for financing Jewish welfare facilities were raised not only by a radical sector of Christians. It is worth noting that the law defining the system of *kehillas* since 1927 (in Warsaw since 1916) indicated institutionalized assistance to the poor as one of the goals of these communities' activities.[51] On the other hand, their nature was determined by religious persuasion, making members of the communities—and, in fact, public-legal corporations—all persons declaring observance of Mosaic religion (Judaism). The ability to collect certain fees from coreligionists gave the communities authority, which meant that the *kehillas* had budgets that enabled them to organize charity. They also had at their disposal properties potentially serving this purpose directly or through rental profits. In addition, the communities were institutions embedded in religious tradition and law. They coordinated the religious life of Jews, managed ritual baths, kosher slaughter, and so on. With all this, they had an apparatus of clerks, accountants, and lawyers. They were able to take actions that translated into social reality, giving individuals a sense of participation in determining their priorities through a democratic formula for electing governing bodies. Thus even before the economic collapse of the late 1920s and early 1930s, Jewish communities were seen as important tools for meeting diaspora needs (religious, social, national). This opinion did not change, and perhaps even strengthened, during a period of uncertainty and rising antisemitic sentiment.

As long as municipal subsidies remained a reliable income for nursing homes' budgets, only supplemented by donations or occasional collections, the role of *kehillas* in maintaining them remained marginal. Religious communities provided various kinds of support to the societies running the institutions, if only by lending space for general assembly sessions, but little more than that. This clearly began to change in the 1930s. Year after year, Jewish social activists and politicians faced increasingly serious difficulties in fighting for the existence of the institutions entrusted to them. Although threats to eliminate subsidies to Jewish institutions were openly raised, mainly by circles affiliated with the National Democrats, their impact reached far beyond the opposition benches. Talks with the ruling camp and negotiations at the local government level yielded results that were short-lived at best. Localized compromises were burdened with significant concessions and were sometimes broken after just a few weeks. The hope that with an improvement in the country's economic situation there would be a return to subsidizing old people's homes at a level even close to the previous one seemed to be fading. In such a situation, seeking help from the Jewish religious community was becoming a true gesture of despair.

The expectations placed on the *kehillah* authorities did not always prove to be justified. This is evidenced, among other things, by their passive attitude toward the liquidation of the elderly section of the Main Shelter Home in Warsaw. And yet the religious community had all the tools to play a leading role in solving the problems plaguing the establishments. For example, in Pińsk, where the Jewish community had to face the consequences of the incorporation of the Karolin community, the *kehillah* authorities managed two old people's homes from the early 1930s, and within a few years brought them together under their supervision.[52] The efficiency of the communal management of the Pińsk institution is evidenced primarily by the fact that it quickly resumed operation after a tragic fire in 1936.[53] In Białystok, two institutions with similar goals—a *hekdesh* (originally a home for the poor) and an old people's home—survived into the interwar period, competing for municipal subsidies and support from the local Jewish community. The profile of their residents was essentially identical. The conflict over this issue escalated in 1929, shortly after the *hekdesh* building underwent a major renovation. The local press reported plans to turn the old people's home into a facility exclusively for the elderly and the *hekdesh* into a shelter for single individuals with disabilities. These efforts coincided with the expectations of the Christian authorities, who looked unfavorably on the existence of two similar Jewish institutions dependent on the municipal budget.[54] Eventually the institutions were merged under management of the *kehillah*, while maintaining their formal separation. This process was not easy and took about five years. It turned out to be possible only thanks to the authority of the religious community, which was able to influence both the *hekdesh* representatives and the intelligentsia involved in the old people's home.[55]

Documents from the interwar period bear ample testimony to the influence of community-wide politics on the situation of institutions for the elderly. Evidently, influences of this kind made themselves known in cities where political parties had strong enough roots to take responsibility for the fate of relief institutions. This was the case, for example, in Baranowicze, where the Zionists held a conspicuous position in the Moshev Zkenim society (alongside several other associations). While in other cities, large and medium-sized, meetings of charitable societies were sometimes held in Jewish community buildings, here the annual gatherings were held rather in the Jabotinsky People's Home. The old people's home itself lived to see modern premises in 1929, which the founder—a local businessman sympathetic to Zionism—handed over for use by the Jewish community. However, already in the first weeks after the building was inaugurated, a conflict of competencies arose between the retirement home committee (actually the society's board of directors) and the *kehillah*. A compromise was reached on the matter and a new committee was elected only during a special meeting held in the community building. The institution was then led by a local Zionist activist, who headed it until the outbreak of war.[56]

However, the friction did not cease, and even escalated after the municipal elections in 1933, which were victorious for the Orthodox. In mid-1935, during the next meeting of the association's members, a heated disagreement ensued over problems with balancing the establishment's budget. Representatives of the Jewish community, dominated by Hasidic circles, announced their readiness to help, but on the condition that a few seats be reserved for them on the next board. This was met with a categorical refusal by Zionist activists, in response to which the representatives of the religious community left the meeting.[57] In 1937—during the same term of the *kehillah*—some members of the Baranowicze Jewish community council demanded an increase in fees from the wealthiest users of the ritual bath. The additional funds were to support relief institutions, including the home for the elderly, and among the arguments in favor of this solution it was pointed out that the higher fees would only burden those who do not otherwise pay for "national institutions," which meant, therefore, the Orthodox. This argument failed to convince the religious majority. In a tense atmosphere, the proposal was rejected as not promising a significant increase in revenue.[58] After the 1938 elections, the relationship between the community and the society's authorities improved. Perhaps political fragmentation and the reluctance of voters to support partisan representatives contributed to this. The religious community's budget estimated for 1939 provided a subsidy to the old people's home. It was not a large one, but it was more than what was planned before the elections, and therefore gave hope for better cooperation with the new *kehillah*.[59] The management of the old people's home did not cease in its appeals for greater involvement of Jewish representatives.[60] A conference of the association's board of directors, held at the Jewish community's headquarters in early 1939, is some evidence of concerted action.[61] However, leaving aside the atmosphere of social mobilization, it is difficult to conclude that it was intended to herald a more serious agreement in favor of the old people's home. A few months later, World War II broke out.

Conclusion

Despite the serious economic stresses of the interwar period, the society of reborn Poland managed to implement pioneering solutions to the welfare and pension security systems in most areas of the country, and the Jewish minority took part in their development. Social activists and politicians representing Jews concentrated their efforts on providing social security for their immediate support base, operating within the religious community, as well as through partisan local politics and on a national level in the Polish parliament. The issue of assistance for the elderly was one of the main concerns raised in almost all forums of public activity. The catastrophe of the Great War deprived many care facilities of secure sources of income. At the same time, there was a growing awareness among members of the Jewish community that nursing homes could provide a dignified alternative for aging outside a family home. Arranging institutional budgets under conditions of political struggle proved to be a very difficult task. Subsidies from municipal coffers obtained under the existing law rarely covered more than half of the necessary annual expenses and, especially in the 1930s, they were reduced or for other reasons went unpaid. On the eve of the outbreak of World War II, however, most Jewish nursing homes in Poland were still operating with the benefit of municipal subsidies, even if in many cities this support was minimal, something Jewish communities perceived as harassment.

After September 1939, the fate of Jewish nursing homes became uncertain overnight. In areas occupied by the Germans, it was only possible to maintain their existence through the enormous efforts of the Jewish population. Many of these institutions continued to operate, even though living conditions deteriorated dramatically, hunger prevailed, and there was no hope of improvement. The home on Górczewska Street still housed a group of elderly people at least until the summer of 1940.[62] The residents of the main shelter, which had been moved to Broszków in 1933, had been forced to return to Warsaw to live in a facility in the ghetto. The cruel conditions of the ghetto took their toll in the final years of that institution, which Janusz Korczak called a *szlachtuz* (slaughterhouse). A similar institution existed in Płock until the fall of 1940 and was maintained by the Jewish Council with funds from the Joint (American Jewish Joint Distribution Committee), among other organizations. The home's approximately forty residents were then sent to the camp in Działdowo (Soldau), where they were probably shot. In Lublin, the local Jewish orphanage and old people's home shared its cramped building with officials from the Judenrat (the German-established Jewish council). Thanks to the generosity of the Jewish population, however, it was able to continue operating until the ghetto was liquidated in 1942. In contrast, in the territories occupied by the Soviet Union, most of the nursing homes were preserved, albeit at the cost of nationalization and the loss of their strictly Jewish character. But with the outbreak of the German-Soviet war in 1941, the fates of their residents were sealed.

Notes

1 Paweł Grata, "System emerytalny Drugiej Rzeczypospolitej," in *Ludzie starzy i starość na ziemiach polskich od XVIII do XXI wieku (na tle porównawczym)*, ed. Agnieszka Janiak-Jasińska, Katarzyna Sierakowska, and Andrzej Szwarc (DiG, 2016), 398–400; Grata, "Polityka społeczna Drugiej Rzeczpospolitej wobec cyklu życia," *Problemy Polityki Społecznej: Studia i Dyskusje* 1, no. 28 (2015): 55–58; Anna Jarosz-Nojszewska, "Ubezpieczenie emerytalne pracowników umysłowych w Drugiej Rzeczypospolitej," in *Od kwestii robotniczej do nowoczesnej kwestii socjalnej: Studia z polskiej polityki społecznej XX i XXI wieku*, vol. 5, ed. Paweł Grata, (Wydawnictwo Uniwersytetu Rzeszowskiego, 2017), 34–50.

2 "Ustawa z dn. 16 sierpnia 1923 o opiece społecznej," *Dziennik Ustaw* 1923, no. 92, item 726, supplemented, among others, by "Ustawa z dn. 16 sierpnia 1923 o opiece społecznej," *Dziennik Ustaw* 1924, no. 56, item 576; "Rozporządzenie Prezydenta Rzeczypospolitej z dn. 6 marca 1928 o rozgraniczeniu obowiązków opiekuńczych związków komunalnych," *Dziennik Ustaw* 1928, no. 26, item 232, and others.

3 Grata, "Polityka społeczna Drugiej Rzeczpospolitej wobec cyklu życia," 58. The first Jewish old people's homes on Polish soil were established in the 1830s and 1840s in Poznań and Warsaw. A preliminary study of this issue, based, among other things, on *yizkor bikher* (Jewish memorial books) literature, was presented by Shaul Stampfer in his article, "What Happened to the Extended Jewish Family? Jewish Homes for the Aged in Eastern Europe," in *Studies in Contemporary Jewry*, vol. 14, *Coping with Life and Death: Jewish Families in the Twentieth Century*, ed. Peter Y. Medding (Oxford University Press, 1999), 128–41.

4 "Nasze postulaty w Sejmie," *Inwalida Żydowski*, March 1, 1929, 1–2. See Paweł Grata, "Stanowisko parlamentarzystów żydowskich wobec polityki

podatkowej państwa polskiego w okresie Wielkiego Kryzysu," in *Rola Żydów w rozwoju gospodarczym ziem ziem polskich*, ed. Janusz Skodlarski and Andrzej Pieczewski (Wydawnictwo Uniwersytetu Łódzkiego, 2014), 157–74.

5 "Memorjal," *Di Shokhtim Shtime*, April 11, 1929, 3–5.

6 "Nowa ustawa emerytalna," *Nowy Dziennik*, February 18, 1932, 10.

7 "Kronik: Di shtelung fun di baamtn tsu di proyektn fun sotsiale gezetsn," *Dos Fraye Vort*, April 1, 1932, 6.

8 "Tsoln mer un bakumen veyniker: Proyekt vegn reformirn di sotsiale farzikherung," *Der Moment*, February 17, 1933, 10; B. Chilinovich, "Velkhe enderungen firt-arayn dos naye gezets vegn sotsiale farzikherungen?," *Der Moment*, February 21, 1933, 4, and March 1, 1933, 4.

9 Janusz Falowski, *Mniejszość żydowska w parlamencie II Rzeczypospolitej* (AFM, 2006), 61–80.

10 The censuses carried out in Poland in the interwar period showed a gradual aging of the Jewish population. The proportion of those over the age of sixty in this group increased from 6.8 percent to 8.6 percent within a decade (1921–31). This phenomenon deepened in the 1930s, marked by economic crisis. See *Pierwszy powszechny spis Rzeczypospolitej Polskiej z dnia 30 września 1921 roku: Mieszkania, ludność, stosunki zawodowe* (Główny Urząd Statystyczny 1927), 20–21; *Drugi powszechny spis ludności z dn. 9.XII 1931 R. Mieszkania i gospodarstwa domowe: Ludność* (Główny Urząd Statystyczny, 1938), 21.

11 Szyja Bronsztejn, *Ludność żydowska w Polsce w okresie międzywojennym: Studium statystyczne* (Zakład Narodowy im. Ossolińskich, 1963), 236.

12 Bronsztejn, 140, 169.

13 "Z dyskusji budżetowej w Sejmie," *Inwalida Żydowski*, July 1, 1928, 1–3; "Premjer Bartel zapowiada," *Nowy Dziennik*, November 30, 1928, 2; "Nasze postulaty w Sejmie," *Inwalida Żydowski*, March 1, 1929, 1–2.

14 "Renty inwalidzkie, emerytury i pensje (Obrady komisji budżetowej Sejmu)," *Inwalida Żydowski*, December 31, 1934, 2–3; *Prawda o emeryturach "zaborczych," traktatach i konwencjach pokojowych oraz przejętych przez Rząd Polski funduszach emerytalnych b. Austrji* (Kraków, 1936).

15 Speakers on the issue included MP Henryk Rozmarin, "Sprawa emerytur na komisji sejmowej," *Nowy Dziennik*, January 14, 1933, 2.

16 For example, "Zarządzenie Ministra Wyznań Religijnych i Oświecenia Publicznego z dnia 28 grudnia 1936 r. o pensji i emeryturze rabinów i

podrabinów oraz o zabezpieczeniu pozostałych po nich wdów i sierot," *Monitor Polski*, March 15, 1937, item 60.

17 "Obniżyć granicę wieku dla świadczeń emerytalnych!," *Nowy Dziennik*, September 30, 1934, 8.

18 I. Fridman, "Hilf fun di landsmanshaftn far undz poylishe Yidn," *Folks Hilf*, January 1, 1939, 37.

19 Ha-Roe, "Michtavim me-arey ha-sde," *Ha-Melitz*, September 7, 1902, 2–3; *Memuarn fun Isroel Bunimowitsh* (Levin, 1928), 86–98.

20 See Żbikowski, *Żydzi krakowscy i ich gmina w latach 1869–1919*, 234–35.

21 A. Litvin, "Yechezkiel Kotik un zayn kaviarnie," in A. Litvin, *Yidish neshomes*, vol. 4, *Poyln* (New York, 1917), 9.

22 *Ognisko dla Starców Inteligentów* (Towarzystwo "Dom Starców," 1929).

23 "80-yerike zkeynim muzn shteyn far an ekzamen in Moyshev Zkeynim," *Unzer Ekspres*, May 7, 1929, 6.

24 Even the announcement calling for attendance at the meeting was to be printed only in Polish, while the society's annual activity reports were published bilingually (in Polish and Hebrew) thanks to the personal involvement of one of the board members. N. Z., "Fun yidishe institutsyes: Oyf der algemeyner farzamlung fun 'Moyshev Zkeynim,'" *Der Moment*, April 30, 1930, 5.

25 Ben-Ir, "Fun yidishn lebn in Radom," *Der Moment*, October 28, 1919, 4; Prof. P. Muszkatblith, "Portret (zikhroynes): H. r' Reuven Bekerman z"l," *Radomer Cajtung*, May 1, 1925, 2–3.

26 For example, in Radom, a new statute was prepared only in the second half of the 1930s, although the Ministry of Social Welfare had been courting it since 1927 ("W trosce o Dom Sierot Żydowskich," *Trybuna*, November 21, 1936, 9; "Vos iz mitn moyshev-zkeynim?," *Radomer-Kielcer Lebn*, December 18, 1936, 7).

27 Barbara Michniak, "Biblioteki żydowskie w Polsce w dwudziestoleciu międzywojennym," *Biuletyn Żydowskiego Instytutu Historycznego* 3, no. 187 (1998): 36–42 (36).

28 Leon Weinstock, "Oaza miłosierdzia żydowskiego w Poznańskiem: Wrażenia z Bojanowa," *Ewa*, March 25, 1928, 5–6; "'Ściśle koszerne letnisko w Wielkopolsce,'" *Kurjer Poznański*, July 27, 1938, 7.

29 Iks, "Brif fun Vilne," *Der Moment*, July 22, 1921, 4.

30 Ben-Henoch, "Vi azoy der Lodzer magistrat 'bazorgt' di interesn fun der oremer Yidisher bafelkerung," *Der Moment*, February 17, 1926, 2.

31 L.P., "Der shtotisher budzhet oyfn yor 1929–30," *Lodzer Veker*, February 15, 1929, 3.
32 Sh. I. Stupnicki, "Magistrat un yidisze kehile," *Lubliner Togblat*, January 9, 1928, 2; Af., "Z Rady Miejskiej: Budżet miasta w krytycznem świetle liderów stronnictw," *Ziemia Lubelska*, September 19, 1928, 2.
33 " 'Yidish' zitsungen in Sht. Rat," *Unzer Veg*, May 18, 1928, 1, 4.
34 "Radni narodowi w walce o polskość Przemyśla," *Dziennik Wileński*, June 17, 1935, 7.
35 "Opłakany bilans gospodarki kahalnej w Przemyślu," *Chwila*, July 16, 1932, 8.
36 Ferri, "Nokh vos zitsn mir in Shtotrat?," *Podlasier leben*, June 3, 1932, 2.
37 A.M., " 'Wydział Powiatowy' kimat in gantsn geshtrokhn di yidishe subsidyes: Oyserordntlekhe zitsung fun Shtot Rat," *Baranovitsher Vokh*, September 25, 1938, 4.
38 "Groyse Yidn-debate in Shtot-Rat," *Kalisher Lebn*, March 11, 1932, 1.
39 "Fun brisker lebn," *Brisker Vokhnblat*, February 3, 1928, 3.
40 "Shtot-rat-zitsung," *Mezritsher Tribune*, January 6, 1931, 3; "Der traditsyoneler bal in moyshev-zkeynim," *Mezritsher Vokhnblat*, June 19, 1931, 3.
41 "Notitsn," *Baranovitsher Vokh*, December 23, 1932, 2.
42 "Bazukh fun voyevode Siderski in Baranovitsh," *Baranovitsher Vokh*, August 30, 1935, 4.
43 "Interwents in voyevodshaft vegn hilf far 'Beys-Yesoymim' un 'Moyshev-Zkeynim,' " *Baranovitsher Vokh*, March 20, 1936, 3.
44 Ing. A. Levitas, "Der yor-budzhet in di shtot-ratn un di 'yidishe pozitsyes,' " *Brisker Vokhnblat*, January 24, 1930, 4.
45 Sabina Lewin, "Warszawski dom sierot (Dom Schronienia) w XIX w.," *Biuletyn Żydowskiego Instytutu Historycznego*, no. 123–24 (1982): 31, 38.
46 "Projekt ustawy zasadniczej o opiece społecznej," *Biuletyn Ministerstwa Pracy i Opieki Społecznej* 1, no. 5 (1919): 172–78 (177); *Sprawozdania Komisji Rewizyjnej m. st. Warszawy: Fundacje i zapisy dobroczynne* (Warsaw, 1936), 8–11.
47 Hanna Kozińska-Witt, "Polityka społeczna m.st. Warszawy względem żydowskich mieszkańców stolicy (1919–1939)—według relacji prasowych," *Kwartalnik Historii Żydów*, no. 267 (2018): 495–96.
48 Hilel Tseytlin, "A bisl mer mitgefil tsu mentshn," *Der Moment*, January 4, 1934, 4; "A sheynem takhles makht der magistrat fun yidishe institutstes," *Haynt*, January 25, 1934, 5; "A 'duel' tsvishn inzh: Kerner un dem endek

Ilski beys a diskusye vegn yidishn Moyshev Zkeynim," *Haynt*, January 26, 1934, x; "5-ta Rano," January 27, 1934, 4.

49 "Di endekishe intrige kegn hekhern Yidishn magistrat-baamtn inzh. Rotmil iz nisht gelungen!," *Unzer Ekspres*, April 25, 1934, 7; "Regirungs-prezident Kościałkowski rehabilitirt a hechern Yidishn baamtn," *Der Moment*, April 25, 1934, 5.

50 For more on Broszków, see Marek Tuszewicki, " 'Nie chcemy iść do grobu za życia': Wokół przeniesienia pensjonariuszy Głównego Domu Schronienia Starozakonnych w Warszawie do Broszkowa," *Kwartalnik Historii Żydów* 4, no. 280 (2021): 957–85.

51 Adv. Jakub Grynsztejn, "Ustawodawstwo dotyczące gmin żydowskich w niepodległej Polsce," *Głos Gminy Żydowskiej* 2, nos. 10–11 (1938): 322–23; "*Gmina wyznaniowa*," in *Żydzi w Polsce: Dzieje i kultura. Leksykon*, ed. Jerzy Tomaszewski and Andrzej Żbikowski (Cyklady, 2001), 108–15.

52 "A shturmishe zitsung fun der Kehile-Farvaltung," *Pinsker Vort*, March 6, 1931, 6; I. H-n, "Fareynikung," *Pinsker Vort*, April 20, 1934, 5; "Barikht fun der kehile-zitsung," *Pinsker Vort*, June 8, 1934, 4.

53 "A Kehile zitsung," *Pinsker Vort*, November 19, 1937, 6.

54 A. R-r, "Mit a kranker kop in a gezunter bet: A sikhsekh tsvishn tsvey institutsyes," *Dos Naye Lebn*, September 27, 1929, 2; Homo, "Vu tuen mir ahin di 'gevezene' mentshn? Di kehile muz makhn a tolk!," *Naye Bialistoker Shtime*, October 4, 1929, 4–5; "Vos hert zikh in Bialistok? Nit keyn hekdesh, nor a pensyonat," *Dos Naye Lebn*, October 15, 1929, 2; Z. Weinstein, "Tsdoke-konkurents tsvishn Polyakn un Yidn in Bialistok," *Der Moment*, January 19, 1930, 3.

55 A. M. Trzonowicz, "Dos yidishe Bialistok hoybt on tsurik uftsulebn," *Unzer Ekspres*, January 5, 1931, 4.

56 "Vos iz mitn moyshev-zkeynim," *Baranovitsher Lebn*, November 15, 1929, 4.

57 "Af der kehile ligt itst der khoyev! (Tsu der yor-farzamlung fun 'Moyshev-Zkeynim')," *Dos Fraye Vort* (Baranovitsh), July 19, 1935, 4; "Yerlekhe algemeyne farzamlung fun 'Moyshev-Zkeynim' Gezelshaft," *Baranovitsher Vokh*, August 9, 1935, 4.

58 "Di bale-batishkayt fun undzer kehile (3 un 4-te budzhet zitsung fun Kehile-Rat): Subsidirte mitsves . . . ," *Baranovitsher Vokh*, December 31, 1937, 2.

59 M., "Vayterdike budzhet-zitsung fun Kehile-Rat: Ongenumen do hoytsoe-teyl," *Baranovitsher Vokh*, January 3, 1939, 2; Baruch Galay, "A por verter tsu di budzhet shtraytn in kehile," *Baranovitsher Vokh*, January 13, 1939, 2.

60 Di Farvaltung, "Ofener briv tsu der kehile-farvaltung fun Baranovitsher 'Moyshev Zkeynim,'" *Baranovitsher Vokh*, January 27, 1939, 3.

61 "Di kritishe lage in 'Moyshev Zkeynim,'" *Baranovitsher Vokh*, March 3, 1939, 2.

62 After the establishment of Warsaw ghetto, the Górczewska Street home happened to be located outside of its boundaries. It is possible that it was forcibly evacuated in the autumn of 1940, but there is no official documentation on this matter.

3

"THE TRAGEDY OF OLD AGE IS NOT THAT ONE IS OLD, BUT THAT ONE IS YOUNG"

Antonia Jacoby and Elderly Jewish Migration to Japan

Niamh Hanrahan

The early 1940s saw thousands of Jews fleeing Europe to escape Nazi persecution, utilizing global routes to find safety. Antonia Jacoby and her mother, Fanny Behrendt, were a part of this movement. Their wartime migration took them from Breslau, Germany (today's Wrocław, Poland), in 1940, through the Soviet Union, Manchuria, China, and Korea before reaching Kobe in Japan, where Antonia remained until 1947. Antonia and Fanny's journey to and their time in Japan are noteworthy, as they were women traveling independently of other family members and were also advanced in age—Antonia was sixty-one and Fanny was eighty-three years old when they arrived in Kobe.[1] This chapter contributes to our understanding of older Jewish refugees fleeing Nazi persecution and the trajectories available to them, on a more globalized scale than is typically considered in historiography. Through a focus on the journey of Antonia Jacoby and Fanny Behrendt from Germany to Japan, the chapter highlights how categories such as gender and economic status figure into traveling, connecting literature on elderly survivors of the Holocaust, gender, and transnational wartime migration.

Only one record related to Antonia Jacoby can be found in a public archive, a letter held by the Wiener Holocaust Library in London.[2] The letter, sent in June 1940 from Antonia in Kobe to family member Marie

Behrendt in Argentina, gives some insight into Antonia and Fanny's journey to Japan. Other material on the women exists in a private archive of their relatives in Israel.[3] Antonia's writing is often reflective of her position in the world: as a daughter caring for an elderly mother, as a Jew encountering and escaping persecution, as someone disconnected from family through migration, and as someone herself aging. In fact, Antonia included the titular quote from *The Picture of Dorian Gray* by Oscar Wilde in a letter to her son in 1947, in which she contemplated becoming older during their time apart throughout the war. It also speaks more widely to the role Antonia assumed during her exile—as a person having to reconfigure her surroundings and thus learn new things, but also as a child, caring for a parent.

This chapter first considers the journey that Antonia and Fanny undertook and the planning that went into their wartime movements. Elderly emigration during the Holocaust is an understudied area in scholarship on wartime migration. Additionally, this chapter explores the global element of this discussion, which has not yet been a significant focus of historians. In one of only a few works focusing on the wartime migration of elderly Jews, historian Melissa Jane Taylor considers their flight from Vienna to the United States. She notes that, for elderly refugees closer to the end rather than the beginning of their lives, the risks and challenges of travel were different from those faced by younger refugees.[4] This chapter does not aim to be an overview of elderly migration experiences to Japan; rather, it hopes to build on Taylor's approach and integrate individual accounts into migration studies.

There has been a great deal written on the intertwining of gender and migration, especially in the social sciences, with the focus of migration studies shifting from solely the working-class male head of household to incorporating women.[5] Johanna Leinonen, a historian of migration, remarks that "the bulk of the scholarship focuses on the reproductive role of migrant women (e.g., as family members, caregivers, domestic workers, or sex workers)."[6] When older women are considered within this framework, it is often through questions surrounding how they are cared for by their children, whether or not they will leave their homelands, and how they will readjust to new environments. The example of Antonia and Fanny provides this chapter an opportunity to move past issues of the immobility of older women in this context, toward a discussion of older people as active participants in migration. The chapter will also consider Antonia and Fanny's time in Kobe, where they spent a considerable period. For most Jewish refugees, Japan was a brief stopping point, from a few months to a few years. Therefore, that Antonia remained in the city until 1947 is significant.

Age studies in Holocaust research is a growing field, with key contributions being made in areas such as age determination, agency, and care.[7] Within this, elderly welfare is also a topic of increasing interest and is largely understood through aid and charity organizations or family members and associates coming to the assistance of those in need. Focusing on the case of Antonia, who at sixty-one-years-old continued to be the main caregiver for her elderly mother, pushes our conceptualization of caregiving during the Holocaust. Few studies consider elderly Jews who undertook forced migration during the Holocaust, especially older women, and those that do tend to focus on trajectories that remain within the West or the Soviet Union.[8] This chapter aims to push this geographic focus, highlighting one example of older people undertaking transnational journeys outside of Europe.

Letter Writing

This chapter reconstructs Antonia and Fanny's trajectory as understood through Antonia's letters. It focuses on the already mentioned letter Antonia's relatives donated to the Wiener Holocaust Library in 2011, also drawing on other letters (as well as a small number of photographs and telegrams) held privately by her family in Israel.[9]

Several publications have considered older people's correspondence during the Holocaust, with a focus on the letters of Jewish grandmothers. At the beginning of a chapter on tracing transatlantic family correspondence during the Holocaust, language and literature scholar Bettina Brandt briefly discusses the fate of the grandmother of a family, Nelly Lehnert. When the family fled Vienna in 1939, they were forced to leave her behind and she was deported to Theresienstadt. "There, in 'the Old Age Home on the Elbe' as the Nazis had deceivingly marketed Theresienstadt to German and Austrian elderly, Nelly died from starvation and disease shortly after her arrival."[10] Brandt describes one of the granddaughters, Trudie, finding letters from Nelly in her attic when she herself was eighty

FIGURE 3.1. Antonia Jacoby. Courtesy of Yael Naaman.

years old, and wanting to reconnect with her grandmother's experiences later in her own life. In the same volume, historian Atina Grossmann traces events and emotions by considering letters sent by her own grandmother, bringing together her own family archives and academic research.[11] Also using material from her family, Holocaust survivor and writer Renata Polt highlights a collection of letters written by her grandmother and aunt, who were killed in concentration camps in 1942.[12]

Letters as source material can offer insights into moments of a person's life, but they also bring challenges. As historian Shirli Gilbert notes, letters can be elusive resources.[13] They were not written with the intention of becoming sources and, therefore, there are "layers of negotiation" with which to contend, for both the historian and writer as well as relatives, archivists, and future readers.[14] Letters that become historical sources, such as Antonia's, have an afterlife that was unanticipated when being written, often moving from the intimate sphere into a public archive. Indeed, Antonia's letter housed in the archives of the Wiener Holocaust Library was written to a family friend with whom she had previously been close when they lived in the same area. She remarks, "only when I tell you all the little things do I still have the feeling that I'm at home with you like before, when we told each other all the everyday things."[15] She refers to people and places in the letter in a style designed for her recipient—not for a researcher in the archives decades later.[16] Historian Charlie Knight suggests when discussing the "shared world" between author, recipient, and researcher, that "in many cases, the researcher unrelated from the family concerned is excluded from the epistolary dialogue and thus creates absences within the context."[17] It is important that researchers coming into contact with these sources are aware of these absences that they will encounter—and also of the power they hold through their highlighting of these sources. Through their research, "they help decide not only which lives will be known by successive generations, but also what parts of those lives, and why."[18] In the case of this letter, there is also a fourth party in this shared space—the future relative. Yael Naaman, Antonia's granddaughter, transcribed and annotated the letter and, along with a photocopy of the original, submitted it to the archive. The resulting document, a product of both 1940 and 2011, incorporates her relatives' attention to how future, unconnected readers can gain insight into her words.

A further consideration when utilizing letters as sources is access. Despite the family having further correspondence from Antonia, this is the only letter that they gave to the Wiener Holocaust Library, donated to a country Antonia neither migrated through nor lived in. Thus it exists as a fragment of her experiences. This letter is also one part of a conversation—we do not know of the reply from Marie, or if there even was one. We do know, however, that Antonia asks for Marie to enclose a copy of her letter in her reply so that Antonia can keep it for her records. Since that letter exists and was donated by Antonia's relatives to the library, we can deduce that the request was met. Other material on Antonia's experiences remains with her family as a private archive. Negotiating private archives can be a complex matter, involving parameters on research, locating relevant materials, and questions of how knowledge should move from private space into the public sphere. Judith Szapor, a historian researching the Hungarian Jewish Polanyi family in private archives, sums up these dilemmas well in relation to her own research: "What may have been an exciting discovery to the historian, highlighting an important episode in the history of twentieth-century physics and, by extension, the intellectual migration of the 1930s, was an intensely private matter to the Polanyis."[19]

Antonia's letters give us valuable insight into her understanding of the world she lived in and the information she felt was valuable to pass on to family members. While working with epistolary-based sources certainly has challenges, these letters—and the decision of the family to donate one of them—allow us to follow a multilayered trajectory in the preservation and dispersal of knowledge.

Journey Planning and Mobility

In a letter sent from Kobe in 1940, Antonia described the preparations she undertook to leave Germany and make the journey to Japan. This letter marks the first time that Antonia was able to recount her life in Germany and her escape to East Asia. She expressed her relief at finally being able to describe what had happened to her and sought to relay the last one-and-a-half years of her life. Much of the preparation involved financial affairs: having to pay the Reich Flight Tax (*Reichsfluchtsteuer*) to leave Germany, selling the family property before she left, and at the same time looking to the future by paying to secure and maintain gravesites.

According to her relatives, Antonia had been married, but her husband Siegfried Jacoby had died in 1928. She had four children, Paul (born 1905), Konrad (1906), Heinrich (1909), and Hans (1918), who were all born in Königsberg (now Kaliningrad, Russia) where Antonia was also born. By the time World War II had begun, three of her children were already married and had children of their own, and all were living in Mandatory Palestine. Little is recorded about their migration. However, in 1933, Heinrich was fired from his position as a violist in a Frankfurt orchestra due to anti-Jewish discriminatory laws.[20] That same year, he moved with his wife and children to Istanbul. A year later, in 1934, the family relocated to Jerusalem, where Heinrich played a key role in founding the Conservatory of Music. The early migration of her children perhaps explains why Antonia made the journey to Japan without any younger family members. In considering gender and migration practices, historian Nancy Green notes that "families—and the family is a gendered unit if anything is—have been central to many explanations of how migration functions."[21] For Antonia and Fanny to be migrating as members of the same family, but without the expected structure of a family (a mix of ages and genders), requires us to think further about the reasoning behind and methods of their migrations.

What we can learn of Fanny comes only through how Antonia describes her mother, and the photographs and information collected by her family. Fanny was born in 1857 in Winzig, a city close to Breslau, and died in Kobe in 1945. She married Heinrich Behrendt, and had two children, Antonia and a son, Kurt. Heinrich died in 1920 and Kurt in 1936. Antonia was her sole remaining child and both women had been widowed, so Fanny accompanied her daughter on the journey to Japan. At eighty-three years old in 1940, Fanny was a very elderly woman to be making an international journey. Antonia often mentioned Fanny's need to rest or to recuperate from an injury. Here an older person is looking after her elderly parent, when in another context she might have been looked after herself. Antonia describes caring for Fanny in her 1940 letter and in records collated by her relatives in Israel. One explanation for Antonia's role was that, as an adult migrant child, caring was a moral rather than strictly medical decision.[22] Indeed, nowhere in her letters does she question having to look after her mother. Whether or not she thought differently outside of the letters is unknown—but within them she seems to have accepted the role of Fanny's caregiver.

Antonia wrote about having to coordinate the sale of a house in Güntherstraße, which had been designed by her cousin, and noted that selling the house was a miracle, given the increasingly fraught financial situation for Jews in Germany. Although not stated, the house was probably sold after November 1938, when Nazi "Aryanization" policy changed such sales from "voluntary" to "forced," meaning that whatever Antonia earned from the sale of the house amounted to probably much less than it was worth.[23] Antonia also described organizing the financing for her own gravesite, making sure that its maintenance was paid (along with two other gravesites, potentially those of other family members) four years into the future. The notes added to this section by her granddaughter in 2011 express surprise at this—"it really is amazing that Toni [as the family called Antonia], a shrewd realistic person, was trying to secure her grave for 4 years in advance, when the near future was so obscure!"[24] Antonia noted that the cemetery would only accept payment for four to five years in the future. At several points early on in her letter, Antonia mentioned having to pay the 25 percent Reich Flight Tax placed on the assets of Jews attempting to emigrate. This tax was one of several measures imposed on Jews in Germany, aiming for their economic destruction. Antonia states that she had to pay 27,500 Reichsmarks (RM) before leaving, and a property tax of 32,800 RM. To provide some context, in 1935, a summary of price and wage levels showed almost half of German workers earned around 18 RM a week, below the poverty line.[25] Historians Christoph Kreutzmüller and Jonathan R. Zatlin further highlight the devastating economic effects placed on German Jewry attempting to flee: "In 1935, Jewish emigrants lost eighty pennies on every single Reichsmark they tried to take with them into exile. By 1937, the World Jewish Congress estimated, losses amounted to 95 percent."[26] A measure to further impoverish Jews limited the amount of money allowed to be withdrawn from bank accounts. Antonia also mentions this, stating that she was only able to take out 225 RM from Fanny's pension account because her own had been blocked. Antonia recalled the increasing stress she felt in Breslau: "Life became more and more oppressive, each day new measures were taken to isolate us as much as possible. From one day to the next I couldn't buy anything—not even milk, potatoes, and bread—on my street. [. . .] It is impossible to describe the humiliation we were subjected to."[27]

Antonia noted that while she and Fanny were still in Germany, she had contacted the Allianz insurance company, where her mother had a pension. Despite Fanny stating that it was "completely pointless," Antonia wrote to request partial repayment of it, evidencing a take-charge attitude. Allianz agreed to give her 3,300 RM after Fanny underwent a medical examination and produced a *Lebensbescheinigung* ("life certificate" to confirm that she was still alive), supplied by a relative.[28] Antonia recalled that Allianz wanted to pay the rest into a blocked account, but she asked them to reconsider and was given 5,200 RM.[29] Antonia did not go into further detail about this, but it was unusual that she was granted access to the pension money within a system where it was common for Jews to lose much of their life savings to blocked accounts. Despite Fanny's often depending on Antonia to look after her physically, her pension gave her a measure of financial agency, which was crucial in enabling the two women to leave Germany.

Later in the letter, Antonia described her increasing knowledge of deportations and actions taken against Jews in Stettin (Szczecin) and Kattowitz (Katowice) in early 1940 and her feeling that these would soon spread to Breslau.[30] Antonia wrote that she felt relieved that she was able to make it out of Germany, now not caring that she had very little money, which had not been her feeling before she left the country.

Antonia and Fanny traveled from Breslau to Berlin by train to try to secure the necessary exit documentation. Antonia noted that she had tried to do this from Breslau by telephoning the travel agency, *Hapag-Beamte*, but had been advised that although the visas for her and Fanny had been issued, they had been returned due to the "J" stamped on their passports.[31] Going in person was her next step. Antonia described giving the agency an ultimatum—either they sort out her travel arrangements within two days or she would change to travel via Vladivostok and not use their services any longer. Antonia's continued persistence in her bid to leave Germany, in the face of increasing restrictions on movement and racist legislation, is notable. Rather than working around difficulties, she appears, from her own descriptions, to have quite obstinately faced these obstacles head-on, demanding that organizations aid her in her plans to flee. This instance also highlights one of the challenges of using letters as a central source in research, as Antonia does not explain why she chose this travel agency, or this route, over another—the letter is the only information available to us. The travel agency was able to arrange the necessary documentation, and Antonia and Fanny traveled from Germany to Moscow by plane. She also did not explain why they took a flight instead of a train (which was widely used by Jewish refugees escaping via Moscow), but that they were able to afford to fly suggests that the two had enough financial resources to facilitate more high-class travel.

Moscow

During journeys of flight from Nazi Europe, there were along the way many periods of immobility for Jewish refugees: waiting for visas, waiting for connections, and waiting for transportation onward.[32] Many of these stops often brought encounters with different people and new cultural experiences, some of which stayed with them throughout their lives. For Jews headed for Japan, Moscow was a memorable stop along their journey. While in the city, Antonia wrote that she left Fanny to sleep in the hotel and was able to go on a sightseeing tour, noting that she saw (among other sites) the Kremlin and Lenin's tomb. Several other Jewish refugees who similarly encountered the city while fleeing Europe, such as Adolf Schneider and Ada Winsten, also recalled seeing the Kremlin and Lenin's tomb and going to the zoo.[33] Giving their testimony in the 1990s, some fifty years later, these are the experiences they highlighted from their journeys. Rabbi Moshe Hertzman, of the Mir Yeshiva, described in his United States Holocaust Memorial Museum oral testimony that kosher food was available in the hotel in Moscow: "we ordered oranges in February in Russia during a war, as well as kosher sardines from Poland."[34] Antonia also mentioned a conversation she had with two German-speaking young women from Moscow, who conducted her tour of the city. Having described in depth the art and architecture she had experienced there, she asked them what impressed them the most. They replied, "that the streets had been made four times their width in recent years." Antonia was underwhelmed by this answer ("which is a pain to walk across").[35] This could speak to the fact that Antonia's stopover in Moscow was brief, and so (like a tourist might be) she was much more impressed with the new cultural sights she saw than the everyday usability of the city.

"Finally, First Class": Train Travel

Upon leaving Moscow, Antonia and Fanny traveled to Manchuria by train. Antonia noted that, despite booking train travel in advance, she was given a second-class ticket, rather than first class. This resulted in having to share with a "Russian-Mongolian farmer's wife and her 12-year-old son . . . a narrow compartment."[36] Her annoyance at this arrangement could reflect some ethnic prejudices, given that she notes the background and occupation of the family in her letter; however, Antonia later states she came around to her "very nice" companions. Yet she remains frustrated at not having been given the correct class seat and noted in her letter that she had written a complaint to the train company.[37] Similar to Antonia's demands of the travel company, here we see her continued insistence to be given what she is entitled to (and ready complaint if she does not get it), as a woman accustomed to certain comforts and expectations. That she mentioned this instance in a letter written a significant time after the journey took place also shows that the discrepancy was important to her.

One location along the train journey Antonia highlighted was Korea. Antonia and Fanny traveled from Charbin (now Harbin) in Japanese-occupied China to Fusan (now Busan) in Korea by Asia Express train, before taking the ferry to Shimonoseki in Japan. In his work on contemporary Holocaust education in South Korea, historian Ho-Keun Choi writes that "Holocaust education in Korea has to begin from the fact that the country has no direct association with the historical event itself."[38] This is a common perception about the role of Korea during the Holocaust; however, given that Jewish refugees like Antonia and Fanny used Korea as a space of transit suggests that, while the connection remains small, Korea had more contact with Jewish escapees from persecution than may be currently understood. Antonia Jacoby described their journey through Korea:

> The next morning in the Asia Express observation car—now finally first class—on to Hsinking [Changchun], there again a few hours of rest with lunch and then wander in an express, which drove us through the rest of Korea to Fusan [Busan]. All bed tickets were sold out, but our courier managed to get us two good beds past Mukden [Shenyang]—after midnight. We travelled in this train until the following evening, then in Fusan we boarded the ship. The landscape in Korea is somewhat higher, very beautiful low mountain ranges similar to the Giant Mountains, in the greatest contrast to Russia very densely populated, in the beautiful wide valleys certainly not a mile of uncultivated land. We saw the industrious people, the men dressed only in trousers and large hats, the women mostly in white ruffled robes, children always tied to their backs, standing in the rice fields or bringing in the corn harvest, all the houses nested closely together and without stopping along the railway (In Japan the same picture, the cities actually never stop). At the train stations a swarm of people, always 20 people greeting or saying goodbye to someone arriving or departing. Everything is done with the greatest calm, friendliness and emphatic politeness. The ride was wonderful.[39]

From this description, three themes emerge. The first is the experience of Antonia and Fanny while on board the Asia Express train, a high-class service, fast and luxurious, operated by the South Manchurian Railway between 1934 and 1943. Antonia and Fanny traveled "finally now in first class," which assuaged Antonia's disappointment with the previous train journey when they were accidentally placed in second class. The insistence on first class might not have only been a class consideration, but also one related to the age of the two women and the amount of traveling they were undertaking. At several points in her letter, Antonia mentions doing activities while leaving Fanny behind to rest (as she did in Moscow). Therefore, it is important to consider age (if not her own, then certainly her mother's) as a potential factor as to why Antonia was insistent on getting certain accommodations, and why she was annoyed when this was not delivered. In this section, Antonia also highlighted the Korean landscape, relating the unknown mountains to the more familiar Sudety range that she knew from the Czechoslovak-Polish border. Describing the scenery en route in oral testimony is also commonplace for Jewish refugees who took the Trans-Siberian Railway through the Soviet Union, with many recalling the endless countryside. However, here monotony, rather than wonder, is a more frequent descriptor. Indeed Leo Melamed, a Jewish refugee on the Trans-Siberian Railway, described that route as "black and white, there was no color."[40] Antonia also noted the people she observed out of the window, emphasizing their clothing and their quiet, "industrious" attitude. While it could be the case that she was simply observing what she could ascertain from inside a train carriage and brief encounters at train stops, her comments demonstrate more "orientalizing" attitudes and stereotyping in Jewish refugees' recollections of their time in Asia.

Kobe

The creation of networks, both organizational and local, was key to aiding incoming Jewish refugees in Kobe and setting them up to be able to support themselves in a new environment. Antonia and Fanny's connections in Kobe, and the length of time they spent in the city (seven years, from 1940 to 1947), meant that they occupied different spaces and interacted with different groups than many of the other Jewish refugees in the city. For example, they utilized different support structures. JEWCOM was the central agency providing relief and support for Jewish refugees in Kobe, run by members of the Ashkenazi Jewish community there, and financially supported by larger organizations such as the American Jewish Joint Distribution Committee (JDC). When Antonia and Fanny arrived in Kobe in June 1940, they did not receive aid from JEWCOM or the JDC, as they had a family network already established in the city. These connections also explain why the two chose to flee to Japan in particular. The women were received by family friends Eva and Hans Mendelsohn and taken to a guest house, since the Mendelsohns' home was too small. Antonia described that they quickly moved from the guest house to rented rooms in a house in the suburbs of Kobe, twenty-five minutes from Hans and Eva. Inconvenient as this may have been (Antonia notes that, in order to see Eva and Hans, Antonia and Fanny needed to take a car, as Fanny was not able to walk the distance), it was likely more comfortable than what some fellow refugees made do with. Many refugees who received assistance from JEWCOM lived in twenty-three shared houses on Yamamoto-Dori Street in Kobe. Susan Bluman recalled sharing a house with thirty other refugees, some ten or twelve people to a room.[41] Yamamoto-Dori is quite far from the areas of Kobe where Antonia and Fanny would have resided (around fifteen kilometers), thus evidencing the range of experiences different refugees had in the city, depending on the ways in which their accommodation was facilitated. While much of this chapter is focused on large-scale movement, which sees the pair move across borders and between continents, Fanny's more everyday physical mobility constraints were also a factor Antonia had to take into consideration when planning trips with Fanny.

Eva and Hans Mendelsohn also appear in the memoir of another Jewish refugee family who came to Japan from Germany via Korea. In *The Wolves at My Shadow: The Story of Ingelore Rothschild*, the Mendelsohn family also welcomed the Rothschilds to Kobe:

> During our stay in Kobe I considered Hans Mendelsohn my favourite uncle. He and his wife had met in Berlin at the home of one of Hans' friends where Eva was the children's governess. They were married a week before they immigrated to Japan. Six months later, my family arrived in Kobe. The Mendelsohns helped us adjust to this strange new land. They introduced us to their friends, showed us around the city and its neighbourhoods, and secured the villa that was our home.[42]

Further documents in the family archive reveal that the house that Antonia and Fanny moved to, with a lodger named Anni Victorius, was in the Nada district on the outskirts of Kobe. While Antonia's letter gives little information on Anni, refugee location lists in the Arolsen Archives reveal that she was also a Jewish refugee originally from Germany and a musician.[43] Helping Fanny communicate with fellow German speakers and finding a social community were important to Antonia. In their original guest house, the only language spoken was English, which Fanny did not know, and so once they moved in with Anni and entered the new community, Antonia wrote, "she will be able to speak German and play bridge with a lot of people there."[44]

The desire for a community can be seen in other instances of elderly emigrating Jews. Grete Katz, whose daughter had tried to convince her to go to Shanghai, finally decided that she would make the trip because friends had decided to go. "She was not so much worried about what she would lose by leaving Vienna, so much as she was worried about what change would ensue and about maintaining certain cultural aspects, characteristics associated with elderly émigrés."[45] According to Antonia, Anni was very nice, but Antonia was to make Fanny breakfast and dinner. Again, this sentiment shows Antonia taking on a caregiving role. In her writings, the only time Antonia discussed being taken care of was when she was ill and received medical attention. Otherwise, she wholly placed herself in the caregiver role, learning new skills and developing connections to provide herself and Fanny with an easier life.

From mid-August to late October 1941, the majority of Jewish refugees who remained in Kobe (around one thousand people) were ordered to move from the city, which was a major port and naval base. Most of them were relocated to Shanghai by Japanese military forces, in light of Japan's war preparations and in the lead-up to its attack on Pearl Harbor.[46] Therefore, the documentation on Jewish refugees in Japan at this time reflects a major location change, either to Shanghai or having secured onward movement to places such as the United States, Palestine, or Australia. Antonia and Fanny remained in Kobe until well after this period (and in Antonia's case, until 1947), which was an exception. Antonia's relatives have ascertained that Antonia and Fanny were probably able to remain in Kobe because of the intercession of the Mendelsohn family and due to their German documentation, as most of the Jewish refugees who settled in Kobe were from Poland. In an interview with the United States Holocaust Memorial Museum, another German Jewish refugee, Hanni Vogelweid, recalled that upon arrival in Kobe, her family was told to move on from the city. "You're not Polish. You're German. German, you have to go to Yokohama."[47] Thus there may not have been a large national community into which Antonia and Fanny could incorporate themselves in Kobe. However, thanks to their family connections they did have a network of contacts that they could use to be able to stay.

Letters from 1945

Given that the 1940 letter is written in the month that Antonia and Fanny arrived in Kobe, the sentiments it expressed reflect future plans rather than details of what her seven years in Kobe were like. For insight into this, we must turn to documents saved by her relatives in Israel. Antonia wrote very little between 1940 and 1945, after which she was able to send mail to her children in Jerusalem. Similar to the letter from 1940, those written in 1945 sum up the events of the previous few years of Antonia's life. Through these letters, she becomes a witness not only to Nazi persecution in Europe but also to the US bombing campaigns in Japan, writing about the horror of the firebombing of Kobe in 1945, which left huge areas devastated. In addition to these large-scale events, Antonia updates family news, stating that Hans Mendelsohn had been arrested (it is not mentioned why) in 1941 and that he was not released until 1942.

Along with detailing her care for her elderly mother, Antonia's later letters also highlight instances where Antonia was sick herself and had to balance Fanny's needs with receiving her own treatment. Antonia wrote that in 1942 she had been diagnosed with uterine cancer and had to be operated on in Osaka. To facilitate this, she procured a nurse to stay and look after Fanny. In later letters, Antonia shares that in 1943 Fanny broke her femur, resulting in her leg being amputated. Fanny did not properly heal from this, and she moved permanently to the International Hospital, living separately from Antonia. Antonia then moved in with Eva and Hans Mendelsohn. Fanny remained in the hospital into 1945, when Kobe was the target of hugely destructive incendiary bomb attacks by US forces.[48] Antonia wrote, "I could see with horror the fire in the sky of the city and I could feel 20 km from Kobe the continuous shock waves of the explosions. It was only two days later that I learned that the hospital was not damaged."[49] Antonia's letters often expressed her emotions, but her description of the firebombing in the near-distance while she did not know if her mother fell within its range is particularly charged. Here Antonia and Fanny, who until this point had been together in both their migration and settling in Kobe, were cut off from one another for days. Fanny was separated from her caregiver daughter and Antonia was unable to protect her mother or to know if she was alive or dead. After suffering a stroke, Fanny died in April.[50]

Upon her death, Fanny was buried in Kobe. We do not know Fanny's wishes toward her burial site, if any. However, having a set resting place was something clearly on Antonia's mind—as discussed earlier, Antonia paid years in advance for the upkeep of her own (and several other) gravesites in Germany. Ultimately, both women found their final resting places far from where their wartime migration began (when Antonia died in Jerusalem in 1968, she was buried there), with their burial locations shaped by shifting circumstances and practical considerations. For those fleeing persecution, choosing where to be buried can be extremely difficult. In an anthropological study of migrants in France, sociologist Claudine Attias-Donfut considers the ramifications of aging and death: "the only two options are either to break with the dead (and be buried in the host country) or to break with the living (and be buried in the home country)."[51] This dilemma underscores the complex and potentially painful choices faced by refugees, as people whose lives and attachments are shaped by multiple countries. Despite Antonia's careful initial planning, both her migration onward from Japan and the wartime context ultimately influenced decisions about where she and Fanny would eventually be laid to rest.

In an August 1945 telegram, Antonia wrote to her children, emphasizing that she was safe but that Fanny had died in Kobe. This is one of a small number of correspondences that Antonia wrote that was not a letter and, as a telegram, required her to condense large amounts of information. This also evidences the difficult role of having to deliver painful news to relatives across the globe via post rather than in person, especially after the war. Her telegram reads: "Received Telegram Kobe stop. Grandmother Deceased April. We are well, unharmed. Endeavor Immigration. How is Eva's family else Jacoby stop."

Given that Antonia was sharing information from events that had occurred in April, it is safe to assume that the family had had little to no contact since then. Between April 1945 and late August, Kobe had been heavily firebombed by US forces and atomic bombs had been dropped on Hiroshima and Nagasaki (Hiroshima only being around 250 km from Kobe). Therefore, there was good reason for Antonia to reassure her family members that she was well and unharmed. The words "endeavour immigration" in the telegram above suggest Antonia was searching for ways to leave Kobe from 1945 onward. Fanny was also mentioned in further letters between Antonia and her family. In 1945, Antonia wrote: "She died in April. What a favour we have done to her; the 88-year-old was spared the horror of the Hiroshima-style atomic bomb landing on Kobe too."[52]

Conclusion

Antonia's letter in the Wiener Holocaust Library serves as a starting point for connecting traces of Antonia Jacoby and her Kobe networks in other archives. From information in the letter, she can be found on a JDC list of Jews living in Kobe in 1946 under the name "Toni Jacobi."[53] According to the list, by 1946 she was living in the same house as Eva and Hans Mendelsohn, as we know she did following Fanny's move into hospital. The list states that they lived in Shioya, a small port town about twenty kilometers from the center of Kobe.[54] After departing Kobe in 1947, Antonia's transnational journey did not end. Leaving Japan via Yokohama, she sailed to the US, and traveled through France and Egypt before landing in Haifa, where she reconnected with her children. The content of her wartime letters not only speaks to her own and her mother's trajectory, but also to wider narratives around gender, age, and class related to migration during Holocaust.

Antonia and Fanny's lives were fundamentally changed by Nazi persecution. The two women were forced to flee their home country while contending with further economic persecution in the form of Nazi "Aryanization" policies. Despite this, resources that remained available to them meant that they were able to successfully emigrate, and to do so in relative comfort—traveling in first-class accommodations and by plane. Finances also enabled Fanny, an eighty-three-year-old woman with limited physical independence, to take some agency in their flight by providing the two women support from her pension savings.

These letters give us an important insight into the international nature of their lives in migration, but it is important to remember that it is only a glimpse into the moments that Antonia chose to share and that have been saved. We do not know much about Antonia's everyday life in Kobe, nor do we have any responses to her correspondence. The insights we do have, however, allow us to reconstruct trajectories that reach beyond the dominant Eurocentric approach, and to focus on how Antonia communicated topics such as elderly care, death, and arranging their flight.

In literature focused on the migration of elderly people during the Holocaust, there is a dominant focus on them as either immobile or needing aid to facilitate any potential movement. As Dan Stone states:

> Having been among the most likely to be left behind when their children and grandchildren emigrated or fled, among the first to be selected for deportations (in the Vilna and Łódź ghettos, for example), and among the first to be selected for death at Auschwitz, by the end of the war elderly Jews were, with the exception of young children, the least likely members of the Jewish community to have survived.[55]

While this is doubtless true, statistically speaking, the migration of Antonia Jacoby and Fanny Behrendt from Germany to Japan shows that the exceptions, too, are worth investigating, offering a fuller and hence more accurate picture of elderly migration experiences. Not only did the two women survive persecution and successfully flee Nazi Europe, Antonia's letters evidence how they did so by their own organization and agency.

Notes

1 Determination of what constitutes "old age" varies. However, in Holocaust research this is often understood at around sixty years of age, with some analyses even lowering this to around forty-five years old—thus placing both Antonia and her mother within this category. See, for example, Dan Stone, "'Somehow the Pathetic Dumb Suffering of These Elderly People Moves Me More Than Anything': Caring for Elderly Holocaust Survivors in the Immediate Postwar Years," *Holocaust and Genocide Studies* 32, no. 3 (2018): 384–403; Melissa Jane Taylor, "Family Matters: The Emigration of Elderly Jews from Vienna to the United States, 1938–1941," *Journal of Social History* 45, no. 1 (2011): 238–60.

2 Antonia Jacoby Collection, Wiener Holocaust Library (henceforth WHL), ref. no. 1823.

3 I would like to thank Yael Naaman, Antonia's granddaughter, for allowing me to access and use some of this material in this chapter.

4 Taylor, "Family Matters," 238–60.

5 Mirjana Morokvasic, "Birds of Passage Are Also Women," *International Migration Review* 18, no. 4 (1984): 886–907. See also Claudia Mora and Nicola Piper, "Gendering Transnationalism: Migration and Mobility in Longue Durée," in *The Palgrave Handbook of Gender and Migration* (Springer International Publishing AG, 2021), 42.

6 Mora and Piper, *Palgrave Handbook*, 42.

7 For a further (but not exhaustive) historiography of age studies in Holocaust research, see Debórah Dwork, *Children with a Star: Jewish Youth in Nazi Europe* (Yale University Press, 1991); Tara Zahra, *The Lost Children: Reconstructing Europe's Families After World War II* (Harvard University Press, 2011); Stone, " 'Somehow the Pathetic Dumb Suffering,' " 384–403; Anna Hájková, *The Last Ghetto: An Everyday History of Theresienstadt* (Oxford University Press, 2020).

8 See Samuel Honig, *From Poland to Russia and Back, 1939–1946: Surviving the Holocaust in the Soviet Union* (Black Moss Press, 1996); Mark Edele, Sheila Fitzpatrick, and Atina Grossmann, eds., *Shelter from the Holocaust: Rethinking Jewish Survival in the Soviet Union* (Wayne State University Press, 2017); Michael Brenner, *After the Holocaust: Rebuilding Jewish Lives in Postwar Germany* (Princeton University Press, 1997).

9 For an overview of the Wiener Holocaust Library's holdings of papers from German-speaking Jewish refugees, see Howard Falksohn, "The Wiener Library: A Repository of Schicksale," in *Refugee Archive: Theory and Practice*, ed. Andrea Hammel and Anthony Grenville, vol. 9 of *Yearbook of the Research Centre for German and Austrian Exile Studies* (Brill Rodopi, 2007), 27–40.

10 Bettina Brandt, "Nelly and Trudie: Deciphering a Transatlantic Family Holocaust Correspondence," in *On Being Adjacent to Historical Violence*, ed. Irene Kacandes (Walter de Gruyter GmbH, 2021), 315.

11 Atina Grossmann, "I Thought She Was Old, but She Was Really My Age: Tracing Desperation and Resilience in My Grandmothers' Letters from Berlin," in *On Being Adjacent to Historical Violence*, 323–40.

12 Renata Polt, ed., *A Thousand Kisses: A Grandmother's Holocaust Letters* (University of Alabama Press, 1999).

13 Shirli Gilbert, "A Cache of Family Letters and the Historiography of the Holocaust: Interpretive Reflections," *Journal of Holocaust Research* 36, no. 4 (2022): 281–98.
14 Margaretta Jolly, "On Burning, Saving and Stealing Letters," *New Formations* 67, no. 67 (2009): 25.
15 Antonia Jacoby Collection, ref. no. 1823, WHL.
16 For more on this negotiation, see Hannah Holtschneider, "Narrating the Archive? Family Collections, the Archive, and the Historian," *Shofar* 37, no. 3 (2019): 331–60.
17 Charlie Knight, "Constructing Narratives: Considerations in the Letters of Theodor M. W. Hirschberg and His Family," *Jewish Culture and History* 23, no. 4 (2022): 396.
18 Gilbert, "A Cache of Family Letters," 291.
19 Judith Szapor, "Private Archives and Public Lives: The Migrations of Alexander Weissberg and the Polanyi Archives," *Jewish Culture and History* 15, nos. 1–2 (2014): 95.
20 The Law for the Restoration of the Professional Civil Service was passed on April 7, 1933, directed mainly at Jewish civil servants and then widened to also include orchestra musicians, actors, and other artists.
21 Nancy L. Green, "Four Ages of Migration Studies: Men, Women, Gender and Sexuality," trans. Siân Reynolds, *Clio: Women, Gender, History* 51 (2020): 191.
22 Agnieszka Radziwinowiczówna, Anna Rosinska, and Weronika Kloc-Nowak, *Ethnomorality of Care: Migrants and Their Aging Parents* (Routledge, 2018).
23 "Aryanization" was a way of economically marginalizing Jews by taking material goods and property. See Christoph Kreutzmüller and Jonathan R. Zatlin, eds., *Dispossession: Plundering German Jewry, 1933–1953* (University of Michigan Press, 2020).
24 Antonia Jacoby Collection, ref. no. 1823, WHL.
25 Ian Kershaw, *Hitler, 1889–1936: Hubris* (W. W. Norton, 1998), 576.
26 Kreutzmüller and Zatlin, *Dispossession*, 11.
27 Antonia Jacoby Collection, ref. no. 1823, WHL.
28 Life certificates are still used by the German government today. They must be signed by the pensioner and certified by an authorized agency, to provide confirmation that those receiving their pensions are still alive.

29 The Nazi regime "legally" blocked access to Jewish bank accounts in Germany and Austria, meaning many Jews could not access their life savings, which were then confiscated by the Nazis. Insurance companies like Allianz benefited financially from "Aryanization" policies. Any Jewish insurance claims after *Kristallnacht* in 1938 were seized by the Nazis, and many life insurance policies were revoked or not paid out.

30 In February 1940, some one thousand Jews from Stettin were "resettled" to Lublin. Late 1939 saw deportations from Kattowitz, Vienna, and Moravská Ostrava in the Protectorate to Nisko camp. This camp was shut down in March 1940, with many prisoners then deported further within the Nazi camp system.

31 In autumn of 1938, all German Jewish passports were declared valid only if stamped with a red letter "J." While Antonia does not make it clear exactly why, it appears Antonia and Fanny's onward visas had been rejected due to their passports identifying them as Jews.

32 Especially on waiting for visas, see Marion Kaplan, *Hitler's Jewish Refugees: Hope and Anxiety in Portugal* (Yale University Press, 2020).

33 Adolf Schneider, interview 4675, *Visual History Archive*, USC Shoah Foundation, September 17, 1995; Ada Winsten, interview 8363, November 6, 1995.

34 Oral history interview with Moshe Zupnik, Jeff and Toby Herr Oral History Archive, United States Holocaust Memorial Museum (henceforth USHMM), RG-50.494.0007.

35 Antonia Jacoby Collection, ref. no. 1823.

36 Antonia Jacoby Collection, ref. no. 1823, WHL.

37 Antonia Jacoby Collection, ref. no. 1823, WHL.

38 Ho-Keun Choi, "Holocaust Education in a Country Without Holocaust Experience: Facing Burdensome Past with Rescuer Stories in South Korea," *Contemporary Review of the Middle East* 3, no. 3 (2016): 269, doi:10.1177/2347798916654582.

39 Antonia Jacoby Collection, ref. no. 1823, WHL. Current names of locations mentioned have been added by the author.

40 Oral history interview with Leo Melamed, Jeff and Toby Herr Oral History Archive, USHMM, RG-50.494.0006.

41 Oral history interview with Susan Bluman, Jeff and Toby Herr Oral History Archive, USHMM, RG-50.494.0015.

42 Ingelore Rothschild, *The Wolves at My Shadow: The Story of Ingelore Rothschild*, ed. Darilyn Stahl Listort and Dennis Listort (Athabasca University Press, 2017), 194.
43 Photostat list concerning Jewish refugees, of the o/m nationalities, who were living in Japan at the o/m localities in early 1946, 3.1.1.3/ 8803130/ ITS Digital Archive, Arolsen Archives.
44 Antonia Jacoby Collection, ref. no. 1823, WHL.
45 Taylor, "Family Matters," 251.
46 On Jewish refugees in Shanghai, see Sara Halpern, "The Integration of Jewish Refugees from Shanghai into Post–World War II San Francisco," *American Jewish History* 104, no. 1 (2020): 87–114; Irene Eber, *Wartime Shanghai and the Jewish Refugees from Central Europe: Survival, Co-Existence, and Identity in a Multi-Ethnic City* (De Gruyter, 2012).
47 Oral history interview with Hanni Vogelweid, Jeff and Toby Herr Oral History Archive, USHMM, RG-50.494.0013.
48 A well-known account of the effects of this bombing campaign can be found in the 1967 book 火垂るの墓 (*Hotaru no haka / Grave of the Fireflies*), later adapted into the film *Grave of the Fireflies* (1988).
49 Antonia Jacoby Private Collection, 1945 letter.
50 Antonia noted that in June the hospital burned down in a second wave of incendiary bombs.
51 In *Ageing in Contexts of Migration*, ed. Karl Ute and Sandra Torres (Routledge, 2016), 92.
52 Antonia Jacoby Private Collection, 1945 letter.
53 Photostat list concerning Jewish refugees, of the o/m nationalities, who were living in Japan at the o/m localities in early 1946, 3.1.1.3/ 8803130/ ITS Digital Archive, Arolsen Archives.
54 The Rothschild family members are also on this list, also living in Shioya.
55 Stone, "'Somehow the Pathetic Dumb Suffering,'" 397.

4

OLDER JEWISH REFUGEES IN CHINA

German and Austrian Exile Artists in Shanghai

Xin Tong

Introduction

With Hitler's rise to power in the 1930s and the increasingly severe antisemitic acts of the Nazi regime, countless European Jews were forced to leave their homelands and flee to various parts of the world. More than twenty thousand Jews, mainly from Germany and Austria, sought refuge in China following Hitler's rise to power. They settled in Chinese cities such as Harbin, Tianjin, Beijing, Qingdao, Nanjing, Shanghai, Chongqing, and Hong Kong. The majority resided in the port metropolis of Shanghai, where a Jewish refugee community of over fifteen thousand people was established.

In recent decades, scholarly works on Jewish exile in China have provided a relatively systematic study of the political, social, and cultural history of Jewish refugees in Shanghai. This research is undergoing a transition from a historical narrative of the "other" in both East and West to a multidirectional dialogue of memories. At the same time, academics have yet to adequately focus on the subgroups within the Jewish refugee community in Shanghai, such as the elderly. With the continuous international expansion of Holocaust studies, social factors such as age, gender, ethnicity, and class have been incorporated into the scope of research, leading to a deeper exploration of the experiences of the elderly during the Holocaust.

Considering that the advanced age of Jewish refugees in China is an understudied factor, this chapter primarily focuses on two representative cases of elderly Jewish artists from Germany and Austria. As accomplished artists and cultural elites, their experiences in Shanghai are better documented and have the potential to contribute to a rich cultural memory of the Jewish community in Shanghai. By investigating their life stories, the study aims to provide insight into the collective experiences of elderly artists among the Jewish refugees in Shanghai and to reexamine the history and memory of Jewish exile in China. For these older Jewish artists who fled from Europe to China with their families, the role of aging in their exile experiences and its impact on their life decisions are key issues of investigation. This study intends to discuss how advanced age influenced their prewar, Holocaust, exile, and postwar experiences, and what kinds of insights might be drawn for our future understanding of the connections between the elderly, the Holocaust, and exile.

The Jewish Exile in China: A Reflection on Global Scholarship

In post–World War II historiography on the Holocaust and exile, Jewish refugees' flight to China was long considered to be "emigration on the fringe"[1] and an "exile of the little people."[2] It was not until the 1970s that historian David Kranzler first systematically studied the Jewish refugee community in Shanghai.[3] In the half-century since then, international scholarship on Jewish refugees in China has resulted in considerable achievements in academic studies and memory practices. This history has become familiar to a broader international public through film, museum representation, and media dissemination, thus transforming itself from what German scholar Aleida Assmann terms a "memory reservoir" (*Speichergedächtnis*) into a functional and prominent cultural memory.[4]

Reviewing the historiography and commemoration of this period over the past fifty years reveals a notable characteristic: the relevant historical research and memory discourse have transitioned from a Western-dominated "Orientalist writing" to a phase of "self-Orientalizing narratives" by Chinese scholars, ultimately evolving into a shared history and a multidirectional memory dialogue. On one hand, for the Jewish refugees, China represented a last resort for escape and a transit point for their postwar immigration to Western countries such as the United States. This perception profoundly influenced mainstream Western scholarship on Jewish exile since the 1970s. In numerous memoirs and historical works, Jewish exile to Western countries like the United Kingdom and the United States is considered "normal," while fleeing to low- and lower-middle-income countries is often regarded as a "special exception." W. Michael Blumenthal, a noted Jewish refugee who came to Shanghai and later served as the secretary of the US Treasury, wrote:

> Thus, the Jewish refugees lived for several years isolated and crammed together in a ghetto in China, a most peculiar and special variation of the emigrant fate of German Jews in other parts of the world. There the emigrants tried to settle into a new society [. . .]. We saw Shanghai only as a temporary shelter. Everyone wanted to leave again as soon as possible, to more "normal" countries, some—at least in the beginning—even went back to their so-called homeland.[5]

This "exceptionalism" narrative essentially underscores a storyline in which Western, Jewish civilization endures hardships in an exotic Oriental land and ultimately achieves self-salvation within the historical context of the Holocaust and exile. This perspective remains embedded in a colonialist binary logic of self/modern/advanced versus other/premodern/backward, failing to fully release from the framework of Orientalism in its view of non-Western countries. In his discussion of Orientalism, American literary critic and philosopher Edward Said incisively points out that it alienates, marginalizes, and symbolizes the Orient, crafting an imagined Oriental world to highlight the superiority of Western culture and thereby affirm Europe's own subjectivity and cultural identity.[6] Chinese scholars have also noted that "the image of China in the Western eye [. . .] has always been historically shaped to represent values that are considered different from Western ones. China, India [. . .] have all served as foils to the West at one time or another, either as idealized utopias, alluring and exotic dreamlands, or lands of eternal stagnation, spiritual purblindness, and ignorance."[7]

These stereotypes of China are directly reflected in some historical accounts of Jewish exile.[8] Therein, China is often portrayed merely as a backdrop for stories centered on Western, Jewish protagonists, and Shanghai, the city with the highest density of Jewish refugees, is simultaneously depicted as both a "sin city" and a "city of hope,"[9] perpetuating an illusionary view of Oriental culture.

Meanwhile, in the context of China's economic reform, Chinese scholars began, from the 1980s onward, to translate, introduce, and draw upon the research of Western historians of this period. By building on the Eurocentric "Orientalist writing," they augmented it with the collection, collation, and research of Chinese historical materials. This effort gradually developed into "a Chinese reading of its own"[10]—a Sinocentric perspective that emphasizes China's specificity in related historical narrative and memory discourse. For instance, Chinese historian Jian Wang at the Shanghai Jewish Studies Center concludes as follows: "This historical memory of Jewish refugees taking refuge in Shanghai during World War II constitutes a unique component within the international Holocaust research community. While other places commemorate the deceased, Shanghai stands out as a special place of commemoration for the living, for their survival and being rescued. The Sino-Jewish friendship forged amidst adversity shines as the most humane chapter in the tragedy of the Holocaust."[11]

However, when viewed in the context of the global history of the Holocaust and Jewish exile, such alternative conclusions about China as a "unique" place of exile are undoubtedly debatable. Behind this narrative of "auto-Orientalism" lies China's own consideration of diplomatic issues and the tensions of memory politics. Especially since the establishment of diplomatic relations between China and Israel in 1992, attention and commemoration of the history of Jewish exile in China have taken on a pronounced trend of politicization and diplomatic instrumentalization. Former sites like the Hongkew ghetto and the Shanghai Jewish Refugees Museum have not only become tourist attractions drawing foreign visitors but also a "quasi-compulsory program"[12] for many Western dignitaries when they visit Shanghai. As Chinese historian Lu Pan aptly observed: "The Shanghai Jewish Refugees Museum can be seen as a process with which Chinese authorities could present China as a mirror image of the West. The museum epitomizes a historical self that is eager to be affirmed in the eye of the others, that is, by assertion from the West. In this sense, this endeavor to be in line with the West, discourse serves as a means of articulating the spectacle of China's imagined modernity."[13]

The memory discourse of Jewish exile in China has been therefore jointly shaped by both Chinese and Western perspectives, depicting the past as a historical narrative of the "other": Jews were not only social outcasts expelled from their European homelands, but also foreigners in the eyes of the Chinese locals. Conversely, China and its people constituted the Oriental other from the perspective of Western Jews. The total and uncritical acceptance of this writing of other and the specificity of exile in Shanghai may internalize its Orientalist and colonialist historical premises to some extent. This may unconsciously reinforce the cultural hegemony underpinned by certain political memory struggles, potentially relativizing the global history of Jewish exile during the Holocaust.[14] The inherent complexity, diversity, and heterogeneity of each exile location may also be obscured and diminished. In view of a new global history, it is essential to reexamine the history and memory of Jewish exile and consider whether and why it possesses a certain "locality." The notion of locality here should not be a simple substitute for the historical narrative of other and the discourse of exceptionalism, nor should it be narrowly interpreted as a symbolic relationship between Jewish refugees and their places of exile. Instead, within a framework of cultural transnationalism, global archives, and international cooperation, it should uncover both the genuine uniqueness and universal spiritual core and value embedded in this history and memory.

Since entering the twenty-first century, a shift within this research field can be observed, from a limited Jewish and Western perspective to one simultaneously global and local.[15] Taking China as an example of an exile location, firstly, this history of Jewish exile occurred in China and is always about China. Regardless of the perspective from which it is written, ethnic and social groups living in China at that time, including the Chinese themselves, were all key actors, participants, and witnesses in this history.[16] Secondly, as relevant historical materials accumulate and shape a rich culture of historical memory, various ethnic and social groups, including the Chinese people, have also become core constructors and disseminators of this past. Under the perspective of postcolonial theory, American literary critic and scholar Michael Rothberg has proposed the concept of "multidirectional memory,"[17] emphasizing the fluidity and openness of memory, wherein the histories and memories of different ethnic and social groups can intersect, refer to, dialogue with, and learn from each other. The history and memory of Jewish exile in China are being passed down from generation to generation around the globe, from the Harbin Museum of Jewish History and Culture and the Shanghai Jewish Refugees Museum in China to the Jewish Museum Berlin and the United States Holocaust

Memorial Museum. In this regard, the Jewish exile experience in China has built a bridge that transcends time and space, not only carrying the shared history of different nations and peoples, but also creating opportunities for cross-cultural memory dialogue among diverse ethnic and social groups to seek common values of all human beings.

Older Jewish Refugees in China

Against the above context, it is worth noting two further points when considering the relationship between the Holocaust, Jewish exile in China, and the social group of elderly refugees. First, as mentioned earlier, the past of elderly Jewish refugees in China is a shared history interwoven with the experiences of different ethnic and social groups. Therefore, the historical inquiry should not be solely centered on the elderly Jewish refugees themselves. Instead, it should utilize transnational archives and documents, incorporating perspectives from various actors, such as local people and institutions, to examine the relationship between elderly Jewish refugees and other ethnic and social groups in the local society in as many dimensions as possible. Second, the history of elderly Jewish refugees in China should be viewed from a global historical perspective and not in isolation. This approach requires both a diachronic temporal dimension and a synchronic geographical dimension. The former examines the role of aging within the broader context of large-scale global exile and migration and involves analyzing whether and how advanced age had an impact on the escape routes, temporary stops, and final destinations of Jewish refugees. The latter takes cases of elderly refugees in other global exile locations into consideration and conducts comparative and cross-sectional analyses of different exile sites. Taking Jewish exile in Shanghai as an example, this paper does not intend to offer a detailed historical review of the historical situation at that time nor to carry out a rigorous and comprehensive sociological survey. Instead, it seeks to reinvestigate the historical overview and individual experiences of Jewish refugees from the standpoint of aging and the elderly.[18]

At a time of an aging society, the World Health Organization defines individuals aged sixty and above as older adults.[19] However, different periods, countries, and cultural contexts have varied understandings of what constitutes an elderly person, distinguishing between birth age, biological age, psychological age, and social age. In the twentieth century, various factors influenced life expectancy. In 1930, the life expectancy at birth for American men was fifty-eight years and for women sixty-two years (life expectancy for German men in 1934 was comparable at 59.9 years).[20] At that time, the average life expectancy in China was less than forty years.[21,22] Therefore, there is no strict, uniform, and unequivocal definition of "older Jewish refugees."

The number of elderly Jews who fled from Europe to China, enduring a long and arduous journey, was not significant. The majority of German and Austrian refugees arrived in Shanghai by sea, typically departing from Italian ports, a situation that lasted until Italy entered the war in 1940, while Polish refugees often traveled by land, taking trans-Siberian trains. By the time Germany invaded the Soviet Union in 1941, the land route became impassable. As a result, both the sea and land routes to China were severed. There were few elderly people who possessed the physical, familial, and financial means and could obtain the necessary immigrant visas and documents to successfully seize this opportunity within its small window of time. Therefore, the population of Jewish refugees in Shanghai was predominantly composed of middle-aged men. Due to variations in the statistical methods employed by different agencies at different times in registering the entry of Jewish refugees, there is no precise data on the number of elderly individuals within this social subgroup. According to German historian Petra Löber, Jewish refugees in Shanghai represented a wide range of professions, and their overall "age structure" (*Altersstruktur*) and living conditions were highly unfavorable: "The refugees were already over 40 years old and most of them arrived physically and mentally exhausted in an unfamiliar environment where the language and living conditions were foreign and unknown to them."[23]

Among the refugees, the elderly faced particularly difficult circumstances. They usually fled Europe with their families or joined relatives already settled in Shanghai. Those who arrived before 1938 were, in the strict sense, not yet considered refugees but rather expatriates, residing in the former International Settlement and French Concession in Shanghai. But after *Kristallnacht* in 1938, the influx of Jewish refugees from Europe to Shanghai significantly increased, greatly challenging the city's capacity to accommodate them amid its own wartime struggles. Many of the later-arriving refugees were housed in temporary shelters in Hongkou, which were rented or purchased and converted by the Committee for the Assistance of European Jewish Refugees in Shanghai (CAEJF).[24] Upon arrival in Hongkou, many refugees wished to leave the shelters, but finding rental housing or employment was not easy. Under such circumstances, relief organizations were unable to provide comprehensive and in-depth support for the elderly in terms of housing, food, medical care, and social assistance.[25] Compared to younger people, the elderly in general faced greater challenges in settling down and making a living in Shanghai.

At the individual level, whether elderly Jewish refugees could genuinely adapt to and peacefully endure their years of exile in China depended not only on a comprehensive range of factors such as their age, gender, occupation, personality, family, skills, and physical condition, but also on their experiences before and during their time in China. By combing through historical materials, this chapter categorizes the elderly Jewish refugees coming to China into two types: the first fled Europe in middle age but aged gradually during their exile in China, transitioning into old age; the second category consisted of refugees who were older, aged fifty-five and above, when they fled to China.

Examples of the first category were members of the musical group the Wolf Brothers (die Gebrüder Wolf) from Germany. The Wolf brothers came from a family of Jewish musicians in Hamburg, two generations of which had been actively touring across Germany and Europe under this stage name as well as in duets. The songs they wrote had been widely sung in the local area. Before World War II, these Jewish musicians had a remarkable influence on jazz and popular music in Europe, and in particular contributed to the genre of cabaret. Following *Kristallnacht*, James Iwan Wolf (1893–1981), a core member of the Wolf Brothers, was arrested and transported to the Sachsenhausen concentration camp, and later released upon submitting proof of permanent emigration from Germany. Between 1939 and 1947, he and his younger brother, Donat Wolf (1902–84), found refuge in Shanghai. There they rebuilt the Wolf Brothers ensemble to carry on the family's musical tradition, performing in Shanghai's theaters and makeshift Jewish refugee homes. After the war, they immigrated to the United States and continued to perform under their family name. Today their life stories and music remain celebrated and remembered in Germany, with Hamburg honoring them as "sons of Hamburg" through various commemorative events.[26]

Similar to the Wolf brothers, Adolf Josef Storfer (1888–1944), an Austrian-Jewish journalist and publisher born in Romania, resumed his professional endeavors in China. As a student of Sigmund Freud, Storfer served as the president of the Vienna Psychoanalytic Press before World War I. At the age of fifty he fled to Shanghai and, despite being penniless and exhausted, miraculously established the exile newspaper *Gelbe Post* (the Yellow Post) within a few months.[27] Although Storfer lived in Shanghai for only three years, his newspaper was rated as the best German-language newspaper in Asia at that time.[28] The *Gelbe Post* featured rich content curated by Storfer, showcasing his profound scholarship and his team of authors and editors who were experts on China. The newspaper systematically introduced Chinese history, culture, art, and society to European refugees, while also tracing the history of Jews in ancient China. Dr. Ho Feng-Shan (何凤山), later known as China's "Oskar Schindler," also contributed articles to the *Gelbe Post*, showing great sympathy towards Jewish refugees. In 1941, following the Japanese occupation of the International Settlement and French Concession in Shanghai, Storfer continued his exile in Australia, where he ceased his journalistic activities and died three years later due to illness.

The examples from the first category of exiles—those who aged gradually in exile—elucidate that despite advanced age and significant challenges, Jewish refugees actively endeavored to establish themselves in Shanghai. Amid their struggles for survival, they also dedicated themselves to creating and providing intellectual and artistic support for themselves and other refugees. The following section focuses specifically on the second category—exiles fifty-five years or older at the time of their flight to Shanghai—to offer a glimpse of the inherent heterogeneity of older Jewish refugees in China.

The Flecks and the Wittenberg Family: Two Cases of Elderly *Shanghailänder*

Luise Fleck was born into a non-Jewish French aristocratic family and was the second female film director in the world to achieve prominence following the renowned French director Alice Guy-Blaché. In 1910, she cofounded Austria's first film production company, Wiener Kunstfilm-Industrie (Vienna Art Film Industry) with her first husband Anton Kolm and the Jewish cinematographer Jacob Fleck, who later became her second husband. In the 1920s the Flecks directed a number of films for the German film company UFA, achieving great success and becoming famously known in Europe as the "director couple" (*Regieehepaar*). After Nazi Germany annexed Austria in 1938, the couple was imprisoned for sixteen months in the Dachau and Buchenwald concentration camps—Jacob for being Jewish and Luise for remaining in their intermarriage. They were fortunate to escape with the help of their friend, the renowned German director William Dieterle. In 1940, Luise, aged sixty-seven, and Jacob, aged fifty-nine, endured great hardships along with many other Jewish refugees and arrived in China, where they began a seven-year period of exile.[29]

Around the same time, in 1939, fifty-eight-year-old Alfred Wittenberg fled to Shanghai with his wife, Paula Wittenberg, who was fifteen years younger, and his sixty-six-year-old mother-in-law, Eva Fuss.[30] As the last disciple of the globally renowned Hungarian-Jewish violinist Joseph Joachim, Alfred had already established himself as an eminent violinist and pianist in Europe before World War II. In Germany, in addition to his time as the first violinist at the Royal Opera House for many years, he had also taught violin for decades, accumulating extensive teaching experience.[31] However, similar to the Flecks, the escalation of Nazi antisemitic atrocities compelled him to make up his mind to relinquish his prestigious position in the Berlin music scene and join, along with his family, the wave of refugees.

TABLE 4.1. Basic Information About the Fleck and the Wittenberg Families

Name	**Gender**	**Birthplace**	**Year of Birth and Death**	**Years in Shanghai**	**Occupation**	**Postwar Destination**
Luise Fleck	Female	Austria	1873–1950	1940–1947	Film Director	Returned to Austria
Jacob Fleck	Male	Austria	1881–1953	1940–1947	Photographer Film Director	Returned to Austria
Alfred Wittenberg	Male	Germany	1880–1952	1939–1952	Musician	Stayed in China
Paula Wittenberg	Female	Germany	1895–1944	1939–1944	Nurse	n.a.
Eva Fuss	Female	Germany	1873–?	1939–?	?	n.a.

What similarities and differences can be observed about these two refugee families in Shanghai, all members of which were elderly and of the cultural elite? How did the factor of age play a role in their lives in China? Based on the previous discussion, the following analysis will focus on these questions from both global and local perspectives. First, by examining the chronological processes of the two families' escape, transit, and postwar trajectories, it can be seen that age was a crucial and unavoidable factor in their decision-making processes. If it was fortuitous that they fled to Shanghai (the Wittenberg family originally attempted to flee to the United Kingdom but failed, and the Flecks fled Europe only at the last minute), they then made choices based on age both during the exile and postwar years when they had more autonomy. Before the outbreak of the Pacific War, Wittenberg's German students and musician friends who had immigrated to the United States invited him to move there with his family. However, he repeatedly declined: "He said that he was old, had a wife and mother-in-law, and did not want to travel far across the ocean."[32] The Flecks similarly considered age in their postwar choice to return to their homeland, Austria, after the war to enjoy their retirement and the final chapters of their lives. "At that time, they were both over sixty, Jacob was 66 and Louise was 74 years old. They had reached the age of retirement. They seemed no longer engaged in new film production."[33] Their intermarriage, too, may have bolstered their confidence in opting to go back to Vienna.

It is noteworthy here that aging often comes with an increased likelihood of being widowed, making the confrontation with one's own mortality and that of a partner an inevitable challenge for these former Shanghai Jews. In this regard, a synchronic comparison with cases of elderly *Shanghailänder* from other parts of the world can bring different insights. Confronted with widowerhood in their later years, Alfred, who stayed in China, and Jacob, who returned to Austria, chose to live alone. In contrast, James Iwan Wolf, who immigrated to the United States, remarried at the age of seventy-two.[34] From the perspective of social constructionism, aging and the accompanying adjustments and changes are unique personal processes that depend on each individual's own social cognition and construction of reality. Therefore, widowerhood might have presented new opportunities for self-development for these refugees.

However, for Max Ludwig Berges (1899–1973), another Jewish refugee who also fled to Shanghai and later immigrated to the United States, widowerhood in old age marked the beginning of waiting for death. The playwright, who like the Wolf brothers came from Hamburg, fled with his wife from 1935 to 1938 through Dalian, Shanghai, Hong Kong, and Manila, before immigrating to California. While in Shanghai, he completed the novel *Cold Pogrom*,[35] in which he had already foreseen the escalating persecution and massacre of Jews under the Nazi regime. After living in the United States for many years, and following the death of his wife, who had been his companion for forty-two years, the elderly Max ended his own life.[36]

Returning to the cases of the Flecks and the Wittenberg family: Beyond situating their histories into a global perspective, it is perhaps even more crucial to examine the relationships between elderly Jewish refugees and local ethnic and social groups in China, especially the localized social construction of elderly refugees at that time. On one hand, aging and being elderly indeed brought more inconveniences and disadvantages to their lives in exile. Alfred, as he aged, experienced a decline in hearing, which often resulted in inaccuracies while playing the violin. In addition, he suffered from a hunched back and frequent back pain, and by the age of seventy he "could no longer walk continuously but had to stop after each step."[37] His wife, Paula, suffered from mental illness and died at the age of forty-nine. Shortly thereafter, the elderly mother-in-law, Eva, also died due to the loss of her daughter and the hardships of life.[38] (The date of Eva's death is not recorded, but it is estimated between 1944 and 1945 based on available data).[39] The prolonged impoverished living conditions significantly reduced the Flecks' weight, which made them physically much weaker as they aged. In 1941, Luise weighed 120 jin (around 132 pounds), but by 1945 her weight decreased to 83 jin (approximately 91 pounds); similarly, Jacob's weight dropped from 162 jin (179 pounds) in 1941 to 110 jin (121 pounds) in 1945.[40]

On the other hand, as elderly refugees, both the Flecks and Alfred Wittenberg continued their preexile achievements in Shanghai in their own ways, leaving behind significant spiritual legacies and cultural imprints in China. In this process, old age not only did not become a hindrance but rather played an exceptionally positive role. Shortly after arriving in Shanghai, driven by their professional interests, the Flecks showed great concern for the development of the Chinese film industry. They visited film institutions in Shanghai and thereby became acquainted with the distinguished Chinese film director Fei Mu (费穆). Fei Mu was China's first director to incorporate Chinese traditional music into silent films and the first Chinese director to shoot color films, and therefore was revered as the "pioneer of modern Chinese cinema."[41] As the forerunners in their respective national film industries, both parties were genuinely delighted by this unusual encounter and expressed a desire to collaborate on film projects. Fei Mu warmly invited the Flecks to direct films and offered them generous directorial remuneration, which became a lifesaver for the couple, as refugees in a foreign country. Fei Mu held that, "given the state of the world, amidst the raging fires of war, the Flecks left their homeland and came to China, their sympathy for China goes without saying. I think they can cooperate with us in China, and their rich experience and knowledge will contribute significantly, at least in terms of the improvement of technical standards."[42]

Ultimately, after extensive participation and refinement by both parties, they developed a screenplay titled *Children of the World* (*Söhne und Töchter der Welt* in German and "世界儿女" in Chinese), which combined narrative elements and characteristics from both Chinese and Western traditions. The film tells the story of several young Chinese people who went through the baptism of war and love. The two male leads love the same woman, but they decide to put aside their personal feelings and go to the battlefield together to fight off the Japanese invaders, placing the good of the whole world first, making them "children of the world." On October 4, 1941, this first collaborative film involving Chinese and foreign film artists premiered at the Jindu Grand Theater in Shanghai, marking a milestone in Chinese cinematic history. The film attracted great social attention and was regarded by Shanghai's film critics as one of the best patriotic and serious films.[43]

At the same time, the Flecks forged connections with some of China's finest filmmakers and established a school called the Academy of Movie Arts, China, in Shanghai. They recruited many well-known local film actors of the time to teach at the academy. This institution was one of the few film schools in Chinese history and played a constructive role in cultivating local film talent. With the outbreak of the Pacific War and the Japanese occupation of the Shanghai concessions, the ongoing screenings of *Children of the World* were forcibly halted and later banned. The film school was also forced to close. However, the Flecks, with their extensive expertise, broad international perspective, and rich practical experience in film production and talent development, left an important mark on the history of Chinese cinema.

Similar to the Flecks, Alfred Wittenberg's profound musical qualifications and superb violin and piano skills gave him opportunities to host chamber music concerts soon after arriving in Shanghai. Afterward, he became well known and began to recruit local students. Many of his Chinese students were musicians who had already made their own mark at that time, such as Tan Shuzhen (谭抒真), known as the "founder of Chinese violin production," and Fan Jisen (范继森), the former dean of the piano department of the Shanghai Conservatory of Music. Hence, Wittenberg came to be revered as the "professor of professors."[44]

Wittenberg himself was remarkably talented, yet modest and approachable. The German newspaper *Berliner Volkszeitung* wrote in an article celebrating his fiftieth birthday: "His large circle of students reveres him as an artist and a human being, and his magnificent art as well as his modest kindness have earned him numerous loyal friends."[45] Upon arriving in Shanghai, Wittenberg maintained this world-class demeanor of a maestro, combining a quest for artistic excellence with affableness toward others. Despite being "in his twilight years, he continued to perform alongside his students and younger colleagues, sometimes accompanying them on the piano, always approaching these engagements with the same meticulous attention to detail as he did when collaborating with the world's leading musicians in his youth."[46]

Wittenberg's Chinese students formed deep friendships with the elderly musician and treated him as a guest of honor. Many of his former Chinese students later became masters in Chinese music history and held their teacher in great esteem, in accordance with traditional Confucian values deeply rooted in Chinese society of respecting teachers and elders. They eagerly acquired extraordinary skills and profound musical knowledge from him, while also caring meticulously for him and his family.[47] In this way, they built a cultural bridge of emotional resonance and mutual understanding through music. It was precisely because "the Chinese students treated him so well, with deep affection between teacher and students, that he was unwilling to leave them and seek a new life elsewhere."[48] Therefore, despite multiple invitations to move to the United States, Wittenberg stayed in China and continued teaching at the Shanghai Conservatory of

Music after the war. As a representative figure of Jewish musicians in exile in Shanghai, Wittenberg lived in China for over a decade, considering Shanghai his home. He passed away there in 1952, to rest peacefully among his beloved Chinese students.

Examining the experiences of the Flecks and Alfred Wittenberg in Shanghai, it is clear that as accomplished artists, their seniority and aging played a positive role in their exile years. With the increased age and experience, they endured more challenges and difficulties. They demonstrated strong adaptability in maintaining the continuity of their careers, a resilient spirit, and remarkable mental fortitude. In addition, they possessed broader and deeper social networks than young people, enabling them to quickly establish connections within their existing circles as soon as they arrived in Shanghai. They also courageously transcended cultural barriers, forging relationships with China's intellectual elites and collaborating with cultural and artistic institutions in Shanghai. This allowed them to expand their local resources and support networks, ultimately gaining recognition and acceptance both professionally and personally.

FIGURE 4.1. Alfred Wittenberg and his Chinese students. Photo credit: Guozhang Tan, private collection.

From the perspective of role theory, as older refugees both the Flecks and Alfred Wittenberg defied expectations: they did not confine themselves to the fixed lifestyle they had had in Europe.[49] Instead, they constantly adjusted to changes in their social environment. They actively engaged in social and cultural activities in Shanghai, seeking new secondary roles and relying on their own strengths to regain control over their lives and maintain a sense of purpose in China. In doing so, they infused their lives with cultural character and significance. Following their passing, stories and memories about them continue to be recounted and preserved. In 1986, the Flecks and Fei Mu collaboration *Children of the World*, preserved by the China Film Archive, was exhibited in Hong Kong; in 1991, the Vienna International Film Festival specially selected this film during a retrospective exhibition of Chinese films. Whether in the Flecks' hometown or their place of exile, Shanghai, this film by Sino-Austrian film artists serves as a historical testimony and also testifies to the memory and respect that later generations have for the Flecks and Chinese film artists. Regarding Alfred Wittenberg, many of his Chinese students have produced valuable historical materials about their mentor. In 1999, Chen Yifei's (陈逸飞) film *Escape to Shanghai* (逃往上海) was the first film in China to focus on the Holocaust and Jewish refugees in Shanghai. The film shows Wittenberg and his students as the protagonists and reviews the history of Jewish refugees in China. In 2005, the Shanghai Oriental Television Music Station (上海东方电视音乐台) produced the documentary *Jewish Musician in Shanghai* (犹太音乐家在上海), revisiting Wittenberg's former residence in Shanghai as a tribute to this musical maestro.

Meanwhile, local actors (individuals, communities, institutions, and organizations) involved in both the Flecks' and Wittenbergs' experience in China reflect a social and historical picture of China and the cosmopolitan spirit and inclusiveness of Shanghai. Since the late nineteenth century, Shanghai has become a highly diverse, heterogeneous cultural space, where traditions from all over the world collide and interact. This urban character exemplifies a modern version of Chinese civilization that integrates various regional cultures. From the 1920s to the 1940s, known as the Golden Age of Shanghai cinema, the city emerged as one of the most significant film centers in Asia. It attracted international capital and talent, witnessed the establishment of various film companies, and fostered an exceptionally prosperous film culture. Collaborative films, such as *Children of the World*, epitomized Shanghai during that period as an international metropolis and cinematic hub.

As far as music is concerned, Chinese music historian Tang Yating summarizes the key role played by exiled musicians like Alfred Wittenberg in the development of Chinese modern music: "To some extent, we can say that it was primarily Jewish musicians and Soviet musicians who cultivated Western art music culture in China: before and after World War I, it was musicians from Belarus and Russia; before and after World War II, it was Central European—mainly German and Austrian Jewish musicians, and in the 1950s, it was Soviet musicians."[50]

At that time, there were many globally renowned music masters in Shanghai, like Alfred Wittenberg. Some Jewish refugee musicians joined the Shanghai Municipal Council Orchestra (the predecessor of the Shanghai Symphony Orchestra), known as "the first orchestra of the Far East," while others were employed in various departments of the National Conservatory of Music (the predecessor of the Shanghai Conservatory of Music), thereby leaving behind a precious musical legacy in China.[51] Therefore, recounting the Flecks' and Wittenbergs' history of exile from the perspective of older refugees and relevant local actors also points to multilayered memory cultures, facilitating multidirectional dialogues among different ethnic groups, histories, and cultures.

Conclusion

This chapter takes older German and Austrian exile artists in Shanghai as a starting point to reexamine the history and memory of Jewish exile in China within a new context. By exploring the cases of several elderly, culturally elite Jewish refugees, it preliminarily discusses the different roles that aging plays in their exile experiences. This study serves as a catalyst, aiming to lay the groundwork for future in-depth, nuanced, and rigorous research on older Jewish refugees in China. Examining the history of the Holocaust and exile centered on age somewhat bridges the gap between past and present, them and us, there and here. For this still-developing study, perhaps the crucial aspect lies not in how to define aging and the elderly, but rather in investigating how they understood themselves and society from both global and local perspectives. Additionally, it depends on how society construes them, and how aging intersects with other analytical categories such as gender, occupation, and ethnicity, and engages in dialogue with multiple dimensions of cultural memory. The cases of the Flecks and Alfred Wittenberg demonstrate that age as a multilayered category reaches beyond the narratives that tend to highlight the vulnerability and passiveness of older Jewish refugees who fled Europe. Both the Flecks and Wittenberg successfully navigated the aftermath of the atrocities and played a role in the cultural modernization of Shanghai. Case studies of well-known artists provide a framework for future scholarly attention to older Jewish refugees in exile in China.

While this chapter focuses on examples of elderly Jewish cultural elites, it also raises numerous unresolved questions that require further exploration. For example, Eva Fuss, the mother-in-law of Alfred Wittenberg, arrived and died in Shanghai at an advanced age, yet she remains an "ordinary" older, female Jewish refugee who did not leave behind historical records. Who was she? What did she go through? What did she leave behind? Who else like her existed? What other experiences did they go through? What else did they leave behind? Such questions await investigation.

Notes

1 Alfred Dreifuß, "Schanghai—Eine Emigration am Rande," in *Kunst und Literatur im antifaschistischen Exil: 1933–1945*, vol. 3, *Exil in den USA*, ed. Eike Middell et al. (Röderberg, 1980), 447.

2 Jan Hans, "Geschichten aus der Exilforschungsgeschichte: Gründung und Arbeiten der 'Hamburger Arbeitsstelle für deutsche Exilliteratur,'" in *Exilforschungen im historischen Prozess*, ed. Claus-Dieter Krohn and Lutz Winckler (Edition Text + Kritik, 2012), 93.

3 David Kranzler, *Japanese, Nazis and Jews: The Jewish Refugees Community of Shanghai, 1938–1945* (Yeshiva University Press, 1976).

4 Aleida Assmann, *Erinnerungsräume: Formen und Wandlungen des kulturellen Gedächtnisses* (C. H. Beck, 1999), 134.

5 Translated by this author from the German, in *Leben im Wartesaal: Exil in Shanghai, 1938–1947*, exhibit catalog, ed. Amnon Barzel and Jüdisches Museum Berlin (Jüdisches Museum Berlin, 1997), inside cover.

6 Edward W. Said, *Orientalism*, twenty-fifth anniversary edition (Random House, 2014), 2.

7 Longxi Zhang, "The Myth of the Other: China in the Eyes of the West," *Critical Inquiry* 15, no. 1 (Autumn 1988): 127.

8 Kranzler, *Japanese, Nazis and Jews*, 40; Barzel and Jüdisches Museum Berlin, *Leben im Wartesaal*, 21; Sybille Baumbach et al., eds., *Atmen und halbwegs frei sein: Flucht nach Shanghai* (Museum für Hamburgische Geschichte, 2011), 28.

9 Elisabeth Buxbaum, *Transit Shanghai: Ein Leben im Exil* (Steinbauer, 2008), 25.

10 Françoise Kreissler, "Europäische Emigranten (1933–1945) in der chinesischen Geschichtsschreibung: Zwischen Politik und Geschichte," in *Exilforschungen im historischen Prozess*, ed. Krohn and Winckler, 237.

11 Jian Wang, *Escape and Rescue: Jewish Refugees and Shanghai in World War II* (Shanghai Jiao Tong University Press, 2016), 305.

12 Kreissler, "Europäische Emigranten," 233.

13 Lu Pan, "Remembering the Pain of 'Others': Reflections on the Shanghai Jewish Refugees Museum and Beyond," *Writing the War in Asia—A Documentary History* 2 (March 2014): 6.

14 The imbalance in this politics of memory manifests in multiple dimensions. For instance, within China itself, Jewish exile in other cities (such as Tianjin, Harbin, and Hong Kong) remains relatively underrepresented. The historiography and memory of Jewish refugees in China has also, to some extent, overshadowed the parallel histories of Jewish exiles in other countries like Japan and the Philippines across East and Southeast Asia during World War II.

15 Related studies such as Jüdisches Museum Berlin and Stiftung Haus der Geschichte, eds., *Heimat und Exil: Emigration der deutschen Juden nach 1933* (Jüdischer Verlag im Suhrkamp Verlag, 2006); Margit Franz and Heimo Halbrainer, eds., *Going East—Going South: Österreichisches Exil in Asien und Afrika* (CLIO, 2014).

16 For example, in 1933, in order to protest against the persecution of European progressives and Jews by German fascists, Song Qingling (宋庆龄), Cai Yuanpei (蔡元培), Lu Xun (鲁迅), Lin Yutang (林语堂), and other well-known Chinese intellectuals went to the German Consulate in Shanghai to submit a protest letter. The Chinese Nationalist government during the wartime also planned to resettle Jewish refugees

on a large scale in the Chinese frontier province of Yunnan. See Wang, *Escape and Rescue*, 29.

17 Michael Rothberg, *Multidirectional Memory: Remembering the Holocaust in the Age of Decolonization* (Stanford University Press, 2009), 3.

18 See relevant historical works in recent years: Astrid Freyeisen, *Shanghai und die Politik des Dritten Reiches* (Königshausen & Neumann, 2000); Guang Pan, "The Jews and China: Study of Jews in China After 1840 and Their Relationship with China" (PhD diss., East China Normal University, 2000); Steve Hochstadt, *Exodus to Shanghai: Stories of Escape from the Third Reich* (Palgrave Macmillan, 2012); Irene Eber, *Wartime Shanghai and the Jewish Refugees from Central Europe: Survival, Co-Existence, and Identity in a Multi-Ethnic City* (Walter de Gruyter, 2012); Bei Gao, *Shanghai Sanctuary: Chinese and Japanese Policy Toward European Jewish Refugees During World War II* (Oxford University Press, 2013).

19 "Decade of Healthy Ageing: The Global Strategy and Action Plan on Ageing and Health 2016–2020: Towards a World in Which Everyone Can Live a Long and Healthy Life," World Health Organization, accessed August 10, 2024, apps.who.int/gb/ebwha/pdf_files/WHA73/A73_INF2-en.pdf.

20 "Life Expectancy for Social Security," US Social Security Administration, accessed October 17, 2023, www.ssa.gov/history/lifeexpect.html.

21 In the 1930s and 1940s, China did not have a comprehensive, large-scale census due to the war, but only statistics on the life expectancy of the population in some areas. Data have shown that the overall life expectancy was less than forty years old. See Weizhi Wang, "A Study on Life Expectancy in China," *Chinese Journal of Population Science* 1 (1987): 36.

22 Thomas Rahlf, *Deutschland in Daten: Zeitreihen zur Historischen Statistik* (Bundeszentralefür politische Bildung, 2015), 76.

23 Petra Löber, "Leben im Wartesaal: Exil in Shanghai, 1938–1947," in *Leben im Wartesaal*, Barzel and Jüdisches Museum Berlin, 17.

24 Wang, *Escape and Rescue*, 100.

25 Wang, *Escape and Rescue*, 101.

26 For more on the cultural memory of the Wolf Brothers, see Dieter Guderian, *Die Hamburger Originale Tetje und Fietje: Lebensgeschichte der Gebrüder Wolf und ihrer Familie Isaac* (CARDAMINA, 2006); Xin Tong, *Transmedia Remembering: Eine Fallstudie des Shanghaier Exils in Deutschland und China seit 1990* (Avinus, 2022).

27 Zhiying Yuan, "A. J. Storfer und die 'Gelbe Post,'" *Literaturstraße: Chinesisch-deutsches Jahrbuch für Sprache* 1 (2008): 226.

28 Christian Pape, "Verdrängt, Verkannt, Vergessen? Ein Beitrag zu Leben und Werken von Adolf Josef Storfer," *Chilufim: Zeitschrift für jüdische Kulturgeschichte* 12 (2012): 7.

29 Teng Teng, "'Children of the World' and the Austrian Jewish Film Director Couple Fleck," *New Films* 2 (1997): 51.

30 In contrast to the intermarried Flecks, Alfred Wittenberg and his wife were both born into Jewish families and became members of the Jewish community of Berlin. See Sophie Fetthauer, "Alfred Wittenberg," in *Lexikon verfolgter Musiker und Musikerinnen der NS-Zeit*, ed. Claudia Maurer Zenck et al. (University of Hamburg, 2022), www.lexm.uni-hamburg.de/object/lexm_lexmperson_00002496.

31 Buzeng Xu, *The Jewish Cultural Elite of Shanghai* (Shanghai Academy of Social Sciences Press, 2007), 57.

32 Xu, *Jewish Cultural Elite of Shanghai*, 67.

33 Xu, *Jewish Cultural Elite of Shanghai*, 125.

34 Guderian, *Die Hamburger Originale Tetje und Fietje*, 88.

35 Max L. Berges, *Cold Pogrom*, trans. Benjamin R. Epstein (Jewish Publication Society of America, 1939).

36 Wilfried Weinke, "'I Am Proud to Be a Jew!': Der Schriftsteller Max Ludwig Berges," in *Eine verschwundene Welt: Jüdisches Leben am Grindel*, ed. Ursula Wamser and Wilfried Weinke (zu Klampen, 2006), 253.

37 Xu, *Jewish Cultural Elite of Shanghai*, 67–68.

38 Xu, *Jewish Cultural Elite of Shanghai*, 65.

39 Xu, *Jewish Cultural Elite of Shanghai*, 67.

40 Teng, "'Children of the World,'" 53.

41 Teng, "'Children of the World,'" 51.

42 Quoted in Teng, "'Children of the World,'" 51.

43 Teng, "'Children of the World,'" 52.

44 Xu, *Jewish Cultural Elite of Shanghai*, 60.

45 Quoted in Fetthauer, "Alfred Wittenberg."

46 Xu, *Jewish Cultural Elite of Shanghai*, 60.

47 Xu, *Jewish Cultural Elite of Shanghai*, 63.

48 Xu, *Jewish Cultural Elite of Shanghai*, 67.

49 Michael Banton, "Role," in *The Social Science Encyclopedia*, ed. Adam Kuper and Jessica Kuper (Routledge Taylor and Francis, 1996), 749–51.

50 Yating Tang, *Musical Life of Shanghai Jewish Communities: 1850–1950, 1998–2005* (Shanghai Conservatory of Music Press, 2007), 154–55.

51 Tang, *Musical Life of Shanghai Jewish Communities*, 164.

5

"HEAD OF AN OLD WOMAN"

Nelly Wolffheim and the Voices of the Aged

Christine Schmidt

> Ken vun's Expektaschons
> effer be low enuff? Eefen tryink
> viz ziss relinkvischink
> off Eekgo, ve are all still
> frenkly inzufferapel.
>
> —Sophie Herxheimer[1]

Nelly Wolffheim, a feminist specialist in Freudian-based psychoanalytic pedagogy for young children, was remembered fondly by a former student in her obituary, published in 1965:

> Nelly Wolffheim, who was slight in build and completely white, appeared to me as a wise, old and unshakable institution. Four years later, when I visited her in Oxford, where she lived in very cramped circumstances, she seemed very much younger in outlook, but physically more fragile. Thus, through the years that I knew her, she almost reversed the process of ageing. She mentioned . . . that a young friend had painted a portrait of her . . . and had called it "Head of an Old Woman." This, she regarded as a most inapt description.[2]

Wolffheim struggled to leave Nazi Germany for England in 1939 at the age of sixty, her books burned and her career proscribed. Until settling

FIGURE 5.1. Nelly Wolffheim. Credit: Ida-Seele-Archiv, 89407 Dilligen/Do.

in the Otto Schiff Home for the aged in London in 1956, she lived peripatetically in Oxford and London, never reestablishing herself as a pedagogue in her newly adopted country.[3] A close examination of Wolffheim's life, especially her postwar contributions related to German-speaking Jewish communities in Britain, subverts the idea that older surviving persecutees of Nazism faded into anonymity or inactivity, even while they coped with humiliation, loneliness, dislocation, and loss.

A prolific writer, Wolffheim published numerous essays in German psychoanalytic journals on her pedagogical theories, as well as in the Britain-based *AJR Information* journal regarding communal issues among aging Jewish refugees.[4] Among her notable achievements was her advancement of the creation of a record of Jewish suffering before and during the Holocaust. She conducted at least thirty interviews for the Wiener Library's (now Wiener Holocaust Library) project to record written survivor eyewitness accounts in the 1950s, including with several fellow residents of the Otto Schiff Home, where she "retired" in 1957 at the age of seventy-eight.[5] While her professional career focused on child psychology and development, in later years she turned to documenting her own relationship to Anglo-Jewry and British non-Jews, and to amplifying the voices of the aged. She aimed to ensure that the perceptions and agency of older Jewish refugees were embedded within a collection intended to "salvage" the "immaterial" memories of witnesses and survivors of Nazi persecution.[6] The collection of over twelve hundred accounts was varied, and while there was a basic temporal and thematic framework set for the interviews, there was no set of core questions assigned to the interviewers. Therefore, each interviewer who participated produced accounts shaped by their own subjectivities. Wolffheim's interviewees, primarily middle-class, German-speaking Jews who had fled Nazi Germany before or during the war, ranged in age from thirty-eight- to eighty-six-years-old at the time of their interviews in the late 1950s. Considered collectively, these highly mediated accounts illustrate Wolffheim's own concerns, especially with regard to age, class, and gender—particularly women's experiences—in relation to flight from persecution and survival, as well as professional status, "privilege" (such as might come with "mixed" marriages), and the psychological torment experienced by victims revealed in brief but disturbing "small stories" of abuse and cruelty, as well as rare acts of kindness.[7] A close reading of the corpus created by Wolffheim reveals the concerns and outlook of an older, likely queer, German Jewish woman who aimed to chronicle the lives of other women in her community with whom she shared affinities, friendship, and intimacy.

While she may have been rather exceptional in her position to assess her own and others' experiences as she did, Wolffheim's writing and the accounts she recorded allow us to examine the challenges faced by elderly refugee survivors, particularly but not only those who, as middle-aged or older people, escaped the traumas of early Nazi anti-Jewish persecution before policies radicalized with the onset of war. Through an analysis of the accounts, framed by Wolffheim's biography and her writing as an advocate for the elderly, I argue that early projects to record survivor testimonies are key to recovering the fates of the elderly. They can reveal how the elderly made meaning of their experiences in the postwar period. Building on the work of historian Hannah Pollin-Galay, I will explore the potential "shared conceptual resources" between Wolffheim and those she interviewed, particularly with regard to such markers as class, education, and gender.[8] This subcollection supports Pollin-Galay's identification of continuities in Jewish culture, binding the history of German-speaking Jewish refugees in Britain to their pre-Holocaust pasts as described in life stories.[9] Finally, I will suggest how the content and structure of the accounts Wolffheim developed with interviewees provides a window onto the developing image of the German Jewish refugee taking shape in public consciousness in Britain, a little over ten years after the end of hostilities in Europe.

The Wiener Library's "Early" Eyewitness Accounts

In the mid-1950s, when Jewish historical commissions were beginning to wind down their immediate postwar work of collecting Holocaust documentation, Eva Reichmann, then director of research at the Wiener Library, launched an initiative to gather as many eyewitness accounts of the Holocaust as possible.[10] The project lasted for approximately seven years and amassed over twelve hundred eyewitness reports in seven languages. Reichmann recruited paid interviewers, often survivors or refugees from Nazi persecution themselves, to record accounts with other survivors, whom they found by word-of-mouth in Britain and then, through advertisements in various publications and expansion of the network, in Europe and elsewhere. The interviewers recorded, edited, and produced typewritten accounts, which were checked and verified by Reichmann (including her handwritten notes) and then often signed off by the interviewee.[11]

The methodology of the project was in some ways consistent with other earlier projects, despite its comparatively later launch.[12] Historian Noah Shenker has emphasized that "testimonies are shaped by individually and institutionally embedded practices framed by a wide range of aims extending beyond empirical historical content or visceral impact. In that sense, testimonies are not circulated as enclosed capsules of memory, but as constantly mediated, contested, and fragile acts of remembering."[13] Many (though certainly not all) of the mediations, interventions, and processes Shenker has identified in relation to audiovisual testimony are illustrative for analyzing collections of written early accounts and, in the case of the library's project, can be partly reconstructed from institutional correspondence, made even more palpable in Reichmann's notations incorporated in what were termed the final accounts in the collection.[14] There is no surviving record of the questions that were asked, however, and it is clear that there was no standard template of questions for interviews, since each interviewer produced somewhat different "subcollections" for the project with their own internal consistencies, constructions, and subjectivities. This makes the collection ripe for analyzing and interpreting intentionality and co-construction.[15] In addition to the narrative reports, the library's collection includes court depositions, diary excerpts, letters, poetry, songs, quotes from published memoirs, and other materials submitted as accounts, but not necessarily considered testimony in the traditional sense.[16]

Paid by the library for her work, Nelly Wolffheim submitted twenty-three reports incorporated into the collection between 1957 and 1960, which included interviews with thirty refugees and survivors of Nazi persecution, most of whom were Jewish.[17] Married couples' experiences were usually reported together in a single account, which typically began with brief biographical details as well as the interviewees' parents' professions. The oldest interviewee, Margarete Maison (née Born), was born in 1874 in Berlin, aged sixty-five at the time of her flight first to France, displaced to Britain at age seventy-four, and eighty-six at the time of her interview with Wolffheim. The youngest, Kitty Hillier (née Friedländer), was born in 1921 in Budapest, and aged thirty-eight at the time of her interview. Twenty-four of the eyewitnesses were aged fifty-five or older at the time of their interviews. At least eleven interviews were conducted with coresidents of the Otto Schiff Home, a home for mainly older Jewish refugees in London; others seemed to be Wolffheim's former professional contacts, or members of the Belsize Square Synagogue, which both Reichmann and Wolffheim attended.[18] Twenty-three accounts were developed with women, including eleven single or widowed women. The men who were interviewed were generally interviewed as part of married couples.[19] Wolffheim recorded her own memories of a close friend, Ella Perutz, a non-Jewish woman whose boardinghouse she had frequented in Teplitz-Schönau (Teplice, Czech Republic), whose social relations were primarily Jewish. Perutz died by suicide in 1945 due to the threatened deportation of ethnic Germans; her daughter Helene Hirsch, whose husband was Jewish, helped Wolffheim compile the report.[20]

Clarifying the aims of the project, Reichmann urged the duty of survivors and eyewitnesses to come forward in a 1954 appeal in the *Association of Jewish Refugees* monthly bulletin: "We all have a duty to fulfil towards our past. Political developments on a global as well as on the Jewish level are not too auspicious for keeping alive the memory of German Jewry."[21] Presumably having seen the appeal, Wolffheim submitted her own report, which was compiled by Midia Krause, a London-based interviewer, and received by the library in 1955, with an addendum submitted in 1960.[22] In 1957, the library (on behalf of Reichmann) opened the door to Wolffheim's further involvement with the project, writing to her that "should there be other personalities among the inhabitants of the Otto Schiff House, who have had important experiences for our collections, we would be very grateful—perhaps with prior telephone consultation—if you would collect them for us."[23] Bertha Cohn, who compiled bibliographies for the library, reiterated Reichmann's exhortation to eyewitnesses' "moral obligation" in her letter to Wolffheim on January 22, 1960, after interviews Wolffheim had scheduled were apparently canceled: "It is a great pity that interviews that were promised to you did not take place after all. But I can imagine that, considering the most recent events, some people will see and understand how important our collection is, and that it is actually their duty to record their memories, precisely because they should not be forgotten."[24]

Wolffheim, an Advocate for Older Refugees

Although some experiences and particular challenges faced by older refugees have been broadly described in social and cultural histories of Jewish refugee life in Britain, age in relation to class, gender, and sexuality has not been a primary prism for analysis of Jewish refugees' experiences in Britain, perhaps in part due to their small number.[25] That said, historian Anthony Grenville has noted that although most Jewish refugees who came to Britain experienced poverty, older people suffered more from "a psychological inability to adapt to unfamiliar conditions and a strange lifestyle—there were cases of elderly refugees who were so adrift in Britain that they chose to return to Germany—and especially by the loss of status that shattered their confidence, on which their very identity rested."[26] He finds that older women seemed more adaptable and flexible to their new surroundings, while older professional men often lapsed into "enforced idleness." Historian Marion Berghahn has described the impact of emigration on different generations of refugees, noting that because their lives had been interrupted at a formative time, there persisted a greater feeling of inferiority among the younger over older refugees, who could call upon a "solid psychological, cultural and social base," as well as a reclamation of German Jewish culture through association with others in Britain, to provide a degree of emotional, if not financial, security.[27]

While there is now a vast body of literature focusing on child refugees who came to the UK and elsewhere via the *Kindertransporte*, elderly refugees remain a faint outline. They are often presented as a foil to younger Jewish refugees in the literature at best, and at worst, reduced and infantilized by fellow, younger refugees who observed or interacted with them. Lily Wagner, a German Jewish émigré who set up a boardinghouse for refugees in London, captured some of the most persistent and troubling characterizations of elderly refugees, whom she observed with pity: "Humiliation and illness in the face of old age have swept away their zest for living, in many cases their very desire to live. How precious is the sympathy of anyone who can understand the seemingly strange ways of those who [were] once respected and prosperous [who] have now to accept and even to beg for alms."[28] She describes the struggle for language adaptation among older refugees: "They are just like children, these refugees, helpless and irresolute, dependent on others and grateful for every kindness and advice. If you think of it, you realise the tragedy of these people, who so well deserve a rest, both physically and mentally, and now in their old age have to learn strange languages, new habits and foreign customs."[29]

Wolffheim's life, writing and interviews nuance the discomfiting, reductive picture Wagner painted, even while her work and interviews reflect, to some extent, the difficulties that the scholarship describes. Of central concern to Wolffheim was the interviewees' gender, their ability to cope with the loss of professional status and activity, their struggle to earn money, life in a new language, as well as loneliness and grief. At the same time, Wolffheim aimed to ensure that the experiences, aspirations, and contributions of older people, and the fullness of their lives (including her own) as individuals with agency were not overlooked or reduced. A brief consideration of her biography helps us gain a clearer picture of the themes prevalent in the interviews she conducted and their potential meaning for Wolffheim.

Wolffheim, born in 1879 in Berlin, grew up in an upper middle-class, secular Jewish household. She was influenced early on by feminist movements in Germany, and pursued an education to support herself in the future.[30] She never married, and most of her intimate friendships were with women. While she expressed romantic desire toward female mentors and preferred to develop friendships with women, it is unclear whether she herself ever pursued sexual or romantic relationships with them, even though it seems she wished for one.[31] In 1896, she enrolled at the Pestalozzi-Fröbel-Haus in Berlin to focus on early childhood education and modern pedagogy. Although chronic ill health and anxiety suffered since childhood prevented Wolffheim from working regularly in her field, she opened her own private kindergarten in 1914. She then suffered a mental health crisis, and during her recovery, began to incorporate Freud's theories both in her own published psychoanalytic research and her curriculum development. The Nazis' rise to power abruptly interrupted her work, however, and she was no longer able to write or hold public lectures.[32] Her book, *Psychoanalyse und Kindergarten*, was banned and burned in 1933, and she recalled: "Suddenly everything was ended, not only my work but also all the ideals which had been important for me. Principles for which I had fought my whole life became invalidated. It was very painful for me to watch as my work became useless."[33]

She opened a kindergarten teacher school for female Jewish students who were no longer accepted at training centers, to help prepare them to emigrate. As students dwindled and the Nazis implemented further restrictions, she closed the school in 1939 and faced the daunting prospect of emigration herself.[34] Wolffheim, a single, older, likely queer woman, with limited professional opportunities at the age of sixty, would have found it difficult to find the required guarantor for immigration to the UK since she had no relatives abroad to help and her friends who had emigrated were in no financial position to sponsor her.[35] Eventually, colleagues and friends, the psychoanalysts Karen Horney (in the United States) and Ilse Seglow (in Britain), did help her, and Seglow placed an advertisement in the *Church Times*, after which a wealthy woman in London agreed to the sponsorship.[36] She recalled: "My own emigration, which was planned for the middle of March, was delayed by my illness. I was lying in the Jewish hospital in Berlin because of a heart condition. . . . I lay there right up until I flew to London in May 1939. It was not until after the war that I was able to settle down to becoming a writer."[37]

Most of her account punctuates her experiences in Nazi Germany by an almost singular fixation on when and how she might be able to write again. After she came to England, she lived in London until 1940 when the threat of air raids drove her to Oxford, sometimes sleeping on the couches of friends when she was unable to find housing.[38] To earn a living, she took on odd jobs, tutored children, became a portrait model ("capitalizing on my ugliness," as she said), and made children's toys.[39] Correspondence with Anna Freud reveals that she applied to the Claims Conference for support, with the help of Eva Reichmann's husband, Hans Reichmann.[40] She briefly considered returning to Germany after the war, but she saw no chance of reviving her former professional circles. Her ability to write, which she returned to not long after her emigration to England, provided not only an outlet for the development of her psychoanalytic theories and reclamation of her intellectual pursuits but also a means to express her existential concerns and to transmit the voices of older refugees. Wolffheim's writing on aging provides a useful interpretive framework for understanding recurring themes in her interviews, reflecting her own insight into the lives of older Jewish refugees, as well as a space where she found a new home and kinship network.[41]

In the October 1954 issue of *AJR Journal* (a few years before she moved to the Otto Schiff Home), Wolffheim addressed a painful condition experienced by elderly refugees and survivors: loneliness. She drew *Journal* readers' attention to "Jewish Friendship Clubs," which were organized by the League of Jewish Women in cooperation with the United Synagogue Welfare Committee. With a sensitive eye on gendered experiences of aging, she pointed to the great value of the clubs for women and men over sixty: "I emphasise women, as they are in the majority, although a more mixed attendance would, of course, be desirable."[42] The aim of the clubs was to provide elderly, potentially lonely, people a meeting place one afternoon a week. "Thus they have 'a date' for two and a half hours every week, and that means a great deal to many elderly people, especially those who live on their own." Wolffheim reports that she met many women who attended several clubs each week, "to enjoy the cosy atmosphere and also to escape loneliness."

In another reflection, Wolffheim wrote about the trepidation that engulfed her decision to move to the Schiff Home and her self-perception of "being old": "One must first be emotionally ready, feel old enough, before one can look forward to going to an Old Age Home. Going into an Old Age Home—whatever may be one's attitude to it or one's reasons for going—means a completely new life."[43] Evoking historian Guy Miron's concept of "home" and the daily struggle for private space among German Jews, she describes the spatial contours of her "new life," which ended her residential drifting:

> Anyone who, for eighteen years, has been living in furnished rooms, containing for the most part unwanted furniture and a collection of undesirable bric-a-brac, will fully appreciate the effect on us of the beautiful colours and simple design of the rooms of the Home. That secret yearning for a flat of my own, vanished; here my room was once more a real home, a place that belonged to *me*.[44]

She explains in detail (and with wry humor) the care given toward considerations for the residents—ample space, walls with insulation from sound that prevented people from disturbing each other ("unavoidable with a large number of inhabitants who are hard of hearing"), color, and furnishings. Medical care was more than suitable: "The frequently expressed regret of refugees that there are no 'Continental sanatoria' in England, is something we never feel, we are so well looked after."

But the care Wolffheim felt at Otto Schiff Home stretched beyond the spatial consideration of the rooms or furnishings and spread to a sense of "belonging" and "community," even if she longed for more social gatherings, especially for those who did not observe Shabbat.[45] This desire was set against the concurrent impulse she had to "perform gratitude" to establish herself as a "deserving refugee": "Are all these things that we are being given too much? Are we being 'spoilt'?" She provides an impression of a social worker who visited the home and who expressed an "outsider's" (or nativist) view, which separated elderly Jewish refugees from the British elderly population:

> To many outside people this may appear to be the case, for they do not know what lies behind it all. I was recently visited by an English social

> worker, whose special field of activity is care for the aged. She, too, like many of my visitors, was amazed and delighted by the beautiful modern rooms, but I felt a certain reserve in her manner and I think I saw what was passing through her mind: "Here we have all this luxury; how does it compare with the sort of places our old people live in?" I felt almost ashamed of our better circumstances, and yet she could hardly be expected to understand that the possibility of creating this Home came out of our own sufferings and that it is the result of a desire to try to give those who had suffered a peaceful and contented old age. But what has been given to us gives us a responsibility too; the responsibility of appreciation.[46]

Wolffheim's sentiments echo both the "othering" and apprehension many German-speaking Jewish refugees encountered from the British (Jewish and non-Jewish) population, both before and after the war, as well as the postwar pressure placed on Jewish refugees to perform gratitude to their "hosts, including by members of the Anglo-Jewish community, for having been spared the horrors of the Holocaust."[47] This can only have contributed to what historian Yael Siman has called an "undefined space of belonging" for Wolffheim, and further interference with her attempts to redefine and reclaim herself amid displacement and exile.[48] These interferences are keenly observed by Wolffheim in the accounts she gathered for the Wiener Library, where she is not a passive recorder of others' experiences but an active participant in the articulation and transmission of memory.

Co-Constructed Narratives of the Aged

The interviews Wolffheim conducted echo her experiences of displacement and loneliness, loss of profession, and desire for self-sufficiency. In addition to the remarkably wide-ranging individual experiences the interviews describe, the corpus of interviews can be considered an extension of Wolffheim's preoccupation with the state of "old age," even though they don't specifically reflect on aging (likely because Wolffheim did not ask questions about this). They also reveal Wolffheim's intellectual interests in child psychology and Freudian theory, as well as her focus on the upper middle-class Jewish milieu, its genealogy and fate. Among the short biographical details at the top of each account, Wolffheim listed the profession of the interviewee and the interviewees' parents. Changes in social status are commonly discussed in her interviews.

Unsurprisingly, Wolffheim had a keen eye for the psychological impact of terror, including on children, experienced by Jews in Germany prior to their emigration. In an account of a couple, LW and RW (kept anonymous), although the description is titled and framed as the wife's experience, Wolffheim briefly analyzes the childhood of RW, the husband, who had suffered neglect. She states that "these childhood experiences may have been the reason for his work with needy children in adult life, as well as his strong leftist political convictions."[49] LW, a former nursery school teacher, also worked with children with special needs, and presumably was Wolffheim's professional acquaintance. The account describes the violence of *Kristallnacht*, including formerly friendly neighbors who spat at them. Wolffheim homes in on the impact of the violence on the couple's children, who were eight and ten years old at the time; a porter beat the younger child, and the older child attempted suicide. After the family fled to England, RW set up his own psychoanalysis practice, although he found the work physically taxing and he died of a heart attack. Wolffheim concludes the account noting that the children were still impacted by the events, with one of them "slightly unstable" and the other making a "conscious effort to avoid talking about the Hitler years."[50]

The Austrian specialist in child psychology and education, Helene Plohn, née Goldbaum, recorded her account for the library at the age of seventy-seven, which was received and edited by Wolffheim in January 1960 (Plohn was not necessarily interviewed by Wolffheim).[51] Plohn, born in 1883 in Trutnov, then Czechoslovakia, was a head teacher of a training college for schoolteachers in Vienna, and like RW also probably a member of Wolffheim's professional circles. Hers is one of the few accounts gathered by Wolffheim written in the first person. Like Wolffheim, Plohn was fired from her post in March 1938, and she describes receiving multiple prank calls from former students, "informing" her that the SS would soon arrive to pick her up. She recounts other cruelty, including being kicked out of a café as a Jew. She and her husband (who remains unnamed in the account) managed to emigrate to Shanghai in January 1939, since she had a relative there. They remained in Shanghai until 1947, and Plohn attached a copy of an article about her teaching there, which she had already published in the Viennese journal *Soziale Berufe* in 1953. The account of life in Shanghai is harrowing, due to the difficult living conditions, air raids, and severe health problems she and her husband suffered, exacerbated by the climate. The couple decided to return to Vienna in 1947. She stresses: "Then we had to start building a new life. . . . We were fortunate to get our old age pensions, and I had and still have some pupils whom I tutor, and thus we were able to continue living comfortably."[52]

Wolffheim was particularly concerned with women's struggles to emigrate, as well as their professional, financial, and other losses brought on by persecution and forced migration. The signed narrative of Lotte Lewin, recorded in March 1960 after an interview with Wolffheim when Lewin was sixty-eight years old, opens immediately with a remark that "following inflation, the salary rate at the university [of Breslau, where Lewin worked] worsened considerably," which compelled her to move into her father's textile industry.[53] Lewin was overheard by a male (non-Jewish) employee of the company referring to Joseph Goebbels as the "spawn of filth and fire" (in the style of Faust). Her words were reported to the Gestapo, and she was imprisoned for three days. The account takes an interesting "editorial" turn in which Wolffheim describes the Jewish community of Breslau as seemingly unaware and unresponsive to the growing threat of Nazism. A rare direct quotation from Lewin, who apparently agreed with her assessment, then appears next; she wrote: "One was more angry than fearful." Wolffheim continues her interpretation of Lewin's activities: "Lotte Lewin distinguished herself through a misguided optimism, and following the experience described above [imprisonment], even travelled for Pentecost to see friends in Czechia, Gräfenberg, for 10 days." She was warned not to return to Germany by relatives in England, who promised to help her emigrate.[54] Lewin was brought to trial again not long after, in 1936, for her comments and sentenced to a further nine months in prison. The account describes her experiences and treatment in prison, from which she was freed in July 1937. The account ends with Lewin's emigration to England with the help of relatives.[55]

Wolffheim wrote a piece in 1954 on the psychology of earning money, and in addition to Lewin's report, other accounts revealed her preoccupation with the theme, particularly for women, perhaps not surprising considering her own biography.[56] Betty and Jenny Student were fifty-seven and fifty-six years old at the time of their emigration to England and were interviewed by Wolffheim in the Schiff Home when they were seventy-six and seventy-five. Their account illustrates Wolffheim's fascination with women's earning capacity as well as her perception of some German Jews' naïveté in face of increasing Nazi persecution, or in her words, "how guileless many Jews remained for a long time."[57] The two sisters had run a textiles shop in Giessen, which they sold ("voluntarily," as Wolffheim underlined) in 1936 after non-Jews were forbidden from shopping there. They then visited their brother in London, and not seeming "fully aware of the seriousness of their situation," returned to Giessen. Their brother tried to convince them to stay but, as Wolffheim describes empathetically, financial considerations held sway: "they did not want to stay in England as they dreaded the dependence and believed they would somehow make a living in Giessen through working from home or something similar." After *Kristallnacht*, the sisters understood the danger they were in and left in January 1939. Most notable about their experience, according to Wolffheim, was their reaction to receiving temporary support from their brother, which still troubled them at the time of the interview:

> Despite their wish for independence, they had to accept their brother's support. But even when they talk about it today, you can see how difficult it was for them to accept this. They earned some money through occasionally working from home. 1½ years later, the brother lost his job due to the War, and he was no longer able to support his sisters. The ladies came up with the plan to rent a house, admittedly with borrowed money, and to use it as a boarding house. They discussed this with the refugee committee, but they did not like the idea as it would mean a huge amount of work for the two women.[58]

It is clear Reichmann shared Wolffheim's views about the Students' "guileless" responses. She wrote to Wolffheim: "What is really valuable about this report is the sisters' disbelief that something really bad could happen, and the false sense of security that it gave them to lull themselves into."[59] Reichmann, however, also noted that while this snapshot was valuable, it was "thinner" and provided "less factual material than expected." Moreover, the report repeated themes Reichmann felt were already addressed within the existing collection: "Now, however, it is precisely this psychological attitude that has been expressed very often in our country. . . . in the present case we would have said that you need not go to the trouble because the subject has already been dealt with many times." Here some tension emerged between Wolffheim's primary concerns and Reichmann's institutionally driven aims for the project, which sought a diverse record of experiences that could be "objectively" verified.[60] Although Reichmann determined that these details were "already known" within the collection, Wolffheim's interviews continued to address similar themes.[61]

Other reports closely document Wolffheim's impressions of those from similar socioeconomic circles, chronicling the impact of migration on aging, including health issues of older people exacerbated by forced migration, as well as loneliness. In 1957 Wolffheim submitted a report based on an interview with Wanda Spiwak (née Weiss), a fellow resident at Otto Schiff Home.[62] Wolffheim begins by describing how the Weiss family lost their wealth through a lawsuit, and moved from Schöneck, West Prussia (Skarszewy) to Berlin, when Spiwak was eight years old. Spiwak did not undertake vocational training or work and married her husband (nameless in the account) in 1916. When the Nazis came to power, the Spiwaks took steps to emigrate: first their children left, one for England on a *Kindertransport*, the other to Palestine. The couple left for Palestine in 1938 with what Wolffheim calls "visas for capitalists" (presumably the Haavara Agreement), and remained there until the war in 1948.[63] Their living quarters destroyed, they decided to follow their daughter and son-in-law to Prague, which worsened their impoverishment. With the help of the International Refugee Organization, they managed to reach a displaced persons (DP) camp in Senigallia, Italy, where the conditions were so terrible that they were transferred again to Barletta, near Bari, Italy. The couple lived in the DP camp there for a year, their health falling; both ended up in hospital, with Wanda Spiwak suffering from pleurisy, pneumonia, and a liver affliction. Once she recovered, Spiwak continued to care for her husband until he died in 1954. Wolffheim observes:

> Under these circumstances his death came as a release; but for Mrs. Spiwak it meant continuing her journey. . . . At first Mrs. Spiwak lived on her own before moving into the Otto Schiff House, where she currently lives in a double bedroom. After being flung from one place to another she finally found a home. She has several physical ailments, especially her old liver affliction. A diet and medical supervision will hopefully improve her condition here. . . . Today Mrs. Spiwak is 71 years old.[64]

The reference to Spiwak "finally finding a home" recalls Wolffheim's own desire for dignified living space and a community of support. Likewise, her description of Spiwak's health reflects Wolffheim's lifelong physical and mental health challenges, and hints at the fear she expressed elsewhere of being infantilized and humiliated as an older person. After surgery in January 1957, for example, Wolffheim herself convalesced in a hospital: "I was fed, which made me feel very bad mentally, and meals often ended with me crying. My eating habits, especially the slowness of my chewing, did not match with the rush of the busy nurses. I was also disgusted when bread was pushed into my mouth with fingers that were previously busy with unsavory things. Most of all, something in me rebelled against being fed like a baby."[65]

Finally, Wolffheim's corpus underscores her view that older people remained valuable contributors to society, through connections to their work and intellectual or artistic pursuits. This is evident, for example, in the account she developed with Margarete Maison, her oldest interviewee and fellow resident of the Schiff Home.[66] Maison planned her and her husband's emigration from Munich after the arrest of their close friend, the communist, anarchist essayist Erich Mühsam, and after their own home was searched, and Mr. Maison was deported to Dachau. Upon his release, the couple fled to France in 1939 to join their daughter and son-in-law. They managed to survive, moving around frequently in the southern zone, and eventually made their way back to Paris in 1945 and then moved to England in 1947. This account unusually describes the Maisons' marriage, interlaced with a description of profound loss experienced by Margarete Maison when her husband died. Wolffheim returns to the themes of loneliness and women's financial and emotional stability independent of their spouses, even while her description of their marriage is kind and sincere:

> Throughout the time of their great suffering, the Maisons' marriage was a particularly good one, as it had been from the start. The pain was all the greater when Mr. Maison died suddenly in 1950 after an illness of just six weeks. . . . On medical advice Mrs. Maison began to paint again; she sometimes received portrait commissions and sold pictures from time to time. In this way, she was able to bring herself out of depression. Since November 1956 Mrs. Maison has been living in Otto Schiff House and continues to paint despite her great age.[67]

Wolffheim emphasized that it was not only the lifelong contributions of elderly people that were valuable in retrospect, but that elderly survivors and refugees were *still* active, connected to their previous lives and pursuits. According to her biographer, Astrid Kerl-Wienecke, Wolffheim was acutely aware of "the self-imposed pressure to 'play healthy' in the [Otto Schiff] home, to avoid attracting attention through illness, and not to be a burden."[68] While she praised the staff of the Schiff home, she also "raised the question of whether the residents who were still able should not do some work in the home." She resented the notion that they were "spoiled" or pampered, since she recognized that there was some sense of what she called *Wiedergutmachung* [literally: making good again] behind their care, and a recognition of all that they had suffered.[69] And she decried a "tendency to regard old people as not being of full value . . . there is often a tendency not to trust the elderly, to take them as more frail, . . . or as more mentally regressed than is perhaps the case."[70] Wolffheim ensured that the dignity of the elderly was recorded within these accounts, pointing out the human value of the older generation and reviving the revered status once accorded to its members.

Conclusion: Continuities and Ruptures

My interpretation of the corpus of eyewitness accounts that Wolffheim gathered for the Wiener Library in the 1950s elucidates Wolffheim's focus on the state of aging, and reflects her own experiences as an older woman refugee from Nazi persecution. They are emblematic of a particular social and cultural milieu, which in some ways came to characterize the "Jewish refugee" in Britain. By examining these accounts as co-constructed by Wolffheim, the interviewees, and Reichmann, who had the ultimate say in what was included or excluded, we can unravel some of the overt and tacit narratives they embodied proliferating within the context in which they were collected, which enables us to consider how this archival collection became a site of knowledge production.[71] Moreover, in focusing on Wolffheim's intentions, the accounts demonstrate how Wolffheim interjected her own subjectivities on aging, gender, solvency, and other aspects of refugee experiences she felt important to document. Her biography and trajectory undoubtedly influenced the kinds of questions she was asking, and the accounts reveal the sort of concerns that may have troubled or otherwise shaped the memories of older refugees and survivors in the 1950s, particularly women who came from a similar social and cultural background, with whom Wolffheim evidently felt a particular affinity.

We can also discern from Wolffheim's accounts how the image and role of the German Jewish refugee was taking shape in public consciousness in British society. How did they fit into the paradigm of the emerging "survivor" in the mid-1950s and 1960s? What narratives were already being formed within these communities at this time? As Grenville has noted, "the process of assimilation into the professional middle class [by middle-class] German Jewish refugees, brutally interrupted in Germany and Austria, was to be resumed and accelerated in Britain."[72] But this was not always possible for older refugees. Therefore, among other factors, the demographics of the refugee population quite likely shaped perceptions of Jewish refugees in Britain at the time, and likewise refugees' perceptions of Britain. Wolffheim recounts the ambiguous relationship of German Jews to their new home country, which provoked a certain ambivalence, perhaps especially in the older generation. When news of the end of the war came, she feigned illness to recuse herself from celebration: "I could not bring myself to celebrate the defeat of Germany, much as I had longed for it, with English people. I felt uncomfortable at taking part as one of them. A strange feeling for a Jew, who was certainly more pleased and excited by the announcement of victory than most of the surprisingly passive English people around me. An eternal contradiction lies hidden within the Jewish soul."[73]

Reichmann aimed to build the credibility of the witness by creating legitimate historical "documents" from these accounts. Wolffheim's contributions demonstrate that she felt there was an acute need to include the voices of older people, especially women, illuminating their agency and continued value in society, as well as continuities with their past lives. Perhaps Wolffheim thought this was missing from the emerging sense of the refugee in society. The focus on professional life and identities that came with it—often painfully destroyed, and so personally familiar to Wolffheim—binds the postwar lives of these refugee interviewees to their pre-Holocaust ones, elucidating the major rupture that their lives entailed.

A year before her death, Wolffheim wrote:

> My life (is) varied and satisfying. I, who have suffered so much, now consciously enjoy the fact that I am, at least for the time being, healthier than

> most of the others here [in the Otto Schiff Home]. I walk slowly, but fairly sure, I can still see well, and my hearing has slackened a bit, but not in a way that makes it difficult for me. I'm almost always in a good mood, and I even find myself singing merrily to myself. If I sleep badly or if I am in pain, I do not talk about it to the others on principle. I am not influenced by the weather; if it rains, I am happy that I can stay at home and have an uninterrupted working day; if the sun is shining, I'm especially happy that it shines so nicely in my room. Since I no longer have to pay attention to diet . . . I enjoy my food and also like to drink some alcohol. Some people see me as a *Wundertier* [a colloquial expression emphasizing one's exceptional qualities] because I am still so restless, and above all so addicted to pleasure. The fact that I can still work, which is actually rare in an old people's home, arouses astonishment.[74]

Wolffheim's legacy as a transmitter of the voices and agency of the elderly, especially women, on which she could still work "restlessly" until her last days, sits comfortably alongside her contributions to the advancement of early childhood pedagogy. Her collection challenges the idea of the burdensome or anonymous elderly and demonstrates the importance of early efforts to record survivor narratives. The voices of those whose experiences were marginalized in later years were captured here, and we can mine them to recover the voices of those who have not been central in histories of forced migration or survival.

Notes

1 Sophie Herxheimer, "Expekt Nussink," *Velkom to Inklandt: Poems in My Grandmother's Inklisch* (Short Books, 2017), 53. Here she mimics the sound of her grandmother's German-inflected English through poetry. The quote and poetry collection prompt consideration of the social and cultural characteristics of German Jewish refugee life in England, the setting in which Nelly Wolffheim lived and worked.

2 Erna Wierschowska, "Obituary: In Memory of Nelly Wolffheim," *AJR Information* 20, no. 5 (May 1965), 11.

3 Wolffheim's registration card, held by the World Jewish Relief (formerly, Central British Fund for German Jewry), lists four separate entries for

residences before her move to the Otto Schiff home. "Wolffheim, Nelly," World Jewish Relief Archives; with thanks to Rachel Pistol for this reference. See also Anthony Grenville, "Academic Refugees in Wartime Oxford: An Overview," in *Ark of Civilization: Refugee Scholars and Oxford University, 1930–1945*, ed. Sally Crawford et al. (Oxford University Press, 2017), 50–61.

4 See Anthony Grenville, *Jewish Refugees from Germany and Austria in Britain, 1933–1970: Their Image in AJR Information* (Vallentine Mitchell, 2010).

5 Some accounts have been published in EHRI's *Early Holocaust Testimony*, digital edition, European Holocaust Research Infrastructure, accessed August 8, 2020, early-testimony.ehri-project.eu/exhibits/show/about. See also *Testifying to the Truth*, Wiener Holocaust Library, accessed June 18, 2021, testifyingtothetruth.co.uk, where many are being translated into English and published online.

6 [Eva Reichmann], "Wiener Library's New Programme: Research and Salvage," *Wiener Library Bulletin* 8, nos. 5–6 (1954): 31.

7 Sharon Kangisser Cohen, "Who? Where? And How? Establishing the Story: Early Recollections of a Devastating Past," *Early Holocaust Testimony*, EHRI, digital edition, 2020, https://early-testimony.ehri-project.eu/exhibits/show/about/kangisser-cohen-introduction.

8 Hannah Pollin-Galay, *Ecologies of Witnessing: Language, Place, and Holocaust Testimony* (Yale University Press, 2018), 27.

9 Christine Schmidt, "'We Are All Witnesses': Eva Reichmann and the Wiener Library's Eyewitness Accounts Collection," in *Agency and the Holocaust—Essays in Honor of Debórah Dwork*, ed. Mary Jane Rein and Thomas Kühne (Palgrave Macmillan, 2020), 123–40. See, too, Ben Barkow, *Alfred Wiener and the Making of the Holocaust Library* (Vallentine Mitchell, 1997).

10 Laura Jockusch, *Collect and Record! Jewish Holocaust Documentation in Early Postwar Europe* (Oxford University Press, 2012).

11 On her theoretical justification for the project, embedded in the methodology of contemporary history and the Rankean tradition, see Eva Reichmann, "The Study of Contemporary History as a Political and Moral Duty," in *On the Track of Tyranny: Essays Presented by the Wiener Library to Leonard G. Montefiore* (Vallentine Mitchell, 1960). See, too, commentary on the lack of recognition of an "anthropological gap" between interviewer and interviewee in Tony Kushner, "Holocaust Testimony, Ethics, and the

Problem of Representation," *Poetics Today* 27, no. 2 (2006): 275–95; as well as Kurt Jacob Ball-Kaduri, "Evidence of Witnesses, Its Value and Limitations," *Yad Vashem Studies on the European Jewish Catastrophe and Resistance* 3 (1959): 79–90, on the value of eyewitness accounts as historical evidence.

12 Kangisser Cohen, "Establishing the Story," and Kushner, "Holocaust Testimony," 281–83.

13 Noah Shenker, "Postmemory: Digital Testimony and the Future of Witnessing," in *A Companion to the Holocaust*, ed. Simone Gigliotti and Hilary Earl (John Wiley & Sons, 2020), 537–51; and Noah Shenker, *Reframing Holocaust Testimony* (Indiana University Press, 2015).

14 Schmidt, "'We Are All Witnesses.'" See also Christine Schmidt, "'Historical Meaning Beyond the Personal': Survivor Agency and Mediation in the Wiener Library's Early Testimonies Collections," *EHRI Document Blog*, 2019, accessed May 29, 2021, blog.ehri-project.eu/2019/04/17/historical-meaning-beyond-the-personal/#en-3083-3.

15 In that sense, the library's project was unlike other projects that used standardized questionnaires, such as the one led by the Deportáltakat Gondozó Országos Bizottság (National Committee for Attending Deportees, or DEGOB) in Hungary. See DEGOB, accessed June 19, 2021, http://degob.hu/. On concepts of "co-creation/co-construction," see Shoshana Felman and Dori Laub, *Testimony: Crises of Witnessing in Literature, Psychoanalysis and History* (Routledge, 1992).

16 As discussed by Leah Sidebotham in "Testifying to the Truth: Curation, Presentation, and Mediation," and Madeline White's presentation, for the *Testifying to the Truth Archival "Discovery" Virtual Workshop*, March 23, 2021, YouTube, accessed March 25, 2021, www.youtube.com/watch?v=p-gUgcHU1Q8. On the limits of the term "testimony" to describe dialogues between interviewer and interviewee, see Henry Greenspan and Sidney Bolkosky, "When Is an Interview an Interview? Notes from Listening to Holocaust Survivors," *Poetics Today* 27, no. 2 (2006): 431–49.

17 Wolffheim conducted other interviews Reichmann ultimately did not accept. For example, see correspondence from Reichmann to Wolffheim regarding the Ms K. Lalouve account. Correspondence with Nelly Wolffheim, Wiener Holocaust Library (WHL) 3000/9/1/1573/17, October 6, 1958. See PIII.i.(France) no. 95, or 1656/3/9/95, WHL.

18 Antony Godfrey, *Three Rabbis in a Vicarage: The Story of Belsize Square Synagogue* (Larsen Grove Press, 2005).

19 Wolffheim's submissions included three letters written by Gertrude Hammerstein in 1942 prior to her deportation to Theresienstadt, where she did not survive. Wolffheim received the surviving letters from the author's daughter and son-in-law and submitted them to the Wiener Library: "Three Letters by Gertrude Hammerstein," PIIIc no. 1062, *Testifying to the Truth*, WHL, accessed June 19, 2021, www.testifyingtothetruth.co.uk/viewer/metadata/105301/1/.

20 Account by Nelly Wolffheim of the life and persecution of her friend Ella Perutz, PIIIe no.938, *Testifying to the Truth*, WHL, accessed June 19, 2021, www.testifyingtothetruth.co.uk/viewer/metadata/105557/1/.

21 Here Reichmann likely referred to the emerging Cold War, the focus on the evils of communism, and developments in Israel. Eva Reichmann, "We All Bear Witness," *AJR Information* 10, no. 11:1. On the "moral witness," see Felman and Laub, *Testimony*; Avishai Margalit, "A Moral Witness," in *The Ethics of Memory* (Harvard University Press, 2002), chap. 5; and Carolyn Dean, *The Moral Witness: Trials and Testimony After Genocide* (Cornell University Press, 2019).

22 Nelly Wolffheim, recorded by Midia Krause, PIIa no. 133, *Testifying to the Truth*, WHL, accessed June 19, 2021, www.testifyingtothetruth.co.uk/viewer/metadata/104766/1/.

23 On behalf of E. G. Reichmann to Nelly Wolffheim, August 2, 1957, 3000/9/1/1573/7, WHL.

24 Bertha Cohn to Wolffheim, January 22, 1960, 3000/9/1/1573, WHL.

25 See, *inter alia*, Marion Berghahn, *Continental Britons: German-Jewish Refugees from Nazi Germany* (Macmillan, 2007); Anthony Grenville, *Jewish Refugees from Germany and Austria in Britain, 1933–1970: Their Image in AJR Information* (Vallentine Mitchell, 2010); Werner Mosse, ed., *Second Chance: Two Centuries of German-Speaking Jews in the United Kingdom* (Mohr, 1991); A. J. Sherman, *Island Refuge: Britain and the Refugees from the Third Reich, 1933–1939* (Routledge, 1973); as well as the *Yearbook of the Research Centre for German and Austrian Exile Studies*, vols. 1–18.

26 Grenville, *Jewish Refugees*, 19.

27 Berghahn, *Continental Britons*, 133–135.

28 Lily Wagner, "Emigrant's Daily Life," unpublished manuscript, n.d. (ca. 1940), 4065a, 3, 7, WHL.

29 Wagner, "Emigrant's Daily Life," 22–23.

30 The most comprehensive biography of Nelly Wolffheim is by Astrid Kerl-Wienecke, *Nelly Wolffheim, Leben und Werk* (Psychosozial-Verlag, 2000).

Kerl-Wienecke devotes the most space to the development of Wolffheim's psychoanalytic and pedagogical theories, and the networks of influence from which she drew her ideas. She focuses to some degree on her childhood, familial relationships, life in Britain, and more briefly on her later years, although she does not examine the Wiener Library accounts Wolffheim recorded. On feminist movements in Germany, see Richard Evans, *The Feminist Movement in Germany, 1894–1933* (Sage, 1976) and Marion Kaplan, *The Jewish Feminist Movement in Germany: The Campaigns of the Jüdischer Frauenbund, 1904–1938* (Greenwood Press, 1979).

31 Wolffheim wrote that, after witnessing physical tenderness in a same-sex relationship between two of her teachers, that this "was in no way repulsive for me, as is usually the case with others when they observe same-sex relationships." As quoted in Kerl Wienecke, who concluded that she longed for a relationship with a woman, 41–42.

32 Wolffheim, PIIa no. 133, WHL.

33 As quoted and translated by Kerl-Wienecke, "Nelly Wolffheim, 1879–1965," *Jewish Women's Archive*, accessed June 21, 2021, jwa.org/encyclopedia/article/wolffheim-nelly.

34 For a helpful overview of the responses of older Jews to Nazi persecution, in particular resistance, see Wolf Gruner, "'It Cries to Heaven!' Elderly Jews and Their Individual Resistance to Nazi Persecution in Germany," *Yad Vashem Studies* 50, no. 2 (2022): 29–54; and on gender and Jewish emigration from Germany, Marion Kaplan, *Between Dignity and Despair: Jewish Life in Nazi Germany* (Oxford University Press, 1998).

35 As Gruner notes in "'It Cries to Heaven,'" the Jewish population of Germany skewed older and older due to Nazi persecution. The multiple intersections of Wolffheim's persecution (being Jewish along with her age, class, gender, and sexuality) emerge from her biography and might have been damning had she not managed to emigrate. Because she did not live within a heteronormative marital structure, her chances for emigration were limited. Following historian Anna Hájková, I use the term "queer" to describe Wolffheim's sexuality and same-sex desire. On the importance of the history of sexuality for Holocaust studies, see Anna Hájková, "Why We Need a Queer History of the Holocaust," *Novaria Media* (January 2020), novaramedia.com/2020/01/27/why-we-need-a-queer-history-of-the-holocaust/; Hájková, "Introduction: Sexuality, Holocaust, Stigma," in "Sexuality, Holocaust, Stigma," special issue, *German History* 38, no. 3 (2020): 1–14; and Hájková, *Menschen ohne Geschichte sind Staub: Homophobie*

und Holocaust (Wallstein Verlag, 2021). See also Claudia Schoppmann, *Days of Masquerade: Life Stories of Lesbian Women During the Third Reich* (Columbia University Press, 1996) and Andreas Krass et al., eds., *Queer Jewish Lives Between Central Europe and Mandatory Palestine: Biographies and Geographies, 1870–1960* (Columbia University Press, 2022).

36 According to Wolffheim's Central British Fund registration card, one Mrs. Gair of Ashley Gardens, London, is listed as her guarantor: World Jewish Relief Archives. On Horney and Seglow, see interview with Ilse Seglow cited in "Nelly Wolffheim," *Mit Freud in Berlin*, accessed March 4, 2025, mitfreudinberlin.jimdofree.com/gedenktafeln-mit-freud/nelly-wolffheim/, and excerpted in "Ilse Seglow," *Mit Freud in Berlin*, mitfreudinberlin.jimdofree.com/gedenktafeln-mit-freud/ilse-seglow/.

37 Wolffheim, PIIa no. 133, WHL.

38 Kerl-Wienecke, *Nelly Wolffheim, Leben und Werk*, 213–14.

39 Kerl-Wienecke, *Nelly Wolffheim, Leben und Werk*, 215.

40 Wolffheim to Anna Freud, November 22, 1955, "Anna Freud Papers," Manuscript/Mixed Material, Library of Congress, lccn.loc.gov/mm82049700.

41 On kinship as an analytical framework, see Jennifer V. Evans, *The Queer Art of History: Queer Kinship After Fascism* (Duke University Press, 2023).

42 Wolffheim, "Jewish Friendship Clubs," *AJR Information* 10, no. 10 (October 1954): 6.

43 Wolffheim, "Life at Otto Schiff House: Personal Impressions," *AJR Information* 12, no. 2 (February 1957): 7.

44 Wolffheim, "Otto Schiff," 7, and Guy Miron, "The Home Experience of German Jews," *Past and Present* 243 (2019): 175–212, as well as Berghahn, *Continental Britons*, 128–29.

45 According to Kerl-Wienecke's interviews with contemporaries who knew her, Wolffheim was often dissatisfied with the level of religious observance in the home: Kerl-Wienecke, *Nelly Wolffheim, Leben und Werk*, 254.

46 Wolffheim, "Otto Schiff," 7.

47 Berghahn, *Continental Britons*, 140–50.

48 Yael Siman, *Testimonies Interpretation Workshop*, June 20, 2021.

49 Eyewitness account by an anonymous Jewish Communist of her family's experiences in Berlin and Vienna, PIIc no. 1137, *Testifying to the Truth*, WHL, accessed June 23, 2021, www.testifyingtothetruth.co.uk/viewer/fulltext/104838/en/.

50 Eyewitness account by an anonymous Jewish Communist, 8.
51 Eyewitness account by Helene Plohn, PIIb (Austria) no. 1165, *Testifying to the Truth*, WHL, accessed June 23, 2021, www.testifyingtothetruth.co.uk/viewer/fulltext/104804/en/.
52 Eyewitness account by Helene Plohn, 7.
53 Eyewitness account by Lotte Lewin, PIIc no. 1182, 1, *Testifying to the Truth*, WHL, accessed June 21, 2021, www.testifyingtothetruth.co.uk/viewer/metadata/104842/1/.
54 Eyewitness account by Lotte Lewin, 2.
55 Eyewitness account by Lotte Lewin, 5.
56 Wolffheim, "Zur Psychologie der Geldbewertung," *Der Psychologe* (1954), as discussed by Kerl-Wienecke, *Nelly Wolffheim, Leben und Werk*, 234–37.
57 Eyewitness account by Betty and Jenny Student, "Would the Germans Really Do Anything Wicked?" PIIa. no 916, *Testifying to the Truth*, WHL, accessed June 2, 2021, www.testifyingtothetruth.co.uk/viewer/metadata/104778/1/eng/.
58 Eyewitness account by Betty and Jenny Student, 3.
59 Eva Reichmann to Nelly Wolffheim, July 9, 1958, 3000/9/1/1573/13, WHL.
60 Schmidt, "'We Are All Witnesses.'"
61 On the process of selecting what is to be included and what is "already known," see Ball-Kaduri, "Evidence of Witnesses, Its Value and Limitations," 89–90.
62 Eyewitness account by Wanda Spiwak, P.IV.b no. 753 /1656/4/2/753, Testifying to the Truth, WHL, accessed June 21, 2021, www.testifyingtothetruth.co.uk/viewer/metadata/106562/2/.
63 The Haavara (transfer) Agreement was made between Germany and authorities in British Mandate Palestine that permitted the capital from disposed Jewish assets to be transferred to Palestine through the export of German products. Over sixty thousand German Jews immigrated to Mandate Palestine during the 1930s under the terms of the agreement.
64 Eyewitness account by Wanda Spiwak, 4.
65 As quoted in Kerl-Wienecke, *Nelly Wolffheim, Leben und Werk*, 253.
66 Eyewitness account by Margarete Maison, PIII.i. France no. 1173, *Testifying to the Truth*, WHL, accessed June 20, 2021, www.testifyingtothetruth.co.uk/viewer/fulltext/106534/en/.
67 Eyewitness account by Margarete Maison, 7.

68 As quoted in Kerl-Wienecke, *Nelly Wolffheim, Leben und Werk*, 252.
69 Nelly Wolffheim, "Altersheim 'Otto Schiff House, London,'" *Soziale Arbeit* 6 (1957): 460–62. She noted that it was "no coincidence that I am reporting on this in this issue, even though I am aware that certain luxuries of this old people's home can probably be found elsewhere. I am thinking of details that may provide inspiration for imitation, and above all, I have endeavored to show the atmosphere that seems to be the most important thing if one wants to contribute to making life easier for old people who are often afflicted mentally and physically" (462). Wolffheim used the contested term a few years after the Federal Republic of Germany adopted it to refer to reparations to Jewish victims of the Holocaust negotiated in 1952.
70 As quoted in Kerl-Wienecke, *Nelly Wolffheim, Leben und Werk*, 252.
71 On the process of recontextualizing archived interviews and "hearing with" a collection, see Malin Thor-Tureby, "To Hear with the Collection: The Contextualization and Recontextualization of Archived Interviews," *Oral History* 41, no. 2 (Autumn 2013): 63–74.
72 Anthony Grenville, "Anglo-Jewry and the Refugees from the Continent," *AJR Journal* 1, no. 9 (September 2001): 5.
73 As quoted in Grenville, *Jewish Refugees*, 203.
74 As quoted in Kerl-Wienecke, *Nelly Wolffheim, Leben und Werk*, 255–56.

6

"OLD SOLDIERS" OF THERESIENSTADT

German Jewish War Veterans at Terezín

Michael Geheran

When Edmund Hadra, a retired gynecologist from Berlin, described scenes of people in "despair" as he looked back on his arrival at Terezín (called Theresienstadt by the Germans) in the summer of 1942, he related these events as an observer, not as a victim. Like all the other prisoners, Hadra had been subjected to unspeakable privations at Theresienstadt: fear, anxiety, uncertainty, hunger, illness, separation from home and loved ones, as well as significant physical and psychological torment. Writing in his memoirs, Hadra recalled: "This is not how we envisioned Theresienstadt. No possibilities for weeks on end to get undressed. One was unable to change clothes. One had neither soap, nor a toothbrush, no spoon, no fork, no knife, no comb, no clothes brush. I did not have a pillow, no blanket to cover myself, and, of course, no bedsheets."[1] Yet the sixty-five-year-old Hadra endured this misery by not allowing himself to be cowed into helplessness and inaction. After lamenting over the dirty, overcrowded prisoners' barracks, Hadra's writing abruptly strikes a defiant tone, as he admonishes himself for "complaining" and having gotten "soft." "During the war," he continued, "I had become used to all manner of things. But the long period of peace had undoubtedly softened me up. Back then, during the World War, I could sleep on the bare ground; yes, I had even been able to fall asleep on the stone floor of a church on one occasion."[2] Hadra adapted to the squalid conditions in the ghetto, a resilience the self-described "old warrior" attributed to his time in the army, where he had endured far worse. Theresienstadt was simply another challenge for the aged but battle-tested former officer to overcome.

The incident stands in contrast to much of the existing historiography on the Holocaust, which suggests that elderly Jews were left diminished and powerless by Nazi terror.[3] Of the 42,921 German Jews the SS deported to Theresienstadt between 1942 and 1945, 32,077 were over the age of sixty.[4] At Nazi camps and ghettos, a person's worth was determined by their ability to work, so elderly prisoners were in a particularly vulnerable position after being deported. Old age brought health concerns and physical limitations, and older people were at much greater risk of falling victim to malnourishment, illness, injuries, neglect, and the violence that characterized everyday life in the camps. One of the problems with existing analyses of Jewish victims of the Holocaust is that they give only scant attention to the military background of Jewish former soldiers like Edmund Hadra,[5] who was one of the three thousand Jews deported to Theresienstadt on account of having earned "high decorations" or suffered serious war wounds.[6] This is a significant oversight, for many elderly German Jews who fought in World War I had been shaped by their service in the Kaiser's military. While it would be a mistake to imagine that Hadra's attitude represented a universal Jewish experience at Theresienstadt, many Jewish veterans of World War I shared the conviction that, despite their advanced age, they could endure the hardships as a result of their wartime experiences. These beliefs were not confined to the younger age cohorts, nor did they abruptly end with the Final Solution. Evidence for this is elderly Jews' petitions to ghetto officials demanding better accommodations due to former rank or wartime military decorations, as well as their repeated invocations of World War I in letters, diaries, and memoirs. There are no reliable statistics on how many World War I veterans interned at Theresienstadt were aged sixty-five and older. Yet their writings offer important revelations about hegemonic images of masculinity, which persisted despite advanced age, and how older Jewish men deployed these images in order to cope under the effects of persecution, betrayal, and confinement.[7]

This chapter examines the experiences of elderly Jewish World War I veterans at Theresienstadt, the ghetto the SS established in Terezín as a destination for Czech and elderly German Jews. It outlines the living conditions of older German Jews in the "privileged" ghetto, examines their cultural values, and observes how they coped and survived under Nazi oppression. It follows the trajectory of their experience beginning with the establishment of exemptions for older and war-decorated Jews at the Wannsee Conference in 1942, their "privileged" status as both elderly Jews and former soldiers, and their daily life as prisoners at Theresienstadt. Particular attention will be given to how older Jewish veterans adapted to the shifting circumstances, as well as how they deployed their record of military service in order to increase their chances of survival. A study of elderly Jewish veterans during the Holocaust raises a number of overarching questions. What did they write about? How did they behave? Which developments did they endow with special meaning? What impact did wartime military service have on Jewish veterans' self-perception of age, physical limitations, and masculinity? How did they adapt to daily life in the ghetto, and how did they engage with normative perceptions of age? Did elderly war veterans, like other Jewish men, experience a breakdown in their masculine identities during their confinement? If so, was it possible for them to recover from this crisis?[8]

In order to answer these questions, this study relies on ego-documents by older Jewish veterans interned at Theresienstadt. The ravages of the Holocaust and World War II severely limited the number and type of source materials available, and perhaps the biggest challenge is writing the history of a group of people from which the majority did not survive. Ninety-two percent of German Jews over the age of sixty perished at Theresienstadt.[9] Most of the surviving personal documents were composed by the small number who lived and were healthy enough to write; others would have to have been hidden from the Nazis after the writers were murdered. Contemporary autobiographical sources such as diaries have limitations: many writers were dispassionate recorders and interpreters of dates, events, and broader historical developments, while some sources suffer from self-censorship and imprecise memory.[10] Postwar testimonies are therefore essential because they also describe those who perished.[11] Together, these sources allow us to arrive at some general conclusions about how elderly Jewish veterans experienced Theresienstadt, which coping and survival strategies they developed, and how age and military experience informed their thinking and behavior in the ghetto.

A Place for Jews to "Live and Die in Peace"

On January 20, 1942, representatives from the SS and various German government ministries met at the Großer Wannsee in Berlin to discuss the "Final Solution of the Jewish Question."[12] It was here that exemptions for certain groups of Jews, which, up to this point, had been administered informally or on an ad hoc basis, were codified into official policy. The relevant passage of the Wannsee protocol reads:

> It is intended not to evacuate Jews over 65 years old, but to transfer them to an old-age ghetto—Theresienstadt is foreseen for this purpose. In addition to these age groups—of the approximately 280,000 Jews in Germany proper and Austria on 31 October 1941, approximately 30% are over 65 years old—severely wounded veterans and Jews with war decorations (Iron Cross First Class) will also be accepted in the old-age ghettos. With this expedient solution, the numerous interventions will be shut down in one fell swoop.[13]

The new camp at Theresienstadt would be used to house German Jews considered controversial or "sensitive" cases, in order to avoid complaints from military officials or the German public.[14] Nazi leaders in Berlin were well aware that the persecution of both older Jews and war veterans antagonized military elites and the more conservative elements of the German population, leading to conflicts that ultimately forced the regime to modify its policies in the face of pressure, real or imagined.[15] To be sure, the exemptions were a temporary measure, a stay of execution, a postponement of the "liquidation" of the privileged groups until it could either be carried out in greater secrecy or at a time when it would arouse less controversy among the German public.

In order to reinforce the image of Theresienstadt as an "old age ghetto," a place where elderly Jews and decorated ex-servicemen would be "permitted to live and die in peace"—and obfuscate the fate that awaited the deportees after their arrival—the Nazis devised an elaborate deception to conceal the reality from both the victims and the German public.[16] First, the deportations were presented not as "evacuations," as had been the case with transports heading to the East, but as "changes of residence" (*Wohnsitzverlegung*). Second, building on the image of Theresienstadt as a "privileged" destination, the SS coerced the victims into using their remaining savings to buy private apartments in the new ghetto, as if they were purchasing property in a retirement community. These "home purchase agreements" (*Heimeinkaufsverträge*) guaranteed the buyers lifelong room and board, including subsidized medical and elderly care. The contracts specified that the assets of the undersigned would be transferred to the Reich Association of Jews in Germany (*Reichsvereinigung der Juden in Deutschland*), and used to refurbish living quarters in the ghetto.[17] In reality, the funds ended up in a special bank account of the SS.[18] This nefarious scheme went beyond mere extortion; it allowed the SS to reinforce the illusion of an "old age ghetto" while concealing the genocidal ambitions of the perpetrators from public view.

The deceptions were successful: Theresienstadt had a calming effect. An internal memorandum from the Reich Security Main Office in Amsterdam from October 1943 reported: "the impression the camp leaves on outsiders is favorable . . . generally speaking, the Jews feel good in respect to their circumstances, and have reconciled themselves with their fate."[19] This assessment is supported by a multitude of private sources, which describe Theresienstadt as a positive corollary to the East, an "elite ghetto," where German Jews would enjoy healthier living conditions and better treatment.[20] Writing on July 3, 1942, Victor Klemperer remarked that it was widely believed among the remaining Jews in Dresden that "things are supposed to not be so bad at all. The general mood among Jews is that they do not fear evacuation quite as much as before and now even regard Theresienstadt as a relatively humane place."[21] There was no panic among the deportees when they learned of their upcoming "resettlement" to Theresienstadt, for they could reassure themselves that "Poland was far more dreadful."[22]

"The Paradise of Theresienstadt"

Based on appearances alone, Terezin was an unlikely site for one of Nazi Germany's most infamous ghettos. The nineteenth-century fortress, named Theresienstadt in honor of the Habsburg empress Maria Theresa, was situated about forty miles northwest of Prague in the idyllic countryside of northern Bohemia.[23] After Germany occupied Czechoslovakia in 1939 and created the Protectorate of Bohemia and Moravia, the SS transformed the fortress into a concentration camp for Czech Jews in November 1941. The camp consisted of two fortresses, billets for troops, storage depots, magazines, and residential quarters designed to accommodate a garrison of about ten thousand soldiers and civilians. By September 1942, however, there were more than fifty-three thousand prisoners, all living in an area that encompassed roughly one square kilometer.[24] The hopelessly overcrowded living space, combined with inadequate sanitation, food, and medical care, led to repeated outbreaks of diseases that decimated the prisoner population, exacting an especially heavy toll on the new arrivals from Germany, most of whom were over sixty years old. Of the forty-two thousand German Jews deported to Theresienstadt by war's end, 20,848 (48.5 percent of the total population) succumbed to sickness, infections, or organ failure resulting from malnourishment, overexertion, and lack of proper medical care.[25] An additional 16,098 inmates—some 37.5 percent—were deported to Auschwitz between June 1942 and October 1944, where the majority were gassed on arrival. When the Red Army liberated the camp on May 8, 1945, barely five thousand German Jews were still alive. Thus, the mortality rate of the German Jews at Theresienstadt stood at 85.85 percent, one of the highest of any prisoner group in the "privileged ghetto."[26]

How did older Jewish veterans endure these conditions? Did their status as both elderly Jews and war-decorated soldiers enable them to elude the fate of the other Jewish victims? Like the writings of other Jewish prisoners, older veterans described in horrific detail the brutality of the SS, tensions between the Czech and German prisoners, and the appalling living conditions in the ghetto. Their accounts convey the agony of living in overcrowded barracks where hundreds of people slept on the floors of dust-filled attics; the lack of accessible latrines and washroom facilities; and insufficient rations of food and medical care. Chronic hunger, fatigue, lice, and infections; outbreaks of tuberculosis, typhus, and other diseases; suicides; and the sight of the corpses of those who had died the night before being carried out from the barracks each morning, and stacked onto handcarts for disposal in the crematorium, were features of everyday life at Theresienstadt. Prisoners endured them together, regardless of age, nationality, gender, or past sacrifices for the fatherland.

Most of the victims from Germany had departed the Reich in normal passenger trains, believing that "better conditions" would await them at their destination, clinging to the faint hope that the life promised to them by Nazi authorities would at least be tolerable.[27] The reality came as a shock. From the moment of their arrival, any lingering expectations of privilege were shattered, as it became all too clear that the "old people's ghetto" (*Altersghetto*) touted by the SS had been a ruse. The German and Austrian deportees were placed in the hastily vacated attics of former troop barracks, where they were forced to sleep on bare floors in the dirty, unventilated upper stories of overcrowded buildings, where latrines and washrooms with running water were often located on a lower floor or outside. This meant that each use of a lavatory or water spigot required having to descend—and then climb again—countless flights of stairs. For older people and disabled veterans, this was an excruciating, if not impossible, task. "University professors, the war-wounded, recipients of war medals, wealthy industrialists . . . all lay on the bare floors of attics, in the sweltering heat, amid the unbearable stench, tortured by lice, dust, and their own feces," wrote Benjamin Murmelstein, who served as Theresienstadt's last *Judenältester* (Jewish elder). "Their luggage had disappeared, their medal certificates were useless, and their company was constantly changing."[28] These conditions exacted a devastating toll on the elderly veteran population. In the space of eight months, from July 1943 to March 1944, the Ghetto Health Department recorded that 17 percent of the veteran population perished, mainly from illnesses and infections resulting from insufficient rations, lack of medical attention, as well as stress and overexertion.[29]

Second only to the fear of being deported further east was the constant worry over finding enough to eat. At Theresienstadt, the allotment of food rations was determined solely by an individual's ability to work. While older veterans "with high decorations" like Hadra were guaranteed full rations, in order to qualify for the standard food allotment, elderly prisoners without certain medals or serious war wounds had to perform labor like younger inmates. Most people over sixty-five, however, were either too weak or deemed "unfit" for meaningful employment and therefore categorized as "nonworkers." Those who received nonworker rations faced the prospect of starving to death. This reality hit the elderly particularly hard: They went hungry, lost weight, became susceptible to illness, and witnessed their elderly friends and neighbors dying. Czech prisoners reported seeing elderly Germans picking through garbage, begging for soup, or trading favors with well-off neighbors. Because of their progressing weakness and loss of energy, they were no longer able to observe basic hygiene and eventually lost control of their bodily functions. Many elderly German Jews, war veterans and nonveterans alike, died in the barracks, on the floors, lying in their own excrement. This is why there are so few recorded testimonies from people who subsisted on nonworker rations: nearly all of them starved. To be sure, ex-servicemen like Philipp Manes had good prospects of finding employment in the ghetto self-administration or in the Security Services. Thus they did not endure the suffering of those elderly inmates too frail or too sick to work, many of whom had to beg or scavenge for food, at times "plunging into empty vats, scraping them out with their spoons, even scraping tables where the food was served with knives, looking for leftovers."[30] The numbers paint a horrific picture: 84 percent of elderly German Jews died in Theresienstadt, most of them because of lack of nutrition.[31]

War medals or past military service carried little weight at Theresienstadt, where the native Czech Jews occupied the important positions in the camp bureaucracy.[32] To be sure, veterans' status did exempt war-decorated and war-disabled Jews from the deportations to Auschwitz and Treblinka until fall 1944. However, the exemptions did not include those Jews deported to Theresienstadt under the category "over the age of sixty-five"; even though they had served in World War I, they were not classified as veterans because they had not received "high decorations."[33] Such was the case with Albert Herzfeld of Düsseldorf, who was deported to Theresienstadt on July 21, 1942, due to his age, not his military service record. Herzfeld had volunteered to fight in World War I at the age of forty-eight, ending the war as a senior lieutenant in command of a *Landsturm* (reserve) infantry company.[34] Although he had earned the Iron Cross Second Class, the seventy-seven-year-old former officer did not meet the criteria for a "frontline veteran with high decorations" and was put in the category "Jews sixty-five years and older" when he was deported to Theresienstadt.[35] This distinction proved to be fatal: unlike decorated or war-disabled ex-soldiers, who were entitled to worker rations, Herzfeld was required to perform labor like the other inmates. But because his failing health prevented him from working, he was designated a nonworker and received a reduced rations allotment, consisting of a mere 33½ grams of bread per day.[36] The resulting malnutrition, together with the other stresses of the camp, led to a gradual weakening of his immune system that had dire consequences: Herzfeld became progressively weaker and vulnerable to even the most minor illnesses and infections. He died on February 13, 1943,[37] one of 2,210 Jews who perished in Theresienstadt that month.[38] His wife, Elsa, survived until the following year and was deported to Auschwitz on May 15, 1944 and murdered there.[39] This was the fate of most of the older Jewish veterans at Theresienstadt: they died of hunger in the ghetto or were deported to Auschwitz, as the SS systematically reduced the non-working ghetto population.

Life in the "Privileged Camp"

Survival was not always a coincidence. Those who endured Theresienstadt until war's end were prisoners with important jobs or special exemptions that guaranteed them better rations. We are afforded insight into how older Jewish veterans took advantage of such opportunities through the diaries of Philipp Manes, one of the only surviving contemporary accounts by an older Jewish former soldier at Theresienstadt. Manes kept a precise record of his experiences in the "old soldiers' town," as he called it, and his writings offer an invaluable perspective on veterans' attitudes, their hopes, expectations, and their personal agendas, more vividly than that typically rendered by survivors writing after 1945.[40] He documented life in the ghetto in minute detail, describing everyday events and routines, his role as a member of the Orientation Service (*Orientierungsdienst*), as an organizer of lectures, in addition to observations of other prisoners. Like Albert Herzfeld, Manes was sent to Theresienstadt because of his age, not on the basis of his military service. The sixty-seven-year-old former fur salesman from Berlin had not seen combat in World War I but was a conscript who served in a variety of support roles behind the front lines, far from the actual fighting. But the war left a deep impression, one that held special meaning for him, and he looked back upon that time as "the most interesting" period in [his] life.[41] Manes had been an enthusiastic soldier: he was promoted to the rank of sergeant, awarded the Iron Cross Second Class, and referred to himself time and again in his diary as an "old soldier of the Great War," revealing that his time in the army was central to his sense of self.[42] Manes did not survive the Holocaust: he was deported to Auschwitz on October 28, 1944, and murdered upon arrival.[43] His diaries were entrusted to the care of a fellow inmate, who concealed them in a mattress until the camp's liberation.

Another valuable source is the memoir of Edmond Hadra. Written shortly after liberation, the detailed manuscript offers a compelling glimpse into the experience of an elderly Jewish former officer who was deported to Theresienstadt on the basis of his wartime achievements.[44] Hadra had served as a medical officer with the crack Second Prussian Foot Guards Regiment from 1914 to 1918. He was wounded three times and, in addition to receiving both classes of the Iron Cross, was awarded the Knight's Cross of the Royal Order of the Hohenzollerns (*Ritterkreuz des königlichen Hausordens von Hohenzollern*), an honor rarely bestowed on an officer of such junior rank (he was a captain). Hadra would survive the Holocaust. He briefly returned to Berlin in 1945 before emigrating to the United States in 1947.[45] To be sure, as a convert to Christianity and an upper middle-class, highly decorated member of the old Prussian officer corps, Hadra's background and experience are atypical. Yet like Manes, his fate exemplifies the plight of the elderly Jewish ex-soldier, whose habitus was molded by the Great War and a pronounced German self-image yet struggled to reconcile the loss of status and betrayal by his country. Together with other autobiographical sources, their writings bring to light crucial similarities regarding older veterans' behaviors, survival strategies, and their spiritual attitudes, as they became victims of the Final Solution.

By the time Manes and Hadra arrived at Theresienstadt, they had already endured nine years under National Socialism and witnessed how one veteran's exemption after another had been stripped away by the Nazis. And yet, by mid-1942, they still believed that as former soldiers of the Kaiser's army, they would receive better treatment than the rest of the Jewish population. When the Gestapo informed Hadra that he was going to be deported, he was genuinely shocked that, as a decorated former officer, he had to "relocate" to Theresienstadt along with the other Berlin Jews. "It was unheard of that I, a holder of the Knight's Cross, would be placed on this transport," he wrote. "Even then, I clung to the faint hope that, as a highly decorated war veteran, I would be left alone, or at least be among the last ones deported."[46] When he arrived at Theresienstadt, Hadra expected to receive living quarters befitting of "a Prussian officer and Knight's Cross holder." Yet if Hadra had imagined himself as belonging to a social elite, he quickly discovered that acts of wartime bravery meant very little in the ghetto. It did not matter if one was a sixty-five-year-old former officer who had served in an elite Prussian regiment or a young orthodox Jew from

Berlin; each was forced to sleep on the same wooden bunks, wear the same clothes, eat the same rations, and wait in the same line to use a latrine. Manes, too, was disheartened by the squalor that greeted him at Theresienstadt. But as he saw other prisoners overcome with dismay after seeing the cramped attics and primitive bathroom facilities, he reassured himself: "we men are familiar with this from our time in the military, and it doesn't put us out to constantly be in public . . . the esthete, however, finds it difficult to stomach and endure, and wanders around despairingly."[47]

Hadra and Manes did not succumb to despair. The ability to transcend physical hardships and feelings of self-pity was part of the value system of the older generation of German Jewish veterans. They clung to the values they had cherished since the First World War and proved themselves to be quite resilient at Theresienstadt. As "old soldiers," they saw themselves as the counterpoint to the stereotype of the frail, needy, geriatric prisoner. They were strong, assertive, fearless, and productive. Older Jewish veterans developed a narrative, one that helped them overcome the tragedy that decimated their coreligionists and ascribed meaning to their struggle for survival. They wrote about their ordeals at Theresienstadt as a moral tale of the preservation of honor and dignity in the face of seeming defeat. Their writings leave little doubt that survival at Theresienstadt was not only a matter of coincidence or luck, attributing their resilience to World War I, where they had faced the enemy in battle. At least this is what their writings suggest: They were stronger, more adaptable, and better equipped to cope with hardship than other elderly inmates, "who, with their broken, weak bodies; their worn, uprooted souls; and their unrealizable longing for their far-off children, could not even resist a mild illness."[48]

Manes and Hadra were not the only older Jews to attribute this resilience to their time in the army. "My experiences during the World War," wrote Jacob Jacobson, a war volunteer who had suffered a severe head wound in 1917, "allowed me to easily endure many of the same hardships that caused others great physical and emotional torment."[49] As "old soldiers," they understood the ordeal ahead. Harking back to the dangers they had faced during the war strengthened their resolve to survive their current predicament, overcome self-pity, and never "lay down our arms," as Manes put it.

> We do not want to be resigned to despair. Did we, as we stood at the front and stared so often into the pallid face of death? We stayed upright. Our

> sacred love of the fatherland kept us from losing courage. So it should be now. Have our German men not boldly and bravely faced the danger of being taken captive in the World War, the barbed wire, the distance from home? Here we are also prisoners of war, albeit under better conditions. We should always think about this![50]

The sense of powerlessness that all the inmates experienced also had a damaging effect on male gender identities, yet the testimonies of the veterans suggest that this shame was mitigated by taking action and not being reduced to passivity. For Manes, working in the Orientation Service provided a means for him to revitalize his masculine identity. The Orientation Service was overseen by Karl Löwenstein, head of the *Ghetto-Wache* (ghetto police). Löwenstein appointed war veterans to key positions of authority within his organization, equipped policemen with special uniforms, and even trained them in Prussian drill. Many of the Czech prisoners regarded this as a blatant display of German militarism and reacted with revulsion.[51] The veneration of soldierly tradition struck a positive chord with Manes, however, who saw it as "a reminder of our time in the military (that) delighted us old soldiers of the Great War."[52] Manes regarded himself as a protector of the Jewish prisoner community, a role that reinforced the link between action, selflessness, and a strong male identity. "On the battlefield and in Theresienstadt," he wrote, "Jews put their lives on the line, sacrificed themselves for their people, to make life squashed together in these attics bearable. They did not talk about it; they did not ask questions. They carried out their mission, and many who might otherwise have lived died in the process."[53]

Manes assessed both himself and his fellow inmates according to contemporary gender norms, such as finding work, attaining respectability, and the ability to provide for and shield family from danger. Those were the qualities that defined him as a man at Theresienstadt. As long as he could work and carry out his duty, a chance of survival remained. His writings make clear that performing "very meaningful" work and "serving the public" as part of the Orientation Service had a positive impact on Manes's self-esteem, thrusting him into a role that encouraged him to act as a protector and father figure to the weaker prisoners.[54] He described comforting several "trembling," "frightened," or "clumsy" inmates, and performing "endless acts of mercy [that] were sometimes lifesaving." Often invoking his experience as a soldier in World War I, Manes galvanized many of the weaker prisoners, his leadership and bearing serving by power of example.[55] It mattered immensely to Manes that the commander of the Jewish ghetto police at Theresienstadt considered him a "comrade" and "respected my 68 years, my experience, and my calm, which was still unshakeable at the time."[56] Implicit in this rhetoric was a certain moral superiority over other elderly inmates. Both Manes and Hadra juxtapose their determination to endure the hardships of Theresienstadt against the "helplessness" and passivity of the other prisoners, many of whom had apparently "lost the qualities we were so proud of, extinguished by hunger, fear, grief, and longing."[57] Their writings suggest that they overcame the sense of powerlessness by rising to any challenge, by placing the well-being of comrades and the greater community before self. Theresienstadt did not sever their psychological connection to their former status as soldiers and heroes of the Great War. They behaved as if this status still belonged to them. Even as they were imprisoned and humiliated, honor was redeemed by maintaining one's composure and self-esteem. Manes and Hadra reassured themselves—and each other—that they had survived four years at the front, under hostile fire, surrounded by death, wounds, and mutilation. They had endured unspeakable privations in the trenches, amid the mud and the vermin, where they had no opportunities to wash or bathe, change their clothes, or properly relieve themselves. Therefore, and as historian Anna Hájková has also observed, Theresienstadt did not "impress" them.[58]

These invocations of honor during the darkest hours of the Final Solution point to a search for masculine identity in a community threatened with destruction. In March 1942, Victor Klemperer, who was confined to a "Jew House" in Dresden during this time, remarked that World War I remained "Jews' favorite topic," and this was also the case for many of the Jewish veterans incarcerated at Theresienstadt.[59] The war not only took center stage in veterans' writings; it was also a topic for the public lectures organized by the prisoner community, which stood at the center of the ghetto's cultural and intellectual life.[60] Among the presentations were "The Last Battle of the Marne and Ludendorff's Error," "Ten Days at the Somme, 3–13 July 1916," and "Two Days in Lemberg After Its Fall."[61] Hadra gave several talks about his experiences as a German officer, including a critique of Ludendorff's strategy during the spring 1918 offensive, while Leo Löwenstein, the former chairman of the Reich Association of Jewish War Veterans, delivered a presentation titled "The Jewish Soldier over the Millennia."[62] These lectures emphasized Jews' comradeship with other Germans, their unbroken loyalty to the fatherland, and selfless devotion to a higher cause. Most importantly, however, they were intended to demonstrate that although the Nazis had deprived them of their former status, they still possessed the same inner values as they did "back then," when they were soldiers fighting for Germany. The repeated invocations of World War I in veterans' writings—a constant juxtaposing of their current struggles with the hardships they had overcome "back then"—are striking. They were an attempt to regain lost status and preserve a sense of continuity from the trenches to the present day, for the Great War was the only connection to their past lives before Hitler, when their sacrifices for Germany had been crucial markers of identity.[63] Despite advanced age, this narrative also enabled older Jewish veterans to legitimize a sense of superiority and set themselves apart from the other Jewish prisoners.

"Our Homeland Is and Remains Ours"

Despite enduring two years at Theresienstadt, Philipp Manes's inner sense of belonging to Germany never wavered. He was dismayed after learning that the *Zeughaus* (arsenal), Prussia's grand military museum on the Unter den Linden boulevard, had been reduced to rubble in an Allied air raid, and with it the great monuments to Germany's military past, "the atrium with the flags, the guns, the Schlüter masks of the 'dying warriors', the beautifully curved stairs leading to the Hall of Fame."[64] They had left a far greater impression on him "than the boring history teacher who taught us only dates." Even more devastating to Manes was news of the destruction being wrought on German cities by British and American bombing raids: "That goes right to our hearts—this is our home, our city; our house in which our parents had died, where for half a century we had experienced joy and sorrow as citizens, and with the citizens . . . Our homeland is and remains ours, and whatever evil befalls it also wounds us. We love our parents, honor and respect them even when they chastise us. Should our attitude toward the fatherland be different?"[65]

Manes wrote these passages in summer 1944, three months before he was gassed at Auschwitz. Even in the midst of the Final Solution, after witnessing how thousands of his coreligionists were murdered and countless more deported to an unknown fate, a discernible thread emerges throughout Manes's writing: the struggle to remain German—to preserve an identity that was under threat, or perhaps already lost. Identity offers him a diversion, a coping mechanism to psychologically survive Theresienstadt and make sense of his world. Manes's revelations are a testament to the persistence of older values, suggesting that prewar attitudes played an important role in their attempts to transcend the daily reality of the Holocaust. They also raise important questions about the extent to which the persecution and loss experienced by older Jews engendered a break with their German identity or strengthened a communal bond with Judaism. The majority of the elderly Jewish veterans at Theresienstadt were acculturated Jews or converts to Christianity. Like Manes, they had neither practiced Judaism as a religion nor identified with it culturally for generations. They were German nationals with roots in Germany and identified themselves first and foremost as Germans rather than as Jews. They had risked life and limb for Germany, believed in her cause, and—despite antisemitism—continued to look back on 1914–18 as "a badge of honor."[66] This identification with Germany was, in part, a product of anticipated recognition—the expectation that, after the fighting ended, their suffering would be compensated by social prestige. Veterans demanded reciprocation of their wartime sacrifices, both from the state and from their communities, and it was this reciprocity that created a moral bond between them and the fatherland. This dilemma remained a source of chronic and unresolved tension throughout the Hitler years, as veterans like Hadra and Manes reassured themselves that the German people were not synonymous with the Nazis. But at Theresienstadt everything became questionable, including whether their sacrifices had truly borne any positive results.

By 1942 even the most stalwartly German Jews were deeply shaken. Despite ongoing affirmations of German identity, their writings expose a simultaneous connection with and increasing attachment to the Jewish community, at least culturally and historically. As they struggled to find a way to cope, practically and emotionally, self-described assimilationists like Manes and Hadra drew spiritual strength from a newfound connection to their Jewishness, a means of assuaging the betrayal inflicted on them by their government and coping with the uncertainty of what lay ahead. Nothing contributed as massively and violently to this process as the measures taken by the SS, especially as Jews were seen dying in the thousands in the "privileged" ghetto, and historian Omer Bartov is right in suggesting that "numerous assimilated and converted Jews were forced by the Nazis to regain the Jewish identity they had relinquished, often just before being murdered for what they believed they no longer were."[67]

The acknowledgment of Jewishness, however, should not be conflated with a refutation of German identity. Manes's and Hadra's writings contain little in the way of reflections on God or religion. But as they envisioned their lives after the Nazis had been vanquished, Jewish identity, one centered on shared experience, often promised a more secure postwar world than the thought of resuming their lives as Germans. This gradual transformation is especially poignant in Hadra's memoir: his initial idealism wore away and was steadily replaced by cynicism, anger, and the realization that life in Germany after Theresienstadt would be impossible. He found emotional comfort by cultivating friendships with Zionists, Czech Jews, and fellow German "assimilationists" who shared his disillusionment and could reassure each other that despite the broken promise of the "Fatherland's thanks," they would emerge from this ordeal.[68] A noticeable if less dramatic shift had taken place in Manes's writings, too. "It was only in Theresienstadt, through contact with men from the Zionist movement, with rabbis, and with the head of the Jewish section of the library," the once stalwart German Jew wrote in summer 1944, "that I got to know the past and great intellectual and spiritual development of Judaism."[69]

Based on the writings of Manes, Hadra, and others, a different and far more complicated picture emerges. In the face of the perpetrators' attempts to deprive him of his Germanness, Manes defied his tormentors, refusing to submit to the Nazi stereotype "Jew" by stubbornly clinging to older values, his Germanness. Remaining German was more than a simple diversion or a coping mechanism to psychologically survive Theresienstadt. It was an act of defiance, for it is precisely of this that the Nazis had sought to deprive Jews from the beginning: the assertion of German identity. As Manes struggled to reconcile his identities as a German and a persecuted Jew, expressions of German culture and nationalism transformed an environment of shame and repression into an act of resistance. He found redemption in defying the Nazis. As his world collapsed around him, as he suffered unspeakable indignities and privations at Theresienstadt, remaining German became the impetus to psychologically endure the Holocaust. As his situation deteriorated, his ruptured self-image was preserved by reinforcing the narrative that it was Hitler's regime—not him—that was un-German. He abnormalized the Nazis as aberrations of Germanness, and in doing so psychologically distanced himself from the terror and the degradations, reasserting German nationalism right up to the end. It is impossible to know how Manes reconciled this dilemma in the moments before he was murdered. But amid an atmosphere of profound uncertainty, "before we knew of gas chambers," Manes and other older Jewish veterans like him waged a personal struggle to remain German.[70] It was the final act of resistance against their oppressors.

Conclusion

Elderly Jewish veterans' accounts of Theresienstadt are a testament to the centrality of wartime military service in shaping their lives. The way they talked and wrote about their participation in the Great War, their veneration for Germany's military past, and reassertions of German identity in the darkest hours of the Holocaust is striking; it says something important about the values they embraced and, more crucially, their identity as "old soldiers" and real men. As they described their ordeals at Theresienstadt, they invoked the traits associated with the prototypical soldierly male: courage, energy, resilience, decisiveness, and strong nerves in moments of crisis. These were the qualities that had kept them alive during World War I and they provided a counterweight to the powerlessness that prevailed in the ghetto. This leitmotif was also a means for the older prisoners to ensure that their ordeal would be remembered as one of endurance, not emasculation.[71] Their writings convey that despite being subjected to the most inhuman conditions imaginable, Jewish former soldiers had not been broken. This was not a final, desperate act of self-delusion, of being lost or helpless while pretending to be in control, nor was it a peripheral development in the overall strategy of survival. Rather, it was a conscious attempt to preserve an identity, a sense of agency; and it is reasonable to suspect that for many older veterans, overcoming these trials while maintaining one's dignity was synonymous with retaining their masculine honor.

Elderly Jewish veterans proved themselves to be remarkably resilient and adaptable at Theresienstadt. Endurance had been a core element of older veterans' masculine identity in the "old age ghetto." This revitalized gender identity, grounded in masculine toughness, stood in opposition to stereotypes of frailty and lethargy, tropes attributed to older people not just by the Nazis but also by younger Jews. This glorification of perseverance defied the Nazis' efforts to strip them of their vitality, their honor. Older veterans simultaneously drew attention to their own resilience by emphasizing the diminished coping capacity of the other prisoners. As they recorded scenes of despair in the ghetto, they did not do so as victims; they seemed unaffected by the trials and indignities inflicted upon others. They presented themselves as being tougher, bolder, and more flexible than their overwhelmed coreligionists, who lacked the energy and grit to adjust to the demands of the ghetto. Until September and October 1944, they were able to make use of the opportunities that offered them a greater chance of survival, sometimes prolonging their survival for several months, even years. In the end, however, Manes's and Hadra's resilience—their ability to withstand hardship and recover from setbacks—did not change the fact that the Nazis viewed them, and the elderly in general, as "useless eaters," as inferior, needy, incapable, and, ultimately, unworthy of life.

Notes

1 Edmund Hadra, "Theresienstadt," Leo Baeck Institute—New York (henceforth LBINY), part 2, AR1249.

2 Hadra, "Theresienstadt."

3 For example, see Saul Friedländer, *Nazi Germany and the Jews, 1939–1945: The Years of Extermination* (Harper Collins, 2007), 341–45, 354; and Marion Kaplan, *Between Dignity and Despair: Jewish Life in Nazi Germany* (Oxford University Press, 1998), 143.

4 Rita Meyhöfer, "Berliner Juden und Theresienstadt," in *Theresienstädter Studien und Dokumente* 3 (1996), 31–51.

5 Exceptions in this regard are Michael Geheran, *Comrades Betrayed: Jewish World War I Veterans Under Hitler* (Cornell University Press, 2020); Maddy Carey, *Jewish Masculinity in the Holocaust: Between Destruction and Construction* (Bloomsbury, 2017); and Anna Hájková, "Ältere deutsche Jüdinnen und Juden im Ghetto Theresienstadt," in *Deutsche Jüdinnen und Juden in Ghettos und Lagern (1941–1945): Lodz. Chelmo. Minsk. Riga. Auschwitz. Theresienstadt*, ed. Beate Meyer (Metropol Verlag, 2017), 201–20.

6 A statistical survey published by the International Tracing Service on June 23, 1943, indicated there were 1,005 war-decorated Jews in the ghetto: MS, "KZ Theresienstadt," undated, US Holocaust Memorial Museum (henceforth USHMM), Institut für die Geschichte der deutschen Juden, Hamburg Collection, RG-14.058M. These statistics are also quoted in H. G. Adler, *Theresienstadt 1941–1945: Das Antlitz einer Zwangsgemeinschaft* (Wallstein Verlag, 2012), 828, n299. On war wounded Jews, see "Geschichte des Ghettos Theresienstadt," December 31, 1943, USHMM, RG-68.103M, reel 7, 64–65; and Hildegard Biermann, "Der 'Dank' ihres Vaterlandes: Kriegsbeschädigte in Theresienstadt," *Aufbau* 13 (August 22, 1947): 17.

7 On the concept of 'remasculinization,' see Susan Jeffords, *The Remasculinization of America: Gender and the Vietnam War* (Indiana University Press, 1989).

8 A "crisis" of masculinity is typically defined as a time when men are hindered or prevented from practicing a previously stable gender identity. See Carey, *Jewish Masculinity*, 46–47.

9 Anna Hájková, "Mutmaßungen über deutsche Juden: Alte Menschen aus Deutschland im Theresienstädter Ghetto," in *Alltag im Holocaust: Jüdisches Leben im Großdeutschen Reich 1941–1945*, ed. Andrea Löw et al. (Oldenbourg, 2013), 179.

10 For an insightful analysis of diaries written during the Holocaust, see Alexandra Garbarini, *Numbered Days: Diaries and the Holocaust* (Yale University Press, 2006).

11 Hájková, "Ältere deutsche Jüdinnen und Juden," 201–2.

12 For an overview of the Wannsee Conference, see Christian Gerlach, "The Wannsee Conference, the Fate of German Jews, and Hitler's Decision in Principle to Exterminate All European Jews," *Journal of Modern History* 70 no. 4 (1998): 766; Mark Roseman, *The Wannsee Conference and the Final Solution: A Reconsideration* (Metropolitan Books, 2002); and the collections of essays in *Die Wannsee-Konferenz am 20. Januar 1942: Dokumente, Forschungsstand, Kontroversen*, ed. Norbert Kampe and Peter Klein (Böhlau, 2013).

13 Wannsee-Protokoll, January 20, 1942, 1.1.0.4/82292863–82292878/ ITS Digital Archive, accessed at the USHMM on December 10, 2012.

14 Minutes, "btr. Bericht über die am 6.3.42 im Reichssicherheitshauptamt—Amt IV B 4 stattgefundenen Besprechung," March 6, 1942, Yad Vashem Archives (henceforth YVA) 02–1163.

15 Wolfgang Benz, *Theresienstadt: Eine Geschichte von Täuschung und Vernichtung* (Verlag C. H. Beck, 2013), 35–39; Peter Longerich, *"Davon haben wir nichts gewusst!": Die Deutschen und die Judenverfolgung 1933–1945* (Siedler, 2006), 201–10.

16 Himmler to Kaltenbrunner, "btr. Abbeförderung von Juden aus Theresienstadt," February 16, 1943, German Federal Archives Berlin (henceforth BArch Berlin), NS 19/352.

17 Memo, Reichsfinanzministerium, "btr. Finanzierung des 'Altersghettos' Theresienstadt," December 14, 1942, BArch Berlin, R 2/12222.

18 Adler, *Theresienstadt 1941–1945*, 89.

19 Memorandum, B.d.S. IV B4, "Lager Theresienstadt," October 25, 1943, NIOD Institute for War, Holocaust and Genocide Studies (henceforth NIOD), HSSPF 077/1290.

20 Behrend-Rosenfeld, entry for July 5, 1942, *Ich stand nicht allein: Erlebnisse einer Jüdin in Deutschland 1933–1944* (Europäische Verlagsanstalt, 1949), 163–66.

21 Victor Klemperer, entry for July 3, 1942, *I Will Bear Witness: A Diary of the Nazi Years, 1942–1945* (Random House, 1998), 91–92. Also see Beate Meyer, " 'Altersghetto,' 'Vorzugslager' und Tätigkeitsfeld: Die Repräsentanten der Reichsvereinigung in Deutschland und Theresienstadt," *Theresienstädter Studien und Dokumente* 12 (2006): 129–30.

22 Edmund Hadra, "Theresienstadt," part 1.

23 The standard work on Theresienstadt remains H. G. Adler, *Theresienstadt 1941–1945*, originally published in 1960 (Cambridge University Press published an English language translation in 2017). Also see Anna Hájková, *The Last Ghetto: An Everyday History of Theresienstadt* (Oxford University Press, 2020); and Benz, *Theresienstadt*.

24 Benz, *Theresienstadt*, 38.

25 Miroslav Karny, "Deutsche Juden in Theresienstadt," *Theresienstädter Studien und Dokumente* 1 (1994): 47–48.

26 Karny, "Deutsche Juden in Theresienstadt." Karny lists the total number of German Jewish dead as 36,848, which represented 85.85 percent of their overall population.

27 Testimony, Peretz Peter Gerzon, YVA 0.33–8728.

28 Benjamin Murmelstein, *Theresienstadt: Eichmann's Vorzeige-Ghetto* (Czernin Verlag, 2014), 45.

29 Adler, *Theresienstadt 1941–1945*, 543.

30 Philipp Manes, *As If It Were Life: A WWII Diary from the Theresienstadt Ghetto* (Palgrave Macmillan, 2009), 67–68.

31 Hájková, *The Last Ghetto*, 111–16.

32 Karny, "Deutsche Juden in Theresienstadt," 39–41.

33 Tagesbefehl Nr. 135, "Richtlinien für Ostenstransporte" May 27, 1942; and Tagesbefehl Nr. 272, "Ostentransporte," January 10, 1943; USHMM RG-68.103M, reel 6. For the May 1944 transports, see Arbeitszentrale, "Verzeichnis der eingereihten Mitarbeiter, bei denen objective Transport-Ausschliessungsgründe vorliegen," undated (May 1944), USHMM RG-68.103M, reel 6.

34 Herzfeld kept a detailed diary of his life in Nazi Germany from 1935 to 1939. Albert Herzfeld, *Ein nichtarischer Deutscher: Die Tagebücher des Albert Herzfeld 1935–1939*, edited by Hugo Weidenhaupt (Triltsch Verlag, 1982).

35 Herzfeld was deported on Transport Da70 / VII/1 which departed Düsseldorf on July 21, 1942. See Alfred Gottwaldt and Diana Schulle, *Die "Judendeportationen" aus dem Deutschen Reich von 1941–1945* (Marix Verlag, 2005), 300.

36 Ältestenrat, Tagebefehl Nr. 127, May 17, 1942, USHMM RG-68.103M, Reel 14.

37 "Herzfeld, Albert," *Gedenkbuch*, Bundesarchiv, www.bundesarchiv.de/gedenkbuch/en861682.

38 Manes, *As If It Were Life*, 67–68.

39 *Terezinska Pametni Kniha / Theresienstaedter Gedenkbuch*, Terezinska Iniciativa, vol. 1–2 (Melantrich, 1995), vol. 3 (Academia Verlag, 2000).

40 Manes, *As If It Were Life*, 164.

41 Manes, *As If It Were Life*, 2.

42 Manes, *As If It Were Life*,103.

43 "Manes, Philipp," *Gedenkbuch*, Bundesarchiv, www.bundesarchiv.de/gedenkbuch/en873869.

44 Edmund Hadra, "Theresienstadt," 2 parts, LBINY AR1249. Hadra composed his memoirs between 1945 and 1947.

45 Hadra, "Theresienstadt," part 1.

46 Hadra, "Theresienstadt," part 1.

47 Manes, *As If It Were Life*, 24–25.

48 Manes, *As If It Were Life*, 69.

49 Jacob Jacobson, "Bruchstücke 1939–1945," LBINY ME 329.

50 Manes, *As If It Were Life*, 88.

51 See, for example, Egon Redlich, entry for November 3, 1942, *The Terezin Diary of Gonda Redlich*, ed. Saul S. Friedman (University Press of Kentucky, 1992), 82.
52 Manes, *As If It Were Life*, 103.
53 Manes, *As If It Were Life*, 219.
54 Manes, *As If It Were Life*, 36.
55 Manes, *As If It Were Life*, 39.
56 Manes, *As If It Were Life*, 103.
57 Manes, *As If It Were Life*, 47.
58 Geheran, *Comrades Betrayed*, 189–94; see also Hájková, "Mutmaßungen über deutsche Juden," 190.
59 Klemperer, *I Will Bear Witness*, March 16, 1942, 2:27.
60 Over twenty-three hundred lectures were held by prisoners at Terezin. See Adler, *Theresienstadt 1941–1945*, 594–604.
61 Adler, *Theresienstadt 1941–1945*, 594–604.
62 Hadra, "Theresienstadt," Part 1; Manes, *As If It Were Life*, 131.
63 Hájková, "Ältere deutsche Jüdinnen und Juden"; Kim Wünschmann, "Die Konzentrationslagererfahrungen deutsch-jüdischer Männer nach dem Novemberpogrom 1938: Geschlechtergeschichtliche Überlegungen zu männlichem Selbstverständnis und Rollenbild," in *"Wer bleibt, opfert seine Jahre, vielleicht sein Leben": Deutsche Juden 1938–1941*, ed. Susanne Heim et al. (Wallstein Verlag, 2010), 39–58.
64 Manes, *As If It Were Life*, 97–98.
65 Manes, *As If It Were Life*, 97–98.
66 Manes, *As If It Were Life*, 219.
67 Omer Bartov, *Mirrors of Destruction: War, Genocide, and Modern Identity* (Oxford University Press, 2000), 144.
68 Hadra, "Theresienstadt."
69 Manes, *As If It Were Life*, 178.
70 Hadra, "Theresienstadt," part 1.
71 On the construction of biographical narratives, see Bettina Dausien, "Erzähltes Leben—erzähltes Geschlecht? Aspekte der narrativen Konstruktion von Geschlecht im Kontext der Biographieforschung," *Feministische Studien* 19 (2001): 57–73.

7

"I AM 57, I AM OLD, USELESS, AND I AM ALIVE"

The Fate of the Elderly Survivors of the First Liquidation Action of the Warsaw Ghetto

Maria Ferenc and Katarzyna Person

> Estera Bieżuner is knitting socks in silence, and only every now and then is she sighing deeply. A pair of crutches is leaning on the chair on which she is sitting. Her emaciated fingers are moving the knitting needles in a skillful and practiced way, but the tragic expression of her eyes indicates that her thoughts are focused on something other than needlework.
>
> "How long have your legs been paralyzed?"
>
> Mrs. Bieżuner is grateful for every compassionate gesture, for every bit of cordiality.
>
> "During the Warsaw uprising [in 1944], I broke both my legs. I fell off the stairs, pushed by the crowd. My bones would not knit together. For 5 months, I had to lie down in the hospital in Podkowa Leśna [about twenty km from Warsaw]. Everyone there was good to me; they took good care of me. I can't complain. Maybe that was because I was also good to people.—She sighs again—I suffered so much. I lost all my loved ones, and I was left entirely alone. Daughters.... Both my daughters, young, beautiful, talented, are dead. And I am alive, I am 57, I am old, useless, and I am alive."[1]

This is the opening passage of the postwar testimony of Estera Bieżuner (born 1888), a survivor of the Warsaw ghetto. She was the only member of her family to survive the Holocaust. Widowed before the war, Estera was the mother of two daughters. The elder died of typhus in the Warsaw ghetto at the age of twenty-nine. The younger, twenty-year-old Ruta, earned her living by smuggling food from the "Aryan" side. When the Germans began liquidating the ghetto in the summer of 1942, Estera went into hiding in cellars, pantries, and on roofs. She survived the first and second roundups in Warsaw and continued to live in the ghetto until the uprising in April 1943, when she moved to a prearranged hiding place on the "Aryan" side. Ruta, who also left the ghetto, was constantly threatened with blackmail and denunciation. Forced to keep changing her address, she eventually died in mysterious circumstances, probably murdered by *szmalcowniks* (blackmailers). Estera was more fortunate than her daughter. Her helper on the "Aryan" side was a "good person" who helped some Jewish women. When she gave her testimony to the Historical Commission of the Central Committee of Polish Jews in 1945, Bieżuner was haunted by feelings of despair and guilt that it was she who remained alive and not her daughters. She was completely alone, psychologically crushed, her physical health seriously damaged. She felt that her survival had been pointless.[2] She was not the only one: a member of the Jewish Historical Commission who immediately after the war's end interviewed Ignacy Rozenkranz (born 1883), who fled the Warsaw ghetto and then had to change hiding locations several times because of blackmail, noted that: "he is [now] completely alone."[3]

For many survivors of the Holocaust, survival meant the deepest loneliness. They had managed to stay alive but had lost almost everyone they cared about. If the social world guarantees one's identity, the loss of one's roots in a community that no longer exists can translate into deep suffering for individuals who may feel that their survival is only partial, incomplete.[4] For older survivors like Bieżuner, the fact that they outlived their children or people who were simply younger made this feeling even more acute.

This article belongs to a growing academic field that deploys emotions as an analytical device and a key category of historical analysis.[5] In particular, it looks at emotional responses to wartime, and how the history of the civilian experience of war can be interpreted through the lens of emotions, or in other words, "the degree to which the inner lives and emotional worlds of contemporaries were affected by war but also the ways in which feelings were constructed, adapted, and presented in wartime contexts."[6]

We will attempt to achieve this by exploring the emotional responses of one very particular group and offering a glimpse into the fate of the elderly Jews who survived the first liquidation operation (*Aktion*) in the Warsaw ghetto in the summer of 1942. This group was very small: the elderly, along with children and the sick, who were considered "unproductive," were the first to be targeted for deportation to the Treblinka killing center. And yet some members of this group survived. Who were these people? How did they survive the liquidation of the ghetto? How did they cope with the new reality of life in the Warsaw ghetto after the summer of 1942? What was their fate afterward? Little has been written about the fate of the elderly in the Holocaust as such, and scholarship on the Warsaw ghetto is no exception, although some researchers have included important observations on the issue of age, including the fate of the elderly, in their research.[7]

In this chapter, we are interested in anthropological and psychological questions, which are as important as the historical questions raised above. This study shows the psychological struggles of the elderly who remained in the Warsaw ghetto or left it for the "Aryan" side. What were their emotional landscapes and their roles within transformed families? What were the relationships between the elderly and their children like when their roles were reversed and the adult children had to help and support their elderly parents?

The first question is however that of how we define old age. In her seminal article, "Social Histories of Old Age and Aging," social historian Pat Thane notes that the concept of old age "can be seen, in any time period, as including people aged from their fifties to past one hundred."[8] In his study of elderly Holocaust survivors, Holocaust historian Dan Stone defines this group as aged fifty-five or older,[9] while historian Anna Hájková analyzed people aged sixty or over in the Theresienstadt ghetto, as did Holocaust researcher Emmanuelle Moscovitz in her study of elderly Jews detained in southern France.[10] In her work, historian of aging Elizabeth Strauss adopted the Litzmannstadt ghetto community's designation of sixty years as a general chronological marker to define "older Jews" living in the Łódź ghetto.[11]

Yet as the work of all of these authors demonstrates: "numerical age was not the only factor in determining an 'older person' in the ghetto. Personal, familial, and social identifications provided a critical lens for defining the aged."[12] For the purposes of this chapter, we define "elderly" as people who in 1942 had adult children (or could have them) or who were older than about fifty years of age. While this definition is far from today's understanding of advanced age, it emerges from the personal documents on which we based our research, where fifty years of age constitutes a visible threshold.[13] At the same time, we agree that "being old" is a social construct that varies according to the cultural environment, changes over time, and is rooted in one's relationships with other people, especially one's family. The dynamics of one's relationship with one's children have a particularly strong influence on one's self-perception of age. Being old (or young) is highly relative and drawing the line between different age groups is never easy, but the sources cited here offer a window into people's self-definitions and perceptions. In her diary, Warsaw ghetto survivor Stefania Staszewska recalled her mother's parting words as she encouraged her to leave the *Umschlagplatz* (transfer point): "I am already old, I am 40 and I am sick, you have to live."[14]

First Liquidation *Aktion* in the Warsaw Ghetto and Survival Strategies

At the beginning of the German occupation, according to the census of October 1939, there were 360,000 Jews living in Warsaw, of whom 8.3 percent, or just over 30,200, were over the age of sixty. In January 1942, the Jewish Population Records Department of the *Judenrat* (Jewish council) estimated the total number of Jews living in the Warsaw ghetto (based on the residential registration survey) at almost 369,000, of whom 7.8 percent (29,000) were aged sixty or over (there is no detailed data available on how many were fifty and older). Scholars assume that the number 369,000 is undervalued because some inhabitants of the ghetto consciously avoided registration. It is also worth noting that in the January 1942 survey, the age of as many as 167,000 people (60,000 men and 107,000 women) was not determined, which is a significant drawback of this data set.[15] In July 1942, there were about 380,000 people living in the Warsaw ghetto.[16] Around 90,000 had died of starvation or illness at that point. On July 22, 1942, deportations from Warsaw to the Treblinka killing center began. Although the destination of these transports was initially unknown, panic broke out in the ghetto.

FIGURE 7.1. A female vendor sits on a street in the Warsaw ghetto next to an open suitcase containing her wares that has been covered with a dress to provide some shade. United States Holocaust Memorial Museum, courtesy of Rafael Scharf.

Historian Havi Dreifuss estimates that more than 265,000 victims were deported to Treblinka, 11,000 were sent to transit camps, and around 10,000 were murdered in the ghetto itself.[17] According to official data collected in October 1942, the number of employed Jews who could legally stay in the Warsaw ghetto totaled 35,639.[18] It is estimated that another 25,000 remained in hiding in the former ghetto area.[19] According to official statistics, among those who remained legally in the ghetto in October 1942, there were approximately 3,500 Jews over the age of fifty. Within this group, only about 550 people—just 1.5 percent of the Jewish population of Warsaw in October 1942—were over the age of sixty. Among women (who were less likely to find work in the factories and were more vulnerable to deportation), the figures were about 1,100 and just over 150 respectively. All in all, only 1 percent of all women (and 2 percent of all men) officially living in the Warsaw ghetto in October 1942 were older than sixty.

After the first *Aktion*, the demography of the Warsaw ghetto changed radically, in terms of numbers, gender proportions, and age (see table 7.1). Of the youngest and oldest groups of inhabitants, 99 percent were deported—the past and the future of Warsaw Jewry were gone. Before the deportations

TABLE 7.1. Inhabitants of the Ghetto According to Age and Gender

	Men			Women			
	Number of People		Percentage	Number of People		Percentage	Ratio of Women
Age Group	**Early 1942**	**October 1942**	**Deported**	**Early 1942**	**October 1942**	**Deported**	**to Men After the Deportation**
0–9	25,759	255	99	25,699	243	99	95:100
10–19	35,283	2,183	94	39,790	2,263	94	103:100
20–29	19,747	3,851	81	36,041	4,581	87	119:100
30–39	29,155	6,748	77	40,892	4,791	88	70:100
40–49	21,128	4,319	80	30,652	2,564	92	59:100
50–59	14,758	2,019	87	20,812	948	96	47:100
60–69	8,881	358	96	12,335	143	99	40:100
70–79	2,553	30	99	4,361	15	100	50:100
≥80	287	—	100	603	—	100	—
Unknown	59	185	—	107	148	—	—
Total	157,610	19, 943	87%	211,292	15,696	93%	79:100

Source of data: "Struktura demograficzna ludności żydowskiej pozostałej w Warszawie (wg stanu z końca października 1942 r.)," AJHI, ARG II 308, 11.

to Treblinka, most of the inhabitants of Warsaw's Jewish quarter were women: there were 134 women for every 100 men.[20] By the autumn of 1942, there were more men than women in almost every age group. Families were decimated; many had only one survivor or none at all.[21] Emanuel Ringelblum was painfully accurate when he wrote that "most of the older generation was wiped out."[22] Few older people managed to avoid the first deportation, and yet this, if they survived, was only the beginning of their long and winding road.

The first notices of deportation contained information about the categories of people who would not be deported, including employees of the *Judenrat*, the Jewish Order Service, the Jewish Social Self-Help (Żydowska Samopomoc Społeczna, ŻSS), hospitals, German factories (so-called *szopy*), and the families (children and spouses) of such employees. Parents of workers were not included in the exemption. Their only chance of survival was to obtain work certificates, to hide in the ghetto, or to flee to the "Aryan" side. Although age was not mentioned, it was clear that the announcement excluded those deemed "unproductive," including the elderly. "The vigorous youth, the healthy and productive, were taken to work in the factories. The old, the women, the children were all sent into exile," noted the sixty-two-year-old Hebrew scholar and diarist Chaim Aron Kaplan at the beginning of the deportations.[23]

Some older people used their connections to find legal employment. For example, Gerszon Sirota (born 1874), a famous tenor, cantor of the Great Synagogue on Tłomackie Street, who in 1942 was almost seventy, became a worker in Bernard Hallmann's woodwork *szop*.[24] Emanuel Ringelblum claimed that in the offices of ŻSS there were "many octogenarian cleaning women."[25] The same was true of the members of the *Judenrat*, almost all of whom were over fifty and had survived the deportations in the summer of 1942. However, unlike members of the *Judenrat*, a large percentage of those who were employed and initially exempted from deportation were not safe; the number of those allowed to stay in the ghetto was steadily decreasing. There were many overlapping and conflicting rescue strategies, none of which was universally effective, especially given the fact that the primary goal of the "blockades" was to eliminate the elderly, the sick, and children, and to select those who were considered fit for work in the vast labor camp that the Warsaw ghetto was about to become.[26]

Some people disguised their real age (for example, by dyeing their hair, shaving their heads, or using makeup to look younger) to try to avoid deportation.[27] The perception of a worker's appearance was crucial and could be a matter of life and death. Teenage ghetto resident Mira Piżyc recalled that during one of the blockades the Germans stopped an elderly woman walking near her. Although she had a "life number" (which entitled her to legally remain in the ghetto after the first liquidation), the look on her face was enough for him to drag her out of the crowd and order her to join the group of other "wretches," and finally to kill her after she tried to escape.[28] Sometimes the roundups specifically targeted the elderly. One contemporary diarist noted that in a particular roundup members of the Jewish Order Service sought to catch people who were allegedly over fifty-five and that he—at age sixty-one—miraculously managed to free himself.[29]

The risk of being declared "unfit for work" was a source of constant anxiety for their families. Even people in their forties could not be sure that they would be considered "fit for work."[30] On September 2, a ghetto inhabitant noted:

> They are blocking [the *szop* of] Schulz, where my mother and sisters work. I feel very anxious. My youngest sister stayed at home with a very high fever, and will my mother, who looks much older than she actually is, with completely grey hair—will she survive? [. . .] Recently, a German officer watched the ward, where mother works with other older women, and threatened manager Rudnicki that he would shoot him if Rudnicki did not remove "graues Haar" [grey hair] from the room.[31]

Dressing up or changing one's appearance did not guarantee survival. Rabbis Moshe Bezalel Alter (born 1867) and Icchak Mendel Danziger (born 1880), both employed in German factories, with clean-shaven beards and sidelocks, were nevertheless deported and murdered in Treblinka.[32]

The horror of the fate of the older generation increased when some of the elderly were not deported, but were killed in the Jewish cemetery, together with the sick.[33] As a result, those who had lost hope of improving their situation often decided to go to the *Umschlagplatz* without trying to hide.[34] Among those who did so were prominent figures of Warsaw Jewry: for example, the lawyer Szymon Rundstein (born 1876), former judge of the Hague Tribunal and legislator in the League of Nations, who went to the *Umschlagplatz* with his wife and grandson.[35]

Others tried to avoid deportation by hiding in the ghetto. Among those who were trying to hide were many elderly (as well as women and children). In the last entry in his diary, dated August 4, 1942, Chaim Aron Kaplan wrote: "I have neither money nor a factory job, and therefore am a candidate for expulsion if I am caught. My only salvation is in hiding. This is an outlaw's life, and a man cannot last very long living illegally."[36] Authors of the report *Liquidation of Jewish Warsaw*, composed by the Oyneg Shabes, a clandestine group established by the historian Emanuel Ringelblum, wrote in the autumn of 1942: "People hide wherever they can: in basements, shelters, abandoned buildings, and ruins. [. . .] On the streets, in residential buildings, on squares, and among the rubble there were still many Jews who had gone into hiding and thus avoided deportation to Treblinka."[37]

On the first day of the deportation, Hebrew teacher and diarist Abraham Lewin wrote: "I am thinking about my aged mother—it would be better to put her to sleep than to hand her over to those murderers."[38] Some doctors and nurses who had access to drugs or poisons administered lethal injections to the youngest and oldest ghetto inhabitants. Doctor Adina Blady Szwajger recalled in her memoirs a nurse who asked her to give her sick mother a lethal injection of morphine, fearing that the old woman would be shot in her hospital bed.[39] Offering someone a peaceful death in such tragic circumstances was an act of mercy and often self-sacrifice: "To give someone your own capsule of morphine or cyanide meant giving up the possibility of a peaceful death at a time of your own choosing [. . .]. My mother injected [. . .] a patient with her own morphine," recalled Alina Margolis, a student nurse in the ghetto.[40] Marek Edelman, who worked in the ghetto as a hospital messenger, saw nurses looking for their mothers and fathers in the crowd of people being gathered for deportation, just to give them "a good death"—a morphine injection.[41]

Some people considered taking these measures themselves, which was becoming a much more common phenomenon, especially among the elderly.[42] Jochewed Kantorowicz recalled that her father carried poison with him and kept asking his children whether he should kill himself or wait for the Germans to kill him.[43] Among those who died by suicide was the Polish and Yiddish writer and journalist, former member of the Polish parliament, Samuel Hirszhorn (born 1876).[44]

The fate of the elderly was truly dramatic: they were not protected by their working children and chances of saving them were low. As we have seen, some people focused on offering their loved ones a peaceful death; others chose to accompany them. Emanuel Ringelblum wrote: "The tragedy of parents—the problem of old people—[. . .] [some] went to [the] Umschlagplatz with parents."[45] Teenager Mary Berg remembered that her friend, Ola, was proclaimed "fit for work," but refused to part from her mother and joined her for deportation.[46] However, many elderly parents who saw no chance of survival for themselves encouraged their adult children to seek rescue independently. They felt that it was right for parents to die before their children, and they did not want to be the burden that would reduce their children's chances of survival.[47] For much of the older generation, the priority was to do whatever they could to help the younger generation survive. Some were prepared to sacrifice their lives, believing that this would help their children to survive. Stefania Staszewska's mother, on the way to the *Umschlagplatz*, began to urge her to escape. Staszewska described later: "Suddenly, mom shook my hand. 'Listen to me, child, if the Germans let you go and take me to the wagon, remember, don't follow me, you are young, you have to live.'"

Staszewska experienced a deep inner conflict and fought for years against the shame of having chosen her own survival instead of joining her mother, feeling that this choice had compromised her. Like many others, she felt torn between wanting to protect her life and loving her parents. She felt an excruciating guilt for having survived, which remained with her years later when she wrote her memoirs.[48] Hospital administrator Judyta Braude recalled another situation in which a mother consciously sacrificed her life for the life of her child: Luba Aronson Tennenbaum, a nurse who, because of her work, had received a so-called "life number," died by suicide in order to give the certificate to her daughter, Deda.[49]

The Survivors

Authors of the report *Liquidation of Jewish Warsaw* wrote: "All of them—fathers, mothers, children, the young, the old, craftsmen, factory workers, office workers, scholars, artists, physicians, attorneys, professors, musicians, and pedagogues—suffered the same fate."[50] However, slim chances of survival remained, and depended on several factors, such as age, gender, social class, and, importantly, luck. This was also true for the oldest group of Warsaw ghetto inhabitants.[51]

An important and socially visible group of older men who managed to survive the first liquidation of the ghetto were those who were spared because of their communal functions and social position. Marek Lichtenbaum, who replaced Adam Czerniaków as head of the *Judenrat* after July 23, 1942, was sixty-six years old (born in 1876) at the time. Some of the leading officials of the welfare and self-help organizations were also in their fifties and sixties. For example, Itzchak Giterman, former director of the American Jewish Joint Distribution Committee (JDC) and one of the heads of ŻSS, was born in 1889. Gustaw Wielikowski, a lawyer and one of the leading figures in the organization of Jewish self-help in Warsaw, as well as a member of the *Judenrat*, was also born in 1889. Stanisław Szereszewski, also active in ŻSS and head of the financial department of the *Judenrat*, was born in 1881, as was Józef Jaszuński, who worked for ŻSS, the statistical department of the *Judenrat* and organized vocational training in the ghetto. Among the members of the *Judenrat* there were more elderly officials, such as Tadeusz Bart (born 1873), head of the trade and public housing department; Bernard Zundelewicz (born 1886), head of the Jewish Order Service department; Abraham Gepner (born 1872), businessman and merchant, head of the supply department (Zakład Zaopatrywania), the organization responsible for supplying the ghetto with food; and Gepner's deputy, Edward Kobryner (born 1880), who had also directed the activities of the Warsaw ghetto bank. None of the above survived the war; some of them perished during the second liquidation *Aktion* in January 1943 and some were murdered during the Warsaw Ghetto Uprising or later. Some of the elderly who survived the first liquidation died later in the ghetto.

On the "Aryan" Side of Warsaw

Survival in the ghetto never felt complete. Warsaw's Jews lived in constant fear and anxiety—after it became clear that the deportees had been murdered in Treblinka, the inhabitants of the Warsaw ghetto expected the worst—the resumption of deportations—to happen at any moment. Their death was only a matter of time. Older members of other socially privileged groups, such as doctors (including some older ones, such as Natan Mesz, Julian Ajzner, and Ludwik Hirszfeld) or those who had enough money, tended to look for a hiding place on the "Aryan" side, which seemed to offer the best chance of survival. People representing higher social classes in the ghetto were more likely to have resources that increased their chances of survival on the other side of the ghetto wall: financial, cultural (such as fluency in Polish or knowledge of customs that enabled them to pass as Poles), and social (such as connections and friends on that side who could help them).

Seeking refuge on the "Aryan" side could be a strategy of the entire family, but those who had less money had to make what literary scholar Lawrence Langer called "choiceless choices."[52] Families had to split up because they could not afford to send everyone to the "Aryan" side. Bracha Karwasser's father, like many others, decided to save his adult children rather than himself. Karwasser recalled that before making the decision, her father had visited a rabbi he was friends with and asked for advice. The rabbi told him to send the children to the "Aryan" side in the hope that one of them would survive. Karwasser's father divided his valuables and jewelry among his sons and daughters, telling them to "save themselves."[53]

Most of the elderly survivors of the Warsaw ghetto who gave testimony after the war hid at some point on the "Aryan" side of Warsaw. They had different survival strategies: Anna Szenicer-Matusiak (born 1880) disguised herself as a beggar to hide her Jewish appearance. She received financial help from the friends of her son, the doctor Stanislaw Szenicer.[54] Sabina Gantz (born 1882) had "Aryan" papers and knitted and sold sweaters to support herself.[55] Wacław Sterling (born 1878) only occasionally left the apartment where he was hiding, but his wife had obtained German papers and moved freely on the "Aryan" side, buying and selling various things.[56] Irena Guranowska (born 1888) never went to the ghetto and lived on the "Aryan" side with her husband until his arrest in the summer of 1942. He was transferred to the ghetto, and Irena and her son moved to a different hiding place.[57] Mieczysław Centnerszwer (born 1874), a professor of chemistry, left the ghetto and hid on the "Aryan" side with his non-Jewish wife, whom he divorced in 1940 to divert attention from her.[58]

While hiding on the "Aryan" side, the elderly, like any other Jews in hiding, experienced blackmail and were forced to change locations frequently.[59] Blackmail, denunciation, and activities of the Gestapo posed a huge risk, and many Jews in hiding were murdered. Among the elderly who fled the Warsaw ghetto and were killed on the "Aryan" side were neurologist Władysław Szterling (born 1877) and his wife.[60] Centnerszwer, too, was denounced and killed in his wife's apartment.[61] Prewar director of JDC and wartime inspector of ŻSS Aron Artur Reinberg (born 1887) and his wife, Judyta, who after the liquidation of the Warsaw ghetto hid in the countryside near Radom, were also murdered.[62]

Some people who could not survive on the "Aryan" side chose to return to the ghetto. Anna Fajnberg (born 1892) escaped to the "Aryan" side after the death of her husband and two sons but returned to the ghetto at the end of 1942. Anna went to the "Aryan" side again during the final liquidation in the spring of 1943; she was ill and wounded but managed to survive the war. Her friend later described her as sick and powerless. She had no one left.[63]

The Price of Survival: Elderly on the "Aryan" Side of Warsaw

Some of the parents who lived longer than their children experienced a painful sense of inadequacy or even inappropriateness to their own lives. Karol Rotgeber (born 1887), a merchant and dental technician, author of a memoir written in hiding on the "Aryan" side of Warsaw, opened the text with a dedication to his son Paweł, born in 1929, who was deported to Treblinka in August 1942. "To you, my dearest son, Pawełek, the only meaning of my life, I dedicate this memoir. You were taken from my protection by misfortune, where are you now?" Rotgeber, who survived the operation in the summer of 1942 in the brush makers' *szop*, continued to fantasize about rescuing the boy, while at the same time mourning his presumed fate. For Rotgeber, his diary became a space for reflection, where he could come to terms with what had happened, while at the same time never ceasing to ask how it could be. Rotgeber's hope that his son had somehow survived clashed with his understanding that he had lost his only child.[64]

According to some theorists, the dyad of two people (the individual and his or her interactional partner) is a fundamental social relationship. The closer the partners are, the more difficult it is to replace one of them. A person who outlives his counterpart dies with them on a symbolic level, because the relationship cannot be continued.[65] The sense of shame that Rotgeber experienced arose from the burden of individual survival. The feeling that the Holocaust was based on injustice manifested itself in the guilt felt by the survivors: If everyone is condemned to death, why did some manage to avoid it?

Karol Rotgeber and his wife managed to survive the war. They obtained "Aryan papers" and lived in the Praga district of Warsaw, where they remained after the liberation. Karol donated his diary to the Jewish Historical Commission in 1945. Both Rotgebers registered as survivors in 1946, shortly before emigrating to Venezuela.[66]

On the surface, their fate was similar to that of Samuel Kahan (born 1877), one of the oldest survivors of the Warsaw ghetto: he was sixty-eight at the end of the war. Their trajectories were, however, very different: Kahan dedicated his memoirs, written while in hiding on the "Aryan" side of Warsaw, not to a deceased member of his family but to his granddaughter, who lived in Brazil. The difference, it seems, is that Kahan's was able to be a dedication in hopefulness, since he was certain his granddaughter would live, in contrast to Rotgeber's despairing one. When the liquidation of the ghetto began in 1942, Samuel was sixty-five and his wife, Franciszka, fifty-eight. For a while, they had worked in one of the *szops*, and had also been hiding in the ghetto, but at their respective ages they had no hope of surviving frequent selections. Their only chance to save themselves was to flee to the "Aryan" side. Kahan later wrote: "This life [in the ghetto] was terrible. We could have been caught at any moment. We decided to cross over to the Polish–Aryan side."[67] Samuel and Franciszka had "Aryan papers," but because of the threat of denunciation, they had to keep changing apartments and the names they used. Samuel Kahan and his wife survived the war and registered with the Central Committee for Polish Jewry. In 1946 they left for Brazil, where their son, daughter, and granddaughter lived.[68] In both Kahan's and Rotgeber's cases, age was not a decisive factor in their survival strategies on the "Aryan" side of Warsaw. For Samuel, his age was one of the motives for his escape, while for Karol it was a point of reference in his reflections on his prematurely deceased son. Their memoirs, however, are strikingly different: Rotgeber's is a testimony to grief and loss, while Kahan's is a story of survival.

Conclusion

Older people had a minimal chance of surviving the first liquidation *Aktion* in the Warsaw ghetto and a tiny chance of surviving until the end of the war. There were only a few hundred people over the age of sixty in the Warsaw ghetto in October 1942. Some of them held important social or organizational positions and most of them were men. Class and gender were important factors in individual chances of survival.

Avoiding deportation from the Warsaw ghetto and staying alive was a constant struggle for everyone, an effort that required creativity, resources, and sheer luck. It was even more difficult for those deemed inherently dispensable, who were considered useless as laborers and void of a future—the elderly. Even those elderly people who had no children of their own felt that children's lives were more important: Menachem Mendel Kon (Kohn) (born 1881), businessman, social activist, and one of the central figures of the Oyneg Shabes group, wrote in the diary he kept during the first *Aktion* in the Warsaw ghetto: "I decide not to go into the cellar. I don't want to take up space where more children could be hidden. Children should be the first to be rescued."[69]

Some of the young survivors felt that they had their lives ahead of them and that they had a chance to start again, albeit with the unbearable burden of the past. Older survivors, who had seen the death of their families and, in many cases, their children, who had witnessed the collapse of their entire world and had no hope of participating in its reconstruction, had a very different perspective. Many of them, like Estera Bieżuner, whose testimony opened this chapter, felt "old and useless" and could not stop thinking about the death of their loved ones, without whom their own survival felt not only incomplete but also, as in the case of Karol Rotgeber, hard to accept. Few were fortunate enough to have their family survive and to be able to lead a successful life after the war.[70]

While age may not have been a factor in determining one's fate on the "Aryan" side, it was crucial in determining how people felt about their survival. Some of those who had lost their loved ones and were the sole survivors in their families felt that their survival was pointless and their lives worthless. Their testimony shows us how emotional responses to wartime experiences continued to shape both postwar social dynamics and individual postwar lives. The emotional register also provides insight into their particular circumstances and burdens. In the case of the elderly, these were close to impossible both in the war and in its aftermath.

Notes

1 Testimony of Estera Bieżuner, Archive of the Emanuel Ringelblum Jewish Historical Institute in Warsaw (henceforth AJHI), 301/468, 1.

2 Bieżuner, 1–2; see also Maria Ferenc, "The Feelings of Survivors of the First Deportations from the Warsaw Ghetto," in *Jews and Non-Jews: Memories and Interactions in the Perspective of Cultural Studies*, ed. Lucyna Aleksandrowicz-Pędich and Jacek Partyka (Peter Lang, 2015), 155–67.

3 Testimony of Ignacy Rosenkranz, AJHI, 301/1441.

4 Zygmunt Bauman, *Mortality, Immortality and Other Life Strategies* (Polity Press, 1992), 40.

5 On history of emotions, in particular in the context of wartime, see among others: Lucy Noakes et al., eds., *Total War: An Emotional History*, Proceedings of the British Academy (British Academy Scholarship, 2020), accessed March 17, 2024, doi.org/10.5871/bacad/9780197266663.003.0001; Stephanie Downes et al., *Writing War in Britain and France, 1370–1854: A History of Emotions* (Routledge, Taylor & Francis, 2019); *Emotions and Mass Atrocity. Philosophical and Theoretical Explorations*, ed. Thomas Brudholm and Johannes Lang (Cambridge University Press, 2018); and Michael Francis Laffan and Max Weiss, *Facing Fear: The History of an Emotion in Global Perspective* (Princeton University Press, 2012).

6 Claire Langhamer et al., introduction to *Total War*, ed. Noakes et al., 1–20.

7 Barbara Engelking and Jacek Leociak, *Getto warszawskie: Przewodnik po nieistniejącym mieście* (Stowarzyszenie Centrum Badań nad Zagładą Żydów, 2013); Havi Dreifuss, *Geto varsha: Hasof* (Yad Vashem, 2018); and Agnieszka Witkowska-Krych, *Dziecko wobec Zagłady: Instytucjonalna opieka nad sierotami w getcie warszawskim* (Wydawnictwo Żydowski Instytut Historyczny, 2022).

8 Pat Thane, "Social Histories of Old Age and Aging," *Journal of Social History* 37, no. 1 (2003): 93.

9 Dan Stone, " 'Somehow the Pathetic Dumb Suffering of These Elderly People Moves Me More Than Anything': Caring for Elderly Holocaust

Survivors in the Immediate Postwar Years," *Holocaust and Genocide Studies* 32, no. 3 (Winter 2018): 384–403.

10 Anna Hájková, "Mutmaßungen über deutsche Juden: Alte Menschen aus Deutschland im Theresienstädter Ghetto," in *Alltag im Holocaust: Jüdisches Leben im Großdeutschen Reich 1941-1945*, ed. Andrea Löw et al., (Oldenbourg Wissenschaftsverlag, 2013): 179–98, (179); Emmanuelle Moscovitz, "Caring for the Elderly: The Efforts of the General Chaplaincy of the Jews in France on Behalf of the Elderly Jews Detained in Southern France, 1940–1944," *Yad Vashem Studies* 50, no. 1 (2022).

11 Elisabeth C. Strauss, "'Cast Me Not Off in My Time of Old Age . . .': The Aged and Aging in the Łódź Ghetto, 1939–1944" (PhD diss., University of Notre Dame, 2014).

12 Strauss, "'Cast Me Not Off,'" 42.

13 This was not a unique situation. For example, in the fifth liquidation action in Borysław in February 1943, people over the age of fifty were considered to be unproductive and thus targeted for murder. See Yitzhak Arad, "German Policy and the Fate of the Elderly Population in the German-Occupied Soviet and Polish Territories," *Yad Vashem Studies* 50, no. 1 (2022): 66.

14 Diary of Stefania Szochur Staszewska, AJHI, 302/167.

15 See Ruta Sakowska, *Ludzie z dzielnicy zamkniętej* (Wydawnictwo Naukowe PWN, 1993), 33; Maria Ferenc Piotrowska, "'Isle of Death': The Demographic Grounds of Social Changes in the Warsaw Ghetto," *Annales de démographie historique* 136 (2018): 145.

16 Tatiana Berenstein and Adam Rutkowski, "Liczba ludności żydowskiej i obszar przez nią zamieszkiwany w Warszawie w latach okupacji hitlerowskiej," *Biuletyn Żydowskiego Instytutu Historycznego* 26 (1958): 80.

17 Havi Dreifuss, "The Leadership of the Jewish Combat Organization During the Warsaw Ghetto Uprising: A Reassessment," *Holocaust and Genocide Studies* 31, no. 1 (2017): 51.

18 Engelking and Leociak, *Getto warszawskie*, 745–46; "Struktura demograficzna ludności żydowskiej pozostałej w Warszawie (wg stanu z końca października 1942 r.)," AJHI, ARG II 308.

19 Engelking and Leociak, *Getto warszawskie*; Berenstein and Rutkowski, "Liczba ludności żydowskiej," 81.

20 Ferenc Piotrowska, "Isle of Death," 144.

21 Stanisław Sznapman, Diary, AJHI, 302/198, 36–37.

22 Ringelblum, *Notes from the Warsaw Ghetto: The Journal of Emanuel Ringelblum*, ed. Jacob Sloan, (Schocken Books, 1974), 322.

23 Chaim Aron Kaplan, *The Warsaw Diary of Chaim A. Kaplan*, ed. Abraham I. Katsh (Collier Books, 1973), 385.

24 *Archiwum Ringelbluma: Konspiracyjne Archiwum Getta Warszawy*, vol. 34: *Getto warszawskie*, part 2, ed. Tadeusz Epsztein (Żydowski Instytut Historyczny i Wydawnictwa Uniwersytetu Warszawskiego, 2016), 214.

25 Emanuel Ringelblum, *Notes from the Warsaw Ghetto*, 322.

26 The houses in the ghetto were blocked by the Jewish Order Service (Jewish police) so that inhabitants could not leave them and try to escape the roundup during the deportations. Józef Gitler-Barski, "Likwidacja getta warszawskiego (relacja świadka)," *Biuletyn Żydowskiego Instytutu Historycznego* 97, no. 1 (1976), 100; Hilel Seidman, *Togbuch fun varshever geto* (Tsenṭral farband fun Poylishe Yidn in Argenṭine, 1947), September 8, 1942; Engelking and Leociak, *Getto warszawskie*, 749–50.

27 Ringelblum, *Notes from the Warsaw Ghetto*, 310; Stanisław Adler, *Żadna blaga, żadne kłamstwo . . . Wspomnienia z warszawskiego getta*, ed. Marta Janczewska (Stowarzyszenie Centrum Badań nad Zagładą Żydów, 2018), 341.

28 Kopel Piżyc and Mirka Piżyc, *Po wojnie, z pomocą bożą, niebawem*, ed. Havi Dreifuss (Stowarzyszenie Centrum Badań nad Zagładą Żydów, 2017), 148.

29 Journal of Menachem Mendel Kohn, AJHI, ARG II 249, 4.

30 Stefan Szpigielman, *Trzeci front*, ed. Marta Janczewska (Żydowski Instytut Historyczny, 2020), 263.

31 Testimony of Leyzor Czarnobroda, AJHI, ARG II 244, 11–12.

32 Biographical notes of the Warsaw ghetto rabbis, AJHI, ARG II 313, 1, 4.

33 Dreifuss, *Geto varsha*, 220; Piżyc and Piżyc, *Po wojnie*, 138.

34 Abraham Lewin, *A Cup of Tears: A Diary of the Warsaw Ghetto* (Basil Blackwell, 1988), 162; Dreifuss, *Geto varsha*, 195.

35 Stanisław Gombiński (Jan Mawult), *Wspomnienia policjanta z warszawskiego getta*, ed. Marta Janczewska (Stowarzyszenie Centrum Badań nad Zagładą Żydów i Żydowski Instytut Historyczny, 2010), 95.

36 Kaplan, *Warsaw Diary*, 399.

37 *The Ringelblum Archive: Underground Archive of the Warsaw Ghetto*, vol. 3: *Oyneg Shabes: People and Works*, ed. Aleksandra Bańkowska and Tadeusz Epsztein (Żydowski Instytut Historyczny im. Emanuela Ringelbluma, 2020), 380, 389; see also Adler, *Żadna blaga, żadne kłamstwo . . .*, 359.

38 Lewin, *Cup of Tears*, 136.
39 Adina Blady Szwajgier, *I więcej nie pamiętam* (Świat Książki, 2010).
40 Alina Margolis-Edelman, *Tego, co mówili nie powtórzę* (Siedmioróg, 1999), 76.
41 Marek Edelman, *The Ghetto Fights* (Bookmarks, 2013), 50. See also Gombiński, *Wspomnienia policjanta*, 73.
42 Szpigielman, *Trzeci front*, 222.
43 Testimony of Jochewed Kantorowicz, AJHI, 301/2493, 3.
44 Gombiński, *Wspomnienia policjanta*, 247.
45 Ringelblum, *Notes from the Warsaw Ghetto*, 322.
46 Mary Berg, *The Diary of Mary Berg: Growing Up in the Warsaw Ghetto* (Oneworld, 2006), 175–76; see also Adler, *Żadna blaga, żadne kłamstwo . . .*, 341.
47 Barbara Engelking, "Życie codzienne Żydów w miasteczkach dystryktu warszawskiego," in *Prowincja noc. Życie i zagłada Żydów w dystrykcie warszawskim*, ed. Barbara Engelking et al., (Wydawnictwo Instytutu Filozofii i Socjologii Polskiej Akademii Nauk, 2007), 205–6.
48 Diary of Stefania Szochur Staszewska, AJHI, 302/167.
49 Testimony of Judyta Braude, Yad Vashem Archive (henceforth YVA), O.3/2360.
50 *Ringelblum Archive*, vol. 3: *Oyneg Shabes*, 360.
51 Stone, " 'Somehow the Pathetic Dumb Suffering,' " 385.
52 Lawrence Langer, *Versions of Survival: The Holocaust and the Human Spirit* (State University of New York Press, 1982), 36.
53 Testimony of Bracha Karwasser, YVA, O3/3484.
54 Testimony of Anna Szenicer-Matusiak, AJHI, 301/6147.
55 Testimony of Sabina Gantz, AJHI, 301/1105.
56 Testimony of Władysław Sterling, AJHI, 301/5295.
57 Testimony of Irena Guranowska, AJHI, 301/1123.
58 Halina Lichocka, "Mieczysław Centnerszwer (1874–1944)," in *Portrety uczonych: Profesorowie Uniwersytetu Warszawskiego 1915–1945: A–Ł*, ed. Piotr Salwa (Wydawnictwa Uniwersytetu Warszawskiego, 2016), 163–70.
59 Testimony of Ignacy Rozenkranz, AJHI, 301/1441.
60 *Archiwum Ringelbluma*, vol. 27: *Żydowska Samopomoc Społeczna*, ed. Aleksandra Bańkowska and Maria Ferenc Piotrowska, 849–50.
61 Lichocka, "Mieczysław Centnerszwer."
62 *Archiwum Ringelbluma*, vol. 6: *Generalne Gubernatorstwo: Relacje i dokumenty*, ed. Aleksandra Bańkowska, 176.

63 Testimony of Adam Kirsz, AJHI, 301/5639.

64 Jacek Leociak, "'. . . rozmawiałem z Bogiem (uśmiechacie się! tylko z nim mogę jeszcze rozmawiać!)': Modlitewne lamentacje w pamiętniku Karola Rotgebera z getta warszawskiego," *Zagłada Żydów: Studia i Materiały* 15 (2019): 274–304.

65 Howard Becker and Ruth Hill Useem, "Sociological Analysis of the Dyad," *American Sociological Review* 7, no. 1 (1942): 13–14.

66 Jacek Leociak, "Karol Rotgeber," *Nowa Panorama Literatury Polskiej*, accessed December 19, 2023, https://nplp.pl/artykul/karol-rotgeber-1887/.

67 Diary of Samuel Kahan, AJHI, 302/166, 26.

68 Diary of Samuel Kahan, AJHI, 302/166, 26.

69 Journal of Menachem Mendel Kohn, AJHI, ARG II 249, 1.

70 For one such case, see the diary of Anatol Wekszta jn, AJHI, 302/204.

8

POLISH ELDERLY JEWISH REFUGEES AND HOLOCAUST SURVIVAL IN THE SOVIET UNION

Lidia Zessin-Jurek and Katharina Friedla

A bare 0.5 percent of Polish Jews who had survived the war and were waiting in German and Austrian displaced persons' (DP) camps for foreign visas in early 1946 were people aged sixty and older. They had survived the war in areas controlled by Nazi forces. When they were soon joined by Polish Jews returning from wartime exile and incarceration in the USSR, the percentage of older people among their ranks rose to two. This means that, although still dramatically low, the figure quadrupled.[1]

This chapter focuses on elderly Polish Jewish survivors of the Holocaust whose experiences during wartime carried them deep into the Soviet Union. Forced migration—and this one covered many thousands of kilometers—is nearly always an age-selective process in which the elderly are least represented. Given the deadly effects of the German occupation, however, even the small number of elderly people who were part of the Soviet displacement was very significant in terms of intergenerational continuity and cultural transmission. Concerted research into the Asian geography of Holocaust survival over the past decade has emphasized one important fact that, although previously known, has finally taken on its proper significance:[2] three-quarters, or about 230,000, of those Polish Jews who survived (out of 3.3 million before the war) endured the war in areas to the east of their homeland.[3] The importance of this displacement is therefore crucial in any study of the extermination and survival of Polish Jews.

FIGURE 8.1. Polish refugees during the German invasion of Poland in 1939. Polish National Digital Archives (Narodowe Archiwum Cyfrowe), 3/2/0/-/5926.

Their path east led them along the only available routes to escape from the advancing Wehrmacht: from their homes in Poland to the eastern Polish borderlands soon occupied by the Soviets. What follows, therefore, is both a refugee story and a story of (subsequent) Soviet deportation to forced labor in various conditions: vast Siberian territories, sub-Arctic regions in the north, and the desert-steppe zone in Central Asia. As might be expected, neither of these two categories of experience—refugeeism and deportation—favored the elderly. Both required, above all, physical fitness and strength to overcome the challenges of being uprooted from home, traversing long distances in deplorable conditions, performing forced labor, enduring food shortages, and being exposed to unknown diseases and extreme weather (the searing cold of Siberia and the scorching heat of Central Asia).

The question naturally arises about who should be considered elderly. Studies of the Holocaust have used varying approaches to define this group.[4] For this chapter, rather than specifying a fixed age range, we examine, as far as possible, each individual's role within the community and his or her ability to cope with the new pressing challenges of the time of war.[5] Instead of picking a minimum age as the starting point to define the elderly, we see the category as describing people old enough to have had adult children and thus grandchildren; in other words, not only people's physical condition is determinative but also their social functions, including in the family.

In most cases, the decision to flee ultimately led to deportation deep into the USSR, while the decision to stay put meant an individual was likely to fall into deadly Nazi hands. The conditions of eastern exile were far removed from any organized form of refugee relief. As a result, the mortality rate among the most vulnerable individuals was particularly high. The paucity of migration statistics kept either by the collapsing Polish state or by the occupying German and Soviet regimes makes it impossible to describe with any exactitude the scale of the flight and removal among the older cohort. Most of those who escaped by fleeing from German occupation toward Soviet-occupied Poland were arrested by the People's Commissariat for Internal Affairs (NKVD) in the spring of 1940 and deported to the Soviet Union for forced labor in the faraway taiga settlements and in the Gulag. Earlier wartime deportations in this direction (conventionally referred to as "Siberia") included residents of eastern Poland who were considered class and state enemies (families of army officers, landowners, wealthier peasants, and local elites). In the case of the Jewish population resident in former eastern Poland, the first to be selected were representatives of various factions of political associations, religious Jews, and those declared capitalists. In addition, Jewish refugees from other parts of Poland who refused to accept a Soviet passport were automatically put on deportation lists, which are kept in Moscow archives and difficult to access. The same is true for the lists of inmates of the camps and forced labor settlements, as well as lists of amnestied Polish citizens.[6] On July 30, 1941, after the German attack on the USSR, the Polish government-in-exile signed an agreement with the Soviet authorities that changed the status of most Poles in the USSR from that of prisoners to allies who were supposed to support the common military effort against the Germans.

For the reasons mentioned above, and in recognition of the value of this still underexploited corpus of sources, this chapter relies heavily on narrative testimonial material. Testimonies reveal the perspective of those who actually participated in these events. Our chapter presents the Soviet experience of elderly Polish Jews as recounted mainly by their younger relatives (who were there with them), both immediately after the war and many years later. This material—along with documentation on any survival of European Jews—has been steadily growing since the early postwar years and has taken the shape of an impressive number of published memoirs, especially over the past three decades.[7]

The structure of the chapter corresponds to the successive stages that mark the experience of Polish Jews during the war and their trajectory toward the Soviet Union, starting from the stage of wartime flight, through deportation, the so-called postamnesty period, and finishing with return to Poland. Each of these stages witnessed an accelerated, unnatural shrinking of the number of representatives of the older generation among the group of survivors, albeit to differing degrees. The largest proportional change in the demographics of this group happened already during flight and was related to the decision of who would become a refugee and who would not.

Elderly as Refugees

In terms of demography in any wartime situation, population changes occur not only due to direct casualties but also due to various types of ensuing displacement. Among patterns of displacement produced by the conflict, Germany's invasion of Poland resulted in one of the classic types: Mostly it was young men who became displaced, either because they were active combatants or because they fled to avoid targeted violence on men of military age. In addition, they were assumed to be the fittest and thus expected to pave the way for the others to evacuate.

Deciding to flee or stay was conditioned upon more than the immediacy of war violence. Any conscious decisions about escape were made within the wider context of individuals' lives, and this context varied considerably in terms of geography, social background, and political beliefs. Central factors, however, were demographic: gender and age. Leaving aside other categories, we focus here on the context as defined by the age of the individuals. We believe age was also the most important determining factor in this particular refugee story, even more important than gender. Although women refugees were significantly outnumbered by men, far more young Jewish women chose to head east than did members of the older generations.

Historical, biological, and psychological reasons related to age played a role in their views regarding escape. The generation with adult children at that time clearly remembered World War I and often raised arguments based on their experiences of that war. Some regretted that they had sought shelter in eastern regions during that previous conflagration and had had to endure many years of deprivation and hunger as a result. Some took from this period the belief that German soldiers were more cultured than the Russians in particular, and they were thus not convinced that exposure to the latter was a better alternative than staying where they were. Anna Pasternak recalls her grandmother's reaction when the family wanted to take her along: "Grandmother protested, arguing that the Germans would be kind to her because she was old and sickly and even spoke some German. After all, they were nice, educated people."[8] Max Blauner, born in 1919 in Grybów, recalls the discussions about the possibility of fleeing to Soviet-held territory: "My father said, he served in World War I, he was an officer in the Austrian army, and he met Germans, he went through that war, so it would be perhaps the same."[9]

Although the oft-repeated motif of "civilized Germans" was not the only vision shared by the older generation, it undoubtedly played an important role. The younger generation found it difficult to effectively oppose their own fears of the "new Germans" against the previous first-hand life experience of their parents and grandparents. This argument about the civilized German nation might have stemmed not so much from the elderly's misjudgment of the risks or wishful thinking as a desire to reassure younger people who were leaving home not to worry about the relatives they were leaving behind. After all, many older people were concerned that their physical condition and abilities were insufficient to cope with the challenges of refugee routes. Ryszard Leciński (Jakub Rotenstein) explains in an interview that his mother considered herself too old and weak to undertake the strenuous and dangerous flight, but she drove him and his sister out in the direction of the Bug River to Luboml, where the border crossing was.[10] Leciński adds that there were refugees who later crossed back over the border and returned to retrieve their parents, "but I didn't do anything. I couldn't imagine her risking her life. It was probably my duty [to bring my mother to the Soviet side], but I didn't do it [cries]. This is perhaps the greatest sin I have on my conscience."[11] Leciński's experience parallels that of many other young refugees. Even though a long time had passed since those events, what is striking in the witnesses' accounts is that many former refugees still felt traumatized and guilty of having abandoned their elderly parents or grandparents.

Physical condition was the most important factor in decision-making when considering escape. This "biological determinant" is mentioned in countless sources and followed by descriptions of a farewell scene between the adolescent or adult children and their parents. For instance, Helena Wojtowska's parents were too "sick, physically and mentally broken" to go with her.[12] A typical situation of that time, Wojtowska's parents decided to stay in their home in Płock, while she fled to the Soviet zone with her two sisters; a third sister stayed to look after their sick parents.[13] An oft-repeated argument by the older generation, in this story as in refugee stories more generally, was that if they were to die, they would rather do it in their own home than while wandering. Some older people attributed their decision to stay to an attachment to the land of their ancestors, which they felt obliged not to leave.[14]

This points to the third important factor in their decision-making, the psychological, which is involved in a life-course perspective in the migration process. As people anticipated what the war would mean—albeit without foreseeing the genocide—and the possibility of fleeing from its path, many thought they were too tired to revisit the refugee fate. Among the psychological factors that can be read from the testimonies, besides tiredness and the fear of setting out on a difficult journey, of leaving possessions that could not be easily regained at that age, older individuals also harbored concerns that they would slow down younger people along these routes. In this context, the decision to stay was a form of agency on the part of the elderly and only seemingly a passive gesture.

In virtually all families, heated discussions broke out. Accounts like the one written down by Ben Zion Wacholder from Ożarów can be multiplied by many dozens: "Should the family stick together and whatever will be, will be, or should we separate to increase the chances of survival of one of us? The arguments in favor of the family staying together seemed most compelling."[15] Indeed, in researching the case of the small town of Hrubieszów, historian Eliyana Adler established that family consensus was an important factor in decision-making.[16] While for Hrubieszów's case this translated into a decision that either the family stays as a whole or leaves together, more generally opinions on that issue were far from unanimous. Some believed that in a situation of war families should stick together, while others held that it was better to separate. Eventually, the common pattern was for the younger and fitter to volunteer or be encouraged to go.[17]

In a small number of cases, older people succumbed to persuasion and tried to flee with their children. In the early days of the war, in the oft-described "rivers of refugees" heading east, elderly people were certainly seen everywhere on the roads. Janusz Bardach noted: "Men pulled carts carrying small children and elderly people; old people pushed wheelbarrows filled with their belongings; the infirm hobbled along with canes."[18] Eleven people of the Geller family, including grandparents, set off together from Oświęcim toward the Soviet-occupied zone. This typical escape was particularly hard and dangerous for the elderly members of the family:

> It was difficult to drive through the crowded road, which was constantly being bombed and shot at by German airplanes. We hid in ditches and it took a long time for us to find one another. We lost Grandma and didn't find her until a few hours later, injured in the forest. A doctor in a town tended to her wounds. Our horses were killed by the bombs, and we had to go on foot and carry Grandma on [our] backs until Father bought new ones. Grandma moaned in pain and asked us to leave her behind. [. . .] We went to Jagielnica [. . .]. Grandma fell ill on the way and stayed in a peasant's barn for two weeks. We didn't think she would pull through. But God helped her, and we carried on.[19]

In summarizing this section, it is important to emphasize that of the different stages of Jewish survival in the USSR, the greatest loss of the older generation occurred immediately during the first period of flight. For all of the reasons discussed above, the elderly were the least likely to opt for flight.

Elderly as Deportees

As soon as the Soviet regime gained control of the eastern Polish territories, they began deporting Polish citizens into the interior of the USSR, but it was between February 1940 and June 1941 that four main deportations took place. The largest group of Polish Jews was deported in June 1940. The majority of these deportees (the so-called *bezentsy*, or refugees) came from the groups described in the previous section. They fled to the Soviet-held zone, refused to accept Soviet citizenship, and registered to return to their former houses in the German zone. But as mentioned earlier, those deported also included Polish Jews who had resided in eastern Poland all along. Among them was the family of Esther Hautzig, who described several years of Siberian exile in her memoirs.[20] The nine-year-old girl was deported from Vilnius with her mother and grandmother. Her account—detailing her grandmother's role during the years of exile—is one of the very few published testimonies in which a grandparent actually lived to see the end of the deportation and returned to Poland.

The deportation trains left toward the Arctic, Siberia, Kazakhstan, and the Urals. The conditions under which people were transported over the course of several weeks were atrocious: crowded stock cars with no sanitary facilities, with forced intimacy, inadequate food rations, very little water, and no access to medical supplies. Each of the thousands of boxcars heading east had its own internal crowd dynamics, which could be the subject of a separate study. Age played a role in the wagons and raised a number of questions: Where to place whom? How much to give everyone to drink and eat? "Should the children get more because they are growing, less because they are smaller, or the same as the adults? Hunger made everyone shrill—and reckless."[21] Elderly people and children were at the highest risk during this journey. The dead bodies of the elderly and infants dominated among the corpses removed from the transports during the long journey.

Thirteen-year-old Jaffa Iras escaped with her mother, two siblings, and her grandfather to the Soviet-held side. Since they were separated from her father, who had gotten stuck under the German occupation, her mother and grandfather registered to return. In June 1940 they were arrested by the NKVD. In her testimony, Jaffa recalled the typical circumstances of deportation:

> One day, on Friday night, we were woken by the knocking of gunstocks on the door. NKVD-ers told us to pack. Our old grandpa and the children burst into tears. [. . .] We were loaded into a freight car, sixty people in each. [. . .] It was crowded in the car; people lay on top of each other. The doors were sealed. [. . .] The stuffiness was awful. [. . .] Many people were ill, [and] a few died. We demanded that the dead be taken away, but the guards pretended not to hear our request, and only when we tried to break the door open at one of the stations did [some] NKVD-ers appear and take away the bodies.[22]

Psychological factors continued to differentiate the responses of the elderly during the deportation phase; the mental and emotional stresses burdened the well-being of older refugees more than other age groups. Firstly, as in many cases of elderly displacement, their physical fragility must be added to the fatigue of experiencing more hostile events throughout their longer lives. Secondly, for the elderly, being uprooted from the natural environment and habits that kept them in shape despite their age caused an even more serious mental strain. Their age often made it more difficult for them to adjust than younger deportees. There are many accounts of elderly men who tried to continue their religious and kosher observances at all costs despite starvation, which added to their weakness.[23] Wherever they were settled, the deportees heard the same words from the NKVD functionaries, that this would be the place of their final stay (and death) and they would never return to Poland. In the face of such a prospect, discouragement and passivity struck each generation in a slightly different way. While younger and middle-aged people were at least inwardly rebellious, older people often felt that surviving their remaining days under such conditions was not worth the extra strength and willpower needed to continue living.

After a three-week journey, Jaffa's family arrived in the Novosibirsk Oblast, Serovsky district, and was transferred to a special settlement located in a forest. Like Jaffa's family, most of the refugees deported in June 1940 were placed in NKVD-supervised settlements, mostly located deep in the taiga, known as *specposioleks*. The people there performed forced labor, mostly clearing forests, mining for lead or coal, and building roads and railroads. The oldest and youngest were usually not taken to work. In Jaffa's case, her fifteen-year-old brother Mosze was the only breadwinner in the family of five. Food was very scarce. The deportees were so hungry that they overate grass and roots, and many contracted dysentery. Some managed to recover, but rarely were the oldest generation among them. One girl whose family became sick reported: "The first to die was my grandmother, who was sixty years old. The same night my grandfather died."[24] Jaffa's grandfather likewise became ill, and, in his case, "they didn't want to admit him to a hospital as he was too old. He died a few days later and was buried in the forest, where the *posiolek* (special settlement) was located."[25]

Given the near total lack of available medicine and the fact that the most the hospital could offer was a little warmth and cleanliness, the elderly were virtually excluded from any medical intervention. Hanna Prager describes the passing of her beloved grandfather, Isroel, in similar terms to Jaffa's. Isroel joined the fleeing children at the last minute and was taken with them to Archangelsk Oblast, Kargopolsky Rayon. He developed a boil on one of his ankles that had a little pus in it, which was a typical effect of the avitaminosis rampant among the deportees. Although the wound did not seem serious, there was nothing to treat it with. The medics did not even want to examine him after they found out he was sixty-two years old. Hanna heard it said that he was "an old man and they had nothing for him anyway." In her view, her grandfather was still a strong man with bright eyes and all that was wrong with him was "this miserable little sore on the ankle."[26] The wound grew more serious, however, and Isroel died a few weeks later.

More such stories are among the accounts of Jewish children compiled by the writer Henryk Grynberg, one of the first ones who worked with the deportees' testimonies: "Grandfather fell ill with dysentery, but they would not admit him to the hospital because he was too old, and after a few days he died. We buried him in the forest and Moishe carved his name on a tree so we could visit his grave. We missed Grandfather a lot because whenever we had had hunger pangs he would tell us stories and we would forget our hunger."[27] Even worse was the situation of the elderly in the Gulag. Gustaw Herling-Grudziński titled his testimony *A World Apart* (one of the most well-known on the topic), a just reference to how Soviet prison logic diverged from the basic rules of human coexistence. Only prisoners who had not completely lost the capacity to work were treated with some minimal medical measures: "No attempt was made to cure complete physical exhaustion, various forms of hunger, dementia, night-blindness, and advanced vitamin deficiency which resulted in ulceration of the body and loss of hair and teeth—these qualified directly for the mortuary. [. . .] For old men, for prisoners with incurable heart disease, protracted pylagra [pellagra], or tuberculosis the hospital was only a temporary resting-place before death or removal to the mortuary."[28] Yitzkhak Erlichson, reporting on the labor camp near Kolyma, mentioned how dead bodies were thrown directly into the water and were eaten by sharks.[29] In some other places, due to the ground freezing for most of the year, the corpses were sometimes piled up and attracted forest animals as scavengers.

The elderly had a much better chance of survival outside the Gulag, in settlements where whole families were deported. Accounts suggest that families could support and care for elderly relatives if the majority of their members were not disabled and worked. This was the case of the

Cwibel family from Kraków, who was deported from Lwów (present-day Lviv, Ukraine) to a special settlement near Asino. Jehoszua and Saba Cwibel were over the age of sixty and exempted from work, but they were supported by their five children, who all were older than sixteen and who worked. They were thus able to buy meals from the camp's shop.[30] Similarly, Józef Geller noted that his family, consisting of eleven people, was able to provide for his grandparents. The elderly couple was exempt from work, but ran the household and took care of the smaller children.[31] In conditions where the family, or part of it, remained together, the elderly provided continuity by assuming caregiving roles, which often proved to be a necessity for survival, as they enabled the children's parents to work.

For researchers of the subject, the first thing that becomes obvious when studying the policy of Soviet repression is that Soviet regulations were far from consistent. This is evidenced by the significant differences in the conditions under which deportations deep into the USSR were experienced. It was clear that the obligation to work in the forest, in the mines, or on railway construction covered all adult men. Disparities in forcing labor involved teenagers (some had to work, others—although less often—were allowed to attend school), women, and the elderly. Rabbi Izrael Halberstam was deported together with his seventy-year-old father to one of the special settlements in the Omsk Oblast. Both had to work in forest harvesting. After a few weeks of this exhausting work, Halberstam's father died.[32] The work of older people like Israel's father was by no means an isolated case. The elderly who were forced to work could not keep up the pace in their work brigades. The fewer trees they felled, the worse food rations they got, and the less strength they had to work the next day. They usually were the first to fall victim to exhaustion.

At this point, it is not possible to determine the mortality rate of the elderly during the phase of deportation and ensuing phase of forced labor and starvation in the cold taiga. Even if there are some estimates, the available data aggregates the casualties both among the elderly and children, as well as among men due to work accidents, and other adults struck by disease. As long as it existed, the Polish Committee of the Memorial Association in Moscow responded to individual requests to provide basic information on family members on the deportation list. These lists contained, in addition to the name and place of deportation, also the date of birth of the deportee. At some future point, it will hopefully become possible to conduct further work to detail the statistical demographics of the deportees, including Polish Jews. These could then be collated with the list of those who returned to the country.

From previous studies based on Moscow databases, historians estimate that Jews constituted around 30 percent of all Polish citizens deported to the USSR. Aleksander Gurjanow used Soviet sources to estimate the total number of Polish citizens repressed by the USSR between 1939 and 1941 at around 490,000, which includes those arrested, sentenced, and/or exiled.[33] Gurjanow maintains that, based on the NKVD's statistical reporting of deaths of all civilian deportees made available to him, it is impossible to isolate the number of Polish citizens who died (amid Ukrainian, Lithuanian, Latvian, Russian, German, and other nationalities). Nevertheless, based on his approximate calculations, the mortality of this group up to the amnesty in 1941 was around fifty-eight thousand, which gives a per year average of around 8 percent. Among the deported, some were taken to prisons or the restrictive Gulag camps, some to the *specposioleks*. Older people only rarely left the prisons or the Gulag alive. About twenty-five thousand deportees to the special settlements, which "housed" around sixty-eight percent of all Polish repressed, died by the summer of 1941, which gives an average of around 7.5 percent for this phase of the "survival in the East." A comparison of these very rough figures with the baseline mortality of Poles before the war—for the year 1937, around 1.4 percent—suggests that the mortality during this phase of Siberian exile was about 5.5 times higher than normal.

Elderly as Amnestees

One of the most common themes in memoirs from Siberia is the outbreak of the German-Soviet war in June 1941, which marked a turning point in the lives of most of the deportees and prisoners.[34] The authors often express the belief that if it had not been for this war, they would not have been able to survive much longer in the conditions of displacement to Siberia. With the start of the war, diplomatic relations between the Polish government-in-exile and the USSR were restored. Most of the detained Polish citizens were amnestied. In addition, the agreement provided for the creation of a Polish army in the USSR, the so-called Władysław Anders' Army, to support the war against Germany.

Polish Jews, like most other able-bodied Polish citizens, rushed south to the central Asian Soviet republics, where Polish military units were being formed. In addition to joining the fight, they hoped for better living conditions, a more temperate climate, and easier access to food. The areas surrounding Samarkand, Bukhara, Tashkent (Uzbekistan), Jambul (today's Taraz, Kazakhstan), and Jalal-Abad (Kyrgyzstan) soon contained the largest concentrations of Polish refugees in Central Asia.

Having been away from home for two years and enduring exhaustion throughout this time, most were sick, famished, and lacked adequate clothing and food. The long journey southward, which often began on homemade rafts, was very strenuous, especially for the elderly and children. Józef Geller's family, including his grandparents, was initially exhilarated to be released from the special settlement in Tavda, Sverdlovsk Oblast. Soon enough, however, they realized that what awaited them was further hunger and, added to it, malaria and typhus.

> We were [already] certain we would die from hunger and exhaustion when we learned about the Amnesty. [. . .] We went to Bukhara. The journey took four weeks. [. . .] We suffered terribly from starvation until we reached our destination. In Bukhara we had no place to stay—we slept in the mud, resting our heads on our boxes. [. . .] There were people lying in the streets ill with fever, and sometimes corpses, which no one paid any attention to.[35]

This moment of partial liberation is paradoxically the point, when according to documents from the Polish Embassy in the USSR, the mortality rate among the weakened refugees was the highest, between 25 and 30 percent.[36] As before, the elderly and infants were the most likely to succumb to illness. Among the victims were Józef Geller's grandparents, who made it that far, but died in Uzbekistan: "The whole family fell ill with typhus and everyone recovered. We got back from the hospital completely famished and ate wild herbs, after which we fell ill with dysentery. My grandma, Róża Szpajchler, age sixty, and my grandpa, Pesach Szpajchler, died at that time."[37] Izrael Ferster from Majdan Kolbuszowski recounts a similar story about his family, which left Altai Krai for Bukhara: "Epidemics like typhus and dysentery ravaged the population and the refugees. Out of our family, Grandpa, Grandma, my aunt, her husband, and [her] child died from these diseases within a short time. [. . .] Out of fifteen people in our family who were deported to Russia, there were three people left, not including the three children who were in the Polish children's center."[38] Izrael's family, as was usually the case, received some minimal support from the Polish diplomatic post, the so-called Delegation (Delegatura). These offices were established by the Polish Embassy that represented the London-based government-in-exile. The Polish delegations were able to create an impressive array of more than four hundred welfare institutions throughout the southern part of the Soviet Union, including orphanages, sleeping and feeding centers, hospitals and medical aid posts, homes for the disabled, the so-called invalid homes, and old people's homes.[39] Their help, however, was only a drop in the ocean. The December 1942 report stated that, due to limited financial resources and overwhelming relief needs, priority was given to rescuing children and young people. The number of elderly was smaller than children generally, and the number of homes for the elderly and disabled was much smaller than the number of orphanages (66 to 338).[40]

Polish diplomats were simultaneously searching feverishly for many notable individuals missing from public and social life. Some of them perished in Katyn, where the Soviets committed the mass murder of twenty thousand members of the Polish officer elite (which, in addition to professional military, included scientists, doctors, engineers, lawyers, teachers, civil servants, and entrepreneurs) in the spring of 1940. Some others—especially older ones—had not survived forced labor. One of the most respected politicians of prewar Poland and a rabbi, Moses Schorr, belonged to the latter group. He died of exhaustion at the age of sixty-seven in the Uzbek camp in the summer of 1941, but the Polish authorities did not learn about his death until many months later.

Cooperation between the Polish authorities based in London and the Soviets, which allowed a modest level of support for refugees, lasted less than two years. In the spring of 1943, when the German army advancing eastward discovered the bodies of Polish officers murdered by the NKVD and buried in the Katyn Forest, Polish-Soviet diplomatic relations were again severed. This revelation also accelerated the tense evacuation of the Polish Anders' Army to Iran, which had already been underway since mid-1942, to supply the southern front of the war against Germany (via Palestine to Italy).

There is a large body of scholarship outlining the many difficulties Polish Jews faced when enlisting in Anders' Army.[41] Many factors played a role, along with overt discrimination, starting with the limited number of places in the army and including the official reason—their physical condition. Antisemitic sentiments were strongly influential, something that some examiners did not even bother to conceal from Jewish candidates. For many Polish Jews, this bitter rejection at recruitment stations became the ultimate reason for their postwar renunciation of Poland.[42] Still, four thousand Jewish soldiers were accepted into the army and many of them left testimonies, like Menachem Begin (later Israel's Prime Minister). But as a route out of the USSR, Jews represented just 5 percent of the seventy-eight thousand, plus about sixteen hundred Jewish civilians, who were evacuated with Anders' troops. Many of them would later fight and die at Monte Cassino.[43]

There were no elderly among the Jewish soldiers. Among the evacuated group of civilians accompanying them, there were a small number of older Jews. One of them was a sixty-year-old Wilhelm Lichtblau from Tarnów. He left Siberia for Samarkand. Only thanks to the support of his children, who lived at that time in Palestine, and as Lichtblau stated, "had a lot of contacts and influence in London," was he able to get personal protection from Polish general Szyszko-Bohusz, who secured his evacuation. Wilhelm Lichtblau concluded: "Not everyone was this lucky. Thousands of my acquaintances left [their] *posiołki* to join the army and weren't accepted. [. . .] In Samarkand, I was present at the opening of a new Jewish cemetery, and when I was leaving a few months later, there was no more space in that cemetery."[44] A recently discovered source—the Jewish death book from Samarkand—confirms the high mortality rate of refugees.[45] At the same time, it shows that there were still older people in this group: the oldest Polish Jews who died in Samarkand in 1942 and 1944, respectively, were seventy-nine and eighty-one years old.[46]

Following their split with the Polish government in London, the Soviets closed Polish social welfare institutions and arrested many of their employees. Eventually, some little help to refugees came from a new Communist Polish organization created by Stalin, the Union of Polish Patriots (Związek Patriotów Polskich). The latter was also responsible for preparing Polish citizens for their return to Poland in its newly redrawn borders. Before this possibility was announced, however, the death rate skyrocketed. People were still starving and ill, the prospect of leaving the USSR was uncertain, and the fear of what they would find in Poland was acute.

This was a period of further physical and mental breakdown for Polish refugees. Even those in their prime went through serious psychological crises as some struggled to prove to the Soviet authorities that they were Polish citizens before the war. As recounted by Roma Talasiewicz: "We were alone [. . .] and trapped. Life became more and more hopeless. [. . .] Abram and I started talking about ending our lives."[47]

Elderly as Repatriates and DPs

The history of elderly Polish Jews at the end of the war and the circumstances of their departure from the USSR are the least represented in the sources we have accessed. At this stage, the number of older people was very low. Their chance to leave Soviet exile came with the agreement signed by the Soviet Union and the Provisional Polish Government of National Unity (under Soviet patronage) on July 6, 1945, which served as the foundation for repatriation to Poland. By the end of 1946, Jews accounted for some 136,000 Polish citizens on official repatriation lists.[48] Among them were also elderly people. According to the statistics for the first half of 1946, there were 10,100 Jewish repatriates aged fifty-six and over: fifty-five hundred men and forty-six hundred women.[49]

The hunger and disease they had endured during their exile in Siberia and Central Asia had left a strong mark on their physical condition. However, the worst blow was yet to come and further affected their emotional state: the country they had left in 1939 no longer existed, and their immediate neighbors, homes, and families had disappeared. What followed was a profound sense of longing and isolation. Regina Kesler from Suwałki had fled with her elderly parents to Vilnius, from whence the family was deported to Novosibirsk. After the amnesty, they settled in Osh, Kyrgyzstan, where they all managed to survive the Soviet hardship and eventually returned as part of the repatriation movement to their hometown. Regina reported, "Our first impression soon gave way to a harsher reality. The town, now dead and desolate, had no Jews. My aunts and uncles had perished with their families. Strange Polish people occupied their homes and apartments. [. . .] My parents had no social life and could survive only with help from my mother's brothers in America."[50] This loss of social and family ties was not only a source of great pain and social isolation, but it also had significance in terms of security. Jews often returned to find that they were not welcome in their former homes. Anti-Jewish violence continued to sweep through many Polish cities and provinces in the early days after the war. In this respect, those returning faced the same problems as the survivors under the German occupation. This atmosphere culminated in the July 1946 pogrom in Kielce, in which an estimated forty-two Jewish survivors were killed. Following these events, most Polish Jews opted to move out of the country and rebuild their lives elsewhere.

Most of those who emigrated went to the American occupation zone of Germany, where a number of displaced persons camps operated.[51] Very soon, Polish survivors from the USSR formed the majority of Jewish displaced persons.[52] The Nazi extermination policy had left almost no elderly Jews and few Jewish children. Concentration camp survivors staying in the DP camps and the camp administrators were genuinely stunned by the arrival of Polish Jews who returned from further east because among them were also whole families.[53] As was mentioned in the opening of this chapter, the influx of "Siberian deportees" changed the age structure in the DP camps, stabilizing it at 2 percent elderly among the survivors, a statistical figure that is corroborated by data collected in Poland. Among the nearly twenty-six thousand registered in the Jewish organization in Łódź in 1945, survivors over fifty-five years of age and children under six accounted for between 1.9 and 2.3 percent.[54] Emil Sommerstein, a politician and activist who survived in the East, recalled how his traditional gray beard inspired awe and curiosity in Jewish children upon his return to Poland—children for whom such a sight had become unfamiliar.[55]

As is the case with any migration, regardless of whether it might be in Poland or in a DP camp or another country that would be the last stop in their migration (e.g., the United States, Australia, or Israel), adapting to life in new surroundings and often also to a new language was more difficult for older people than for all other age groups.

Conclusion

Throughout their struggle for survival in the USSR during World War II, older Polish Jews faced a significantly higher risk of failure compared to the younger refugees. This disparity was primarily due to their physical

FIGURE 8.2. Portrait of Mordechai and Sheindl Rajs, in the Ulm displaced persons camp, 1948. United States Holocaust Memorial Museum, 38598.

condition, which determined their ability to endure the harsh realities of displacement, deportation, forced labor in Siberia, and eventual exile in Central Asia, where they encountered unfamiliar diseases and climates that were especially challenging for Eastern Europeans. However, their difficulties were not solely physical. In terms of generational contingency, Miriam Keppler, who survived in Siberia as a child, observed that although her experience was undeniably harsh, survival seemed easier for children compared to the older generation. Both the youngest and the oldest were most vulnerable to rapid health deterioration, but the Soviet system treated these generations in different ways. Whereas the Nazis targeted children for extermination, seeing them as a threat to the future of Germany, just as they did with adults, the Soviet system sometimes embraced "enemy" children, viewing them as potential vessels for Soviet ideology.[56] The elderly, however, were not afforded this regard. In the Soviet logic, their limited capacity to contribute to physical labor, shorter life expectancy, and resistance to political indoctrination rendered them the least useful of all deportees.

Despite the significant differences between the Nazi and Stalinist regimes, the survival rate of elderly Jews was in effect very low under both. It was notably lower among older Jewish refugees in the USSR than among other age groups who escaped the Nazis. While elderly Polish Jews in the Soviet Union were not directly targeted for immediate extermination, they were nonetheless effectively regarded as expendable by both regimes. The topic of elderly Polish Jews' escape to the East and their deportation to the USSR can hopefully be further explored in the future based on sources that become newly available.

One concluding point that can, however, be highlighted concerns memory. As we mentioned earlier, most of the information about the elderly's experience comes from the accounts of their children and grandchildren. That is, it is a mediated perspective. This is because the longer, published testimonies of Holocaust survivors, those that have largely shaped our view of this period, were penned primarily by younger witnesses of the war.

Not only are the accounts of those born in the nineteenth century far fewer, but they also mainly take the form of short, unpublished testimonies collected immediately after the war by Jewish organizations. For political reasons, those who stayed in Poland could not engage in describing the true picture of their Soviet experience. Moreover, in the postwar period, when survival in the USSR was generally interpreted as comparative good fortune, the good fortune of having extricated oneself from the Germans, these early accounts, also given by older people, focused on describing the beginning of the German occupation (before their flight and deportation eastward). As for Siberia, they often ended with a one-sentence explanation that the witness managed "to escape to Russia, where s/he survived the war."[57] The elders' perspective is generally better represented in the yizkor bikher (memorial books), which after the war collected information about the life and fate of individual Jewish communities. These accounts, however, were mainly intended to record the time before 1939 and document events in the given localities during the war; Siberia hardly fit in that picture. Therefore, the extent one can know the elderly perspective on Holocaust survival in the USSR remains sorely limited. By the time the true "era of the witness" came about, and the publishing boom of memoir literature took place, those who had already been elderly during the phase of survival in the East were no longer there.

Notes

1 Lidia Zessin-Jurek's research for this paper was supported by the ERC-Project "Unlikely Refuge? Refugees and Citizens in East-Central Europe in the 20th Century" under the European Union's Horizon 2020 research and innovation program. Calculations based on JDC reports and work by Irit Keynan, *Holocaust Survivors and the Emissaries from Eretz Israel: Germany 1945–1948* [in Hebrew] (Tel Aviv, 1996), as quoted in Na'ama Seri-Levi, " 'These People Are Unique': The Repatriates in the Displaced Persons Camps, 1945–1946," *Moreshet* 14 (2017): 62.

2 See e.g., Mark Edele et al., eds., *Shelter from the Holocaust: Rethinking Jewish Survival in the Soviet Union* (Wayne State University Press, 2017); Markus Nesselrodt, *Dem Holocaust entkommen: Polnische Juden in der Sowjetunion (1939–1946)* (De Gruyter, 2019); Lidia Zessin-Jurek and Katharina Friedla, eds., *Syberiada Żydów polskich: Losy uchodźców z Zagłady* (Żydowski Instytut Historyczny, 2020); Eliyana R. Adler, *Survival on the Margins: Polish Jewish Refugees in the Wartime Soviet Union* (Harvard University Press, 2020); Markus Nesselrodt and Katharina Friedla, eds., *Polish*

Jews in the Soviet Union (1939–1959): History and Memory of Deportation, Exile, and Survival (Academic Studies Press, 2021).

3 It is difficult to estimate the exact number of Polish Jews who survived the Shoah in Poland. Despite the fact that the Central Committee of Polish Jews kept the records of the surviving Jews, the unstable situation of the community of Polish Jews after the war interfered with the statistics. See Anna M. Rosner, *Obraz społeczności ocalałych w Centralnej Kartotece Wydziału Ewidencji i Statystyki CKŻP* (Żydowski Instytut Historyczny, 2018).

4 In a major text on the subject, Dan Stone starts at fifty-five years of age. Dan Stone, " 'Somehow the Pathetic Dumb Suffering of These Elderly People Moves Me More Than Anything': Caring for Elderly Holocaust Survivors in the Immediate Postwar Years," *Holocaust and Genocide Studies* 32, no. 3 (Winter 2018): 384–403. Studies on the wartime history of European Jewry that have drawn attention to the importance of the question of age and also provide the background for this text include Anna Hájková, "Speculations About German Jews: Elderly People from Germany in the Theresienstadt Ghetto," *Yad Vashem Studies* 50, no. 2 (2022): 55–84; Michael A. Meyer, " 'Cast Us Not Off in Days of Old Age': Elderly Jews in Nazi Germany," *Yad Vashem Studies* 50, no. 1 (2022): 77–101.

5 Herbert C. Covey, "The Definitions of the Beginning of Old Age in History," *International Journal of Aging and Human Development* 34, no. 4 (June 1992): 325–37.

6 The exception here is the valuable resource regarding the names of Polish citizens (including Polish-Jewish deportees) who registered themselves having reached Polish diplomatic posts in the Soviet Union. More than thirty thousand survivors' depositions, along with twelve thousand NKVD release certificates and other related documentation, are stored in the archives of the Polish Ministry of Information and Documentation, the Ministry of Foreign Affairs, Anders Collection, and of the Polish Embassy on the Soviet Union in the deposit of the Hoover Institution Library and Archives at Stanford University.

7 Lidia Zessin-Jurek, "Whose Victims and Whose Survivors? Polish Jewish Refugees Between Holocaust and Gulag Memory Cultures," *Holocaust and Genocide Studies* 36, no. 2 (Fall 2022): 154–70.

8 Anna Pasternak, *The Untold Story of a Young Girl During WWII* (Page, 2017), 141.

9 Max Blauner, interview 33607, September 18, 1997, tape 2, *Visual History Archive*, USC Shoah Foundation.
10 Ryszard Leciński, interview 18144, August 1, 1996, tape 3, *Visual History Archive*, USC Shoah Foundation.
11 Leciński, interview 18144.
12 Protocol 182, testimony of Helena Wojtowska, in *I Saw the Angel of Death: Experiences of Polish Jews Deported to the USSR During World War II*, ed. Maciej Siekierski and Feliks Tych (Hoover Institution Press, 2022), 579.
13 Protocol 182, testimony of Helena Wojtowska.
14 Irena Kowalska and Ida Merżan, *Rottenbergowie znad Buga* (Ludowa Spółdzielnia Wydawnicza, 1989), 105.
15 Ben Zion Wacholder, *Wspomnienia*, ed. Łukasz Rzepka (BOŻnica, 2018), 96.
16 Eliyana Adler, "Hrubieszów at the Crossroads: Polish Jews Navigate the German and Soviet Occupations," *Holocaust and Genocide Studies* 28, no. 1 (Spring 2014): 1–30.
17 Lidia Zessin-Jurek, "Belated Flight?" (unpublished manuscript).
18 Janusz Bardach, *Man Is a Wolf to Man: Surviving the Gulag* (University of California Press, 1998), 16.
19 Protocol 181, testimony of Józef Geller, in *I Saw the Angel of Death: Experiences of Polish Jews Deported to the USSR During World War II*, ed. Maciej Siekierski and Feliks Tych (Hoover Institution Press, 2022), 574.
20 Esther Rudomin Hautzig, *The Endless Steppe* (Holt, Rinehart and Winston, 2002).
21 Aleena Rieger, *I Didn't Tell Them Anything: The Wartime Secrets of an American Girl* (SunPetal Books, 2015), 88.
22 Protocol 151, testimony of Jaffa Iras, in *I Saw the Angel of Death: Experiences of Polish Jews Deported to the USSR During World War II*, ed. Maciej Siekierski and Feliks Tych (Hoover Institution Press, 2022), 481.
23 For example, in Jaffa's case: "My grandfather could barely stand up; he didn't want to eat the soup because it was non-kosher and he ate only dry bread with cold water," Protocol 151, testimony of Jaffa Iras.
24 Henryk Grynberg, *The Children of Zion* (Northwestern University Press: 1998), 143.
25 Grynberg, *Children of Zion*, 143.
26 Hanna Prager Kogosowski, *The Times of My Life* (self-pub., 1991), 126.
27 Grynberg, *Children of Zion*, 143.

28 Gustaw Herling-Grudziński, *A World Apart* (Arbor House, 1986), 100.
29 Yitzkhak Erlichson, *My Four Years in Soviet Russia* (Academic Studies Press, 2013), 66.
30 Protocol 40, testimony of Chaim Dawid Cwibel, in *I Saw the Angel of Death: Experiences of Polish Jews Deported to the USSR During World War II*, ed. Maciej Siekierski and Feliks Tych (Hoover Institution Press, 2022), 97.
31 Protocol 181, testimony of Józef Geller, in *I Saw the Angel of Death*, 575.
32 Protocol 216, testimony of Rabbi Izrael Halberstam, in *I Saw the Angel of Death*, 680.
33 Aleksander Gurjanow, "Sowieckie represje polityczne na ziemiach wschodnich II Rzeczypospolitej w latach 1939–1941," in *Exodus: Deportacje i migracje (wątek wschodni): Stan i perspektywy badań*, ed. Marcin Zwolski (Instytut Pamięci Narodowej, 2008), 27.
34 On the meaning of Operation Barbarossa for Polish Jews and its significance as the start of a full-scale genocide under German occupation while at the same time enabling the release of Polish Jews deported to Soviet forced labor camps, see Lidia Zessin-Jurek's presentation at the conference *Between War and Mass Murder—80 Years to "Operation Barbarossa,"* June 22–24, 2021 (from 1hr., 06min.) YouTube, www.youtube.com/watch?v=S8KhkusMYos.
35 Protocol 181, testimony of Józef Geller, 576.
36 As reported in January 1943, Hoover Institution Library and Archives (HILA), Poland. Ministerstwo Informacji i Dokumentacji Records (MIiD), box 47, folder 1, Działalność opiekuńcza ambasady R.P. w Kujbyszewie.
37 Protocol 181, testimony of Józef Geller, 576.
38 Protocol 109, testimony of Izrael Ferster, in *I Saw the Angel of Death*, 316.
39 HILA, MIiD, box 46, folder 7, Notatka do Pana Ministra, February 2, 1943, London. A number of Jewish organizations, such as the JDC and the Jewish Agency for Palestine, supported refugees by sending food and funds: HILA, Poland. Ministerstwo Spraw Zagranicznych Records (MSZ), box 148, folder 19, "Brief Outline of Relief Work Amongst the Jewish Refugees in the USSR, Through the Parcel-Service, Charles Passman, Jerusalem, February 25, 1944," 1–4.
40 HILA, MIiD, box 47, folder 9, Sprawozdanie działu opieki społecznej ambasady R.P. w Z.S.R.R., 1. grudnia 1942, 20, 25.

41 Yisrael Gutman, "Jews in General Anders' Army in the Soviet Union," *Yad Vashem Studies* 12, (1977): 231–96.

42 Lidia Zessin-Jurek, "On a Melting Ice Floe—Polish Jewish Wartime Refugees in Central Asia," *Journal of Genocide Research* 26, no. 3 (June 2023): 286–306.

43 The total number of Polish evacuees with the Polish Army from the USSR included more than forty-one thousand civilians. Even if Polish Jews constituted around 30 percent of all Polish citizens in the Soviet Union, only 5 percent succeeded in enlisting as soldiers or civilians for evacuation. HILA, MSZ, box 143, folder 11, "Report on the Evacuation from the USSR, May 6, 1944, Tehran"; Polish Institute and Sikorski Museum Archive in London, Ministerstwo Spraw Zagranicznych, A.11, folder 380, "Notatka w sprawie opieki nad Żydami w Persji i Palestynie."

44 Protocol 173, testimony of Wilhelm Lichtblau, in *I Saw the Angel of Death*, 554.

45 Na'ama Seri-Levi, *Digital and Spatial History of Jewish Refugeedom: Newly Discovered Burial Registry Book of Samarkand* (Claims Conference, forthcoming).

46 *Burial Registry Book of Samarkand*, YVA O.41/2395.

47 Suzanna Eibuszyc, *Memory Is Our Home* (Ibidem Verlag, 2015), 205.

48 Albert Kaganovitch, "Stalin's Great Power Politics, the Return of Jewish Refugees to Poland, and Continued Migration to Palestine, 1944–1946," *Holocaust and Genocide Studies* 26, no. 1 (Spring 2012): 74.

49 Albert Stankowski, "How Many Polish Jews Survived the Holocaust?," in *Jewish Presence in Absence: The Aftermath of the Holocaust in Poland, 1944–2010*, ed. Feliks Tych and Monika Adamczyk-Garbowska (Yad Vashem, 2014), 212.

50 Regina Kesler, *Grit: A Pediatrician's Odyssey from a Soviet Camp to Harvard*, ed. Michael G. Kesler (AuthorHouse, 2009), 92, 101.

51 Atina Grossmann, *Jews, Germans, and Allies: Close Encounters in Occupied Germany* (Princeton University Press, 2007); and Margarete Myers Feinstein, *Holocaust Survivors in Postwar Germany, 1945–1957* (Cambridge University Press, 2007).

52 Polish Jewish repatriates constituted almost three-fourths of the postwar Polish Jewish population and thus formed the largest group (up to two-thirds) among the Jews in DP camps: Zeev Mankowitz, *Life Between Memory and Hope: The Survivors of the Holocaust in Occupied Germany* (Cambridge University Press, 2002), 19.

53 Na'ama Seri-Levi, "'These People Are Unique,'" 61.

54 Ewa Koźmińska-Frejlak, *Po Zagładzie: Praktyki asymilacyjne ocalałych jako strategie zadomawiania się w Polsce* (Żydowski Instytut Historyczny, 2022), 102.

55 Adler, *Survival on the Margins*, 241.56 Interview with Miriam Keppler (née Weintraub) by Lidia Zessin-Jurek, Yonkers NY, October 29, 2024 (author's collection).

56 Interview with Miriam Keppler (née Weintraub) by Lidia Zessin-Jurek, Yonkers NY, October 29, 2024 (author's collection).

57 Hersz Engelberg (born 1881), Protokół zeznania, Relacje Ocalałych (1947), Jewish Historical Institute Archive (henceforth AJHI) 301/3212, 2; Aleksander Lubasz (born 1896), Wiadomości o Jarosławiu, Relacje Ocalałych (1948), AJHI, 301/332, 2.

9

POSTWAR HUMANITARIAN PHOTOGRAPHY

The Jewish Committee for Relief Abroad's Photographs of Older Jews in Postwar Europe

Roxy Moore

In June 1947, an article in the Anglo-Jewish newspaper the *Jewish Chronicle* reported that German Jewry was becoming "a community of elderly people," the responsibility for whose care lay with "world Jewry."[1] Although, as historian Dan Stone has noted, the number of elderly or older survivors in postwar Europe was "very small" and certainly a minority, as the above extract from the *Chronicle* attests, they existed.[2] And indeed, in some places, as Jewish Relief Unit (JRU) aid worker Charles Zarback observed from Berlin in 1946, they formed "a good proportion of the population," alongside the middle-aged.[3] Older Jews, then, were present across postwar Europe and, due to their traumatic and difficult wartime experiences and advanced age, were also in need of tender care and humanitarian aid. As such, older Jews' needs were carefully considered by aid agencies such as the JRU throughout the postwar period and their plight was subsequently captured and discussed in the organization's regular field reports and extensive collection of photographs.

This chapter looks specifically at examples from the latter: it considers how and why images from the JRU's photograph archive depict older displaced persons (DPs) and survivors in postwar Europe, and in what ways these photographs can deepen our understanding of approaches to this group as well as postwar Anglo-Jewish humanitarianism.[4] To do so, it first examines the JRU's intentions in capturing images of and portraying older Jews, before turning to consider styles of photography specifically, looking first at portraiture and then activity and event photographs. It argues that photographs of older Jews in the JRU archive allow for an appreciation of the complexities of life in postwar Europe for this age group and, in turn, a greater understanding of the diversity of Anglo-Jewish care and support delivered to them (and, indeed, the consistent dedication of the JRU to this group). By considering a range of images and styles, it highlights both how the JRU drew on traditional Jewish cultural conceptions of elderly care, as well as the active engagement of older Jews in their own rehabilitation. And yet it also highlights how older Jews' lived experience of postwar Europe was often different from that captured through a lens, and how contemporary intentions and uses in particular mediated the images we see today.

The JRU was the operational arm of the Jewish Committee for Relief Abroad (JCRA), an Anglo-Jewish humanitarian aid organization founded on January 24, 1943, to provide relief to DPs and Holocaust survivors in the aftermath of World War II.[5] From its base in Endsleigh Square, London, the JCRA deployed personnel across Europe and North Africa until its closure in 1950, providing a variety of different services to aid DPs' physical and psychological rehabilitation. Although a comparatively small organization (with just 213 field workers), the impact of the JCRA was notable.[6] Not only were the JRU's activities with DPs consequential, but as the primary manifestation of Anglo-Jewish aid in response to the Holocaust, its actions are particularly important in understanding the historical development of Anglo-Jewish humanitarianism. Yet in spite of this historic importance, the existing scholarship focusing on the JCRA and JRU is sparse and, as a result of this dearth in the literature, the organization is often overlooked or mischaracterized as a short-lived, pro-Zionist agency operating almost exclusively in Germany and based on outdated philanthropic ideas as opposed to the methods of modern humanitarianism which it actually sought to emulate.[7]

The type of care that older survivors across Europe needed varied greatly depending on individual circumstances and experiences during the war. Accordingly, the JRU facilitated a range of different types of support for this group, from the reconstitution of old age homes to the tracing of loved ones—as well as help with tasks such as reparations forms, pensions, and work placements. Visual depictions of this care for older Jews appear regularly throughout the JRU's extensive collection of photographs held at the Wiener Holocaust Library (WHL) in London, although, like the organization itself, these images are rarely the subject of serious scholarly research. Indeed, in this respect historian Isabel Wollaston's statement regarding photographs of the Holocaust can equally be applied to those, such as the JRU collections, of its aftermath: "there is a tendency to rely heavily on a relatively small number of images, some of which have become iconic, functioning as visual shorthand for the Holocaust or aspects of it."[8] During the JRU's lifetime, however, photographs of its work with the elderly were often used to illustrate articles in the pages of contemporary publications such as the *Jewish Chronicle*, *CBF News*, *JRU News*, various fundraising pamphlets, and British newspapers more widely. As this list of publications suggests, the origins of the photographs collected by the JRU were also wide-ranging: images were sent in from field workers, bought from photograph agencies on the ground, as well as commissioned and taken from contemporary news reports, among other methods.

Today, the JCRA's photograph collection housed at the WHL constitutes twenty-three albums containing 2,509 photographs. The albums can broadly be split into two categories of provenance. The first set is contemporary, curated, and hand-annotated (although by whom it is unknown). These albums are divided thematically into each country and place that the JRU was stationed and were likely created as the archive itself was collated in the early 1950s.[9] The second group of albums is an "artificial" collection, composed of formerly loose photographs that have been amalgamated into archival albums by WHL photo archivists (and again sorted into country and place of work). Noting the physicality of the collection here is important because the form in which these photographs are presented directly shapes how the images are understood. In particular, it highlights that these photographs were originally viewed in a different context to that in which we see them today: at the time of their capture, these images (where disseminated at all) were usually not viewed as part of albums (which were created later) but rather as individual images or as series of images at events or in contemporary publications. There is then a distinction to be made between the contemporary purpose(s) for which the images in the JRU collections were taken and used, which were wide ranging, and the secondary purpose that they served by subsequently being stored, organized, and curated into albums.

Furthermore, it is also crucial to note that the images within the collection are primarily *not* photographs taken by DPs, but rather photographs *of* DPs. This is not to say that those pictured did not contribute in some way to the image produced, or that the photographs rob those depicted of agency or dehumanize them, as the scholarship discussing humanitarian photographs—often correctly—concludes.[10] Rather, it is to highlight that the intentions and ideas that shaped the final images found in the archive today came from a variety of sources. Yet it is equally important to recognize, as visual arts expert Terence Wright argues, that in many cases photographs of DPs in this era (and, indeed, photographs of refugees today) were expected to satisfy preconceived ideas about what this group should look like, and how they should act.[11] And, accordingly, identifying whose ideas shaped the images produced, and how, is vital to understanding what and who they depict, and why. A letter written by Joy (Billie) Rothe, for example, a JRU aid worker deployed to Egypt and then Italy, where she worked alongside the American Jewish Joint Distribution Committee (JDC), to her family in 1945 sheds light on how aid agencies' ideas directly shaped the images produced in this period:

> Today Mr Brooks of the Joint came with his usual battery of press cameras so you can hope for a picture soon. All Joint Reps work like this for its [*sic*] necessary to squeeze the shekels out of the American Jews. He was almost sorry to see that my stay here had made the children look so much better and happier for they weren't half such good propaganda.[12]

DPs, then, were supposed to be destitute, desperate, and hungry, and images attesting to clear physical and psychological improvements (while, in this case, the reality of the situation) did not always feed this preconceived notion in the way that aid organizations, to inspire donations, required.[13]

As Rothe's letter and contemporary use of the images in press articles indicate, photographs of aid work in postwar Europe were taken to document the relief being facilitated, but also to inform the target audience of their continuing responsibility. In Rothe's words, the images created, bought, used, and stored by the JRU were also "propaganda": by ensuring the Jewish community was kept informed of their activities and the need for them, the JCRA (the JDC and others, too) attempted to directly connect their target audience to these events to inspire the crucial financial donations needed to sustain each respective organization. As Heide Fehrenbach and Davide Rodogno, authors of *Humanitarian Photography*, explain, "since the late nineteenth century, humanitarians, journalists, and missionaries have used visual props and narratives to summon attention and funds. These visual props—often photos—were not just 'evidence'; they were rhetoric," which "gave form and meaning to human suffering, rendering it comprehensible, urgent, and actionable for European and American audiences"—or in the case of the JRU, for Anglo-Jewry in particular.[14] As this chapter will demonstrate, a consideration of these intentions in creating and curating images of older Jews is crucial to fully understanding both the Anglo-Jewish approach to this group on the ground and older Jews' lived experience as they navigated life in postwar Europe.

Portraits

A significant number of the photographs featuring older Jews within the JRU archive take the form of portraits. Portraiture was, and remains, a popular form of humanitarian photography, largely because its intimate nature gives a human face to causes, encouraging an emotional connection between the viewer and the subject. Indeed, the JRU repeatedly emphasized to its field workers the importance of promoting individuals' stories, with Rose Henriques, head of the JRU's Germany Department, for example, instructing field worker Milly Polatchik in 1946 to "let me have any news or interesting stories about the work, as I am in constant need of material for the various speakers who attend the CBF [Central British Fund for Jewish Relief and Rehabilitation] gatherings, and the more intimate pictures we can present to the audience, the more likely are we to get the funds."[15] In utilizing intimate, individual stories the JRU employed what Heide Fehrenbach has termed "strategies of emotional address": strategies that "played upon the emotional resonance of familiar, and sometimes familial, photographic genres and practices" and were "cast in languages of national, imperial, religious, or civilizational responsibility."[16] In the case of photographs of older Jews, these strategies drew directly upon cultural understanding of Jewish communal and religious responsibilities toward the elderly. The Torah repeatedly advocates respect toward older members of society, for example, in Leviticus 19:32: "Stand up in the presence of the elderly, and show respect for the aged." And while, as historian Eugene Black explained, "this responsibility devolved, in the first instance, on the family," where "children and grandchildren cared for parents and grandparents who had not or could not provide for themselves"; but the "aged spinster or bachelor, the man or woman who had the misfortune to outlive his or her family, or those whose children would not or could not care for them became communal obligations."[17] Throughout the nineteenth and early twentieth centuries in Britain, these Jewish communal obligations were addressed largely by philanthropic organizations, which provided both material supplies and spiritual guidance. Where possible, this support was facilitated within the recipients' homes—in line with the principle of self-help that dominated British (and Western) philanthropy at that time—or, where unfeasible, in almshouses or old age homes.[18] By the 1940s, when the JRU was operating and publishing pictures of older Jewish DPs and Holocaust survivors in Europe, conceptions of elderly care and communal responsibilities toward older Jews were concretely embedded within the Anglo-Jewish community. By using portraits of elderly Jews, the JRU sought to forge a familiar sense of kinship between the Anglo-Jewish viewer in Britain and the subject of the photograph in Europe, encouraging a feeling of social responsibility and, in turn, emotional and financial investment in their cause.

Figures 9.1 and 9.2 provide a clear example of this methodological thinking in practice. The two photographs portray Raphael Feger, a DP from Lublin, at Bad Harzburg, a Jewish rest home opened by the JRU in 1947.[19] Bad Harzburg cared for a range of people, although the elderly were particularly common among its residents. In both photographs, Feger is pictured alone, dressed in a thick cardigan and, in figure 9.1, reading from a newspaper. While relaxed, Feger also appears aged. Both photographs are featured as part of one of the curated photo albums documenting the JRU's activities in Germany and, more specifically, in Bad Harzburg. In this album, captions accompany the images: alongside figure 9.1, "Feger Raphael, a D.P. from Lublin, in the reading room of the Jewish Rest Home" and, alongside figure 9.2, "A face lined through years of suffering . . . Feger Raphael, a D.P. from Lublin, finds rest and comfort

FIGURE 9.1. Raphael Feger, a displaced person from Lublin, Poland, pictured in Bad Harzburg, Germany, ca. 1946–49. Jewish Relief Unit Photograph Albums, 35/1/9/10, The Wiener Holocaust Library Collections.

at the Jewish Rest Home."[20] These captions demonstrate how the JCRA, when constructing albums documenting their work, used text to direct and anchor specific meanings and interpretations to images. In the first photograph and caption, the viewer's attention is drawn to focus on Feger's rehabilitation—the activity being pursued (reading) and their location, in a Jewish rest home funded by the JRU. In the second, Feger's wartime persecution is foregrounded—the photograph is cropped to focus solely on Feger's face, and the caption foregrounds their suffering and subsequent difficulties. And yet the second half of the latter caption again reminds the viewer that Feger "finds rest and comfort at the Jewish Rest Home." Feger's hard and seemingly lonely situation, the viewer is consistently reminded, was alleviated by the work of the JRU.

Notably, however, contemporary documents and reports of field workers from the home, as well as other images in the same photograph album, contrast the downcast depiction of older Jews with portraits of the group. Bad Harzburg was usually busy, if not full, and the communal

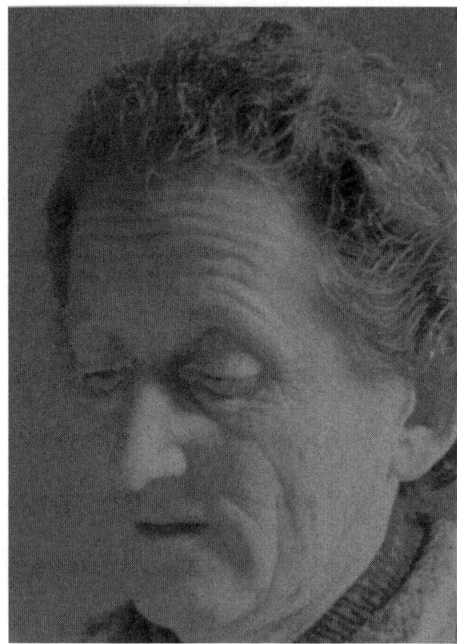

FIGURE 9.2. A further portrait of Raphael Feger, a displaced person from Lublin. Jewish Relief Unit Photograph Albums, 35/1/9/8, The Wiener Holocaust Library Collections.

spaces within the home provided room for these numerous residents to gather, socialize, and meet others in a similar situation. Where the lone nature of the images of Feger emphasizes individual suffering, images of the home functioning more generally (and indeed, the nature of the home itself) evidence that Bad Harzburg was in fact a communal setting—a distinct Jewish space that allowed residents a sense of kinship and company in the aftermath of shared persecution. This disparity suggests a difference between the lived experience of the home, including the care that the elderly were receiving there, and the limited presentation of it in portrait photographs.

Contemporary uses of the photographs of Feger allow more insight into this disparity, and the purpose behind it. When used in publications at the time, Feger was not named as the individual portrayed in the image. Rather, the portrait was used to broadly indicate the heartrending situation in Germany for the aged more widely and the comfort being provided to them by representatives of Anglo-Jewry. In a fundraising pamphlet from the late 1940s, for example, CBF utilized an image of Feger (figure 9.1) among a montage of others.[21] However, they did so without using a caption—or indeed without giving any other context to the photograph; the image was used merely as an illustration to imply to the reader what the JCRA's work with the elderly entailed without giving any specifics. In doing so, Feger is not accorded any real agency and, despite the intimacy provided by the portraiture style of the photograph, becomes another anonymous subject of persecution. The focus shifts from Feger as an individual to what the JCRA (funded by the CBF) was doing for them—on how Feger was recovering and under whose guidance. On the one hand, to the historian viewing these images as part of a series within a curated album, the photograph of Feger evidences the regular presence of older Jews at Bad Harzburg (and indeed, in other images from the album, their use of communal spaces—a source of company and comfort) as well as allowing for a glimpse into the types of rehabilitative care and activities offered to the elderly at the rest home. On the other hand, when viewed as individual images as they were disseminated at the time, the portraits of Feger (and others) also shed light on how the elderly as a group were symbolically used by the JRU as a longstanding, recognizable, and pitiable visual plight. This served to remind contemporary viewers of their communal obligation to the elderly and inspire further financial donations.

While intimate in style, photographs of older Jews were often used in an arguably shallow manner. Beyond the basic facts given in the caption (Feger's name, birthplace, and location at the time of the photograph), neither the contemporary nor modern viewer can glean even cursory knowledge of Feger. The caption is not clear if their suffering was a result of hiding, incarceration in a concentration camp, or exile in the Soviet Union, and it does not indicate what their rehabilitation actually consisted of, other than reading. Overall, the clearest summary of the portrayal of Feger that emerges from these pictures is that of a lone, previously persecuted individual, who subsequently benefitted from rest facilitated by the JCRA in Germany. This use of photography was typical of aid agencies at the time. In a similar vein, for example, historian Silvia Salvatici has described the photographs of the United Nations Relief and Rehabilitation Administration (UNRRA), alongside which the JCRA worked: "Although the photos appeared to be telling the story of the women and men in the camps, the real protagonist was UNRRA itself. Sometimes it was present through the insignia or uniforms worn by personnel; more often it was invisible but still dominating through the idea of effectiveness and professionalism conveyed by the photos."[22]

One notable difference, however, between UNRRA and the JCRA's use of imagery was that although both organizations used photographs to highlight their own activities, the JCRA also utilized emotion in a way that UNRRA did not. As Salvatici observes, UNRRA did not use photography "to stir up stark emotions. Instead, their purpose was to explain their mission and persuade, reassure, and familiarize the postwar public with a new vision of humanitarianism as modern, professional, and thoroughly international."[23] Although the JCRA largely shared UNRRA's commitment to this new incarnation of modern humanitarianism, their patchy funding base—which was, through the CBF, in part reliant on private donations, as opposed to an international funding pot—meant that their aim in taking and using imagery differed: they did not seek to simply assure the Anglo-Jewish public that they were doing a good job, but to draw on the deep communal obligations toward the elderly in order to serve the JCRA's fundraising aims.

And yet, as suggested above, this portrayal is neither a thorough nor accurate indication of the JCRA's actual field work with older Jews: on the ground, the elderly were not simply vessels used by the JRU to induce guilt. Indeed, the JCRA's real mission, as stated in their organizational aims below, was rehabilitative, rooted—as was UNRRA's—in modern conceptions of social care, psychology, and humanitarianism: "The J.C.R.A. has been created by the Jewish community of Great Britain to assist in the relief of their suffering brethren, whose spiritual and physical needs they feel themselves best qualified to understand and meet; and, working with other like bodies on the C.O.B.S.R.A. [Council of British Societies for Relief Abroad], to do all in their power to relieve suffering wherever it may be found."[24] On a base level, the JRU's work with Feger and their presence in Bad Harzburg evidence these aims in action. But, crucially, as the contemporary *use* of Feger's image attests, the organization also had to make calculated, practical considerations in its use of photography, decisions that often differed from DPs' lived experience of interactions with the JRU, for the organization to be financially viable and sustainable. Images had to be digestible and compelling, even where this meant deviating from thorough or perhaps more accurate visual presentations of the difficulties and nuances of life for older Jews—and indeed Jewish DPs more widely. In some ways, as anthropologist Lynda Mannik writes, this "failure of photography to accurately capture experience force[d] the viewer to rethink stereotypical tropes about refugee identity."[25] Following this thinking, DPs became more than their physical or psychological injuries: their diverse portrayal humanized them. Furthermore, the target audience is also important to consider here: after the horrors of World War II, many viewers did not *want* to see in vivid detail the continuing grim realities of the aftermath of persecution. Many felt they had seen enough despair and desperation to last a lifetime, and thus photographs such as Feger's, which provoked emotion but also, with their indications of JRU's rehabilitation, hope, were more likely to be engaged with and thus more impactful.

The portrayal of Feger is not an exception: other photographs of older Jews in the JRU archive also utilize portraiture to foreground the difficulties or loneliness of the lens' elderly subjects. Figure 9.3, for example, depicts an older man artistically illuminated by a stream of sunlight while seated at a table in Camp Two of Bergen-Belsen, leaning on one hand and staring into the distance. Half a loaf of bread sits before him, and various cooking pots are stowed by the man's feet beneath the table. Several copies of this photograph exist throughout the JRU archive. In the curated album on the JRU's work in Germany, the image is captioned: "Aged D.P.'s [*sic*] in their rooms at Camp 2—Belsen. As many as ten people share one room."[26] In this photograph, the elderly gentleman is portrayed as the lone, sad (or at the very least, forlorn) subject in a lonely and depressing scenario, and the viewer instinctively pities him. The caption reinforces this pity, labeling the man as "aged" and highlighting that while the man appears alone, the rooms are in fact subject to overcrowding—he does not even have the luxury of privacy. In the Anglo-Jewish press, this image was used in the October 1947 edition of the *CBF News*, illustrating an article that updated readers on the JCRA's work in Germany. Despite the article making no other mention of the elderly, the caption accompanying the photograph highlighted how "there is so little left for the aged in a place like Belsen—except what we can give them."[27] Again, the role of the JRU and the Anglo-Jewish community was foregrounded ("what *we* can give them"), juxtaposing the

FIGURE 9.3. An unknown older man, pictured at a table in Bergen-Belsen Displaced Persons Camp, ca. 1945–50. Jewish Relief Unit Photograph Albums, 35/6/3/197, The Wiener Holocaust Library Collections.

depicted elderly man's otherwise seemingly lonely life. Likewise, figure 1.1, discussed in Dan Stone's chapter, which depicts an elderly woman in bed, was used in the 1946 CBF annual report.[28] Captioned "ALONE in Belsen without known relatives in the world," the rest of the report focuses on the broader care and activities facilitated by the JRU over the course of the year, mentioning the "hospitalisation of old people" but without going into specific details.[29]

As with the image of Feger, the publications featuring these two images contain no further information on the identity of either individual, their experiences, or their plans for the future. In a similar vein to the photographic policy of UNRRA explored by Salvatici, those portrayed in these unnamed photographs are anonymous; even where "the captions offered details about their supposedly personal stories, the portrayed recipients were in fact standardized and depersonalized."[30] Portraits of the elderly were thus used simultaneously to indicate the work being done by the Anglo-Jewish community and what was still left to be done, rather than as profiles of individuals in their own right. Indeed, it is unsurprising that the issue of *CBF News* in which the photograph of the older woman in bed is featured opens by outlining how "the Central British Fund is experiencing a financial crisis similar in some respects to the national one," pleading: "surely, the Community will not fail to renew its support of those few who now look to us for help," and concluding, "is it too much for us to give [so] that they who remain in Europe, particularly the young and the aged, may be saved at this, the eleventh hour?"[31] Despite otherwise stressing the progress being made by the JRU in Germany, images of children and the elderly were disproportionately used to compel the reader to acknowledge the work that remained. Indeed, the JRU repeatedly stressed how, "as well as facts and figures, 'human interest' stories are needed to stir the feelings of the audiences" for "fund-raising meetings all over the country."[32] The JRU's work could not continue without funding, and thus representations of what this work looked like and meant were calculated toward achieving this aim.

In summary, the JRU often portrayed older Jews through portrait photography, the intimate nature of which sought to connect the Anglo-Jewish public to the subject and evoke emotion by drawing on cultural understanding of communal obligations toward the elderly. The ultimate intention behind many of these types of images was to use certain individuals, such as Feger, to indicate the wider plight and continuing problems of older Jews in postwar Europe and prompt financial donations. They also continue to serve a secondary, documentary purpose by being placed and maintained in the JRU archive. In this regard, unless viewed as part of a series, such as within the album mentioned, these portraits only reveal glimpses of the JRU's humanitarian rehabilitative methods and very little detail about the individuals photographed. And yet their existence and prevalence within the archive—and their widespread dissemination in contemporary publications—speak to how older Jews were a key and consistent priority for the JRU throughout its existence. Anglo-Jewish philanthropy had long catered to the elderly, and Anglo-Jewish humanitarianism continued this trend in their work abroad.

The other major style of photography that dominates the JRU's archive is more directly documentary. These photographs usually focus on a specific event or activity, rather than a person, and, due to their nature, typically (but not always) depict celebrations or events of particular note. Given this, the activities photographed were often associated with communal reconstruction. Figure 9.4, for example, depicts one such notable occasion: the silver wedding anniversary celebration of Mr. and Mrs. Siegmund and Henriette Falk, two survivors of Theresienstadt, which was held at the Jewish Old Age Home in Berlin.[33] With Allied flags hanging in the background of the room, Mr. and Mrs. Falk are surrounded by their guests, eating and drinking at long, shared tables. While this focus on notable communal events is perhaps unremarkable in itself (especially in a period where photography was common but still relatively costly), the fact that the JRU actively chose to visually document these moments is important. It shows that, in contrast to the emphasis of much of the existing scholarship on the organization, which focuses overwhelmingly on its links to Zionism and emigration, the JCRA was continually committed to the reconstruction, and not just rehabilitation, of European Jewry.[34] Indeed, for the elderly, who, for various reasons, were more likely to resettle in their former countries of residence, these events and the JCRA's communal efforts more widely were particularly significant.

Another example of event photography being used to depict an important communal occasion is a series of postliberation photographs that show the baking of the first matzo at the Sarotti bakery in Tempelhof, Berlin

FIGURE 9.4. The silver wedding anniversary of Mr. and Mrs. Siegmund and Henriette Falk, two survivors of the Theresienstadt ghetto, in Berlin. Jewish Relief Unit Photograph Albums, 35/6/4/302, The Wiener Holocaust Library Collections.

(figure 9.5).[35] At the time, the JRU's primary field officer based in Berlin was Charles Zarback, a social worker from East London, who highlighted the importance of the event in a letter penned to the military public relations office in 1946, writing it was "of the greatest significance that in Berlin, the centre of Fascism, Jews are preparing to celebrate their religious festivals in their own particular way."[36] Given this, Zarback naturally hurried to report the occasion and send photographs to Leila Pierce, the JCRA's press and information officer.[37] Figure 9.5 is one example from this series, and pertinent to the discussion here due to the presence of an older man. The photograph depicts the man alongside a middle-aged woman, both of whom are engaged in the breadmaking process. Within the JRU photograph album documenting the organization's activities in Germany into which it was later incorporated, the photograph was captioned as "a further photograph in the preparation of Matza. This family has been engaged in Matza baking for five generations."[38] In the photograph, the visual depiction of the unknown older man—who, in his position looking over the woman's shoulder, appears to be guiding the process—contrasts dramatically in style and emotion with

FIGURE 9.5. The first matzo baking at the Sarotti bakery in Tempelhof, Berlin, 1946. Jewish Relief Unit Photograph Albums, 35/1/2/19, The Wiener Holocaust Library Collections.

the portrait photographs described above.[39] As discussed, because of their intended use, the portraits depict elderly Jews alone, often stylistically highlighting their difficult or desperate situations, even where these are being addressed through rehabilitation. The elderly gentleman photographed in figure 9.5 is presented not as a passive figure or a communal responsibility, but as a still-active, knowledgeable contributor—as someone who has valuable expertise and, as such, is playing an important communal role.

During his time in Berlin, Zarback also assisted with and arranged for photographs to be taken of the celebrations for the 1946 Purim and Passover festivals, which were the first of each to take place in Berlin following the end of World War II. For Purim, for example, a special "Old Peoples' Purim Party" was held for the seventy inhabitants of the Iranische Strasse Old Age Home as the official Berlin *Gemeinde* (Community) Purim party was held "many miles from the Old Age Home," which made it "impossible for the old people to attend."[40] Most of the inhabitants of the home were survivors of Theresienstadt. Describing the group, Zarback wrote of their bleak situation: "these people, whose grey hair and lined faces exaggerate their years, are for the most part sole survivors of their families. Only two or three have managed to remain together as husband and wife during their suffering, the rest have been parted from their loved ones for ever."[41] The party, coorganized by the director of the home, Mr. Fiedler, the JRU, and the JDC, thus not only provided a space for the residents to further reconnect with their prewar communal traditions, but to do so together, providing a familial sense of community to those who were no longer able to celebrate with family, neighbors, and friends. Indeed, this sense of community is further evident in photographs of Passover celebrations from the same year, where older members of the community are seen socializing alongside other generations at tables in a packed, formal party setting.[42] Many of those close to the photographer are turned to face the camera, while in the background others enjoy the food and conversation around them. The choice to mark this occasion with photographs, and subsequently archive them, points to a desire not only to document the event, but also to its poignance for all involved. After the fall of the Third Reich, this was an important moment for German Jewry, but also for European Jewry. Furthermore, visually capturing others celebrating this shared religious festival across the continent further served to remind contemporary viewers in Britain of the communal ties that bound the Anglo-Jewish community to the wider world, and, given these, the reason behind their work.

As well as specific celebratory events, everyday rehabilitative activities were also photographed. Figure 9.6, for example, evidences how older Jews were also included in skills classes and work placements.[43] The photograph, taken at the Sedan Kaserne DP camp in Ulm, Germany, foregrounds two women, one of whom appears significantly older and wearing glasses, in the sewing center at the camp. Both women are looking down, focused on the material in front of them, while various sewing ephemera litter the front of the image, and other men and women work on similar tasks in the background. While not particularly striking in itself—there are many images that depict the JRU's rehabilitative activities, several of which feature older Jews—this image, and others like it, are incredibly important when considering photographic depictions of older Jews in postwar Europe more widely. Although we know almost nothing specific about the women or men in the picture other than their physical location, their placement side by side allows the older woman an element of agency that many portraits, despite providing the viewer a sense of connection and often direct personal information, do not. This photograph instead offers

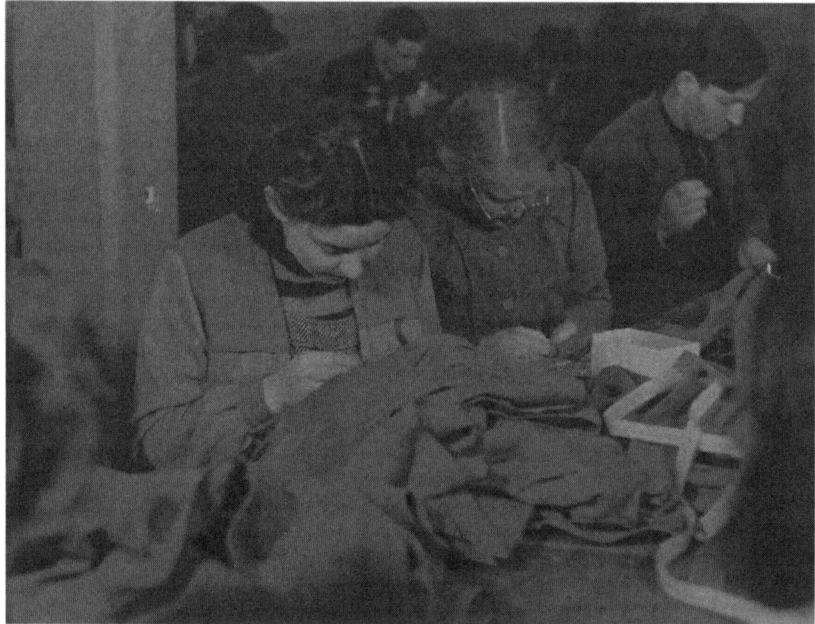

FIGURE 9.6. Two women sewing at the Sedan Kaserne Displaced Persons Camp in Ulm, Germany, ca. 1945–50. Jewish Relief Unit Photograph Albums, 35/6/25/11, The Wiener Holocaust Library Collections.

an impression of the everyday and shows some of the more general rehabilitative tasks that older Jews took part in alongside other DPs. While the outlook for older Jews in postwar Europe was often distinctly bleak, these activities demonstrate engagement, not resignation to loneliness, and draw attention to the skills and social value inherent in the elderly, in defiance of their persecution.

Collectively, these photographs allow not only for a greater appreciation of older Jews' lives in postwar Europe, but also a deeper understanding of Anglo-Jewish humanitarian approaches to and activities with them. In other words, they depict what the JRU actually did on a day-to-day basis, outside of trying to fundraise, which, while important, certainly did not fill the days of field workers on the ground. More specifically, they evidence the active *engagement* of older Jews, an element of elderly Jewish survivors and DPs' lives often unexpressed in the static portrait photography that, as noted, was typically favored for contemporary publication. This engagement does not gloss over the bleaker elements of many older

Jews' lives in postwar Europe: the photographs of Purim and Passover in 1946, for example, speak to both the loneliness of Jewish old age in the immediate post-Holocaust years and the sense of company and comfort found in reinstating communal traditions. Moreover, these photographs also evidence the ways in which older Jews were turned to as upholders of tradition and sources of communal knowledge and pride: the elderly were not simply a burden or a group to be cared for; they were active and important participants in the reconstruction of European Jewry, despite their paltry numbers.

Finally, these photographs also demonstrate the JRU's unwavering commitment to the communal reconstruction and support of local actors and *Gemeinden* (communities)—reconstruction particularly important for those, often elderly, Jews who could not or would not emigrate. With this in mind, it is clear that these types of photographs were taken with a different intention than for portraits, so often used to put a "human face" to the JRU's activities. Event and activity photography intended to document the JRU's actions in postwar Europe. They were not necessarily taken to show *why* Anglo-Jewry should be helping DPs (although this was often a side-effect), or to evoke sympathy, but rather to document *how* exactly the JCRA was aiding rehabilitation and reconstruction. And part of this, as the photographs evidence, was forming and reforming relationships, between the old and young, between long-separated family members or partners, and between aid officers and Jewish DPs. Viewed in this light, these photographs perhaps give a more accurate depiction of the "human" side of the JRU's activities than the portraits—which ironically intended to do exactly that.

Conclusion

The diverse array of photographs of older Jews within the JRU's archive allows for a sense of both the types and breadth of care and support delivered to the elderly by the JRU (whether through rest homes, hospitals, skill development workshops, cultural celebrations, or communal reinvigoration) throughout the organization's existence, the complexities of life in postwar Europe for older Jews, as well as the intentions behind capturing specific moments. Moreover, many of these images—and specifically those that document activities or events—also speak to the active engagement of older DPs in the rehabilitation and reconstruction of postwar Jewry. Older Jews were not simply passive recipients of care, but rather they continued to be engaged actors in the transient and permanent communities of postwar Europe, whose expertise was drawn on to facilitate Jewish reconstruction, and, in turn, highly valued.

And yet this engagement is not necessarily obvious in *all* photographs of older Jews within the archive. There is, then, a difference between the lived experience of older Jews in postwar Europe and photographic depictions of them. In seeking to explain this disparity, beyond the natural fluctuation in each individual's experience, this chapter has emphasized the photographic strategies employed and, more specifically, the intent behind and use of each image. In portraits in particular, for example, the subjects of each image typically appear as sad, lonely recipients of care, in need of further help. While life for many older Jews in postwar Europe was indeed often bleak, the choice behind the style of these images specifically emphasized this, encouraging empathy from the Anglo-Jewish audience and prompting financial donations.

On the surface, this decision can appear somewhat mechanical. But it is important to remember that this was not the JRU's intention: as a charity, they were reliant on donations to the CBF to facilitate their activities with older Jews (and others). Humanitarians were not, as we often paint them to be, uncomplicated seraphim, but rather arrived in postwar Europe with their own ideas and agendas. And, regardless, as is revealed in glimpses through these portraits (especially when viewed as part of a series documenting, for example, the Bad Harzburg convalescent home) or in event and activity photography, the JRU's activities with the elderly in fact sought to empower them, to include them, to rehabilitate them, and to alleviate loneliness, irrespective of their photography strategy. But as obligations to the elderly were a longstanding Jewish communal tradition, this group (alongside children) was an obvious choice to be featured in such fundraising campaigns. It is an unfortunate side effect that, despite their style, the portraits in the archive do not allow for a deeper sense or understanding of the individuals and their experiences.

There is not, then, a single narrative or presentation that emerges from depictions of older Jews within the JRU's photo archive but a variety, which arguably reflects the complex nature of the care provided and diversity of those thought of as "older Jews." The long-term outlook for older Jews and for Holocaust survivors more widely was indeed often extremely sad, but they also found moments of joy, comfort, love, and celebration in postwar Europe. The JRU not only regularly interacted with and cared for but also thought carefully about older Jews, and their commitment to documenting their interactions with this group suggests a deep, institutional obligation to the elderly as individuals and as active members of the postwar European and worldwide Jewish community.

Notes

1 "German Jews' Plight: Legal and Spiritual Aid Needed," *Jewish Chronicle*, June 13, 1947, 6.

2 Dan Stone, "'Somehow the Pathetic Dumb Suffering of These Elderly People Moves Me More Than Anything': Caring for Elderly Holocaust Survivors in the Immediate Postwar Years," *Holocaust and Genocide Studies* 32, no. 3 (Winter 2018): 384.

3 Charles Zarback to Henry Lunzer, February 25, 1946, HA6A-1/20/3/C, Lady Rose Henriques Archive (henceforth LRHA), Wiener Holocaust Library (henceforth WHL).

4 This chapter forms part of a wider project charting the history of the JCRA, which is funded by the Arts and Humanities Research Council/Techne DTP, AH/R01275X/1.

5 The terms JRU and JCRA are both used to refer to the organization throughout this chapter.

6 Tom Sampson, "Anglo-Jewish Humanitarianism and the Jewish Relief Unit, 1943–1950," *German History* 4, no. 2 (2022): 222.

7 There are two articles that focus solely on the JRU: Sampson, "Anglo-Jewish Humanitarianism," and Hagit Lavsky, "British Jewry and the Jews in Post-Holocaust Germany: The Jewish Relief Unit, 1945–50," *Holocaust Education* 4, no. 1 (1995). The most prominent other discussions of the organization appear in Amy Zahl Gottlieb, *Men of Vision: Anglo-Jewry's Aid to Victims of the Nazi Regime, 1933–1945* (Weidenfeld & Nicolson, 1998); Norman Bentwich, *They Found Refuge: An Account of British Jewry's Work for Victims of Nazi Oppression* (Cresset Press, 1956); Hagit Lavsky, *New Beginnings: Holocaust Survivors in Bergen-Belsen and the British Zone*

in Germany, 1945–1950 (Wayne State University Press, 2002); Joanne Reilly, *Belsen: The Liberation of a Concentration Camp* (Routledge, 1998); Lea Weik, "'In the Religious Field Great Strides Have Been Made'—Jewish Relief Organizations and the Supply of Religious Objects to Jewish Communities in the British Zone (1945–1950)," in *Jewish Life and Culture in Germany After 1945: Sacred Spaces, Objects and Musical Traditions*, ed. Katrin Kessler et al. (De Gruyter, 2022); and Dan Stone, who notes that the JRU was "the most important of relief organizations in the British zone" in Germany. Dan Stone, *The Liberation of the Camps: The End of the Holocaust and Its Aftermath* (Yale University Press, 2015), 122.

8 Isabel Wollaston, "The Absent, the Partial and the Iconic in Archival Photographs of the Holocaust," *Jewish Culture and History* 12, no. 3 (2010): 439.

9 Rose Henriques coordinated the deposit of the JCRA's archive at WHL in the early 1950s while Margot Pottlitzer (a former JRU field worker) was employed to arrange the material in 1953. The collections relating to the JRU were later expanded upon and also reorganized. There is no record of who exactly created the contemporary hand-annotated photograph albums.

10 On this, see, for example, Lynda Mannik, "Public and Private Photographs of Refugees: The Problem of Representation," *Visual Studies* 27, no. 3 (2012): 262; Liisa H. Malkki, "Speechless Emissaries: Refugees, Humanitarianism and Dehistoricization," *Cultural Anthropology* 11, no. 3 (1996); and Terence Wright, "Moving Images: Media Representations of Refugees," *Visual Studies* 17, no. 1 (2002).

11 Wright, "Moving Images," 57.

12 Joy Rothe, "Jewish Committee for Relief Abroad and the Jewish Relief Unit: Organizational Papers," September 23, 1945, 1232/2, WHL. In this context, Rothe likely used the term "shekel" as a reference to silver coins, rather than to the later currency of Israel.

13 On how the JDC commissioned and used photographs for fundraising campaigns, see, for example, the discussion of the photographer Roman Vishniac's work in Hildegard Frübis, "Europe as Transit: Jewish Displaced-Persons Camps and the Photographs of Roman Vishniac," in *Rethinking Postwar Europe, Artistic Production and Discourses on Art in the late 1940s and 1950s*, ed. Barbara Lange et al. (Böhlau Verlag, 2019).

14 Heide Fehrenbach and Davide Rodogno, "Introduction: The Morality of Sight," in *Humanitarian Photography: A History*, ed. Heide Fehrenbach and Davide Rodogno (Cambridge University Press, 2015), 6, 4.

15 Rose Henriques to Millie Polatchik, October 29, 1946, HA6B/1–4/7/E, LHRA, WHL. The CBF was one of two core funders of the JCRA's work.
16 Heide Fehrenbach, "Children and Other Civilians, Photography and the Politics of Humanitarian Image-Making," in *Humanitarian Photography*, 192.
17 Eugene Black, *The Social Politics of Anglo-Jewry, 1880–1920* (Basil Blackwell, 1988), 172–73.
18 On this, see Black, *Social Politics of Anglo-Jewry*, 173–77.
19 Dudley Osbourne, "Proposed List of Guests to Attend Official Opening of Bad Harzburg Home, on the 10th January 1947," 1947, HA6B/1–5/17/K, LHRA, WHL.
20 Jewish Relief Unit Photograph Albums, 35/1/9/10 and 35/1/9/8, WHL.
21 Pamphlet, CBF, 1946–48, HA2-3/7/13/B/N, LRHA, WHL.
22 Silvia Salvatici, "Sights of Benevolence: UNRRA's Recipients Portrayed," in *Humanitarian Photography*, 216.
23 Salvatici, "Sights of Benevolence," 211.
24 "Minutes of Meeting of the Executive Committee," April 20, 1944, JCRA and the JRU: Organisational Papers, 1232/1, WHL.
25 Mannik, "Public and Private Photographs of Refugees," 265.
26 JRU Photograph Albums, 35/1/9/79, WHL.
27 "Germany," *CBF News: Bulletin of the Central British Fund for Jewish Relief and Rehabilitation* (October 1947).
28 CBF, *Towards the Future: Annual Report 1946* (London: Steler & Young, 1947), 4.
29 CBF, *Towards the Future*, 4.
30 Salvatici, "Sights of Benevolence," 218.
31 H. Oscar Joseph, "The CBF Has a Crisis Too," *CBF News* (October 1946), 1.
32 Lilian Neuberger, "To All Field Workers," March 20, 1947, HA21/2/15/18, LRHA, WHL.
33 JRU Photograph Albums, 35/6/4/302, WHL.
34 On this, see, for example, Lavsky, "British Jewry and the Jews in Post-Holocaust Germany."
35 Charles Zarback to Major Doyle, "Jewish Affairs," February 21, 1946, HA7/3–15/3/C, LRHA, WHL.
36 Zarback to Doyle, "Jewish Affairs."
37 Charles Zarback to Leila Pierce, April 2, 1946, HA7/3–15/24/M, LRHA, WHL.

38 JRU Photograph Albums, 35/1/2/19, WHL.

39 While the man depicted in the photograph is not identified, matzo is often made under rabbinical supervision and so it is possible that he is a representative of the Berlin rabbinate. On the other hand, he could also be a member of the family running the bakery.

40 Charles Zarback, "Old Peoples' Purim Party," March 23, 1946, HA7/3-15/29/N, LRHA, WHL.

41 Zarback, "Old Peoples' Purim Party," March 23, 1946.

42 Jacobson Sonnenfeld, "Passover Berlin April 1946," JRU Photograph Albums, 35, WHL.

43 JRU Photograph Albums, 35/6/25/11, WHL.

10

THE MOST TRAGIC OF ALL SURVIVORS?

Elderly Displaced Persons in US-Occupied Germany

Kierra Crago-Schneider

Born in New York in 1881, Gemma Gluck, *née* La Guardia, was raised in Hungary, where she met and married her husband and, as a result, lost her American citizenship. At the age of sixty-three, Gluck found herself in a peculiar situation. As the sister of New York City's influential mayor throughout World War II, Fiorello La Guardia, the Nazis considered Gluck a possible pawn in hostage exchanges with the Americans. They arrested her in 1944 and held her in concentration camps, Ravensbrück via Mauthausen, where she was confined in the "elite" barracks with slightly better conditions than those in the rest of the camp and was not subjected to forced labor. Her daughter and grandson were also in Ravensbrück, but Gluck did not learn of their presence for nine months. The three were moved to Gestapo headquarters in Berlin and from there to the Kaiserdamm prison in Charlottenburg in April 1945. Realizing the war was lost and trying to save themselves, the prison guards released the three prisoners. Gluck was able to contact her brother, who was a former congressman, director of the Office of Civilian Defense, and head of the United Nations Relief and Rehabilitation Administration (UNRRA) after the end of the war. He informed Gluck that he would not use his position to whisk the remaining family from Germany to the United States and that she, her daughter, and grandson would have to wait their turn for a visa to get to the United States. Gluck regained her US citizenship in 1946, when her husband was declared deceased, but she had to wait for her daughter and grandson to qualify for US visas. They made it to New York in 1947. In her memoir, Gluck shared her thoughts and emotions as an older Holocaust survivor:

> I was so utterly helpless at that time, knowing neither the country nor people.
>
> My daughter and I still knew nothing of our husbands, and we had lost all—home, possessions, clothing, certificates of birth and marriage. We had nothing. It is a bitter thing to have nothing in one's old age. One is almost too weary to start a new life.[1]

Unable to emigrate upon their liberation, and for most Jewish survivors, the first three years after that, Jewish DPs (displaced persons) remained in centers operated by Allied occupation authorities and later the Federal Republic of Germany. These centers were managed by UNRRA and its successor, the International Refugee Organization (IRO), with the assistance of several international Jewish aid groups and the occupying forces. To those running the centers, as well as to the Jewish DPs, the solution to the Jewish DP "problem" seemed to present itself in 1948 with the creation of the State of Israel and the introduction of the United States Displaced Persons Act (subsequently expanded in 1950). However, more than two thousand Holocaust survivors, mainly the elderly, infirm, sick, and their families, remained in centers awaiting emigration opportunities, until February 1957, when the last Jews-only camp closed.

The Allied military governments and international aid workers understood that the elderly needed attention and care beyond the scope of what the agencies had anticipated and for which they had prepared. Not only were these caregivers faced with people aged fifty-five and over who qualified for retirement and a state pension in Germany, but also individuals who were not yet of retirement age but considered themselves too old to work or restart their lives abroad.[2] This chapter examines the cases of "elderly" survivors displaced in Germany and China who ended up in postwar Germany in the US-occupied zone, and is based on a close analysis of the policies and experiences there. The chapter does not define old age based on birth year, because this meant little in the minds of survivors and their caregivers. In fact, this chapter will use the more traditional understanding of old age, which was "subjective . . . variable and dependent more on the appearance and physical capacities of individuals than on chronological age."[3] Survivors' Holocaust experiences, self-evaluation, and the way aid workers understood their health largely defined how they were categorized in reports and cared for in displaced persons camps and old age facilities. Despite the difficulties of providing for the group classified as elderly, the Allies and international aid agencies' plan for all Jewish survivors was the same: immediate emigration. However, the "aged" were initially believed to have no opportunities for a future outside of Europe.[4] Western countries willing to accept refugees viewed these DPs as welfare cases and the government of the *Yishuv*—the Jewish population in Mandatory Palestine—understood them as a burden the country could not accommodate.[5] Additionally, many survivors who were forty-five and older at the war's end, and who were ready to emigrate at liberation, aged during their long stays in DP camps for Jews. This transformed them into "unattractive" immigrants because of their "advanced" age and ill-health. Despite these labels, the elderly fought for the futures they believed they deserved, reimagining what they hoped for as options for emigration closed.

The "Hardcore"

While constituting only a small number of Europe's Jewish survivors, elderly people made up a significant portion of the "hardcore" DPs, or individuals considered unattractive by immigration workers because of their age, physical disabilities, illness, or mental health.[6] The lack of resettlement options forced the Federal Republic of Germany (West Germany) and international aid workers to keep the camp system open until 1957, create integration plans for these DPs and their families, and build new institutions in West Germany and Israel to care for them.[7] By 1952, the American Jewish Joint Distribution Committee (JDC) considered everyone in the last remaining DP center, Föhrenwald, "hardcore" because they fit the description or were related to someone who did. The need to care for these individuals continued into the late 1950s and was anticipated to be necessary even after all centers were closed in West Germany.[8] For these reasons, separating elderly survivors from other "hardcore" DPs in historical analysis is incredibly difficult because aid agencies reporting on them used "hardcore" as a shorthand. Despite these challenges, this chapter will use the existing materials on the aged to introduce the struggles faced by these survivors.

Notably, "elderly," "aged," and "old" are, unlike "youth," "children," or "young," not usable search categories for most archives, nor do these terms appear in many documents that break down the Jewish survivor population. Instead, folders titled "hard-core," "invalid," "aged," "sick," "work and displaced persons (DPs)" contain files that, if they discuss older survivors, almost always report on child survivors and their care as well. These reports include documentation on mentally and physically traumatized, widowed, orphaned, and sick patients, alongside their medically determined work abilities.[9] Many of the "hardcore" DPs were elderly and ill or suffered from a disability, so distinguishing to which category the individual belonged is difficult. For example, most files titled "hardcore" or "work" grouped people with disabilities, individuals traditionally considered aged, and the sick together in their totals. Reports that did mention the ages of survivors are of little help as they often group people 21–60 together and those 60–65 in the same category.[10] Sometimes these files discuss the tragedy of these groups, including the elderly, concluding that they would remain displaced, never finding the homes they sought. Moses A. Leavitt, JDC director for Germany in 1945, with sadness called the elderly, "probably the most tragic segment of the entire Jewish population. They saw younger and stronger members of their families slaughtered while they lived on. Now they are too old, too weak, too tired to help rebuild. For them there exists no future—only a tragic past."[11]

"Elderly," "aged," and "old" will be used loosely to refer to the group in this chapter, but it is important to remember that this is not the only categorization that could be used to describe them and that many people belonging to this category did not fit our contemporary understanding of the terms. The mixing of different people who felt or seemed elderly into the "hardcore" group is part of the reason that, to date, little scholarship on the postwar period has focused on older survivors, resulting in few articles and references in some scholarship about DPs. This chapter introduces members of this displaced group in the US-occupied zone in Germany and discusses their agency and efforts to secure the resettlement futures they imagined for themselves. These survivors believed their futures lay in countries away from the "cemetery" that was postwar Europe, somewhere that would provide a sense of security. It aims to explain their limited emigration opportunities and will pay special attention to survivors displaced in the US-occupied zone in Germany who lingered in camps, sometimes for up to twelve years, before their resettlement. This chapter relies heavily on testimonies of aid workers and official reports written and collected by international aid organizations because few survivor testimonies link their experiences in postwar Germany with their age.

Elderly Jewish DPs in Germany

Some ninety thousand Jews were liberated on German soil in May 1945. Most were between the ages of eighteen and forty-five.[12] Koppel Pinson, the JDC director of Education and Culture for Jewish Displaced Persons in Germany and Austria, noted with dismay in an April 1947 report that "practically no children and no older persons" had survived.[13] A report compiled in July 1945 by the Institute of Jewish Affairs in London and based on registration numbers from survivors in fifty-five concentration camps confirmed Pinson's assessment. Only 2,104 respondents were over forty-five and even fewer children—1,394—had survived and were living in Germany and Austria.[14] The number of Jewish DPs living in these countries increased drastically in 1946 and 1947 with the arrival of Jews who had survived in the Soviet Union and had tried to return to their homes but fled ongoing postwar antisemitic violence in Eastern Europe, such as the Kielce pogrom in July 1946, which resulted in the murder of forty-two Jews. The arrival of these Jews, known as "infiltrees," increased the DP population to about 250,000 in the Allied zones of occupation. With the influx of these mainly Polish Jews came intact families, with children and elderly members, seeking a haven in Allied-occupied Europe. The number of children grew over the course of the postwar period with births, but the older population remained relatively static as elderly individuals died and middle-aged survivors aged into their fifties while they awaited opportunities to emigrate.

Anyone who fell outside of the eighteen to forty-five age range was considered outside the norm. Aid agencies created programs that would give children a chance at a normal childhood after years of hiding, false identities, camp life, and other Holocaust experiences. Similar programs were established for survivors in the "viable" age range in the form of

FIGURE 10.1. Polish Jewish DPs ("infiltrees") arriving in Vienna with the *Bricha* (Hebrew for "flight" or "escape," and the name of an illegal underground movement of Jews to Palestine), Vienna, Austria, 1946. United States Holocaust Memorial Museum (USHMM), courtesy of American Jewish Joint Distribution Committee.

training schools, university classes, and other learning opportunities that would help them become "more attractive" immigrants.[15] Elderly Jews who resided in DP centers in the American zone of occupation were cared for by local German medical professionals, received rations meant to help keep them alive, and chose to be as involved in the life of the center as they wished. Trivia nights, book clubs, religious celebrations, art shows, movies, classes, and lectures were regular occurrences in the DP camps and open to all residents.[16] However, no specific plans were made for the future of the aged in the US zone. In a 1948 JDC report on ORT (Obshchestvo Rasprostraneniya Truda Sredi Yevreyev, or Society for the spreading of vocational work among Jews) activities in displaced persons camps in Germany, Moses Lukaczer described with anger the addition of training classes for children, people with disabilities, and the elderly. Lukaczer questioned the sensibility of the diversion of a significant part of the funds the JDC provided to ORT to help train healthy survivors for their future lives abroad. He continued by wondering about the "purpose of giving courses of unknown worth and relevance to elderly persons and to children under 17." Grouping together the three above-mentioned categories, Lukaczer asked, "Is it true that invalids can become eligible for emigration, for example to the United States after taking ORT courses or is this just talk?"[17]

However, few elderly and frail DPs who did not have family members to care for them remained in DP centers. The postwar situation for older survivors was far from perfect. The buildings that housed all DPs, including the elderly, were decrepit. The residents were regularly moved from one center to another as better facilities became available and as time passed and the camps and homes for the elderly were closed. Additionally, survivors in these assisted living facilities often fell into the "viable" age range. Still, they considered themselves, or were considered by others, to have aged far beyond their years during the Holocaust.[18]

The three hundred-plus elderly DPs housed at the St. Ottilien DP center in Bavaria lived independently in the camp or in the hospital located therein. Some elderly DPs too ill or frail to care for themselves were moved into *Altersheime* (homes for the elderly). A 1946 fundraising video produced by the Central Committee of Liberated Jews in Germany paid special attention to survivors in facilities for the aged and living in Jewish DP centers. In the film, an older woman is cooking for herself surrounded by packed suitcases. The voice-over states sadly, "*Altersheime*. The young were killed. The old aged left to die. These are the people. Our people. Waiting."[19] When and how would these people achieve their resettlement goals?

In addition to survivors who fell within the contemporary understanding of "old age" (fifty-five to seventy), younger survivors often appeared or considered themselves elderly.[20] Premature aging was noted already during the Holocaust and is clear in Anna Seghers's fictional thriller *Transit*, published in 1944. A survivor, Seghers fled her home in Germany soon after the Reichstag fire of 1933 and escaped to Mexico via France. Her protagonist similarly is a refugee seeking a safe haven. In the novel, the narrator describes with disbelief a scene in a train station in unoccupied France. The narrator recalls:

> [I] had to climb over a woman lying among suitcases, bundles, and piles of guns, nursing a baby. How the world has aged in this single year (1940)! The infant looked old and wrinkled, the nursing mother's hair was gray, and the faces of the baby's two little brothers watching over her shoulder seemed shameless, old, and sad. Old also were the eyes of these two boys

> from whom nothing had been concealed, neither the mystery of death nor the mystery of birth.[21]

The disbelief at how old survivors appeared was shared by Allied military troops and aid workers in the immediate postwar period. George Vida, a Jewish military chaplain and Hungarian Jewish refugee to the United States, was stationed in Germany from 1945 to 1946 and again from 1952 to 1956. Vida visited a home for the aged in Berlin in 1945 and recorded with shock: "Their rooms had wooden boards in place of windows, and hope in the future took the place of the heat! And they were not all old people. There were among them also middle-aged and younger people, all of them huddled in bed, just waiting for the winter to pass and perhaps better days to come. Or else, for death to come and redeem them."[22] In a letter he sent home, American soldier Irving P. Eisner shared his encounter with a Jewish DP survivor in Buchenwald: "He was 30 but he looked like twice that age and acted like that too."[23] This situation repeated itself frequently when aid workers encountered survivors. Faced with a small but constant number of people who felt old, were categorized as elderly, and were sometimes infirm, caregivers were met with new and unanticipated challenges after liberation.

Emigration Opportunities and Obstacles

Emigration was one of the foremost goals for survivors and, on survivors' behalf, those caring for them in postwar Germany. This was especially true for Jewish DPs, many of whom longed to leave Europe. However, immigration quotas, antisemitism, and political issues continued to act as a bar to the mass emigration of Holocaust survivors. And, as early as 1946, Jewish aid workers were evaluating survivors' worth and their likelihood of emigration based on whether any country would accept them and if they were willing to go. Jewish leaders realized there would be Jews left in Germany indefinitely, but they also believed those who remained had no choice; those who were able would leave for Mandate Palestine or elsewhere when the opportunity arose.

World Jewry believed the solution to the "Jewish problem" in Germany, Italy, Austria, and China had finally arrived with the establishment of the Jewish state in 1948 and the passage of the American Displaced Persons Act that same year. However, both emigration options came with their own restrictions, caveats, and exclusions. The DP Act of 1948 was written to exclude as many survivors as possible. Not only did it limit the number of people who could qualify, but it also set the date of December 22, 1945, as the cutoff by when displaced persons had to have registered in an Allied-operated DP center to be considered. Because the infiltrees began to arrive in liberated Europe in 1946, this policy excluded two-thirds of the DP population. While Israel would eventually allow the immigration of all Jews wishing to settle there, its early representatives made efforts to protect the soon-to-be state from an influx of sick, aged, and infirm DPs. They argued that, once established, Israel could not take in DPs during the first few years of its existence—especially not those needing care.[24] Nahum Goldmann of the Jewish Agency argued there was a strong chance the new state would have to adopt a policy of voluntary limited immigration. It was the usefulness of the DP to the new state that would determine their eligibility. Goldman candidly expressed this sentiment when he declared: "Let us face the realities. The Jewish state, in the prevailing terrific situation will have to care for itself, not for refugees. It can use, under the dictate of *sacro egoismo* [egocentric nationalism], only young people who can shoot. It cannot be interested in this time in youth aliyah, in children, in families, and old people. . . . The DPs in general do not represent the human material Eretz Yisroel needs today."[25]

Despite this proclamation, "hardcore" Jewish DPs risked imprisonment in their attempts to reach the *Yishuv*. The "elderly Jews" captured in contemporary images on trains and aboard ships were part of the *Aliyah Bet* illegal immigration to Palestine.[26] Despite the risks and continued obstacles facing aged Jews, the state was the proclaimed great hope for survivors and their caregivers.[27] However, Israel remained largely closed to the "hardcore" for the first seven years of its existence.[28]

The elderly and infirm who did reach Israel were cared for under the auspices of the Malben program (*Mosdot le-tipul be-ʻolim nehshalim*), which provided aid for the aged, people with disabilities, and those with long-term illnesses.[29] The JDC, the United Jewish Appeal, and the Israeli government ran and funded Malben. The JDC assumed control of Malben in 1950 and expanded the program by paying for the building expenses associated with new medical facilities—homes for the elderly and the sick.[30]

As JDC's leader, Leavitt lamented in a 1955 meeting, "What is perhaps most tragic is that the vast majority of the aged under Malben care are healthy and would under 'normal' circumstances—had their families not been exterminated by Nazism and war—not have been compelled to live in institutions at all."[31]

Israel's independence and the expansion of the DP Act resulted in the immigration of three-quarters of all Jewish DPs remaining in occupied Europe. Relocating these survivors to their new homes took almost four years. The visa process was slow, and finding places to resettle hundreds of thousands of DPs took more time than expected. Despite the best efforts of the IRO, the JDC, the Hebrew Immigrant Aid Society (HIAS), the United Service for New Americans (USNA), and several other aid organizations, more than two thousand Jewish survivors categorized as "hardcore" remained in West Germany at the end of 1952, all of them in Föhrenwald, the last remaining Jews-only DP camp in operation.[32] These were the absolute hardest cases to resettle. In a confidential statement issued by the JDC, the author noted with sorrow that perhaps a more fitting name than "hardcore" would be the "unwanted," because they were so difficult to place.[33] Despite the best efforts of international aid workers to negotiate housing abroad, the "hardcore" remained stateless in Germany, Austria, Italy, and China.

China

Where possible, Jews had fled far beyond Europe, including to China, before the war, but dire circumstances in the postwar period led them to seek resettlement elsewhere. It seemed there was hope for many DPs to immigrate to Israel in November 1948, when the new state vowed to accept the twenty-four thousand Jewish refugees—including the elderly and infirm—who had lived out the war in China. These Jews, who ranged in age from young children to individuals in their eighties and older, were put in a ghetto run by Japanese forces during the war and lived in hovels in poverty after liberation.[34] Carl Jacobson (fig. 10.2) was among the Jewish survivors trapped in China. He fled to Shanghai in 1939 from Germany. His age prevented him from working and he was largely reliant on JDC support to survive in postwar China. As an elderly German Jew, his chances of immigrating to the United States were slim and he spent the years after the war's end waiting for his resettlement abroad. While Jacobson and this group of elderly DPs received supplies and care from UNRRA, IRO, and JDC, JDC assumed responsibility for their resettlement to Israel.[35]

Many of these DPs, including the German and Austrian population who were ordered to leave China in 1945, argued they could not go home.[36] While China reversed this order, country quotas from Central and Eastern Europe were so limited in the West that survivors had little chance of qualifying for a visa and overwhelmingly remained where they were. A Jewish Telegraphic Agency bulletin from December 14, 1954, reported that 790 Jews remained in China waiting for a chance to emigrate. Of the total, 115 were under the age of eighteen and three hundred were over sixty years old. Within this group were about 160 individuals who were identified as "hardcore" cases and fifty who were hospitalized.[37] Most of these Jews were between the ages of forty-five and sixty and fell outside of the "viable" group mentioned above. In response to a JDC survey of this population, half of the respondents declared they wanted to settle in Israel. The other half had indicated different countries and that they had no desire to stay in China.[38] JDC asked Israel to provide more visas for those previously denied entry, especially for the "hardcore" survivors, citing Malben's expanded care network.[39] The DPs who refused to settle in Israel were brought to Germany and settled in the Föhrenwald DP Assembly Center where they awaited emigration opportunities.

Chozrim

Zionist propagandists and teachers in the camps portrayed Israel as an idyllic and safe country with rolling fields of flowers and beautiful beaches. However, the reality of malaria, frequent clashes with Arab neighbors, the hardships of daily life in a developing land, and the struggle to find a place to settle were rarely discussed. This disconnect became a problem in late 1948 when the first *chozrim*, or returners, began to trickle back into Germany demanding the reinstatement of their DP status and telling people about the realities of life in the "promised land."[40] The fact that roughly 10 percent of the returners were fifty years old or older and that many of these individuals traveled with their younger family

FIGURE 10.2. "Carl Jacobson reads a newspaper on his bunk in the Hongkew ghetto. Jacobson, who due to his advanced age was unable to work, relied on support from the JDC to survive, both before and after liberation." Shanghai [Kiangsu], China. USHMM, courtesy of the American Jewish Joint Distribution Committee. JDC Photo, 07/1946.

members, helped convince the "hardcore" DPs to fight for resettlement elsewhere.[41] The vast majority of émigrés who came back to Germany had settled in Israel via both the *Bricha* and IRO. However, others returned from the United States, South America, and Australia, where they had been unable to make life work and hoped for a second chance. The returners from Israel crossed—illegally, according to their passports, but legally according to the German government—into Germany and resettled in the remaining DP camps.[42]

The IRO, the Office of the Military Government US, international aid workers, and later the Federal Republic of Germany argued over who was responsible for these returners. However, these offices and organizations had more to worry about than a few dozen *chozrim*. Not only was IRO in the process of consolidating DP camps, but the Office of the United States High Commissioner to Germany was working to transfer its control over all remaining DPs to the Federal Republic of Germany. Both undertakings were met with outraged protests by the remaining DPs, who feared for their continued safety outside of the DP assembly centers where they had lived for so long and for their future lives under their former oppressors. The "hardcore" proclaimed, "We have no desire to be under either the political or legal protection of those who murdered our parents, children, sisters and brothers."[43] They sent letters and published pleas in international papers demanding that world Jewry "do everything to combat this scandal."[44] Despite their best efforts, DPs fell under German control on December 1, 1951. From that point on they were known as *Heimatlose Ausländer* (homeless foreigners), although they continued to be called, and to call themselves, DPs.[45]

Roughly 1,950 people remained in Föhrenwald, with 480 camp inhabitants under the age of fourteen and twelve hundred residents qualifying for JDC aid based on their health and age. These numbers increased slightly with the addition of survivors from Landsburg and Feldafing when these two centers were closed, but again leveled out with an estimated two thousand legal residents living in the camp in September 1952, all identified as "hardcore" by the IRO and JDC.

The massive influx of *chozrim* into Germany took place during these years of change. The trickle of *chozrim* increased between 1948 and 1950, peaking in 1953.[46] The prospect of restitution also drew a significant number of returners to West Germany and slowed down emigration after the May 1950 Bavarian restitution law proclaimed that victims of Nazi persecution who lost family members and continued to suffer from health issues could receive compensation if they lived in Bavaria.[47] Many "hardcore" DPs deemed this law too restrictive and claimed that the compensation payouts, which were determined by the government and based on a doctor's assessment of the level of disability or illness one displayed, were insufficient for their losses. A poster created at a protest meeting in 1950, convened by the Invalids' Union, issued several resolutions and demanded they be included in an adapted version of the law.

Like the legal residents of Jews-only DP centers, the *chozrim* wanted to ensure that they were granted fair compensation for their suffering even if it meant returning to DP camps in Germany. The number of returners began to climb sharply in the 1950s when the compensation negotiations between the Adenauer government and the Conference on Jewish Material Claims Against Germany (Claims Conference) and between the State of Israel and West Germany, culminated in the Luxembourg Agreements and offered compensation to survivors who qualified. This law stipulated that the "Federal Republic of Germany commits itself to delivering goods worth a total of 3 billion DM to the state of Israel over a period of 12 years, for the support, integration, and resettlement of Jewish victims of persecution who gained Israeli citizenship through immigration."[48] Subsection (b) of this law required that West Germany set aside additional funds to help support Jews living outside of Israel and to help integrate and resettle the Jews outside of DP centers. Living in Germany or a German-speaking country made it easier for those seeking compensation to secure these funds because applicants had to show their connection to German language and culture, be seen by a German doctor, and go for reexaminations when, as happened regularly, claims were rejected.[49]

Many DPs begrudged the presence of *chozrim* in their midst as well as the negativity they brought upon the "legal" camp inhabitants. They felt conflicted; they wanted to aid their fellow Jews, but they were concerned about this new competition for resources and emigration visas. By 1953, 4,137 people lived in Föhrenwald and somewhere around 2,738 were forty-six and older.[50] Hoping to staunch the influx of future returners, the DP groups remaining in the last camps asked German and Jewish authorities to seal Föhrenwald to returners. In several reports from August through October 1952, the Camp Committee pleaded with JDC and the Bavarian government to prevent the resettlement of returners in the DP center. Dr. Ludwig Erhard, the German Minister of Economic Affairs, stated that "the Jews themselves demanded protection against the illegals."[51] The pleas of the DPs were not answered in 1952, but with the ever-increasing number of *chozrim* settling in closed portions of Föhrenwald, the Bavarian government decided they must do something. They would never be able to resettle the "hardcore" survivors if more Jews continued to arrive, and ending the DP camp system was a central priority for the government. To this end, Bavarian officials replaced the DP police with German police officers in August 1954. These officers oversaw and enforced the legal entry of all individuals into the camp, which finally led to the stabilization of the number of camp inhabitants in Föhrenwald.

By March 1954, only about 150 ill, infirm, or elderly *chozrim* remained in Föhrenwald, along with some of their family members, bringing the total number of returners in the camp to 175.[52] Many of these individuals were eventually given resettlement grants and integrated into Germany.[53] The German Ministry of Labor and Social Welfare mandated that eighty-four of the remaining returners in Föhrenwald be transferred to the Ludwigsfeld center near Munich.[54] Ludwigsfeld was a "mixed" DP assembly center inhabited mainly by non-Jewish East European DPs. Most of the eighty-four returners who resettled there had valid emigration visas but were not scheduled for immediate departure.[55] Of the total number of cases in Ludwigsfeld, only four were not "persons over 65 years of age, . . . people [who] are unemployable on account of sickness or in cases of women with two children under 14 and who have no husband."[56] Another fifty-four returners in Föhrenwald were booked to depart Germany within weeks.

Integration in Europe

Realizing that many of Föhrenwald's "hardcore" cases would need resettlement opportunities in Germany, JDC began working with the various divisions involved with creating housing in the Federal Republic. One option proposed by Mary Palevsky, JDC's director of Social Services, was to move the elderly DPs, fifty-five and older, into the Munich *Kultusgemeinde* (Jewish community's) *Altersheim*. The *Kultusgemeinde* guaranteed spots in this "new nicely furnished, forty-two bed institution." Palevsky determined that there were sixty-five residents over the age of sixty and forty-seven people older than fifty-five, totaling 112 individuals. Each person was interviewed to ensure they would be a good fit for the *Altersheim*. In the end, only five people qualified, one of whom did not even fit within the JDC's parameters for the "old age project." He was a forty-eight-year-old man who suffered from chronic polyarthritis and was considered a "semi-invalid," according to the report, in which Palevsky noted the "extremely complex character of the individual family situation and the difficulty of fitting it into the projects designed for groups. In other words, each situation seem[ed] to require an individual solution, custom tailored to fit that case." She went on to discuss the "atypical family composition characteristic of the DP group—older men having lost wives and children, are now 'remarried' to women a generation or more younger than themselves. This shows up in our study in the form of 20 wives obviously too young to enter an Altersheim."[57] Additionally, nineteen families with at least one elderly parent refused to consider separation.

Among those who abandoned their plans to immigrate to Israel, despite having registered to do so, were Orthodox Jews who remained in Föhrenwald after 1954.[58] Members of this group were offered places in the *Altersheim* mentioned above, but they proved problem cases, refusing this resettlement option. They specified that the kosher kitchen did not meet their standards and that they wanted to cook for themselves to ensure their food adhered to kashrut. Palevsky stated with annoyance that the JDC offered a *mashgiach* (a Jew who oversees and ensures the kosher status of a Jewish organization) to supervise the kitchen and food, "at considerable expense to AJDC," but this plan was rejected.[59] This group also included families with elderly members and young children. These DPs demanded their integration in Munich in a separate community, away from non-Jewish Germans and non-Orthodox Jews, with all the necessities to live an Orthodox life. Although the number of older DPs had gone down by 1955, the aged still made up 30 percent of Föhrenwald's population.[60] This was double the number of elderly people (defined as sixty-five and older) found in communities across Western Europe.[61] Over the course of the following two years, these DPs fought the German authorities at both the federal and state levels and asserted their agency to determine their community's future outside the DP center. In the end, members of Föhrenwald's Orthodox community forced the Bavarian state and the German federal governments to include them in the process of decision-making. They ended up with all their religious needs met, living in their own gated center located securely within southern Bavaria. The result, while not perfect, was "suitable" according to all involved parties.[62]

The Closure of Föhrenwald

International Jewish aid organizations spent the 1950s reaching out to countries around the world looking to resettle "hardcore" DPs. JDC also set up an office that reviewed each case file, evaluated each family member's chances at success in countries willing to take in DPs, and tried to match survivors with available visas. They also worked simultaneously with the Federal Republic of Germany to create resettlement plans for DPs who could not, or would not, leave Germany. In the end, they were successful. By 1956, DPs were leaving Föhrenwald at an increasingly rapid rate as housing opportunities and visas became available. However, a Claims Conference annual report from that same year recorded that there was a waiting list for acceptance into homes for the aged in Germany, Yugoslavia, and the Netherlands. The author remarked that, "To add fuel to the catastrophe, many aged are alone in the world, and children or other near kinsmen who would normally have rallied to their aid, had themselves lost their lives in concentration camps."[63] For many of the "hardcore," the final months in DP camps were incredibly stressful, as they waited to see what their futures held. Some survivors despaired as their family members qualified for visas to the US but they did not. One extreme and heartbreaking case involved a family of three: an elderly blind father and his two daughters. Although granted two visas, the daughters chose to stay together in Germany as a family, but their father refused to let this happen and died by suicide so they could immigrate. Hard decisions were the only ones available to these survivors.[64]

In the end, Norway and Sweden took hundreds of tubercular patients. Norway also accepted fifty blind survivors, while Belgium took 237 elderly ones. The United States made special accommodations for people with physical disabilities and the Office of New Americans worked with individual communities to arrange for the placement of these survivors on a case-by-case basis. Those unable to qualify for visas elsewhere and willing to go to Israel did so. The remaining eight hundred DPs in Germany were integrated into German society in independent living environments as well as in Jewish assisted living facilities. The closure of the Föhrenwald DP camp in February 1957 ended the Jewish DP era, and only those Jews unwilling to leave Germany until they had a visa to North America remained in non-Jewish camps. While many of the "hardcore" survivors argued they were forced to integrate into society in countries they would never willingly have chosen for themselves, their futures were, in part, shaped by their age, demands, and refusal to emigrate elsewhere. The elderly DPs who had called Föhrenwald home and who were resettled in Germany reported that their new homes were acceptable, and they had integrated into their new lives well.[65]

An analysis of elderly survivors in DP camps in the US-occupied zone of Germany, a group rarely mentioned in discussions about the Holocaust, sheds light on the postwar life of the Jews slated for death by the Nazis and their accomplices. As this chapter illustrated, the definition and understanding of who qualified as elderly changed drastically after the war to include ill, infirm, and middle-aged people, who often argued they were old before their time. Even though these "hardcore" DPs were considered unattractive candidates for emigration, they fought for the futures they imagined for themselves. At present, scholars have only completed a cursory examination of this topic, leaving many unanswered questions. While the documents are scarce and often protected by medical privacy laws, for example with regard to personal information held in archives of the Claims Conference and JDC, research about the elderly can shed light on what happens after genocide and how people of all ages worked to rebuild some semblance of the lives they lost.

Notes

1 Gemma La Guardia Gluck, *My Story* (David McKay, 1961), 100.

2 Dan Stone, " 'Somehow the Pathetic Dumb Suffering of These Elderly People Moves Me More Than Anything': Caring for Elderly Holocaust Survivors in the Immediate Postwar Years," *Holocaust and Genocide Studies* 32, no. 3 (2018): 384–403.

3 Pat Thane, "The 20th Century," in *The Long History of Old Age*, ed. Pat Thane (Thames and Hudson, 2005), 266; Zorach Warhaftig, *Uprooted: Jewish Refugees and Displaced Persons After Liberation*, From War to Peace 5 (Institute of Jewish Affairs of the American Jewish Congress and World Jewish Congress, 1946), 53.

4 Moses A. Levitt, *The Year of Survival 1946 Annual Report the American Jewish Joint Distribution Committee*, JDC Archives, item 1231257, 10.

5 I used the spelling of the JDC Archives for the Hebrew terms throughout this chapter and consulted with an Israeli scholar to ensure consistency and standardization throughout this article.

6 The earliest use of the term "hardcore," "hard core," or "hard-core" that I found appeared in an article in *Life* magazine titled "DPs: Millions of Displaced Persons Stream Across Europe to Their Homes" from July 30, 1945. The two-page article included the subheading, "Those Who Do Not Want to Go Home Are 'Hard Core' of DP Problem." The term "hardcore" will be used interchangeably with "elderly" and "old" throughout this chapter.

7 Mary Palevsky, "Old Age Project—Camp Föhrenwald," August 28, 1953, JDC Archives, item 2638518.

8 Theodore D. Feder, letter from AJDC-Frankfurt to Dr. H. Selveri, Country Directors' Conference, September 26, 1956, Visit to Frankfurt/Country Directors' Reports, JDC Archives, item 2707793.

9 "Chronically Ill DP's Successfully Absorbed Norway Agrees to Admit 78 More for Germany," July 14, 1955, Norway, Refugees TB Patients, 1952–1954, JDC Archives, item 705871, 2.

10 Dr. A. Kohane, Legal Population—Camp Foehrenwald, January 10, 1957, Camp Foehrenwald—Closing, Emigration and Integration 1957–1958, JDC Archives–NY, 2.

11 Moses A. Leavitt, "Ten Years Later, Leavitt, Moses, 1955–1956," November 25, 1955, JDC Archives, item 972233, 6.

12 Koppel Pinson, "Jewish Life in Liberated Germany: A Study of the Jewish DPs," *Jewish Social Studies* 9, no. 2 (1947): 101–26.

13 Pinson, "Jewish Life in Liberated Germany."

14 Warhaftig, *Uprooted*, 53.

15 For more on emigration opportunities and restrictions see USHMM, 1996.A.0454, Citizens Committee on Displaced Persons, 1955–1956.

16 Report of the First Half of 1951, June 27, 1951, Germany, Displaced Persons, 1951, JDC Archives, item 673481, 5.

17 M. Lukaczer, *World ORT Union Weekly Summary*, October 15, 1948, Germany, Displaced Persons, 1948, JDC Archives–NY, 1.

18 For an example of an elderly survivor who remained in a DP center in Austria with her elderly children, see photo 2012.184.1, of a 106-year-old woman, USHMM, collections.ushmm.org/search/catalog/irn46976?rsc=21966&cv=0&x=1885&y=1359&z=1.1e-4.

19 Central Committee of Liberated Jews in Germany, *These Are the People*, Feldafing, Germany, 1946, USHMM, accession number 2001.316.1, RG number RG-60.3361, film ID 2281.
20 Thane, "The 20th Century," 267.
21 Anna Seghers, *Transit* (Aufbau-Verlag GmbH, 1951), 25, www.eriesd.org/cms/lib/PA01001942/Centricity/Domain/691/Transit%20-%20Anna%20Seghers.pdf.
22 George Vida, *From Doom to Dawn: A Jewish Chaplain's Story of Displaced Persons* (Jonathan David, 1967), 25.
23 Letter from Irving P. Eisner, Buchenwald, May 15, 1945, USHMM ACC. 2012.16.1, Irving P. Eisner Collection; *Documenting Life and Destruction: Holocaust Sources in Context*, vol. 5: *1944–1946*, ed. Leah Wolfson (Rowman and Littlefield in association with USHMM, 2015), 57.
24 Abraham Klausner J., *A Letter to My Children: From the Edge of the Holocaust* (Holocaust Center of Northern California, 2002), 164.
25 Klausner, *Letter to My Children*, 170.
26 George Vida, interview by Annmarie Miller, September 29, 1980, USHMM, RG-50.477.1806, accessed February 5, 2024, collections.ushmm.org/search/catalog/irn87735.
27 Surveys filled out by Jewish DPs about their hopes for future emigration often listed Palestine as the first choice and the crematoria as their second option.
28 For a visual example of elderly people illegally immigrating to Palestine, see "Elderly DPs on board a train, say farewell to friends before leaving on the first leg of their journey to British Mandate Palestine, 1947," USHMM, photograph number 10159, collections.ushmm.org/search/catalog/pa1045504 (URL unavailable).
29 For more information about the work of the Malben program, see Joanna Sliwa and Anat Kutner's chapters in this volume.
30 "Tells UJA Mission of Plans to Extend Malben Work in Israel," *JTA Daily News Bulletin*, October 27, 1955.
31 Moses A. Leavitt, Moses A. Leavitt JDC Executive Vice-Chairman, May 30, 1956, Annual Meeting, 1955 [*sic*], JDC Archives–NY, 6.
32 JDC, Current Programs, September 11, 1952, Council of Jewish Federations and Welfare Funds 1952, JDC Archives–NY.
33 Charles Jordan, "The Foehrenwald Story," Legal Records, Report from the JDC, 2/1954, JDC Archives–Jerusalem.

34 "14,000 Jews in Shanghai Slum in Desperate Need of Housing Look Forward to Emigration," *JTA Daily News Bulletin* (New York), March 5, 1946.
35 Table of Contents, International Refugee Organization, IV–XII 1952, JDC Archives–NY, 61.
36 "China Orders Repatriation of Jews from Shanghai to Germany: Thousands Are Panic Stricken," *JTA Daily News Bulletin* (New York), December 16, 1945.
37 "Efforts to Find Temporary Asylum for Shanghai Jews Stepped Up: Haven Sought in Japan," *JTA Daily News Bulletin* (New York), December 20, 1948.
38 "Only 790 Jews Reported Remaining in China: Seek Emigration," *JTA Daily News Bulletin* (New York), December 14, 1954.
39 "Israeli Govt. Agrees to Admit All Jewish Refugees in China," *JTA Daily News Bulletin* (New York), November 19, 1948.
40 For more information on the returner population, see Kierra Crago-Schneider, "Jewish 'Shtetls' in Postwar Germany: An Analysis of Interactions Among Jewish Displaced Persons, Germans, and Americans Between 1945 and 1957 in Bavaria," (PhD diss., University of California, 2013).
41 List for Illegals, list of illegal DPs in Föhrenwald, in Guide of Records of the Displaced Camps and Centers in Germany, box 42A, folder 573, reel 43.223 (RG 294.2), 22–47, YIVO Institute for Jewish Research (henceforth YIVO-NY). I used a sample of 658 returners with listed ages shared with me by Ori Yehudai, author of *Leaving Zion: Jewish Emigration from Palestine and Israel After World War II* (Ohio State University Press, 2020), to come up with this estimate. I confirmed Yehudai's findings in the archival source cited above.
42 The Foehrenwald Story [report], March 1, 1954, Germany, Displaced Persons Camps: Foehrenwald, Jan–Jun 1954 AR 45/54 #327, JDC Archives–NY, 2.
43 Angelika Konigseder and Juliane Wetzle, *Waiting for Hope: Jewish Displaced Persons in Post–World War II Germany* (Northwestern University Press, 2001), 150.
44 Föhrenwald Committee, Zloto, "We Must Not Let This Happen," *Unzer shtime*, November 14, 1951; report from Germany, German Legal Bulletins, ORG 2, Office of General Counsel, JDC Archives–Jerusalem, 1.
45 I use the terms "Displaced Persons" (DPs) throughout this article despite the 1951 name change to eliminate confusion and because this is how the population was referred to internally and in international aid documents.

46 Report by Charles Jordan, "The Story of Föhrenwald," May 1, 1957, C45.072.2, Legal Aid, JDC Archives–Jerusalem, 6.
47 Union of Jewish Invalids, Records of the Displaced Persons Camps in Germany, 1946–1954, series 6, posters of the Action Committee of the Union, YIVO-NY, 1.
48 Conference on Jewish Material Claims Against Germany, "Measures to Compensate for National Socialist Injustice: A Timeline" (Berlin: Federal Ministry of Finance [Germany] Public Relations Division, 2020) 7, accessed October 20, 2024, www.congreso.es/docu/docum/ddocum/dosieres/sleg/legislatura_14/spl_25/pdfs/82.pdf.
49 Nathan Durst, "Emotional Wounds That Never Heal," *Jewish Political Studies Review* 14, nos. 3–4 (2002): 2.
50 Report on Medical and Social Problems in Germany, June 28, 1954, Germany, Medical, 1951–1953, JDC Archives–NY.
51 Ministerrat Bavaria, Auszug aus dem Protokoll des Ministerrats, 1953, Minutes for the Bavarian Ministry Meeting on the Jewish Illegal Returners, Bestand Bayerische Staatskanzlei BayHStA-Munich, 11.
52 Report of the Executive Vice-Chairman to the Executive Committee Meeting Tuesday, January 17, 1956, 1955–1964, JDC Archives–NY.
53 Returners who did not fall into the "hardcore" category were sent to temporary housing while awaiting their return to Israel or their immigration to South America.
54 "Jewish Refugees Transferred from Foehrenwald to Non-Jewish Camps," *JTA Daily News Bulletin*, April 19, 1956.
55 "Jewish Refugees Transferred from Foehrenwald."
56 Monek Einziger, letter from M. Einziger to Mr. Theodore D. Feder, May 4, 1956, Germany: Camp Foehrenwald—Closing, Emigration and Integration 1955–1956, JDC Archives–Geneva.
57 Palevsky, "Old Age Project," 3.
58 Kierra A. Crago-Schneider, "A Community of Will: The Resettlement of Orthodox Jewish DPs from Föhrenwald," *Holocaust and Genocide Studies* 32, no. 1 (2018): 93–110.
59 Palevsky, "Old Age Project," 3.
60 In twentieth-century Europe old age fell between the ages of fifty-five and seventy, usually settling at sixty-five, when someone qualified for a pension. Thane, "The 20th Century," 267.

61 Letter from AJDC, Paris-Budget Department to Miss Dorothy Speiser, Re: Estimated AJDC Budget Requirements, 1956, September 24, 1956, Budget 1956, JDC Archives–Geneva, 16; Pavlesky, "Old Age Project," 4.

62 Feder, letter from AJDC-Frankfurt, 16.

63 Claims Conference, "Conference on Jewish Material Claims Against Germany Annual Report," December 31, 1955, Claims Conference, Annual Report, 1956, JDC Archives–NY, 24.

64 Karlis Kalnins, "Those Who Remain," n.d., Lutheran World Federation report, in Mark Wyman, *DPs: Europe's Displaced Persons, 1945–1951* (Cornell University Press, 1989), 203.

65 Konigseder and Wetzel, "Waiting for Hope," 211–15.

11

CARE FOR OLDER HOLOCAUST SURVIVORS

The Work of the Claims Conference and JDC, 1954–1960

Joanna Sliwa

> The aftermath of brutal Nazism has left in its wake, among the survivors, a large number of widows and widowers, aged parents without sons and daughters, in many European cities. They need and in truth are receiving, the care of the Jewish people among whom they find themselves. Added to this poignant situation is the broader effect, felt universally, of the constantly growing number of the aged in the population as a whole.[1]

This quote derives from a pamphlet that the rescue, relief, and rehabilitation arm of the American Jewish community, the American Jewish Joint Distribution Committee (JDC), issued in January 1957.[2] In the twelve years since the end of World War II, the landscape of assistance for older Jewish Holocaust survivors was evolving. The last displaced persons (DP) camp for Jews, Föhrenwald in Germany, closed in February 1957. By then, survivors who had been at least sixty years old when the war ended had reached the age of seventy-two and above. That same year, JDC conducted a survey of older survivors in Europe to glean their numbers, backgrounds, frameworks of care, and their needs. The findings outlined plans for non-institutional (open care) and institutional (closed care) services. Five principles of assistance emphasized championing the productivity of older adults, fostering their independence, cultivating their creativity, offering closed care as a last resort, and ensuring that older Jews received respectful treatment.[3] The Conference on Jewish Material Claims Against Germany (Claims Conference), created just six years earlier (in 1951) to negotiate with the Federal Republic of Germany (West Germany) for a measure of justice for Jewish Holocaust survivors, followed these objectives when evaluating grant requests.

This chapter examines the early initiatives of the Claims Conference and its member organization, JDC, in assessing the situation of older Jews after the Holocaust, envisioning care for them, supporting age-tailored and need-based projects, and in doing so, establishing a blueprint for advocating for and assisting older survivors. The focus is on the years 1954–60. JDC had been pursuing its programs for older survivors. However, it was not until 1954 that the completed negotiations with the West German government allowed for the transfer of funds to the Claims Conference and for their distribution through JDC. By 1960, shifts in care for older survivors were influenced by the medical needs of elderly Jews, political and social changes, economic factors, population movements, and reparation and compensation programs.

Records in the JDC Archives form the basis for this study, and convey the perspectives of the activists, professional staff, and institutions dedicated to Jewish social welfare. As a major member of the Claims Conference, its advisor on grant proposals, and distributor and overseer of funds, JDC has produced and kept voluminous documentation about its own and the Claims Conference's activities. If JDC channeled relief worldwide, Claims Conference funding for older Jews was designated for those in Austria, Belgium, France, Germany, Great Britain, Holland, Italy, Luxembourg, Sweden, Switzerland, and Yugoslavia (in addition to a few countries in South America). This chapter focuses on care for older Jewish Holocaust survivors in Belgium, the Netherlands, Italy, and Yugoslavia. The material about older survivors in these four countries illuminates the issues that affected how care for older Jews was conceptualized and realized, and what older people were experiencing in the first fifteen years after the war. The four case studies demonstrate, too, a hope for the renewal and future of Jewish life. A focus on those four countries expands the geography of the aftermath of the Holocaust by drawing attention to countries where the situation of survivors has not received much scholarly attention.

If quotations from primary sources and place names repeat the terminology from the past in reference to older adults and care for older people, this chapter employs modern terms that are used in social welfare, international policy, gerontology, and geriatrics.[4] While in the 1957 survey JDC had asked for the numbers of Jews over sixty-five years of age (for men) and sixty (for women) in Belgium, the Netherlands, Italy, and Yugoslavia, thereby defining "older people" according to their gender, the personnel from some nursing homes included individuals as young as fifty-six in their responses. Thus old age was a fluid concept.

A plethora of studies examine care for older Jewish Holocaust survivors today, but the lives of and assistance for them have not been prominent topics of historical inquiry. The efforts of JDC and the Claims Conference reveal how their work has continued to shape the ways in which the unique needs of older survivors have been addressed over the years. A focus on the two Jewish organizations also illuminates aspects of their histories and cooperation. Although the post-Holocaust activities of JDC on behalf of Jews worldwide have been garnering scholarly attention, there is a lacuna in understanding the endeavors of the Claims Conference.[5] This chapter engages in this unexplored part of postwar history.

JDC

Founded in 1914 to assist Jews in Palestine, for whom the outbreak of World War I interrupted aid, JDC expanded its activities to vulnerable Jews elsewhere. With the rise of Nazism, JDC amplified its efforts through material assistance, rescue networks, and medical care. The US entry into World War II in December 1941 forced JDC to officially stop its activities in German-occupied Europe. Still, JDC personnel channeled help clandestinely, serving as a lifeline to Jews.

After the Holocaust, JDC assisted survivors and their children. Care for older survivors figured among its programs. As of fall 1947, JDC supported fifty-three nursing homes in ten countries: one home each in Bulgaria, China, and Greece; two homes in Yugoslavia; three in Czechoslovakia; five in Germany; six in Hungary; nine in France; eleven in Poland; and fourteen in Romania. More than twenty-four hundred older survivors benefited from JDC's assistance (the two homes in Berlin and three in the British zone of Germany did not provide the numbers of people under their care). The largest (registered) numbers of older survivors lived in Romania (835), France (530), Poland (390), Hungary (320), and Czechoslovakia (150).[6]

By 1950, JDC ceased many of its programs in Europe after many survivors had emigrated to the newly created State of Israel. Other reasons for restricting allocations in Europe included fewer funding sources, the removal of JDC branches or impediments to their work in communist countries, and the emergence of new regional priorities. Yet JDC continued to rebuild and support Jewish communities in Europe, especially once it became a major beneficiary of allocations from and, in a way, an operating agency of the Claims Conference.

The Claims Conference

Representatives of twenty-three major Jewish organizations formed the Claims Conference in New York in October 1951 in response to the readiness of West Germany to address Jewish material claims. The organization would negotiate for reparations for heirless and unclaimed Jewish assets, ensure compensation for Jewish Holocaust survivors, rehabilitate and resettle survivors, and reconstruct Jewish life. JDC was an integral part of the Claims Conference from the beginning. At first, this new organization operated from the JDC office in New York City.

Negotiations between Claims Conference representatives, headed by JDC's executive vice chairman, Moses Leavitt, and members of the West German government, culminated in the signing of the Luxembourg Agreement in October 1952 (a separate agreement was signed between West Germany and the State of Israel). Protocol I outlined individual indemnification and Protocol II ensured 450 million DM for the global work of the organization.

While the Claims Conference was the recipient of West German funds for the rehabilitation of Jewish Holocaust survivors and the renewal of Jewish life, the agreements designated JDC as the distributor of the grants. And for the right reasons. The expertise and mission of the Claims Conference focused on ensuring material compensation for Jewish Holocaust survivors. JDC, on the other hand, already had extensive experience responding to the needs of vulnerable Jewish populations. Therefore, every year JDC applied to the Claims Conference for funds, receiving 80 percent of the Claims Conference's annual budget.[7]

Assessing the Situation

Saul Kagan, the Founding Executive Director of the Claims Conference, developed a close relationship with JDC. Through his interactions with JDC professional staff and the documentation that they submitted for Claims Conference funding, Kagan gleaned the aspects of Jewish life that required immediate and long-term responses. This personal and professional context allows us to understand the interdependency of the two organizations concerning assessing the situation of older survivors, evaluating applications for the care of older Jews, conceptualizing such care, and making relevant allocations.

In a meeting at the Board of Directors of the Claims Conference in June 1955, Kagan stated that "the care of aged victims of Nazi persecution is the subject of special attention in the Conference allocations program."[8] In 1954, Claims Conference funds channeled through JDC reached 1,561 older survivors, and in 1955 that number was expected to increase to 1,800 older individuals. To gain a better understanding of the situation of older survivors in Europe, a need for a survey emerged at the October 1955 JDC Country Directors' Conference regarding capital investment in JDC and Claims Conference's areas of operation. The Claims Conference called a meeting on capital investment with JDC headquarters in May 1956. "The care of the aged was recognized as one of the major fields where grants for capital investment would be essential in strengthening and developing the European Jewish communities," reads the text of the survey sent out a year later.[9] One-fourth of all grants for capital investment projects from 1954 to 1956 were channeled for the building, repair, and equipping of nursing homes (the same proportion as for community and youth centers).

In May 1957, JDC published "Serving the Needs of Older People" to offer best practices and ideas. A month later, JDC issued a policy statement regarding programs for "Care of the Aged" and encouraged the Claims Conference to endorse it.[10] Louis Kraft, whom both JDC and the Claims Conference appointed to manage the planning of rebuilding and supporting Jewish communities in Europe, explained to Kagan that "the main purpose is to encourage communities to think in terms of community services rather than the construction of new buildings, as the sole solution to the problem of caring for aged people."[11] Kagan agreed.[12] But while the Claims Conference did not officially adopt JDC's statement, it viewed it as a guiding policy when considering grant applications.[13] In fact, Kagan championed innovative care for older survivors, including residence clubs for single and ambulatory older people.[14] He also explored new and potentially durable avenues of support: from municipalities and governments. Their financial and other forms of assistance, housing legislation for older people, and expertise in geriatric care reflected the Claims Conference's prioritization of administering programs for older survivors and strategizing for a sustainable plan of care once the Allocations funding ceased.

The "Survey on the Care of the Jewish Aged," published in October 1957, illustrates key information about older Jewish Holocaust survivors in selected countries twelve years after the end of World War II. The disproportion of women to men in the older Jewish populations reflected the consequences of Nazi persecution, Jews' survival strategies, and life expectancy for men and women. Another pronounced result of the survey was a comparatively high number of older Jewish people. (The estimate for older people in most Western countries at the time ranged between 8 and 12 percent).[15] The numbers provided in the survey conveyed the near utter destruction of Jewish generations, Jewish communities, and Jewish populations in specific countries.[16]

Elevating Care: Belgium

The Jewish nursing home in Brussels, Belgium, "from many viewpoints, is an eyesore to my American-trained Social worker eyes," Gerda J. Jacobson stated in her letter to Dr. Henry Selver, an expert on social work at the JDC European headquarters in Paris, France. Jacobson asked for help in hiring a woman social worker. The qualifications that she sought in the applicant reflected the diversity of the home's residents and their needs. Jacobson explained,

> The Social worker I have in mind must be firm but kind and patient AND carry authority, some one not too young, she must speak Yiddish, some German, in addition to French, some one [*sic*] who has a heart and is devoted to this kind of complex work, which is far from gay or rewarding in a way. I want a decent human being in this home, which must be organized and I want the Social worker to be in charge of all aspects of the Home,

Survey on the Care of the Jewish Aged, 1957

Age Range of Residents in the 47 Nursing Homes Surveyed	
90 years old and over	56
85–89 years old	237
80–84 years old	542
75–79 years old	615
70–74 years old	474
65–69 years old	339
65 years old and below	315
Total	2,578

Characteristics of the Nursing Homes' Residents			
Gender	Women	Men	Unknown
	1,582	687	309
Marital Status	Couples 167	Singles (likely including widowed people) and of unknown marital status 2,244	
Health	Infirm residents in 28 nursing homes 276		

> except the Administrative side, which will be handled by some one else. The morale of the old people, their emotional well-being, etc., etc., will be strictly and without question the domaine [*sic*] of the Social worker.[17]

In the United States, where Jacobson received her training, social work had been gaining government recognition and professional status since the 1930s.[18] The war delayed such advances in Europe. It was not surprising that Jacobson encountered a lack of interest in her plans in Belgium. Women on the committee overseeing the Jewish nursing home in Brussels, who were traditionally occupied with charitable work, ignored Jacobson's idea to employ professional staff, or at least that was her impression. However, Jacobson found allies in the men on the nursing home's board. This gendered difference may have had something to do with the traditional men's role as managers. It allowed the men to see Jacobson's proposal from a different perspective, one that welcomed innovation and results. Jacobson explained:

> We have 50 to 55 old people here, Russians, Poles, Austrians, Hungarians, Belgian and French, some of the senile, some of them feeble-minded, some of the ailing, others are ill, some of them are quite normal. The morale is rather poor, there is no guidance, no occupational therapy, the emotional and spiritual aspect MUST be improved and I am determined to do what I can in this respect. I have in mind to engage a trained Social worker who has some psychiatric training and perhaps some nursing experience, although we have 2 nurses, one of which I am trying to replace by another one, in addition to them I will hire also a nurses-aid [*sic*].[19]

Nothing came of Jacobson's ideas. As Selver noted to her, hiring social workers qualified to work in nursing homes was something of a novelty, and pursuing the idea could have been impeded by costs and laws affecting hires from outside Belgium.[20]

More information emerged about the Jewish nursing home in Brussels, leading to efforts to address the difficult situation of the home and the inadequate living conditions of its residents.[21] The home, founded in the late nineteenth century, was a two-floor building located in a densely populated area of the city. In 1949, the home underwent improvements with JDC support. In 1956, fifty-five residents, cared for by twelve staff, lived in this home (which had capacity for fifty-nine residents).[22] The needs of the Belgian Jewish community were rising. An estimated twenty thousand Jews lived in Belgium, including about twenty-five hundred older people, or 12 percent of the country's Jewish population.[23] Some of them required institutional assistance, entering a nursing home in Brussels or Antwerp or receiving help from a Belgian Jewish social welfare agency.

Among the approximately one thousand clients of the Aid to Jewish War Victims (Aide aux Israélites Victimes de la Guerre, AIVG), 32 percent were older people.[24] Out of these 350 persons, over one hundred lived in substandard conditions. AIVG gave grants to some of the older Jews to improve their dwellings or to rehouse them. The agency employed one woman to assist older people who were ill. It enabled older survivors to vacation in the countryside. In 1956, ninety people benefited from the program. AIVG also explored creating a club for their clients who lived independently, which points to the agency's efforts to introduce progressive ideas.[25]

To meet their clients' residential and care needs, AIVG supported the construction of a pavilion attached to the current nursing home, and which could accommodate the agency's clients: fifty couples and twenty singles. AIVG reasoned that such a solution could be achieved with the participation of the Belgian government and fall within the state housing plan. This notion of government participation in creating and funding institutions dedicated to care for older Jews was a solution influenced by the war, and quite progressive considering that until the outbreak of World War II, nursing homes fell into the domain of denominational groups.

In 1957, the Jewish nursing home in Brussels applied to the Claims Conference to construct a new home to accommodate ninety beds. At that time, a total of fifty-six older people lived in the home: forty-three women and thirteen men. While the average age was seventy-seven, there were three residents below the age of sixty-five (which again points to the community-specific definition of an eligible older resident), and one person who was ninety-seven years old. Nearly one-half of all residents were former DPs or refugees. Except for three women, all other residents had been born abroad.

A year earlier, a question emerged about the home's viability within five to ten years. Renovations at another Jewish nursing home, in Antwerp, were about to be completed at that time with JDC and Claims Conference funding. It could offer places for people from Brussels, it was hoped. The four-floor building housed forty residents, a little over one-half of them seventy-five years or older. A sizable group of the home's residents (twelve) were Dutch, "which is readily understood if one thinks of the geographical vicinity of Antwerp to Holland and the free movement of the people across the border," the report stated.[26]

More than one-half of all residents in both Antwerp and Brussels were seventy-four years old or younger upon admission. Their entrance into the two Belgian nursing homes was motivated by physical disabilities, mental illness, and social issues (including shortage of housing and isolation). The last reason is particularly important when considering the social and familial networks available to older people from those two homes. Less than one-half of all residents in the two nursing homes had close relatives in Belgium. The older people's marital status also affected their opportunities for remaining in their own dwellings versus seeking institutional support. In both the Brussels and Antwerp nursing homes, out of ninety-six residents, only four were part of couples and the rest were widowed or single.

In 1956, the Brussels home sought from the Claims Conference a recommendation about its future.[27] One perspective emerged in 1958. In a letter to Leonard Seidenman, who led the Belgian desk at the JDC headquarters, Dr. Ladislao Molnar, advisor at the Medical Department at the JDC Geneva office, reported about a waiting list for social services provided by AIVG. On the list were forty-five applicants, most between seventy and seventy-nine years old. All but five had Belgian nationality or had arrived in Belgium before the war. All but nine applicants had relatives in Belgium. Of all the applicants, only eighteen agreed to enter the Brussels nursing home. The hesitancy about entering or refusing to enter the home, known for its inadequate accommodations, demanded a clear direction for the home's future. While institutional care offered the best solution for many AIVG clients, such was not readily available.[28] Then too, older people in Belgium, especially in Brussels, were overwhelmingly refugees, many without relatives. Thus they needed tailored assistance. While it made sense to elevate care for older Jews in Belgium and expand existing homes, the approach did not apply in other places. This view clashed with local, prewar norms of family members assuming care for their elders.

Reconciling Cultural Norms with Postwar Realities: The Netherlands

> In the Netherlands care and housing for the aged is one of the most urgent problems which social work has to solve; it is an even greater problem when it concerns the group of Jewish aged, who, as a result of the last war, has lost so many of her nearest relatives. It is for these reasons that the Board appeals to your assistance and trusts that with your help the project may be realized.[29]

This excerpt from a letter written by Chairman J. A. Polak and Honorary Secretary Susanna A. Meijers of the Home for the Aged in The Hague to the Claims Conference in June 1957 illuminates the issues, expectations, and realities surrounding care for older survivors in the Netherlands. The

Dutch Jewish population as of January 1954 was estimated at twenty-four thousand, of whom just over three thousand were Jews over the age of sixty-five; roughly one-half of them were sixty-six to seventy-two years old, and the rest were seventy-three years old and above.[30] About 60 percent of the Dutch Jewish population lived in Amsterdam, meaning that about eighteen hundred older survivors lived there. Of the total number of older Jews in the Netherlands, 86 percent were Dutch and 9 percent nonnaturalized residents. Many were born in the same city where they entered a nursing home or where they lived prior to admission.[31] This was a starkly different situation from Belgium.

The planned renovations and extensions of existing buildings, and construction of new ones signified hope for the future of Jews in the Netherlands. They also corresponded to the insistence on preserving the continuity of Dutch Jewish customs and conveyed the vitality and stability of the many Jewish communal institutions.[32]

In 1958, the Jewish home for people with disabilities in Amsterdam housed ninety-four residents. The largest group of thirty-seven people consisted of Jews between the ages of seventy and eighty. The three youngest residents were between fifty and sixty years old, and the seven eldest were ninety years old and above. Between 1952 and 1956, 156 residents were admitted to the home.[33] Faced with the urgency to house more older people and confronted with the prevalence of mental health issues among the aging Jewish population, the board decided to expand the home in Amsterdam and construct a Jewish psychiatric institution in Amersfoort (which opened in 1960). The leadership of the home recognized the different needs of the older applicants and was determined not to group everyone together.[34] In addition, the Dutch Jewish leaders requested assistance for older Dutch Jewish Americans who wished to enter nursing homes in the Netherlands. JDC's Seidenman remarked: "It appears that many older people who went to America during the war and who have a small income, now seem to wish to pass their last years back home in Holland. I will be very surprised if the numbers turn out to be rather substantial."[35] In January 1959, that number was five.

The Amsterdam home applied for Claims Conference funding in 1958 to add another wing to its already patchwork building. In 1951, the home moved into the former Portuguese Jewish Hospital. One reason for the decision to remain in Amsterdam was the choice of the older people themselves. "They did not wish neither to live in the periphery of the city nor in a rustic suburb near Amsterdam. It is the wish of most old-aged that they want to live as near as possible to the most vivid part of the town which means to them to be in the middle of life," the chairmen of the home stated in their letter to the Claims Conference in December 1958.[36] Another reason was public transportation access. Many residents had family or friends whom they visited. Out of the 107 residents in December 1958, fifty had children; most were older and could not care for their parents. On the waiting list were 123 more people, with the majority (sixty-one individuals) aged seventy-five to eighty-four. Another issue that explained the need for expanding the Amsterdam home was a housing problem. "Our youth is leaving for Israel, so that for the coming years the problem of the care for the aged will become considerably greater," the letter writers warned.[37]

Two other Jewish nursing homes applied to expand their buildings to accommodate an additional thirty-two individuals in Enschede and forty in Arnhem.[38] According to JDC's Dr. Molnar, adequate facilities for the care of older people in the Netherlands already existed and any expansion should be done in the principal centers of Jewish life.[39] This advice, in turn, purposefully or not, encouraged the concentration of Jews in major urban centers. It was done for the expedient delivery of services, but also, the shrinking of Jewish communities outside major cities raised concern over the continuity of management and leadership. That, in turn, evoked a paternalistic approach toward institutional grant recipients.[40]

The Claims Conference felt compelled to analyze the situation of the Dutch Jewish community's care for older people because of the insistence of the community's representatives and pressure from its influential members. A further analysis strengthened the Claims Conference's resolve, based on JDC's advice, to help the Dutch Jewish community change its approach.[41] That perspective clashed with Dutch Jewish traditions and expectations. The nursing home in The Hague, which applied for a Claims Conference grant in 1957, had been serving fifty-two residents since 1954. Only three years later, the need for places in the home increased drastically. There were seventy-five people between sixty-one and eighty years old on the waiting list. "ALL these people are in urgent and direct need for admission to the Home," Meijers and Polak emphasized.[42] Already in 1954, Dr. Lionel Cosin, JDC medical advisor, observed that the "social admissions" into Dutch Jewish nursing homes may increase "unless there is a well-articulated extra-mural program associated with a preventative health campaign, early medical assessment and physical rehabilitation, to facilitate social reintegration of those individuals back into the community."[43]

In December 1957, the Executive Committee of the Claims Conference reviewed applications for allocations. "The amounts requested by all applicants exceeded by far the anticipated resources of the Conference for the coming year," Saul Kagan stated in his letter to the home in The Hague.[44] Claims Conference leaders faced difficult decisions that could result in disappointment and questioning of the role and work of the organization that affected individual lives and collective fates. Still, the Claims Conference allocated over 35 percent of the requested sum for the nursing home in The Hague.

A JDC study indicated that the Netherlands was the only country with a substantial waiting list (150 people) for nursing homes despite the high ratio of beds to eligible adults. Drs. Molnar and Cosin observed, "it would appear that the excessive demand for beds in Holland is due, not so much to medical and social factors as to customs and cultural patterns."[45] The situation was different elsewhere where substandard living conditions in nursing homes and a low ratio of beds per the older adult population necessitated an inquiry and intervention.

Planning for the Future of a Diverse, Aging Population: Italy

As of May 1958, there were 27,689 Jews registered with Jewish communities throughout Italy.[46] JDC estimated that nearly five thousand of them were sixty-five years of age and older.

> The proportion of the aged in the general population in five major Italian cities of which we possess data ranges from 6 per cent to 10 per cent. The aging of the population shows similar proportions in most western countries and is already the cause of serious concern to social planners. The much larger number of aged among the Jews in Italy [about 18 percent] must, therefore, be viewed as a very serious social problem.[47]

The large number of older Jews in Italy prompted JDC to apply the ratio of seventy beds per thousand people, meaning 350 beds in Italy (in most

Western European countries at the time, the ratio of beds for the institutional care of older people was fifty per thousand older people). JDC estimated that this ratio would be maintained for ten to fifteen years.

Several factors necessitated a solid plan for the care of older Jews. There was a substantial number of foreign-born older Jews without family ties in Italy. The emigration of young Jews left a void in the chain of care. Then too, the lack of activities and services for older Jews, especially in smaller communities, and the transfer of older Jews from Catholic to Jewish nursing homes impelled the need to ensure a Jewish environment for older people.[48] Yet another problem that affected open care was assimilation and intermarriage. Inga Gottfarb of the JDC Office in Rome explained the issue: "Such mixed marriages often create tensions between the old and the young generation and many aged persons prefer to live in an Old Age Home to living with, for example, a Catholic daughter-in-law. It also seems to be a general factor in Italy that a Catholic son-in-law does not have the same responsibilities towards his in-laws as a Jewish son-in-law would have."[49]

"Services to aged persons in Italy, in both the Jewish and general community, are at a lower level than I found in other European countries visited," Deborah Miller, JDC special consultant on care for the aged, reported in September 1956.[50] Her assessment highlights that which was lacking, and which Miller considered essential to creating proper conditions for older survivors: lighting, furniture, space, décor, clothing, recreation, and safety.

In contrast to the situations in Belgium and the Netherlands, few if any older people were on waiting lists for nursing homes. Therefore, it was possible to admit them relatively quickly. An earlier study to establish the number of people sixty-five years and above who were assisted by JDC and who could be interested in entering a nursing home revealed 120 such individuals—forty-eight men and seventy-two women.[51] While eight of the prospective applicants were Italian nationals, most (twenty-two individuals) were Austrian; others came from Bulgaria, Czechoslovakia, Germany, Hungary, Lithuania, Poland, Romania, Russia, and Yugoslavia. Among JDC clients were nine non-Jewish spouses of Jews. Out of the sixty-five documented cases, thirty people were no longer independent. Out of 120 elderly people, 105 were considered ineligible for emigration.

Older survivors who entered Jewish nursing homes were a diverse group. The Milan Jewish Home for the Aged housed its maximum forty-four residents (eleven men and thirty-three women) with an average age of eighty. The residents were of a higher social class than in other Jewish nursing homes in Italy. Miller described:

> Among the residents are: a former teacher, still tutoring in languages (a teenage boy was there for a lesson at the time of our visit); a woman unable to walk, moved about in a chair on rollers (not regular wheelchair); a woman using wooden walking aids; a 91-year-old woman, very alert, but who claimed her legs were giving way; a senile woman; a deaf woman; and a man of 84 (very well preserved) who formerly served as president of the Jewish community in San Remo and who now is the liaison between the Home and the Milan Jewish community, making daily visits there.[52]

The Jewish Home for the Aged in Mantova was different in that it had fewer residents (twenty-seven) than the capacity (forty). Its residents included ten men and seventeen women, aged sixty-five and above (with two exceptions of residents aged forty-five and fifty). With only 150 Jews in the city, the home was a destination for older people from other parts of Italy. Founded in 1810, the home became a multifunctional community center after the war. The municipality contributed some funds. To earn pocket money and to occupy the residents, the administration of the home created work opportunities: washing dishes, cooking, sewing, running errands, gardening, and maintenance.

Miller aimed to gauge the general feeling of each nursing home that she visited and get a sense of the residents' perceptions of the institution. The Jewish Home for the Aged in Rome reached capacity with thirty-two residents, fifteen men and seventeen women, aged sixty-five to ninety-eight, with an average age of eighty. Constructed in the sixteenth century and located at the edge of the historic Jewish ghetto, the nursing home was outdated, which restricted older people's mobility in it. Still, Miller observed:

> As inadequate as the building is, the residents seemed happier here than in any other Home visited in Italy. It confirmed what we know of old people's desire to remain in old known neighborhoods. The atmosphere was extremely cordial and people seemed to feel free. It must give them considerable security, these people who lived in poverty all their lives, to know

> that a hospital is ready to serve them in case of illness, that friends and relatives are close by, that a synagogue is at hand.[53]

This assessment highlighted the role of older people's agency, relationships, feeling of safety, connection to a community, and location as factors that determined older people's contentment with their care arrangements. These were valuable findings, especially when Italian Jewish communities faced an influx of Jewish refugees in the 1950s. They needed to plan for care for an aging, largely immigrant, older Jewish people, composed not only of Holocaust survivors. The Egyptian Welfare Committee of Milan estimated that approximately two thousand Jews from Egypt had settled in Milan alone.[54] Jewish leaders in Italy anticipated that many among the refugees would enter Jewish nursing homes.[55]

Despite the issues they were facing, Italy's Jews saw a future for themselves. For example, a group of Jewish women founded the Hebrew Women of Milan, open to all members of the Association of the Hebrew Women in Italy. Focusing on care for older Jewish women, the group proposed building a summer house, planned for eighteen to twenty beds, on Lake Como.[56] In this case, a local Jewish group emerged to identify a need and devise a way to meet it. This was neither an apparent nor a possible response for other Jewish communities.

Clashing Views Within the Elderly Jewish Community: Yugoslavia

"It is the view of the authorities that the problems of the aged must be faced along with all other social problems and they expect more practical results for the aged from the new trends in social organizations," read a report on the situation of the care for older Jews in Yugoslavia.[57] This meant that social issues were expected to be tackled on the local level, sparked by mutual interest and self-management. JDC observed that older survivors would benefit from these long-term community developments and the extension of retirement privileges. However, the age structure and social conditions of the Jewish population demanded more urgent action.

JDC's survey was, for the Yugoslav Federation of Jewish Communities, an opportunity to analyze the management and activities of the

Home for the Aged in Zagreb.[58] The Federation registered the following numbers of Jews in Yugoslavia (6,116 in total, among them five hundred non-Jewish family members): 2,560 in Serbia, 2,062 in Croatia, 1,308 in Bosnia-Herzegovina, 95 in Slovenia, and 91 in Macedonia. In addition, six hundred individuals of Jewish origin remained unregistered. This was an aging community, with 49 percent between the ages of nineteen and fifty-five, and 31 percent over fifty-five years old.

The Zagreb nursing home, founded in 1909, was the only one in the country. At the time of the Nazi invasion in 1941, eighty residents lived there. When the German authorities confiscated the building, half of the residents were transferred to a provisional home near the city. After liberation, the Yugoslav government allocated a plot and some funds for a new home for Jewish seniors. The new building became a joint venture of local funders, Yugoslavian Jewish emigrants in the US, the Claims Conference, and JDC. In January 1958, the home was opened. The JDC report described it as a modern four-story building surrounded by a park. In 1959, there were 112 residents in the nursing home (and thirty on the waiting list): ninety-three women and nineteen men. Most residents were between seventy and eighty-four years old, and four were over ninety. Most residents (seventy-six) were born in Yugoslavia.[59]

Moses Levine, from the JDC office in Geneva, visited the Zagreb facility in June 1960. "The Home is an excellent one," he observed, although it required certain minor updates.[60] As such, Levine noted, they would not get approved by the Claims Conference. A capital grant, however, was needed for lightning protection, hot water, ventilation and air conditioning, laundry and dishwashing machines, a dining room, and a second television set. Levine stated, "I have a strong personal opinion regarding TV sets in Homes for the Aged: It is a window on the world. Zagreb received Austria, Italy and local programs."[61]

Two months later, Deborah Miller visited the nursing home. She learned about the challenges that this home faced, with clashes erupting among the older people. While the president of the Federation, Dr. Albert Vajs, and the chief medical officer, Rafael Montilijo, had called for a social worker to help "deal with the problems that cause the residents to quarrel," the director of the home (Bogdan Vajs) "felt that what is important are work projects such as Malben has, and which will give people other things to think about than their own complaints."[62] This points to the familiarity in Jewish nursing homes in Europe with Malben (*Mosdot le-tipul be-'olim nehshalim*, founded as the Organization for the Care of Handicapped Immigrants), which JDC operated in Israel between 1951 and 1975. Perhaps one reason why Vajs highlighted Malben was the program's experience with dealing with a diverse Jewish population.

The friction at the home stemmed from the varied demographic composition of its older residents. The director was concerned with keeping the two-thirds of the residents who were younger than eighty years old occupied. He complained about the discord that the generational gap between the sixty- and eighty-year-olds caused. Another issue concerned older people's mobility, or lack thereof. The home's distance from the city center meant that only 20 percent of the residents could visit there. Yet another line of conflict ran along cultural, traditional, ethnic, and religious divides. The home director emphasized the "latent antagonism" between the Sephardim and Ashkenazim, which had been separate communities before the war. Now they were grouped together. Social class was also a trigger: Playing the piano was seen as arrogant, as was speaking French. The situation was so dire that activities were done in small groups, which furthered separateness.

The arrival of a new housekeeper, who, together with the nursing home director, initiated group handicraft projects that ameliorated the tense situation. Miller showed the director the value of engaging older people in activities that boosted their sense of self-worth. In particular, the residents were encouraged to make their own decisions about the type of activities they wished to engage in.[63] All these methods were meant to—and did—diffuse the multiple and multilayered conflicts in the nursing home.

Conclusion

This chapter introduces selected issues surrounding care for older Holocaust survivors in Europe—in Belgium, the Netherlands, Italy, and Yugoslavia—between 1954 and 1960. The correspondence between representatives of JDC and the Claims Conference highlights the composition of the older Jewish Holocaust survivor population, some of the needs of the older people, the range of care that was both envisioned and streamlined, and the obstacles faced by care institutions, the older people themselves,

FIGURE 11.1. Exterior view of the Home for the Aged in Zagreb. JDC Archives NY_09126.

and the organizations that assisted them. A focus on these four countries turns our attention to places that have been rather sidelined in Holocaust scholarship. And yet, during the years considered for this chapter, older Holocaust survivors figured prominently on the Claims Conference and JDC's radars. A future study would reveal how the discussions about care for older survivors in those four countries reflected the situation of their counterparts elsewhere.

The uneven landscape of care for elderly people, the fluidity of defining an older person, financial struggles, personality clashes, and community expectations were some factors that representatives of both major US-based organizations dealt with in these four countries. Other challenges stemmed from the varied backgrounds of the older people. In Belgium, the older survivors were largely refugees and immigrants who required tailored assistance. Prewar cultural norms about what constituted elderly care shaped the Dutch case. In Italy, the emigration of young Jews, assimilation, the concentration of older survivors unable to leave Italy, and the influx of Jews from Egypt necessitated charting a long-term plan. An age gap among residents in the nursing home and rifts along Sephardi-Ashkenazi lines marked older care in Yugoslavia. What all those communities shared was the struggle between decreased and aging Jewish populations versus hope for a renewal and future of Jewish life.

Ideas about how to implement and adjust care for older survivors in times of limited funding, an evolving political situation, and numerous pressing needs illustrate the hardships that Jews endured and the difficult decisions that JDC and the Claims Conference were forced to make. Both organizations struggled, too, with the issue of "how far AJDC/Claims Conference is supposed to act as equalizing factor or where the higher standards prevalent in one country must be reckoned with in distribution of funds."[64] A critical assessment of the two organizations' successes and failures is a line of inquiry that is beyond the scope of this chapter. What emerges in the correspondence is a sense that a viable structure of care for older Jews had been built in advance of an impending closure of the Claims Conference.[65] In 1960, the board of directors of the Claims Conference decided to make the final allocations from the West German fund in 1964. However, the Claims Conference neither closed nor did it cease its efforts to continue to negotiate with the German government for compensation for Jewish Holocaust survivors and to address the needs of the aging survivor population around the world. For JDC, too, care for older survivors, and older Jews in general, has remained a pillar of its work.

Notes

1 "Introduction," December 28, 1956, JDC Archives, item 824514, 1. See also "Care for the Jewish Aged," January 23, 1957, item 824513, and "Serving the Needs of Older People," May 1, 1957, item 2963969.

2 This text stems from my talk at the symposium "Old Age Care in Times of Crisis, Past and Present," Birkbeck and London School of Hygiene and Tropical Medicine, University of London, April 2021.

3 Memorandum from Louis Kraft to Dr. Henry Selver et al., Re: Old Age Program, June 18, 1957, JDC Archives, item, 2963558.

4 See, Marianne Falconer and Desmond O'Neill, "Out with 'The Old,' Elderly and Aged," *British Medical Journal* 334, no. 7588 (February 10, 2007): 316; Joe Pinsker, "When Does Someone Become 'Old'?" *Atlantic*, January 27, 2020, accessed May 31, 2021, www.theatlantic.com/family/

archive/2020/01/old-people-older-elderly-middle-age/605590/; and Linton Weeks, "An Age-Old Problem: Who Is 'Elderly'?" *NPR*, March 14, 2013, accessed May 31, 2021, www.npr.org/2013/03/12/174124992/an-age-old-problem-who-is-elderly.

5 Selected publications about JDC include Avinoam Patt et al., eds., *The JDC at 100: A Century of Humanitarianism* (Wayne State University Press, 2019); Pnina Romem, *MALBEN: Institutional Care and Rehabilitation of the Hard Core Immigrants* [in Hebrew] (Itai Bahur, 2012); and Anna Sommer Schneider, *Sze'erit hapleta: Ocaleni z Zagłady: Działalność American Jewish Joint Distribution Committee w Polsce w latach 1945–1989* (Księgarnia Akademicka, 2014). About the Claims Conference, see Marilyn Henry, *Confronting the Perpetrators: A History of the Claims Conference* (Vallentine Mitchell, 2007); Ronald W. Zweig, *German Reparations and the Jewish World: A History of the Claims Conference* (Routledge, 2013); and Rachel Blumenthal, *Right to Reparations: The Claims Conference and Holocaust Survivors, 1951–1964* (Lexington Books, 2021).

6 JDC-Supported Homes for the Aged as of the Fall of 1947, August 17, 1954, JDC Archives, item 624451.

7 Zweig, *German Reparations and the Jewish World*, 74, 85.

8 Memorandum from Saul Kagan to Board of Directors, June 8, 1955, JDC Archives, item 2963559, 2.

9 Survey on the Care of the Jewish Aged in the AJDC/Claims Conference Areas of Operation in Europe, October 1, 1957, JDC Archives, item 824507, 2.

10 Memorandum from Louis Kraft to Dr. Henry Selver et al., Re: Old Age Program, June 18, 1957, JDC Archives, item 2963558. See also Proposed Policy Statement on Care of the Aged, Presentation for the Country Directors' Conference, October 23, 1957, item 2963549.

11 Letter no. GC 87 from Louis Kraft to Mr. Saul Kagan, July 8, 1957, JDC Archives, item 2963557.

12 Letter no. 1130 from Saul Kagan to Mr. Louis Kraft, July 29, 1957, JDC Archives, item 2963555, 1.

13 Letter from Louis Kraft to Mr. H. Katzki, September 1, 1958, JDC Archives, item 2963546.

14 Kagan joined a committee that explored assistance for older people in Germany, financed by the Jewish Restitution Successor Organization (JRSO) founded in 1947, of which he was secretary. JDC, a member of JRSO,

received funds acquired by JRSO from restitution and indemnity claims. The "residence clubs" that Kagan proposed were first introduced in the US in May 1939. "'Residence Club' Set Up for Elderly Group as Experimental Substitute for Institution," *New York Times*, May 19, 1939, 22.

15 Survey on the Care of the Jewish Aged in the AJDC/Claims Conference Areas of Operation in Europe, October 1, 1957, JDC Archives, item 824507, 5.

16 Survey on the Care of the Jewish Aged, 13.

17 Memorandum from Henry Selver to Mr. Leonard Seidenman, Re: Old Age Home—Brussels, August 27, 1956, JDC Archives, item 2685782, 2.

18 See Ruth E. Dunkle, "An Historical Perspective on Social Service Delivery to the Elderly," *Journal of Gerontological Social Work* 7, no. 3 (1984): 5–18, and Paul H. Stuart, "Social Work Profession: History," *Encyclopedia of Social Work*, June 11, 2013, revised March 26, 2019, accessed June 1, 2021, oxfordre.com/socialwork/view/10.1093/acrefore/9780199975839.001.0001/acrefore-9780199975839-e-623.

19 Memorandum from Henry Selver to Mr. Leonard Seidenman.

20 Letter from Henry Selver to Gerda J. Jacobson, August 27, 1956, JDC Archives, item 2685783.

21 In 1953, Deborah Miller, special consultant to JDC Paris Office, prepared a report about the nursing home in Brussels. I was unable to locate a copy of it.

22 Letter from Leonard Seidenman to Monsieur L. Maiersdorf, June 15, 1959, JDC Archives, item 2685805, 4. See also Letter from President to Conference of Jewish Material Claims Against Germany, Inc., May 15, 1956, item 2685990.

23 About seventy thousand Jews, of whom over 90 percent were foreigners, lived in Belgium in 1940. A significant number of Yiddish-speaking, traditionally religious Jews of Eastern European origin lived in Antwerp. Brussels was home to the more assimilated, culturally French Jewish population. Over 40 percent of Belgium's Jews were murdered during the Holocaust. Over twenty-five thousand Jews survived in Belgium.

24 AIVG, as a social welfare agency, emerged after the war from the transformation of the wartime Jewish and non-Jewish resistance group, the Committee for the Defense of Jews (Comité de Défense des Juifs).

25 Memorandum from Dr. L. Molnar to Mr. Charles H. Jordan, Re: Evaluation of Application for Claims Conference Grant: Old Age Home,

Brussels, September 11, 1957, JDC Archives, item 2685979. See also File Memorandum Concerning Investigation of Application #1103 from the Maison de Retraite des Vieillards and Application #1250 from the AIVG of Brussels, Sept. 1956, September 17, 1956, item 2685991.

26 Survey of the Jewish Homes for the Aged in Belgium, August 1, 1956, JDC Archives, item 2686035, 5.

27 File Memorandum Concerning Investigation of Application #1103.

28 Letter no. 20 from Dr. L. Molnar to Mr. L. Seidenman, Re: Waiting List for Old Age Home, September 19, 1958, JDC Archives, item 2685963. A renovated home with a capacity to accommodate 104 residents reopened in 1961.

29 Letter no. 2222 from J. A. Polak and Susanna A. Meijers to Claims Conference, June 19, 1957, JDC Archives, item 2721505, 2.

30 Nazi anti-Jewish laws in the Netherlands affected about 160,000 people, including about twenty thousand foreign nationals. Out of the 107,000 Dutch Jews deported to camps in German-occupied Poland, about fifty-two hundred were liberated. Most of the thirty thousand Jews who hid in the Netherlands survived.

31 Letter from L. Cosin and L. Molnar to Mr. Charles H. Jordan, Re: Coordination of Medical and Social Care for the Aged Jewish Population of Holland Dr. Cosin's Report, November 26, 1956, JDC Archives, item 2721621.

32 See also Survey of the Jewish Homes for the Aged in Holland Conducted: September 1958, October 1, 1958, JDC Archives, item 2721620; Survey of the Jewish Homes for the Aged in Italy and Holland in Letter no. 23 from Dr. Molnar to Mr. Leonard Seidenman, Re: Old Age Homes in Holland, September 26, 1958, item 2721645; and Letter from Dr. I. Dasberg et al. to Mr. L. Seidenman, October 24, 1960, item 2721678, about the Den Dolder convalescent home.

33 Copy of Letter from Mr. H. Van Dan to Dr. L. Molnar and Dr. L. Cosin, Re: Admissions and Discharges in Our Home for the Years 1952–1956, November 15, 1956, JDC Archives, item 2721588.

34 Jaarverslag Van De Vereniging, De Joodse Invalide over de periode 1 Juli 1958 T/M 30 Juni 1959, July 1, 1958, JDC Archives, item 2721529.

35 Letter from Leonard Seidenman to Dr. S. Shindell, Re: Foundation "De Joodse Invalide"—Amsterdam, January 5, 1959, JDC Archives, item 2721549.

36 Letter from A. Van Santen et al. to Conference on Jewish Claims against Germany, Inc., Re: Meeting held at the end of October at Geneva and the Survey of the Jewish Homes for the aged in Holland, December 2, 1958, JDC Archives, item 2721553, 1.

37 Letter from A. Van Santen et al., 2

38 The old age home in Arnhem was reconstructed with the joint effort of the War Indemnification Board and the Ministry of Housing, which points to the supracommunal involvement in care for older Holocaust survivors. The old age home in Enschede applied for money to cover equipment for a newly built wing.

39 Letter no. 23 from Dr. Molnar to Mr. Leonard Seidenman, Re: Old Age Homes in Holland, September 26, 1958, JDC Archives, item 2721559; Letter #46 from Dr. L. Molnar to Mr. L. Seidenman, Re: Old Age Homes in Holland, November 26, 1958, item 2721554; Memorandum from Health Department to Mr. Charles H. Jordan, Re: Claims Conference Applications: Old Age Home—The Hague and Arnhem, July 29, 1957, item 2721574.

40 Zweig explores this notion in *German Reparations and the Jewish World*. See, for example, 137.

41 Letter no. 5 from Dr. L. Molnar to Mr. L. Seidenman, Re: Claims Conference Application—Holland, August 13, 1958, JDC Archives, item 2721562, 2.

42 Letter no. 2222 from J. A. Polak and Susanna A. Meijers, 1.

43 Letter from L. Cosin and L. Molnar to Mr. Charles H. Jordan, 8.

44 Letter from Saul Kagan to Joods Tehuis Voor Bejaarden, December 23, 1957, JDC Archives, item 2721499, 1.

45 Letter no. 5 from Dr. L. Molnar to Mr. L. Seidenman, 2.

46 Nearly seventy thousand Jews lived in the Kingdom of Italy and in Italian colonies and territories in the 1930s. About 20 percent of Italy's Jewish population was murdered in the Holocaust. Over forty thousand Jews survived, most in hiding. Thirty-five DP camps in Italy housed about seventy thousand Jewish refugees.

47 Memorandum from Medical Department to Mr. Charles H. Jordan, Re: Survey of the Homes for the Aged in Italy Capital Investment Projects, May 13, 1958, JDC Archives, item, 2751910, 1.

48 Memorandum from Medical Department, 2–3. See also Survey of the Jewish Homes for the Aged in Italy, October 1, 1958, JDC Archives, item 845657.

49 Letter from Inga Gottfarb to Dr. L. Molnar, May 13, 1958, JDC Archives, item 2751909, 3.
50 Letter from Henry Selver to Mr. Harold Trobe, Re: Report on Old Age Homes in Italy, September 24, 1956, JDC Archives, item 2751923.
51 Conditions of JDC Assistees 65 Years and Older, Living Outside Institutions, April 16, 1956, JDC Archives, item 2751924.
52 Letter from Henry Selver to Mr. Harold Trobe, 4.
53 Letter from Henry Selver to Mr. Harold Trobe, 16.
54 In fall 1956, after the Sinai Campaign and the Suez War, persecution against Egypt's Jews intensified, and about 25,000 Jews left Egypt.
55 Letter from Inga Gottfarb to Dr. L. Molnar.
56 Rest House in Cremeno—Region of the Jewish Community of Milano-North Italy, July 1, 1964, JDC Archives, item 2751863, 1.
57 "Survey on the Care of the Jewish Aged in Yugoslavia," May 1, 1959, JDC Archives, item 2821646, 5. About seventy-eight thousand Jews lived in Yugoslavia (which encompassed Bosnia-Herzegovina, Croatia, Kosovo, Macedonia, Montenegro, Serbia, and Slovenia) in April 1941. About fourteen thousand Jews survived, mainly in hiding or by joining the partisans.
58 Survey on the Care of the Jewish Aged in Yugoslavia, 4.
59 Memorandum from Moses Levine to Mr. Herbert Katzki, Re: Zagreb Home for the Aged, June 17, 1960, JDC Archives, item 2821627, 8–9.
60 Memorandum from Moses Levine to Mr. Herbert Katzki, 1.
61 Memorandum from Moses Levine to Mr. Herbert Katzki, 3.
62 Memorandum from Deborah Miller to Dr. Molnar, Re: Zagreb Old Age Home, August 25, 1960, JDC Archives, item 2821623, 1.
63 Memorandum from Deborah Miller to Dr. Molnar.
64 Memorandum from Dr. L. Molnar to Mr. Kraft, Re: Brief Outline of Paper "Findings on Surveys of the Homes for the Aged in Italy and Holland," October 8, 1958, JDC Archives, item 2751898.
65 Memorandum from Dr. L. Molnar to Mr. Jordan, Re: Report by Conference Study Committee, August 4, 1958, JDC Archives, item 2751903.

12

SURVIVING IN A NEW STATE

JDC Assistance to Elderly Holocaust Survivors in the First Years of the State of Israel

Anat Kutner

Introduction

In May 1948, with the end of the British Mandate and the establishment of the State of Israel, most of the inhabitants of the country enjoyed fairly good health. A major contributing factor to this stability of public health was the quotas the Mandate government in Palestine set for the number of Jews entering the country each year. The quotas were not only quantitative but also qualitative. Prospective immigrants had to prove that they would be productive citizens and did not carry infectious diseases. The leadership of the Jewish community distributed the immigration quotas according to Zionist political party affiliation. Consequently, most of those who received immigration permits were relatively young former members of European Zionist youth movements. These permits were given to people who could prove they could support themselves or had someone to support them, and approximately one thousand immigrants were approved for entry monthly. Each immigrant could bring dependents—a spouse and children up to the age of eighteen.

The Jewish Agency, which served as the operative branch of the World Zionist Organization (WZO), was tasked by the British Mandate authorities with Jewish immigration to Palestine. It followed a strict medical policy, which was both a reflection of British policy and a result of its requirement to provide medical insurance to immigrants during their first year in Mandate Palestine.[1] Existing medical services covered most of the needs of the population, which was overall young and healthy. The majority of Jewish residents were insured through health funds set up to provide care through local clinics. A small number of hospitals treated the more complex cases.[2]

The situation changed dramatically after the end of the British Mandate and the establishment of the State of Israel. The young independent state faced many challenges. Firstly, Israel was embroiled in a war of independence, which required massive recruitment of both soldiers and arms. Simultaneously, the policy of immigrant screening outlined by the British authorities was abolished and the state's gates were opened to unlimited mass immigration. As a result, the country's population doubled in a short time, while the population's nature and needs underwent a significant transformation. In the first decade of the State of Israel more than seventy thousand elderly people arrived in the country, doubling their percentage in the state.[3]

In this article I will describe the situation of the young State of Israel, both as a nation and in the average age of the population, when this balance changed with the opening of the gates of Israel to unlimited immigration. In a reversal to the previous, British-created, policy, sickly and otherwise needy people entered the state. This different profile of immigrants included elderly Holocaust survivors, who carried the psychological and physical impacts of the difficult times they endured during World War II.[4] I will consider the ways in which the state tried to manage the needs of an elderly population. One of the main contributors of the young state's welfare system was the American Jewish Joint Distribution Committee (JDC). It had been active in Palestine since World War I and was established as the largest Jewish humanitarian organization in the world. However, the JDC's assistance to the nascent State of Israel was not merely a humanitarian response to the needs of the Jewish people. It also reflected a crucial internal need for the organization itself. The JDC, at this juncture, faced a pivotal crossroads. It had to navigate a shift from primarily reactive aid provision to a more proactive and strategic approach, while simultaneously ensuring the continued well-being of Jewish communities worldwide. This internal evolution necessitated a reevaluation of its mission, its operational structures, and its relationships with both beneficiary communities and external stakeholders.[5]

JDC in Europe

At the end of World War II, the fate of European Jews became known around the world, and Jewish aid agencies saw a moral obligation to assist refugees. During this period, JDC reached the peak of its activities in international aid and support work, in which JDC workers were involved around the world, including in Palestine, the Caribbean, South and Central America, Asia, Yemen, North Africa, and, of course, Europe. The organization's work focused on basic physical requirements such as medicine, food, and clothing, as well as on the social and spiritual needs of its constituency, providing religious supplies and vocational and academic training. One of the main goals was the economic rehabilitation of the refugees to enable them to become financially independent.[6]

Across Europe, dozens of orphanages were set up with the help of JDC to rehabilitate and educate parentless children gathered from various hiding places. JDC workers helped reconstruct daily life and build the infrastructure of welfare and other communal organizations. JDC enabled those who wanted to return to their homes or to settle in other places in Europe to do so. It also contributed economically and organizationally to help bring immigrants to Israel.

The first displaced persons (DP) camps were situated in what were concentration camps and labor camps built by the Nazi regime in Germany, and most of the inhabitants were those who were liberated from those camps by the Allies. For this reason, most of the survivors were young people who, although sick and malnourished, were still able to work. There were hardly any young children or Jews over the age of sixty among them.[7] A significant change to the population of survivors in DP camps came with the arrival of Jews who had fled to the territories of the Soviet Union during the war.[8] Some of them had spent many years under difficult conditions in remote areas of Siberia and the eastern parts of the Soviet Union. When they tried to return to their homes, mostly in Poland, they discovered that they had no family left to rejoin and that they were still unwanted there. For this reason, they continued westward to DP camps in the Allied territories in Germany.[9]

With the arrival of wartime evacuees from the Soviet Union, the nature of the DP camps changed in several aspects. The population of elderly Jews grew from .5 to about 2 percent.[10] However, despite the growing number of older people, the aid organizations' attention was directed mainly toward the education of children, efforts to train young people, entertainment activities for the general public, and help finding permanent settlement solutions, both in terms of Zionist training programs (*hachsharot*) and in helping with immigration to Palestine (both legal and illegal).[11]

There were small groups of elderly Jewish Holocaust survivors who managed to survive in Europe. One of those groups was based in former Czechoslovakia and was made up of Jews who had been deported to the Theresienstadt ghetto. Theresienstadt, a fortress town in the northwestern part of today's Czech Republic, became the Nazis' destination for the Jews of Bohemia and Moravia; many German and Austrian Jews, including the elderly and persons of "special merit" in the Reich, such as World War I veterans; and several thousand Jews from the Netherlands and Denmark.[12] Although in practice the ghetto, run by the SS, served as a transit camp for Jews en route to killing centers, it was also presented as a "model Jewish settlement" for propaganda purposes. It is estimated that by the end of the war, more than four thousand elderly Jews survived in Czechoslovakia, many of them from other European countries such as Germany, Denmark, and Austria, and needed the help of humanitarian organizations for their everyday needs.[13] Therefore, in then-Czechoslovakia, a large percentage of relief recipients were aged. Elderly Jews also managed to survive in Austria and Germany through intermarriage, among other reasons, many of whom JDC served in old age homes. Most of the relief work with the elderly focused on trying to assist them in their efforts to emigrate, as many of them were planning to leave Europe to join relatives who already lived abroad, while others intended to emigrate to a place where they could find better conditions.[14]

Successfully settling the refugees naturally led to a reduction of the organization's workload, and the question that hung in the air was, what next? In the summer of 1948, immediately after the establishment of the State of Israel, two key figures helped JDC to answer this question. The first, Joseph Schwartz, was one of the most active field workers during this period and, interestingly, it was he who encouraged the organization's involvement in illegal activities.[15] The second, Edward Warburg, a member of the famous German Jewish family that cofounded JDC, represented the official face of the organization.[16] These two men served as the two pillars of JDC's management, which often opposed each other—the board, which adhered to lofty ideals, and the field workers, who usually acted out of necessity and in accordance with reality. The cooperation between these two generally opposed groups—the field workers' leader on the one hand and the head of the board on the other—shows how acute the problem was perceived to be. Letters of the same wording, some signed by Warburg and some by Schwartz, were sent to the heads of the heretofore apolitical organization. Both wrote of the necessity to set up a meeting to clarify the organization's position in view of the establishment of Israel. Warburg and Schwartz personally addressed the people whose presence at the meeting was crucial and wrote, for example:

> I feel certain you will agree that it is most important to hold such a meeting. The establishment of the State of Israel, a great and momentous event, and the completion of more than three years of gigantic effort in behalf of the Jews in Europe since the war's end, make the meeting a necessity. The time has come for us to examine together what has been accomplished, what problems lie ahead, and what must be done to meet these problems.[17]

One of the decisions made by JDC staff and board members was to divert work from Europe, where needs were dwindling, to Israel, where new challenges demanded urgent solutions. It was clear that one of the main problems facing the Jewish people was the change in the balance of power and needs of the Jewish community in Israel. This was obvious in particular when observing the fundamental change in necessary social services with the establishment of the state.[18]

In the time that elapsed between World War II and the founding of the country, JDC specialized in caring for thousands of needy refugees and developing organizational and professional infrastructures to deal with complex and urgent tasks. The professional knowledge and experience acquired by the staff were much needed in the young country, and therefore, the state logically turned to JDC to request its help in this effort.

A New State Is Born

The emerging state changed not only the balance of power in the Middle East, but also the balance of power of the organizations that operated in it.

The fundamental change in the country was a transition from a sectorial system, based on organizational and humanitarian activities, such as the Jewish Agency, to a formal state system. An effort was made to systematically mobilize all interests for the structural framework of a state and for the definition and prioritization of national collective goals. At the same time, the many needs of the young state could not all be covered.[19]

The first decade of the Israeli state was marked by major changes in the social and political structure, mainly by the absorption of the *aliyah* (new immigrants) and the establishment of the state institutions. In addition, in the first year of its existence, Israel faced a war against five Arab countries. And yet at the time of signing the armistice agreements, the country could point to many achievements, although it had also paid a high price, as more than six thousand Israelis were dead and hundreds wounded. With the end of the War of Independence, and the signing of the armistice agreements, the country turned to the urgent task of absorbing the masses of immigrants arriving on its shores. In a short time, Israel doubled its population, an increase that enabled the establishment of its security hold and also led to a national moral justification for its existence.[20]

Between the years 1948 and1951, about 330,000 people immigrated to Israel.[21] Up until the beginning of 1949, the majority of the new immigrants were detainees from British detention camps. Most of them had been illegal immigrants who tried to enter British Mandate Palestine and were imprisoned by the British authorities in Cyprus.[22] Another large group of Jewish immigrants in need of rescue came from the Middle East, mainly from Iraq and Yemen. Evacuating the displaced persons camps and bringing DPs to Israel, and not to other countries, became a central goal of Zionist policy, and with the establishment of the state, it was necessary to implement it. Most of the immigrants to Israel in the first phase came straight from the DP camps in Europe. The Jewish philanthropic organizations were required to provide assistance, both financial and diplomatic, to help Jews leave Europe.[23]

The rapid pace of population increase and its demographic composition became a central problem. Significant resources were needed in order to provide the new arrivals with basic needs such as housing and nutrition, all of which had been strained before but had intensified with the large waves of immigration. Thousands lived in prefabricated housing in immigrant and refugee absorption camps called *ma'abarot*.[24] On April 26, 1949,

David Ben-Gurion, the first Israeli prime minister, announced a policy of rationing because the difficulties of absorbing the new immigrants forced the government to immediately institute a regime of austerity. Inflation was very high, but it was not the only thing threatening Israel. In the spring of 1949, Israel's economic situation was dire; it did not have sufficient production options, nor did it have foreign currency to pay for the import of food products and basic raw materials, mostly because England froze the state's sterling balances. In addition to its high financial costs, the ongoing war had severely damaged production and put thousands out of work. There was a food shortage due to lack of resources and significant parts of the population needed help to meet their basic needs. People who had lived in Israel for a longer period managed to cope better, especially those who lived in rural areas and agricultural communities, but the older and weaker populations were more affected.[25]

In the middle of 1949, the issue of the seriously ill became a central problem in the absorption of *aliyah*. Many DP camps were gradually being closed, and the sick and elderly who were left there received inadequate medical care in local facilities, and an immediate solution was required for them. Ben-Gurion deeply believed in the idea of the "Great *Aliyah*," which meant opening the gate to whoever wanted to come, including the sick and needy. In government meetings Ben-Gurion tried to establish and build the relationship between the young state and the prestate Jewish organizations, first and foremost the Jewish Agency. According to Ben-Gurion, if Israel restricted *aliyah* it would actually be betraying the central Zionist idea. He was troubled by the fact that the immigrants would be a burden rather than an asset to the young country, and the large number of immigrants made him realize that it was necessary to work on this problem.[26] Israel's Declaration of Independence stated: "The State of Israel will be open for Jewish immigration and for the Ingathering of the Exiles; it will foster the development of the country for the benefit of all its inhabitants . . . irrespective of religion, race or sex."[27] That is, the state should and would take all immigrants who arrived, without discrimination and without screening: old and young, sick and persons with disabilities, even those in very poor health.

Among the leadership in Israel, it was clear that the country would not be able to cope with the economic situation without the help of the diaspora Jews. Therefore, *aliyah* and absorption became the responsibilities of both Israel and world Jewry. The existence of Israel was not only a responsibility of its citizens but was directly related to the entirety of the Jewish people wherever they were. For that reason, world Jewry was obliged to help in all ways possible, including economically and logistically. The Jewish Agency, with the help of funds from Jews and Jewish organizations around the world, took on the project of absorbing the waves of *aliyah*, including unmarried individuals and families. This also meant the elderly who came as part of larger families, as couples, or alone, as well as unaccompanied children and young adults who came via Youth Aliyah (Aliyat Hanoar) either because they had lost everyone or because their families had chosen to stay in Europe or Arab countries for the time being.[28]

Holocaust survivors were a significant portion of the immigrants, young and adult. Some of them were physically and mentally exhausted after the horrors of the Holocaust and the years of difficult living conditions, hunger, and hard work. The traumatic events they witnessed and the physical and mental violence also affected survivors' state of mind. They had already passed through several stations in their long journey, including time in transit camps, DP camps, hospitals, and other assistance centers. The living conditions were complicated in all these places, and these refugees were exposed to changing climates and infectious diseases. In addition, when they arrived in Israel their housing was often overcrowded and unhygienic. Approximately 10 percent of the new immigrants needed medical assistance, among them the chronically ill and persons with disabilities. One of the most common diseases was tuberculosis, which was not only deadly but also very infectious.[29]

Preliminary screening of all immigrants was done in the DP camps in Europe, where immigration offices had been established to help with medical examinations, issue relevant documents, help with the luggage, and regulate those assembled for travel to Israel. Authorities responsible for these medical screenings prevented or at least delayed the immigration of many of the more complex medical cases.[30] However, there were many situations in which screening was not possible, both because of the structure of the camp and the danger to the survivors of having to stay in their countries of origin. At the same time, the long stay of some of the immigrants in the transit camps created frustration that led to attempts to bypass the tests and restrictions, as well as to turning to international organizations for assistance to reach Israel faster.[31]

While the emigration of the elderly and infirm from Europe was urgent, meanwhile in Israel, the immigrant camps were filled to capacity, and the overcrowding was compounded by the difficulties of absorbing the newcomers. The initial plan of the Jewish Agency assumed that the immigrants would stay in these transit camps for a very short period and then be moved to permanent residences. But the plan was not realistic, and a bottleneck resulted in the transit camps, which caused immigration to slow, demoralized the residents, and made them unable to sustain themselves financially. Thousands of needy people, including disabled patients and the elderly, went without services. The reception of "difficult" immigrants was a burden that the system could not handle, administratively, financially, or in providing adequate treatment.[32]

At the end of 1948, the elderly population constituted 3.8 percent of Israeli society and about a decade later had reached over 5 percent. This increase does not seem so dramatic, but when taking into account the general growth of the population, it means that the number of elderly people in the state had tripled. During the period in question, the proportion of elderly people in the European population was much higher (between 9 and 12 percent); however, no place is genuinely comparable, for several reasons. Unlike many of the elderly in Europe, most elderly people in Israel did not live in their native country. Most had arrived in Israel from Europe and North Africa and were survivors of labor camps and concentration camps, without relatives and with few possessions. Even those who could work often held professions that were not sought after in Israel and had to settle for jobs that meant both a decrease in pay and social status.[33]

JDC Moves to Israel

To meet the many and diverse needs of those requiring medical attention and the elderly who poured into the country, there was a need to establish a new organization that could give a holistic response. The name that was given to this organization was MaLBeN an acronym for Institutions for the Care of the Underprivileged (*Mosdot le-tipul be-ʿolim nehshalim*). The word "underprivileged" came from a verse in Deuteronomy (25:18), which referred to those left behind and who could not move as quickly as the rest in the desert. This was intended to include the ill, persons with disabilities, and the elderly who could not support themselves and needed assistance. The State of Israel, the Jewish Agency, and JDC were supposed to be equal partners in the project, but Israel did not have the funds to invest in it and the Jewish Agency diverted its resources toward financing immigration to Israel. Thus JDC remained the only body to manage and fund Malben institutions.

Malben was established by JDC in late 1949 at the height of mass immigration. As a first step, it took over the management of all the old-age residences that had been run by the Jewish Agency and invested in a variety of programs on its own initiative. It built more than fifty institutions, including hospitals, clinics, nursing homes, and sheltered workshops. Malben developed and managed four specialty hospitals for lung diseases and other chronic illnesses and provided funding for the hospitalization of the mentally ill and for expenses related to vocational rehabilitation and outpatient clinics. At the same time, JDC established via Malben a new and innovative institutional infrastructure for the care of the elderly to incorporate, broaden, and build upon the ones already existing.[34] The organization was active in several aspects of geriatric care, the most basic and necessary of which was institutional development. In the years of its existence, Malben established more than twenty institutions for the elderly and supplied the most hospital beds for them in Israel. It founded different and diverse kinds of residences, including villages for the elderly, old people's homes, and geriatric hospitals. Among them were institutions that were meant to respond to specific needs within the population, such as tuberculosis, disability, and other physical and mental health needs.[35]

During the State of Israel's first decade, more than five thousand elderly immigrants were cared for under JDC sponsorship in fifteen nursing homes, old-age villages, and convalescent homes. Malben provided 4,322 institutional beds for older Jewish immigrants, of whom a large part were Holocaust survivors. The services spanned the entire country, from Nahariya in the north to Ashkelon in the south. Malben established a comprehensive and complete organizational structure of institutions according to specializations. In addition, Malben staff established programs for the development of tenants' independence and professional training for care workers, formulating development policies and five-year plans. They also initiated innovative models for elder care outside the institution, and took initiative on interinstitutional coordination, among many other tasks.[36] Or as Dr. Virashevsky, a client who received an apartment at a reduced rent through a program of JDC in Israel, summed it up, "The sun in Israel is great for our old bones, but human warmth is a ray of light for our souls."[37]

Over the years Malben became synonymous with JDC in Israel, and for many people in Israel, including even government officials, JDC or Joint, as it was sometimes called, was the same as Malben. The financial system of JDC in Israel was mixed with Malben's and the stationery was imprinted with both logos. At the same time, the work of Malben was part of the Israeli welfare system, and known as part of the state's response to the needs of the elderly and the underprivileged.

Finding Solutions for Those in Need

Although Malben established institutions to help those in need among the immigrants generally, over the years the organization became known mainly for its system of care for the elderly.[38] It was faced with thousands of new elderly immigrants, many of them Holocaust survivors or returnees who spent the war in Siberia or the Far East, and most of them underprivileged and without means.

Malben was not only a pioneer in gerontology in Israel but also in the world. Older Holocaust survivor immigrants to Israel were referred to Malben institutions to receive the care they needed, but over time, the demand for beds increased and the need to find other treatment and housing solutions arose. Some clients sought some "protected independence," and were integrated into less strenuous jobs that nevertheless utilized their physical and intellectual abilities.[39] The need to free up beds actually resulted in the development of innovative treatment methods that allowed the elderly to return to independent living and a healthier lifestyle while drastically reducing the costs related to treating them.

The second, and most innovative, field of work for Malben was its integration of services into the community. Many elderly did not need institutionalization. There was also a limited number of beds, and so JDC worked to improve living conditions and increase capacity within the community. For this purpose, Malben purchased thousands of apartments throughout the country and adapted them for the needs of the elderly. In addition, JDC established a fund for loans to small businesses working with and on behalf of the elderly, and even helped with professional training for older immigrants to learn skills in demand in Israel. Malben founded community meeting centers for the elderly, an innovative concept at the time that originated in the United States. The centers were a means for the institutions to stay in contact with older clients and to make sure they had opportunities for activity. They also provided a place for the elderly to meet with professionals, specialists, and peers. Offering basic treatment and medical oversight, the centers often circumvented the need for hospitalization.[40]

Skilled personnel trained to work in geriatrics were required to operate these institutions, and Malben established an eighteen-month program for psychiatric and geriatric nurses. In addition, the organization initiated studies and surveys in order to assess the unique needs of the elderly with dementia, especially in terms of the trauma they had undergone during the Holocaust. Because there were many Holocaust survivors among the mentally ill and because their experiences were unique, there was a base and a demand for specific research. The research was revolutionary in dealing with trauma in elderly people, and set new standards of care worldwide. The first *Nursing Bulletin* was published in 1953 and *Le'et Ziknah* (literally, "of old age") started in 1956, both dedicated to new research in the field, to spotlight the work done in Israel and to expose the workers to the latest knowledge in the field.[41]

Along with the practical services Malben provided, the organization also represented the field of geriatrics and gerontology to the wider world. The organization established curricula both at the Hebrew University of Jerusalem and in nursing schools of the Hadassah Women's Zionist Organization of America in new treatment methods for the elderly. Its innovative methods emphasizing the preservation of patients' abilities while improving their health were disseminated through its publications and educational initiatives. The organization's employees served as advisors and members of interministerial policy-making committees and scientific and professional councils.[42]

Initially, Malben's policy was to separate geriatric services from other needed services, such as mental health treatment, which were provided in designated institutions. However, at a fairly early stage, it was understood that elderly Holocaust survivors had special needs. Other aging adults suffered from mental illnesses including dementia, and all needed unique treatment. Special attention was given to the elderly who had undergone significant traumas and who had deeper, more complex issues. It should be noted that psychogeriatric treatment was in its infancy in the world, this was all the more true in Israel. Malben's main goal was to respond to the immediate needs of its residents, as well as to ease the load in the small number of psychiatric institutions in Israel: many of these collapsed under the heavy patient load or struggled to cope with existing demands, exacerbated by numerous other pressing national challenges. It also maintained the therapeutic aim of keeping the mentally exhausted in their own home environment as much as possible in order to maintain their quality of life.[43]

To carry out these aims, the psychogeriatric system set up by Malben included inpatient wards for elderly clients suffering from severe mental illness. The first was at the Sha'ar Menashe Hospital near Hadera, in the northern part of Israel, where the hospitalized were treated with innovative methods. They also conducted studies and tested and reevaluated treatment methods. A transition ward was opened at the Nevah Avot nursing home in Pardes Hanna, the concept of which was to give patients a period of adjustment after completing the intensive inpatient treatment. They had a place to stay and to get used to everyday life as they made their way back to the community. In addition, a psychiatric outpatient unit was established to serve the elderly in nursing homes in the Pardes Hanna area. This meant that they received relevant treatment but were not completely cut off from their community. A work village was also established for the elderly with mental health issues. Additionally, as part of these villages, outpatient clinics were set up for those who did not require daily monitoring.[44]

Conclusion

Malben's work in the first years of the State of Israel's existence filled crucial roles. If not for this organization, many of the needy in Israel would never have received treatment. JDC's mission for Malben was to respond generally to the needs of the displaced persons in Europe after the Holocaust. However, when Malben began its work, the elderly were a significant portion of the needy. Therefore, over the years Malben became recognized for its advances in geriatric care. It began with a focus on the needy, including Holocaust survivors in Israel, and increasingly became an innovating force, setting the gold standard for geriatric care in Israel and beyond.

In addition to the establishment of a comprehensive and complete network of specialized institutions, Malben started programs for the training and professionalization of caregivers. The organization used specialists to develop innovative methods for supporting their clients' independence, along with models for care of the elderly in the community. They also shared and distributed the expertise by publishing several professional journals, both in Hebrew and English.

With time, the numerous crises that overwhelmed the young State of Israel were resolved or held in abeyance and Israel developed to the point that it could care for the elderly on its own. When this occurred, JDC took a step back and gave a parting gift: between the years 1968 and 1975 it gradually transferred all Malben's institutions, including the land and buildings purchased by the organization, to the new nation.

Notes

1 For more about the British Mandate policy, see Ritchie Ovendale, "The Palestine Policy of the British Labour Government 1945–1946," *International Affairs (Royal Institute of International Affairs 1944–)* 55, no. 3 (1979): 409–31; Richard L Jasse, "Great Britain and Palestine Towards the United Nations," *Middle Eastern Studies* 30, no. 3 (1994): 558–78; Roza El-Eini, *Mandated Landscape: British Imperial Rule in Palestine, 1929–1948* (Routledge, 2004); Aviva Halamish, "The Yishuv: The Jewish Community in Mandatory Palestine," *Jewish Virtual Library*, www.jewishvirtuallibrary.org/israel-studies-an-anthology-the-yishuv (2009); Penny Sinanoglou, *Partitioning Palestine: British Policymaking at the End of Empire* (University of Chicago Press, 2019).

2 For more about the health care system in the State of Israel and its establishment, see Yair Zalmanovitch, *Policy Making at the Margins of Government: The Case of the Israeli Health System* (State University of New York Press, 2002); Sachlav Stoler-Liss et. al., *To Be a Healthy Nation Massive Immigration and Public Health in Israel (1948–1960)* [להיות עם בריא באר־צנו: בריאות הציבור בעלייה הגדולה] (Ben Gurion University, 2006).

3 Shimon Bergman, "Aging in a Young Country" [in Hebrew], *Public Health* 10 (1967): 90–94.

4 Although in some of the relevant years agreements were signed with the German government regarding payments to the Israeli government, this

article will not discuss this subject, since Malben institutes were based on JDC funding that came mostly from American Jewry. For more about the negotiations between Israel and West Germany and the Luxembourg Agreement signed in 1952, see, for example, Daniel Siemens, "Reparations and Oil in the Cold War: British Perspectives on the Luxembourg Agreement of 1952," *Journal of Contemporary History* 59, no. 2 (2024): 370–93; Roni Stauber, *Diplomacy in the Shadow of Memory: Israel and West Germany, 1953–1965* [דיפלומטיה בצל הזיכרון: ישראל וגרמניה המערבית] (Shazar Institute, 2022); Jacob Tovy, *Destruction and Accounting: The State of Israel and the Reparations from Germany, 1949–1953* [החורבן והחשבון: מדינת ישראל והשילומים מגרמניה] (Bar Ilan University, 2015); Ofer Bord, *Take the Stolen Money from the Hands of the Killer: The Kibbutz Movement and the Reparations Agreement, Personal Compensation and the Restitution from Germany* [in Hebrew] (Yad Tabenkin, 2015); Yossi Katz, *Forsaken: Israel, the Reparations Agreement and the Question of Compensation and Restitution for the Holocaust Survivors* (Ministry of Defense, 2009); and Yeshayahu A. Jelinek, "Implementing the Luxembourg Agreement: The Purchasing Mission and the Israeli Economy," *Journal of Israeli History* 18, nos. 2–3 (1997): 191–209.

5 For more about JDC, see Yehuda Bauer, *American Jewry and the Holocaust: The American Jewish Joint Distribution Committee, 1939–1945* (Wayne State University Press, 2017).

6 For a comprehensive collection about JDC's history, see Avinoam Patt et al., eds., *The JDC at 100: A Century of Humanitarianism* (Wayne State University Press, 2019).

7 Eric Nooter, "Displaced Persons from Bergen-Belsen: JDC Photographic Archives," *History of Photography* 23, no. 4 (1999): 331–40; Michael Schwartz, "Refugees and Expellees in the Soviet Zone of Germany: Political and Social Problems of Their Integration, 1945–50," *Journal of Communist Studies and Transition Politics* 16, nos. 1–2 (2000): 148–74; Jan Hinnerk Antons, "Displaced Persons in Postwar Germany: Parallel Societies in a Hostile Environment," *Journal of Contemporary History* 49, no. 1 (2014): 92–114; Jessica Stroja, *Displaced Persons, Resettlement and the Legacies of War: From War Zones to New Homes* (Routledge, 2022).

8 For more about the repatriates' demographic statistics, see Na'ama Seri-Levi, "'These People Are Unique': The Repatriates in the Displaced Persons Camps, 1945–1946," *Moreshet* 14 (2017): 49–100.

9 For example, Yosef Litvak, "Polish-Jewish Refugees Repatriated from the Soviet Union at the End of the Second World War and Afterwards," *Jews in Eastern Poland and the USSR, 1939–46*, ed. Norman Davies and Antony Polonsky (Palgrave Macmillan, 1991), 227–39; Hagit Lavsky, *New Beginnings: Holocaust Survivors in Bergen-Belsen and the British Zone in Germany, 1945–1950* (Wayne State University Press, 2002); Gerard Daniel Cohen, *In War's Wake: Europe's Displaced Persons in the Postwar Order* (Oxford University Press, 2012); Hannah Rudderham, "A Strange Half-World: The Lives of Soviet Nationals in Europe's Displaced Persons Camps, 1945–1948," *Constellations* 11, no. 1 (2019): 1–15.

10 "Report No. 316, Subject: Report on Austria," March 25, 1946, JDC Archives, JDC-NY AR 194554/4/17/8/112. About the meeting between emissaries from Israel and Holocaust survivors see Irit Keynan, *Holocaust Survivors and the Emissaries from Eretz Israel: Germany 1945–1948* [לא נרגע הרעב: ניצולי השואה ושליחי ארץ־ישראל: גרמניה 1945–1948] (Am Oved, 1996), 78–80; about the medical assistance see, for example: Dorit Weiss and Hava Golander, "Nurses from Here—Epidemics from There: The Encounter Between Nurses from Eretz Israel and Holocaust Survivors Abroad, in an Effort to Eradicate Epidemics and Morbidity, 1945–1948," *European Journal for Nursing History and Ethics* 4 (2022): 16–37.

11 Niva (Shefer) Ashkenazy, *The Land of Israel Reached Them* [ארץ-ישראל באה אליהם: בתי הילדים של תנועות הנוער החלוציות בבוואריה] (Yad Vashem, 2009); Angelika Königseder and Juliane Wetzel, *Waiting for Hope: Jewish Displaced Persons in Post–World War II Germany* (Northwestern University Press, 2001); Zeev W. Mankowitz, *Life Between Memory and Hope: The Survivors of the Holocaust in Occupied Germany*, vol. 12 (Cambridge University Press, 2002); Avinoam J. Patt, *Finding Home and Homeland: Jewish Youth and Zionism in the Aftermath of the Holocaust* (Wayne State University Press, 2009); Ada Schein, "Educational Systems in the Jewish DP Camps of Germany and Austria" [מערכות החינוך במחנות העקורים היהודיים בגרמניה ובאוסטריה (1945–1951)] (PhD diss., Hebrew University of Jerusalem, 2000); Menachem Weinstein, *Peduyim lezion berinah: Activities of the "Mizrahi-Torah va'avodah" Movement Among the Holocaust Survivors in Germany, 1945–1949* [פדויים לציון ברינה: תנועת "מזרחי-תורה ועבודה" במחנות העקורים בגרמניה 1945–1949] (Zionist Library, 2008).

12 Much was written about this unique ghetto, and the elderly there, for example Hans Günther Adler and Jeremy Adler, *Theresienstadt 1941–1945:*

The Face of a Coerced Community (Cambridge University Press, 2017); Wolfgang Benz, *Theresienstadt: Eine Geschichte von Täuschung und Vernichtung* (CH Beck, 2013); Norbert Troller, *Theresienstadt: Hitler's Gift to the Jews* (University of North Carolina Press, 1991).

13 See Anna Hájková, "Mutmaßungen über deutsche Juden: Alte Menschen aus Deutschland im Theresienstädter Ghetto," in *Alltag im Holocaust: Jüdisches Leben im Großdeutschen Reich 1941–1945*, ed. Andrea Löw et al. (Oldenbourg Verlag, 2013), 179–98.

14 Dan Stone, " 'Somehow the Pathetic Dumb Suffering of These Elderly People Moves Me More Than Anything': Caring for Elderly Holocaust Survivors in the Immediate Postwar Years," *Holocaust and Genocide Studies* 32, no. 3 (2018): 384–403.

15 See Tuvia Friling, *The Web Weaver: Dr. Yosef Schwartz and the Joint's Rescue and Relief Operations* [in Hebrew] (Epublish, 2002).

16 About the Warburg family, see Ron Chernow, *The Warburgs: The Twentieth-Century Odyssey of a Remarkable Jewish Family* (Vintage, 2016).

17 JDC Archives, JDC-NY AR194554/1/1/3/2225.

18 For a brief summary of the information and outcome of this meeting and its aftermath see JDC annual report 1948, JDC Archives, search.archives.jdc.org/multimedia/Documents/NY_RPT/NY_RPT_1948/NY_RPT_1948_0001.pdf.

19 Nadav Davidovich and Shifra Shvarts, "Health and Hegemony: Preventive Medicine, Immigrants and the Israeli Melting Pot," *Israel Studies* 9 no. 2 (2004): 150–79.

20 S. Ilan Troen and Noah Lucas, eds., *Israel: The First Decade of Independence* (State University of New York Press, 2012).

21 Mosjhe Sikron, "The Mass Immigration," *Jewish Immigrants and Absorption Centers* [העלייה ההמונית - ממדיה, מאפייניה והשפעתה על מבנה האוכלוסייה הישראלית], ed. Mordechai Naor (Yad Ben Zvi, 1986); Moshe Lissak, *The Mass Immigration in the Fifties: The Failure of the Melting Pot Policy* [”העלייה ההמונית בשנות ה-50: כישלון מדיניות “הכור ההיתוך] (Bialik Institute, 1999).

22 Nahum Bogner, *The Deportation Island: Jewish Illegal Immigration Camps* [אי הגירוש: מחנות ההעפלה היהודיים בקפריסין] (Am Oved, 1991), 33; Arieh J. Kochavi, "The Struggle Against Jewish Immigration to Palestine," *Middle Eastern Studies* 34 (1998): 146–67; Eliana Hadjisavvas, " 'From Dachau to Cyprus': Jewish Refugees and the Cyprus Internment

Camps—Relief and Rehabilitation, 1946–1949," in *Beyond Camps and Forced Labour: Proceedings of the Sixth International Conference*, ed. Suzanne Bardgett et al. (Palgrave Macmillan Springer, 2020), 145–64.

23 Several studies about some aspects of the institutions were published in Hava Golander and Yizhak Brick, eds., *Mission of Compassion and Brotherhood: The Story of Malben-Joint in Israel, 1949–1975* [המשימה של רחמים ואחווה: סיפור מַלבֵּן-ג'וינט בישראל 1949–1975] (Ehsel, 2005).

24 Miriam Kachanski, "The Ma'abarot," in *Jewish Immigrants and Absorption Centers*, ed. Mordechai Naor, 69–86; Yael Allweil, "Israeli Housing and Nation Building: Establishment of the State-Citizen Contract, 1948–1953," *Traditional Dwellings and Settlements Review* 23.2 (2012): 51–67; Roy Kozlovsky, "Temporal States of Architecture: Mass Immigration and Provisional Housing in Israel," in *Modernism and the Middle East: Architecture and Politics in the Twentieth Century*, ed. Sandy Isenstadt and Kishwar Rizvi (University of Washington Press, 2008), 139–60.

25 Mordechai Naor, "Austerity," in *Jewish Immigrants and Absorption Centers*, ed. Naor, 97–110; Nachum T. Gross, "Israeli Economic Policies, 1948–1951: Problems of Evaluation," *Journal of Economic History* 50 no. 1 (1990): 67–83; Orit Rozin, "The Fight on Austerity: Housewives and the Government" [המאבק בצנע: עקרות הבית והממשלה], *Israel* 1 (2002): 81–118; Guy Seidman, "Unexceptional for Once: Austerity and Food Rationing in Israel, 1939–1959," *Southern California Interdisciplinary Law Journal* 18 (2008): 95–130 (95); Talia Diskin, "Austerity Everywhere: The Policy of Austerity in the Children's Press in the State of Israel at Its Beginning" [in Hebrew], *Zmanim* 141 (2002): 76–93.

26 Shifra Shvarts, "Health Reform in Israel: Some Aspects of Seventy Years of Struggle (1925–1995)," *Social History of Medicine* 11, no. 1 (1998): 73–88.

27 Proclamation of Independence, *Official Gazette*, no. 1, Tel Aviv, 5 Iyar 5708, May 14, 1948.

28 Dorit Weiss, "The Background for the Establishment of Malben as a Joint Institution for the Government, the Jewish Agency and JDC" [in Hebrew], in *Mission of Compassion and Brotherhood*, ed. Golander and Brick.

29 John C. Goldner, "History of Public Health in Israel," *Canadian Journal of Public Health / Revue Canadienne de Santé Publique* 56, no. 8 (1965):

343–46. Shifra Shvarts, "The Birth of the Israel Health Care System: An American Mother and a Russian Father," *Korot* 16 (2002): 9–29.

30 Irit Keynan, *Holocaust Survivors*; Shifra Shvarts, *Health Services, Histadrut and Government: Moves in the Design of the Health System in Israel, 1947–1960* [קופת חולים, הסתדרות, ממשלה: מהלכים בעיצובה של מערכת הבריאות בישראל, 1947–1960] (Ben Gurion University, 2000), 143–54.

31 Dorit Weiss, "The Background for the Establishment of Malben as a Joint Institution for the Government, the Jewish Agency and JDC," in *Mission of Compassion and Brotherhood*, ed. Golander and Brick, 29; Dorit Weiss, "Mission in White Nurses in the Mauritius, Aden Cyprus and Atlit Camps" [שליחות בלבן] (PhD diss., Tel Aviv University, 2002).

32 Joseph Neipris, *Some Origins of Social Policy in a New State: The Formation of Policy Concerning Aged Immigrants in Israel, 1948–1955* (University of California–Berkeley, 1966).

33 Israel: Malben: Comprehensive Report on the Health and Medical Care Aspects of the Malben Program, JDC Archives, G 45–54/4/27/2/P.I.55.

34 About the birth of Malben, see Hava Golander and Issac Brick, "The Birth of Malben Organization" [שליחות של חסד ואחוות אחים], in *Mission of Compassion and Brotherhood*, ed. Golander and Brick, 1–17.

35 Hava Golander, "Malben for the Elderly" [שליחות של חסד ואחוות אחים], in *Mission of Compassion and Brotherhood*, ed. Golander and Brick, 121–80.

36 For more about Malben, see Pnina Romem, *MALBEN: Institutional Care and Rehabilitation of the Hard Core Immigrants* [in Hebrew] (Itai Bahur, 2012).

37 *Doors to Life*, JDC Archives, JDC-023, AJDC Malben 1965, 26–30.

38 Yizhak Brick, *Eshel Institutional Work* [אשל] (Eshel, 2013).

39 Romem, *MALBEN*, 94.

40 Issac Margolez and Moshe Zelzer, "From Our Experience in Home Treatment for Chronic Illnesses" [in Hebrew], *Nurse* 21 (1960): 21–38; Moshe Wasser, "A Guide for Homes for the Aged" [in Hebrew], *For Old Age* 21 (1961): 73–88; Emmanuel Margolis, "Health Care in a Changing Society: The Health Services of Israel," *Medical Care* 13.11 (1975): 943–55.

41 Shlomo Adler, "The Rehabilitation Problems of Mental Exhaustion in Old Age" [in Hebrew], *Le'et Ziknah* 14 (1959): 34–37; Aliza Gueta, "The Nurse's Role in Day Care" [in Hebrew], *Nursing Bulletin* 23 (1960): 48–50;

Issac Margolez, “20 Years of Activity” [עשרים שנות פעילות], in *Towards Social Services in Israel*, ed. Issac Margolez (Trust Fund for Development of Mental Health Services, 1978), 11–16.

42 Golander, “Malben for the Elderly,” 122.

43 Romem, *MALBEN*, 75–77.

44 Golander, “Malben for the Elderly,” 136.

13

ELDERLY CONCENTRATION CAMP SURVIVORS IN POSTWAR VIENNA

Elizabeth Anthony

On October 18, 1945, Gabriele Caro received word from relatives in the United Kingdom. The seventy-seven-year-old had been back in her hometown for about three months after a little more than three years' imprisonment at Theresienstadt (Czech: Terezín), the ghetto and transit camp outside of Prague. Despite living with fourteen other Jewish survivors in a large room at the Seegasse 9 *KZ Rückkehrerheim* (home for concentration camp returnees), Caro was very much alone and thrilled to hear from family. One week later, on October 25, she typed a reply that conveyed a spectrum of emotions. Her delight at hearing from them leapt from the page, but her loneliness and despair were palpable as she detailed her wartime experiences and frustration with postwar conditions. Exasperated by the Allies' continued ban on sending letters abroad and the Red Cross's twenty-five-word limit on outgoing correspondence, the resourceful Caro found a British soldier to carry her letter to London.[1]

She told them of her life in Theresienstadt, where she had worked eight or nine hours a day at tasks like peeling potatoes and plucking horsehair in return for extra sugar and margarine. Malnutrition had weakened her eyesight to the point that she could neither read nor write. Surprisingly, while in the camp she had undergone successful surgery on both eyes and was able to see well enough again with the help of glasses. After her treatment, she moved to a home for the blind, still in Theresienstadt, and did knitting work in return for scarce food rations. Back in Vienna, Caro reported that she was in relatively good health and that she had a job in the

Rückkehrerheim, helping her roommates, some of them also elderly, and others blind or deaf. With this work, she earned additional food rations to help recover the forty-five pounds she had lost in the previous three years.

Caro asked about others she knew to be in the UK and wrote of the tragic fates of friends and relatives, many of whom had been with her in Theresienstadt or about whom she had heard. She had many deaths to report, and she also told of the deportation to Poland of others she had not heard from since their departures from Theresienstadt. She was, however, clear that they had likely been gassed by the Nazis. Caro closed her letter with a plea for warm gloves, socks, and sugar, along with a desperate description of her isolation. "I am completely alone here," she wrote. "My friends are all gone, some have died, many took their own lives or were deported. It really is a miracle that I returned. It is very sad to be so alone at age 77, without a home."[2]

Gabriele Caro was already of advanced age when the persecution began. She turned 70 on March 13, 1938, the day after the *Anschluss*, the annexation of Austria into "Greater Germany," and she was seventy-four years old on June 20, 1942, when the Nazis deported her from Vienna to Theresienstadt.[3] Her experience under the Nazis paralleled that of the many other elderly Viennese Jews left in the city in 1942 to be subject to deportation to the East.

Caro had lived in Vienna's fashionable first district, in a home she had moved to shortly after the death of her husband in 1928. Her postwar victim welfare file (*Opferfürsorgeakte*) reveals that she left that apartment on May 14, 1941, to move to the third district, where she lived in two different residences within seven months. On December 12, 1941, Caro was registered at Taborstrasse 20a/12 in the second district, the historically Jewish residential area.[4] It was from this apartment that she was deported six months later. Such shuffling around the city was not unusual in 1941, as the Nazis moved from a system of forced emigration to one of annihilation. Although never creating a closed ghetto, the Nazis concentrated almost 90 percent of the Jewish population in three neighboring districts–the second, the ninth, and the twentieth.[5] There they were forced to live in *Judenhäuser*, or collective Jewish housing. Some were given just twenty-four hours to evacuate their homes.[6] Gathering them in this one central area of the city made it easier to monitor Vienna's Jews and, ultimately, to deport them.

After almost three years of internment at Theresienstadt, Caro found herself back in her hometown in the summer of 1945,[7] living in the Seegasse 9 *Rückkehrerheim* in Vienna's ninth district, where she resided for the rest of her life.[8] A doctor certified on February 10, 1948 that Caro suffered permanent disability of more than 85 percent, including blindness of the left eye and severe impairment of the right, as well as heart muscle enlargement and degeneration, all of which he deemed to have worsened as a result of her imprisonment.[9] Despite all that, it still took more than fifteen years for her to receive any compensation, and at that point she was over the age of ninety. Ultimately, she lived to be one hundred years old.[10]

Gabriele Caro's experiences under Nazi persecution paralleled those of many older Jews in Vienna, but the fact that she survived was unusual in Europe overall. A convergence of conditions in the city, including the destination of those who were deported from there, enabled a disproportionate number of older Viennese Jews to survive the Holocaust. This chapter will elucidate the various factors that enabled thousands of older Jews to remain alive in or to return to postwar Vienna and will zoom in on the postwar lives of the many hundreds of older concentration camp survivors among them.

This study focuses on Viennese Jews who were over the age of sixty in 1945. Defining "older" or "elderly" is difficult and influenced by many factors. The retirement age for both men and women in Austria at the end of the war was sixty-five, as delineated by regulations set after the *Anschluss*.[11] Other sociological and cultural criteria contribute to a definition of age, though, including one's position in a family hierarchy (e.g., being grandparents), physical appearance, and health concerns related to age. Even with current-day longer life expectancies, the United Nations defines an "older person" as someone over sixty years of age.[12] I have taken all of this into account for the purposes of this study and believe that an age of sixty accommodates those older relative to the general population while also taking into consideration the trauma and hardship Jewish survivors experienced, all of which also contributed to one's relative aging.[13]

Historian Michaela Raggam-Blesch has extensively analyzed the hardships endured by elderly members of the Viennese Jewish population during the war, as well as the community organizations that provided them with support.[14] Other scholars have addressed aspects of their experiences within broader histories.[15] A focused examination of their postwar experiences offers a more nuanced and comprehensive understanding of the continuity of Jewish experiences across this period, particularly given that—as will be demonstrated—individuals over the age of 60 constituted a significant proportion of both the wartime and postwar Jewish population in Vienna. Additionally, this analysis sheds light on the redevelopment of the Jewish community and the reestablishment of essential services in the aftermath of the war.

Many older Viennese Jews lived and survived in the city under the Nazis because of different protected circumstances. Historian Brigitte Ungar-Klein demonstrated that 25 percent of those who survived in Vienna in hiding (termed *U-Boote* [literally, submarines]) were aged fifty-one or older.[16] Dr. Hugo Glaser, a founding member of the U-Boot Verband (the association for those who survived in hiding), was indeed fifty-seven years old at the time of the *Anschluss*.[17] His marriage to a gentile wife shielded him for a while, but he spent most of his time under the Nazis living on false identification papers and moving from hiding place to hiding place. Intermarriage did, however, protect Jews in Nazi Vienna throughout the war. Moritz Freiberger, who was sixty-four at the end of the war, survived because of his non-Jewish wife Mimi.[18] Because the Freibergers and their children were members of the Jewish community, theirs was termed a "nonprivileged mixed marriage," which meant that they found themselves subject to the same treatment as the Jewish population, including their exclusion from staple food rations and eviction from their home. There was actual privilege to their marriage, though, as Moritz was exempt from deportation as long as he remained married to his "Aryan" spouse.[19] The children of intermarriage—so-called *Mischlinge*, like Moritz and Mimi's daughter Lotte—were also protected. An August 2, 1945, report of the Jewish Telegraphic Agency likely overestimated that six thousand of the eight thousand Jews in Vienna (75 percent) were married to non-Jews.[20] Such numbers are difficult to pinpoint, but statistics compiled in 1943 by the *Ältestenrat* (Jewish community leadership reconstituted under the Nazis) indicated only slightly fewer at that time, about sixty-five percent.[21] Historian Jonny Moser counted 4,783 so-called mixed marriages, or *Mischehen*, in Vienna (or about 60 percent) at the end of February 1945.[22] In any case, it is clear that a majority of those who survived in the city were intermarried with gentile Austrians.

Another factor that affected the number of elderly survivors in Vienna after the war was the disproportionate number of elderly Austrian Jews who had been left in the city to be subject to Nazi deportation to camps and ghettos in the East. At the time of the *Anschluss* in March 1938, the number of Jews in Austria totaled 185,028; of them, 169,978 lived in Vienna.[23] It is estimated, however, that more than 201,000 Austrian citizens were subject to persecution under Nazi laws due to their Jewish heritage.[24] Thanks to the extraordinary efforts and tireless work of the Viennese Jewish community, which operated under the extreme pressure of the Nazi authorities and a massive forced emigration program, a total of 146,815 Austrian Jews had fled to other countries by November 11, 1941.[25] A ban on Jewish emigration from the Reich issued on October 23, 1941, prevented any further flight from Austria.[26]

Those who had escaped were mostly younger and middle-aged adults who often organized their departures ahead of their older relatives, with plans to get settled in their new homes and then bring their elders along as soon as possible. Neither the extensive requirements of the Nazi authorities nor those of the destination countries favored older emigrés, and as such the opposing sides inadvertently worked together to leave the remaining Jewish population of Vienna middle-aged or older.[27] Thus the Israelitische Kultusgemeinde Wien (IKG, the Viennese Jewish community) reported that, by the end of December 1939 and after the emigration of 117,409 Austrian Jews, 70 percent of those remaining were over the age of forty-five; 42 percent were over the age of sixty.[28] Older Jews left behind were impoverished and entirely dependent on the IKG for support, and in most cases never managed to get out to join their families.[29]

It is also true that many older Viennese Jews never even sought to emigrate, and others decided too late and missed any small window of opportunity that may have existed. Historian Melissa Jane Taylor argues that the elderly felt they had more to lose, and worried about losing their pensions and property. Some also refused to leave other family members behind.[30] On top of that, older Jews were accustomed to the antisemitism endemic in Viennese society. They had grown up in the late nineteenth century and the early part of the twentieth, and did not necessarily think that this new version would be much different. They thought they knew how to navigate it, or they just did not believe that the Nazis' "racialized," eliminationist antisemitism would last.[31]

But alas it did. Most of the Viennese Jewish community's remaining elderly were deported during the mass deportations of October 1942, which left fewer than eight thousand Jews in Vienna, the majority of whom were intermarried with gentile Austrians.[32] Deportations and, of course, persecution continued in 1943, so that by the end of the year a little more than sixty-two hundred people who were subject to Nazi persecution as "Jews" lived in the city. Many Viennese Jews, including the elderly, were sent to Theresienstadt, where certain conditions improved, even if slightly, older prisoners' chances of survival.

Theresienstadt had specific and important propagandistic purposes. In 1942, the Nazis billed it as a ghetto for elderly German and Austrian Jews, which served to cover up the true nature of the transit camp and ghetto. By offering it as a "preferential alternative," Theresienstadt helped maintain the illusion that other transports to the East were for workers.[33] The Nazis went so far as to require elderly German Jews to sign *Heimeinkaufsverträge* (literally, home purchase agreements) that supposedly bought them accommodation, meals, medicines, and laundry services in Theresienstadt, as well as medical and end-of-life care. With these contracts, German Jews could consider their relocation to be a normal move to "Bad Theresien," as it was euphemistically called, and the Nazis could rob them before their departure.[34] Adolf Eichmann, the architect of this plan to fleece elderly Jews bound for the "spa town," did not bother with any such masquerade for Austrian Jews. The Nazis simply expropriated supposed charitable contributions to the IKG and confiscated their remaining property with the help of the Superior Tax Authority of Wien-Niederdonau, the *Reichsgau* (the Reich's administrative subdivision of annexed Austria) that encompassed the municipality of Vienna.[35]

Theresienstadt was also infamously staged for a Red Cross visit in June 1944 to present it as a seemingly desirable retirement destination for older German Jews.[36] In reality, of course, Czech, German, and Austrian Jews of all ages were collected at Theresienstadt for intended deportation to ghettos and killing centers in the East, but the relatively high number of elderly interned there became a key part of camouflaging the true nature of the deportations. Unlike in other Nazi camps, the elderly were not murdered upon arrival there, and—however terrible—specific housing for the elderly existed. To be clear, conditions in Theresienstadt were horrible and most elderly Jews suffered and died there. Historian Anna Hájková writes that "old people occupied the bottom layer of the sharply segmented inmate community."[37] Non-Czechs and the elderly made up the lowest class of prisoners, so older German and Austrian Jews found themselves in the worst position, and many died in Theresienstadt.[38] Nevertheless, for the elderly among the fifteen thousand Viennese Jews deported to Theresienstadt, the possibility of survival existed, however slim.[39]

Within a couple of days of the Soviets' liberation of Theresienstadt on May 9, 1945, many Czech and other Jews had already left for home, and not long after, buses arrived from cities across Germany to retrieve the German Jews. The Austrian former prisoners, however, remained. Authorities from the city of Vienna had failed to take any action to repatriate around fifteen hundred Austrian Jews who waited there for some action on their behalf; about four hundred elderly and infirm were among them.[40] It took another two months for the Soviets to take over this task and to organize buses to carry them home.[41] The first group of 650 Austrian Jews from Theresienstadt arrived in Vienna on July 7, 1945, and about three hundred more joined them on August 1.[42]

A JTA (Jewish Telegraphic Agency) correspondent described the homecoming of 360 Theresienstadt survivors, all of them Viennese Jews, on August 2, 1945. The reporter was particularly "struck by the fact that they were aged and elderly. There were no children among them."[43] Ralph Segalman of the American Jewish Joint Distribution Committee (the JDC or Joint) estimated that by November 1945 about one thousand concentration camp survivors had returned to Vienna and he, too, specified, "most of them old."[44] His educated guess, however, miscalculated the situation. As of September 1945, from Theresienstadt alone 1,368 Jews had returned to Vienna; about one-third of them were elderly.[45] Still one cannot blame Segalman, as the percentage of older Jews among this group of camp survivors was surprisingly large and nothing an aid worker in postwar Europe was accustomed to seeing.

Through the period of Nazi control, Jewish community properties had been appropriated and by the end of the war the *Ältestenrat* administered just one Jewish hospital in Vienna, at Malzgasse 16, and a nursing home at Malzgasse 7.[46] Soon after their conquest of the city, the Soviets began to enforce the return of IKG medical facilities and the community set up *KZ Rückkehrerheime* to specifically cater to the particular needs of concentration camp survivors.[47] Many arrived in Vienna to find no place to stay. Their former homes were occupied, and their friends and relatives were either long since abroad or murdered. And so those in need turned to the IKG and the *Rückkehrerheime* for shelter and services.

Caring for the special needs of concentration camp survivors was a priority and, by the end of 1945, the IKG operated four facilities for concentration camp returnees with more than four hundred beds in total. A *KZ Rückkehrerheim* at Tempelgasse 3 accommodated thirty residents; another at Untere Augartenstraße 35 was home to fifty-two; the wartime nursing home at Malzgasse 7 served as a postwar hospital with a designated section for twenty-seven concentration camp returnees (in addition to the other eight-two beds in the larger hospital); and the former nursing home at Seegasse 9 was the largest *KZ Rückkehrerheim* with 306 residents.[48]

The home at Seegasse 9 in Vienna's ninth district was in the Servitenviertel, a quarter of the city named for the Catholic Serviten order (Order of the Servants of Mary, The Servites) and its church located there.[49] The neighborhood had been home to a thriving middle- and upper-class Jewish community at the time of the *Anschluss*, and for nearly three hundred years—with the exception of 1943–45—a Jewish medical facility had stood at Seegasse 9. In 1698 Samuel Oppenheimer built a private Jewish hospital on the grounds alongside Vienna's oldest Jewish cemetery and almost one hundred years later, in 1793, the Jewish community took over its formal ownership. In 1890, the IKG constructed a then-modern nursing home on the site and dedicated it to Emperor Franz Joseph I. Further modernizations in 1935 saw the addition of a two-story annex, and in 1936 the home contained 454 beds for elderly residents.[50] The *Altersheim* was situated among many Jewish organizations and religious institutions, including the nearby Müllnergasse temple, which the Nazis burned to the ground during the November Pogrom.

The facility at Seegasse 9 served elderly Jews until mid-1943 when it was the last Jewish nursing home closed and emptied of residents in Nazi Vienna.[51] The German Reich had "purchased" the building from the IKG on August 25, 1942, for a price of 622,000 Reichsmark, but they actually transferred the monies to a fund intended to finance the forced emigration of Jews from Bohemia and Moravia.[52] On May 25, 1943, the Nazis evacuated the last 122 residents and took over the building at Seegasse 9 two days later (May 27, 1943).[53] The Waffen-SS moved in on June 4, 1943, and used the home to billet troops until the end of the war.[54]

When emptying the home at Seegasse 9, the Nazis deported most of the elderly residents to Theresienstadt but resettled a few across the street at the Swedish Mission at Seegasse 16,[55] which helped more than fifteen hundred Jews and Gentiles with Jewish family backgrounds to emigrate from Nazi Vienna.[56] A month later, on June 21, 1943, those remaining at the Swedish Mission were moved to the Jewish nursing home in the second district at Malzgasse 7.[57] The Nazis had dissolved the IKG and formed the *Ältestenrat* in November 1942 after the mass deportations of Viennese Jews in October.[58] They pressed the remaining Jewish community leadership and employees into roles serving the city's remaining Jews, as well as those of mixed ancestry and so-called non-Aryan Christians (Jews who had been baptized). In this way, a Jewish community organization existed and functioned in Vienna throughout the entire Nazi period and included the provision of medical services for Jews left to live in the city under the protected circumstances outlined above. The home at Malzgasse 7 served as the only facility for elderly Jews in Vienna from 1943 through the end of the war, and it also supported the remaining community's only hospital, nearby at Malzgasse 16, when overcrowded conditions demanded it. Malzgasse 7 made space for improvised hospital beds for Hungarian-Jewish forced laborers in the summer of 1944, for example, and continued to accommodate some outpatient clinics that had been established previously in the building.[59]

On July 7, 1945, the IKG reopened the Seegasse 9 facility as a *KZ Rückkehrerheim*, although they had not yet regained formal ownership of the building.[60] On that same day, the first large repatriation transport from Theresienstadt arrived in Vienna and four hundred of the returnees became Seegasse 9's first residents.[61] The facility's furnishings scarcely accommodated the new residents. Seegasse 9 director Nicholas Lazarowitsch reported that properly feeding them was difficult for at least the first eight weeks of the home's operation. Once the US Army arrived in Vienna in August 1945 and assumed occupation authority for the ninth district, the home's food rations began to improve. By the middle of September, residents received forty grams of bread daily with some meat, cheese, or jam, plus a breakfast of coffee with forty ml milk, a half-liter of *Eintopf* (a hearty Viennese meat and vegetable soup) for lunch, and dinner of forty ml broth with various traditional Viennese *Einlage* (noodles, meat, strips of crepes, or dumplings added to soup).[62] By October 1945, Seegasse 9 was one of two shelters for returning concentration camp survivors in the US sector and the largest of the *KZ Rückkehrerheime* in Vienna.[63]

The US Forces in Austria (USFA) assumed official oversight of Seegasse 9 on November 15, 1945. Although an estimated 90 percent of the home's residents were originally from Austria, the USFA's DP section officially classified it as a displaced persons (DP) camp under its supervision.[64] This was unusual, and a phenomenon particular to Vienna. The United Nations Relief and Rehabilitation Agency (UNRRA) defined a displaced person as one displaced *outside* of his or her country of origin. But Brigadier General Ralph Tate, deputy commander to General Mark Clark, the head of the USFA and US high commissioner for Austria, had interceded to change the status of Viennese Jews from "refugees" to "displaced persons," which allowed the US occupiers to help support them by bending rules to accommodate them with services intended for DPs, including medical aid, food, and shelter.[65] Interestingly, there also has been speculation that General Clark had a particular interest in the surviving Jews living in areas under his command. The son of a Jewish mother, he had been baptized Episcopalian during his time at West Point.[66] Policies regarding Jews appeared to have been enforced more strictly in Austria under Clark, and he was known to have been quite vocal about and supportive of the contributions of the Jewish soldiers who served under him.[67]

A list dated October 16, 1947, showed that the home's 291 residents included 43 occupants between the ages of sixty and sixty-nine, 85 over the age of seventy, and 26 over the age of eighty. One of them was eighty-seven.[68] By December 1945, about 60 percent of the population of mostly Theresienstadt survivors at Seegasse 9 were over the age of sixty, which reflected the overall Jewish demographic pattern of postwar Vienna.[69] Seegasse 9's long history of serving Vienna's elderly Jews as a nursing home surely contributed to the high concentration of older survivors, and the home's postwar status as a *KZ Rückkehrerheim* accounts for the density of camp survivors in one facility. The percentages, though, nonetheless closely resemble the significantly high proportion of aged Jews in Vienna.

Many older Jews worked in the Seegasse 9 home tending to daily operations. For reasons of age and health, most were unable to take on outside employment. Those who might have tried to resume careers later in life—as well as their younger returnee compatriots—found regaining trade and business licenses difficult and were delayed or prevented in their efforts to return to work.[70] Elderly residents were paid wages for chores and tasks, like working in the kitchen and—like Gabriele Caro—helping needy roommates.[71] In addition, a central kitchen operated in the neighboring building at Seegasse 11 and employed many of the homes' residents to provide nourishment for IKG facilities across the city.[72] Workers at both Seegasse 9 and 11 received either cash or points to be used for purchase within the DP camp system, or a combination of the two.[73] Some of the elderly also received work exemptions and were allotted a certain amount of money to live, as did the physically impaired, mothers, and those caring for young relatives or other dependents.

The US Army oversaw the operations of the home until 1950, including the provision of food, special items for Jewish holidays, and necessary building renovations and maintenance, including the installation of central heating and the repair of broken windows.[74] The Joint also supported activities at Seegasse 9, as it did in many DP camps. "Care packages" of food and supplies arrived from around the world via Joint channels and those of other international Jewish organizations. Some individuals made direct gifts. Max Hirschmann, a Viennese Jewish émigré who fled to Australia, corresponded directly with Lazarowitsch to offer his and other exiled Viennese Jews' assistance from their community. Over several months, Hirschmann and his group provided many basic supplies for Seegasse 9.[75] The Joint also hosted holiday parties and games for children and funded a *Kindergarten* (daycare center and preschool) for the youngest residents of Seegasse 9 and other youngsters in the community.[76] Religious observances took place for young and old residents alike, including Purim and Hanukkah parties, Passover seders, and services for the High Holidays. A 1948 Hanukkah party included song and dance performances and plays put on by the children of the *Kindergarten*, each of whom also received a gift.[77] The Swedish Mission across the street provided Easter eggs and Christmas trees for the few non-Jewish residents, and USFA personnel were involved in both the oversight of and participation in such activities.[78]

The USFA and the IKG strove to accommodate residents' social and cultural needs in addition to religious observances. Visiting guests and celebrities performed concerts for the residents. Peter Herz and a cast of actors and singers from London gave a "great music hall performance" for several important guests (presumably representatives from the US Army) in attendance on June 28, 1949.[79] Residents showed their gratitude to the US Army with an observance of the first anniversary of the death of former US president Franklin Delano Roosevelt at a formal event on April 12, 1946.[80]

The IKG regained official ownership and control of the building at Seegasse 9 in 1947,[81] although the USFA oversaw facility operations until

1948, and by March 1, 1948, the home was completely self-administered and covered its costs with revenues generated from the residents and the surplus of the Seegasse 11 refugee kitchen.[82] In addition to its initial and stated purpose as a home for those returning from concentration camps, Seegasse 9 opened its doors in later years to include other DPs and refugees—mostly Jews—and continued to host a high number of elderly. The home received, for example, several Jewish refugees returning in 1949 after many years of exile in Shanghai.[83] With funding from the city of Vienna in 1950, Seegasse 9 officially returned to its original role as a Jewish community nursing home, although it retained in part its *KZ Rückkehrerheim* function until the end of 1953; former concentration camp prisoners—including Gabriele Caro—resided there until the mid-1960s.[84] Caro, in fact, passed away at the Seegasse 9 nursing home on April 5, 1968, at the age of one hundred. The IKG finally sold the building to the city of Vienna in 1978, ending the centuries-long Jewish ownership of the property (minus the few years between 1942 and 1945), and opened a new community-run nursing home in another part of the city.

The IKG set out to reassemble and reconstruct its community immediately after the Soviet conquest of Vienna and with the support of the Red Army in their recovery of property and medical facilities. Like the city's other residents, surviving and returning Jews suffered from food and housing shortages, and most became dependent on the IKG for support, including the provision of food and shelter, as well as in their attempts to locate family members. Older Jews were the most helpless and exposed, and concentration camp survivors were the most vulnerable.

As we have seen, the pool of Jews in Vienna remaining after mass emigration abroad had skewed older and left a preponderance of the aged among those left in the city to be subject to deportation to the East. Although older Jews were almost always slated for immediate death in Nazi concentration camps, Theresienstadt was different. Many Viennese Jews had been deported there, and the elderly among them met with circumstances that *might* permit them a chance of survival. And indeed about one-third of Austrian Jewish Theresienstadt survivors had been over the age of sixty.

Returning camp survivors often arrived with nothing and found nothing awaited them in their hometown. They returned to a community under reconstruction, both figuratively and literally, and largely made up of their coreligionists who had survived in Nazi Vienna in marriages to non-Jewish spouses, in hiding, or under other protected circumstances, many of whom were also at least of middle age, if not older. They rejoined a postwar Jewish community that—while small—was disproportionately older, including a surprising number of camp survivors over the age of sixty, for whom *KZ Rückkehrerheime* served specific, desperate needs. Gabriele Caro called her return to Vienna "a miracle."[85] And, indeed, her survival—and that of other older Viennese Jews—was miraculous. The odds certainly had been against them, and one can understand her perception and characterization of being alive and once again home in Vienna after the Holocaust. There were, however, some very real and specific conditions that coincided there to permit the possibility for more of the Jewish community's elderly population to survive.

Notes

This chapter partially draws on research conducted for my book *The Compromise of Return: Viennese Jews After the Holocaust* (Wayne State University Press, 2021). Some passages included in this chapter previously appeared there.

1 Letter from Jella [Gabriele] Caro, doc. 1339, Wiener Holocaust Library (WHL).
2 "Meine Freunde sind alle fort, teils verstorben, viele haben sich das Leben genommen oder sind mit den Transporten weg. Ich bin wirklich wie durch ein Wunder zurück geblieben. Es ist sehr traurig mit 77 Jahren so allein zu sein, ohne Heim." Letter from Jella Caro, doc. 1339, WHL.
3 Abgangsliste des 28. Transportes, 1.2.1.1/11203480/ITS Digital Archive, USHMM.
4 Gabriele Caro victim welfare and compensation file, M.Abt. 208, A36—Opferfürsorgeakten—Entschädigungen, Wiener Stadt- und Landesarchiv (WStLA).
5 Raul Hilberg, *The Destruction of the European Jews*, vol. 2 (Holmes and Meier, 1985), 457.
6 Ilana Offenberger, *The Jews of Nazi Vienna* (Palgrave Macmillan Cham, 2017), 249.

7 List of Austrians who returned to Vienna from Theresienstadt, 3.1.1.3/78805387/ITS Digital Archive, USHMM.
8 Aus den Konzentrationslagern nach Wien Zurückgekehrte, September 1945, 3.1.1.3/78805180/ITS Digital Archive, USHMM; List of home-inmates (Seegasse 9, December 1946), 3.1.1.2/82048260/ ITS Digital Archive, USHMM.
9 Gabriele Caro victim welfare and compensation file, WStLA.
10 From "Biographical History," included in the catalog reference to Caro's letter, doc. 1339, WHL.
11 Rudolf Müller, "Die Entwicklung der Pensionsversicherung der unselbständig Erwerbstätigen," *Das Recht der Arbeit* 6 (2015): 492.
12 "Facilitator's Guide: Working with Older Persons in Forced Displacement," UNHCR website, accessed October 19, 2023, www.unhcr.org/us/facilitators-guide-working-older-persons-forced-displacement.
13 Given the short—at best—life expectancy of elderly Jews the Nazis deported to concentration camps, one could make a good argument that an older Jew in postwar Europe was someone over the age of fifty-five or even fifty at the end of the war.
14 Michaela Raggam-Blesch, "Von der Seegasse in die Malzgasse: Jüdische Altersfürsorge," in *Topographie der Shoah: Gedächtnisorte des zerstörten jüdischen Wien*, ed. Dieter Hecht et al. (Mandelbaum Verlag, 2015), 240–60; and Michaela Raggam-Blesch, "Two Streets in Vienna as a Focal Point of Jewish Care for the Elderly: Between Dissolution, Concentration, and Deportation," *Yad Vashem Studies* 50, no. 2 (2022): 113–39.
15 See Evelyn Adunka, *Die Vierte Gemeinde: Die Wiener Juden in der Zeit von 1945 bis heute* (Philo, 2000); Helga Embacher, *Neubeginn ohne Illusionen: Juden in Österreich nach 1945* (Picus Verlag, 1995); Ilana Offenberger, *The Jews of Nazi Vienna, 1938–1945* (Palgrave Macmillan Cham, 2017); Doron Rabinovici, *Instanzen der Ohnmacht: Wien 1938–1945: Der Weg zum Judenrat* (Jüdischer Verlag, 2000); Herbert Rosenkranz, *Verfolgung und Selbstbehauptung: Die Juden in Österreich, 1938–1945* (Herold Verlag, 1978).
16 Ungar-Klein explains that she analyzed a sample of 1,628 Jewish *U-Boote* plus six Jewish resistance fighters; 406 of the 1,634 were over the age of fifty-one. Brigitte Ungar-Klein, *Schattenexistenz: Jüdische U-Boote in Wien 1938–1945* (btb Verlag, 2021), 95.
17 Ungar-Klein, *Schattenexistenz*, 45.

18 For the complete details of the daily life of Freiberger and his family under Nazi oppression, along with two other intermarried couples, see: Michaela Raggam-Blesch, "'Privileged' Under Nazi-Rule: The Fate of Three Intermarried Families in Vienna," *Journal of Genocide Research* 21, no. 3 (2019): 378–97.

19 Raggam-Blesch, "'Privileged' Under Nazi-Rule," 385–86.

20 "Austrian Jews Return from Theresienstadt to Vienna; Jewish Population Reaches 8,000," *Jewish Telegraphic Agency*, August 2, 1945.

21 Statistics from the Ältestenrat der Juden in Wien, "Bericht über die Tätigkeit im Jahre 1943," as cited in Rabinovici, *Instanzen der Ohnmacht*, 116.

22 Jonny Moser, *Demographie der jüdischen Bevölkerung Österreichs 1938–1945* (DÖW, 1999), 54.

23 Rabinovici, *Instanzen der Ohnmacht*, 39.

24 Moser, *Demographie der jüdischen Bevölkerung Österreichs*, 18–19.

25 Wolfgang Muchitsch, *Österreicher im Exil: Großbritannien 1938–1945; Eine Dokumentation*, ed. Dokumentationsarchiv des österreichischen Widerstandes (Österreicher Bundesverlag, 1992), 8. An estimated 135,000 of the 146,815 Viennese Jews who fled reached safety; the rest fell victim to Nazi persecution in other countries. Ultimately, the Nazis murdered about sixty-five thousand Austrian Jews.

26 Offenberger, *The Jews of Nazi Vienna*, 250.

27 Melissa Jane Taylor, "Family Matters: The Emigration of Elderly Jews from Vienna to the United States, 1938–1941," *Journal of Social History* 45, no. 1 (2011): 238–60 (241).

28 "Report of the Vienna Jewish Community: A Description of the Activity of the Israelitische Kultusgemeinde Wien in the Period from May 2nd 1938–December 31st 1939," RG 17.017M, reel 294, IKG-A/W 126, USHMM. In addition, women comprised 60 percent of the Jewish population left in Vienna at that time.

29 Taylor, "Family Matters," 241–42.

30 Taylor, "Family Matters," 239.

31 For more on Viennese Jews and late nineteenth- and early twentieth-century antisemitism, see Elizabeth Anthony, *The Compromise of Return: Viennese Jews After the Holocaust* (Wayne State University Press, 2021), introduction and chapter 1.

32 At the beginning of 1943, there were only 7,989 Jews left in Vienna and by December the number had dwindled to 6,259. Of these, 1,080 belonged to another confession, 85 were foreign, and 5,094 lived in mixed marriages. Statistics from the Ältestenrat der Juden in Wien, "Bericht über die Tätigkeit im Jahre 1943," as cited in Rabinovici, *Instanzen der Ohnmacht*, 116.

33 Anna Hájková, *The Last Ghetto: An Everyday History of Theresienstadt* (Oxford University Press, 2020), 9.

34 Jonathan R. Zatlin, "The Ruse of Retirement: Eichmann, the *Heimeinkaufsverträge*, and the Dispossession of the Elderly," in *Dispossession: Plundering German Jewry, 1933–1953*, ed. Christoph Kreuzmüller and Jonathan R. Zatlin (University of Michigan Press, 2020), 169–201 (169–70).

35 Zatlin, "Ruse of Retirement," 178.

36 Hájková, *The Last Ghetto*, 10.

37 Hájková, *The Last Ghetto*, 1.

38 Hájková, *The Last Ghetto*, 98.

39 For details of dates of arrivals and total numbers of Viennese Jews transported to Theresienstadt, see Moser, *Demographie der jüdischen Bevölkerung Österreichs*, 80–83.

40 Letter from Ing. Paul Stux, Neuegasse 12, Theresienstadt to Dr. Josef Löwenherz, May 10, 1945, A/W 4035, Central Archives for the History of the Jewish People (CAHJP).

41 George Berkeley, *Hitler's Gift: The Story of Theresienstadt* (Branden Books, 1993), 252. Susanne Kriss mentions her return to Vienna from Theresienstadt on buses provided by the Soviets. See Susanne Kriss interview 378, Dokumentationsarchiv des österreichischen Widerstandes (DÖW).

42 Martin Niklas, *". . . die schönste Stadt der Welt": Österreichische Jüdinnen und Juden in Theresienstadt* (DÖW, 2009), 151.

43 "Austrian Jews Return from Theresienstadt to Vienna; Jewish Population Reaches 8,000," *Jewish Telegraphic Agency*, August 2, 1945.

44 Ralph Segalman, "Letters to my Grandchildren," unpublished memoir, 2001, SC-14902, p. 76, Jacob Rader Marcus Center of the American Jewish Archives, Marcus Repository.

45 List "Heimkehrer aus Theresienstadt," September 20, 1945, 3.1.1.3/78805385–78805407/ITS Digital Archive, USHMM.

46 Hecht et al., *Topographie der Shoah*, 497–504.

47 Memo from Major Judah Nadich, US Army, to commanding General, USFA, APO 777, US Army, October 23, 1945, RG 260, Int Affairs/DP

Div., DP Section, General Records 1945–50, folder 104 through 105, box 16, NARA (United States National Archives and Records Administration).

48 "Vom Leben der Juden in Wien," *Aufbau*, December 21, 1945, 24.

49 A longer, more detailed profile of the Seegasse 9 Rückkehrerheim and its operations in the US Zone of Vienna, in some cooperation with the US Forces in Austria, appears in chapter 3 of my book *The Compromise of Return: Viennese Jews After the Holocaust* (Wayne State University Press, 2021), 115–23.

50 Angelika Shoshana Duizend-Jensen, *Jüdische Gemeinden, Vereine, Stiftungen und Fonds: "Arisierung" und Restitution* (Historikerkommission der Republik Österreich, 2002), 12.

51 Duizend-Jensen, *Jüdische Gemeinden*, 61.

52 Duizend-Jensen, *Jüdische Gemeinden*, 62. On the emigration fund, see Gabriele Anderl and Dirk Rupnow, *Die Zentralstelle für jüdische Auswanderung als Beraubungsinstitution* (Historikerkommission der Republik Österreich vol. 20/1, 2004).

53 Duizend-Jensen, *Jüdische Gemeinden*, 63.

54 Ältestenrat der Juden in Wien, 22. Wochenbericht, 1. Juni 1943, DÖW; letter from Max Birnstein to the director of the Ältestenrat, May 28, 1943, A/W 275 and 1827, CAHJP. An immediate postwar witness statement dated June 3, 1945, also mentioned that under Nazi possession Seegasse 9 had housed a jail, either specifically for or at least also used to detain some Wehrmacht deserters. See "Postwar Witness Statements Concerning the Formation of the Special Detachment Dirlewanger," June 3, 1945, 1.1.0.6/82326879/ITS Digital Archive, USHMM.

55 Bericht über die Tätigkeit des Ältestenrates der Juden in Wien im Jahre 1943, p. 11, A/W 117, CAHJP. The Swedish Lutheran Church established the Swedish Mission in 1920 for the purposes of converting and baptizing Jews. From the time of the *Anschluss* through 1941, however, the staff served mainly "non-Aryan Christians" who were persecuted under the Nuremberg Laws (but also some Jews) to help with their social welfare and emigration needs. Once Nazi deportations to the East began, the home at Seegasse 16 served under the management of the IKG as a hospital and nursing home for Jews and Christians with Jewish family backgrounds, and from June 1943 the Nazis permitted it to continue in existence as a home for couples in "mixed marriages." After the war it also served as a KZ Rückkehrerheim, often working in coordination with the Seegasse 9 home across the street.

See Duizend-Jensen, *Jüdische Gemeinden*, 63, and Brigitte Bailer et al., *Erzählte Geschichte: Berichte von Widerstandskämpfern und Verfolgten*, vol. 3: *Jüdische Schicksale* (Österreichischer Bundesverlag, 1992), 173.

56 Michaela Raggam-Blesch, "Unexpected Alliances and Limits of Solidarity: Non-Jewish Aid Organizations and the Jewish Community Assisting Jews and 'Non-Aryans' in Vienna, 1938–1945," in *Jewish Solidarity: The Ideal and the Reality in the Turmoil of the Shoah*, ed. Dan Michman and Robert Rozett (Yad Vashem, 2022), 158.

57 Bericht über die Tätigkeit des Ältestenrates der Juden in Wien im Jahre 1943, p. 11.

58 Rabinovici, *Instanzen der Ohnmacht*, 241.

59 Hecht et al., *Topographie der Shoah*, 497–504. Special thanks to Dr. Michaela Raggam-Blesch for taking the time to talk through and clarify how best to characterize the two institutions' relationship and cooperation.

60 Letter from Seegasse 9 KZ-Rückkehrerheim director Lazarowitsch to the IKG Amtsdirektion at Schottenring 25, 1010 Wien, August 21, 1948, XXVII, B, e, B31, IKG Archiv Wien.

61 Report by Nicholas Lazarowitsch, manager of the Seegasse 9 KZ-Rückkehrerheim, December 22, 1945, Lazarowitsch briefcase (not cataloged), 1, IKG Archiv Wien.

62 Report by Nicholas Lazarowitsch, manager of the Seegasse 9 KZ-Rückkehrerheim.

63 Memo from Major Judah Nadich, US Army.

64 Report by Nicholas Lazarowitsch, manager of the Seegasse 9 KZ-Rückkehrerheim; letter from Lazarowitsch to the IKG Amtsdirektion, August 21, 1948, IKG Archiv Wien.

65 Report to Rabbi Max Nussbaum written by Harry A. Freidenberg, administrative officer, Military Government Section, Vienna Area Command, US Army, May 25, 1947, p. 2, 45/54–143, JDC Archive.

66 Benjamin Ginsberg, *How the Jews Defeated Hitler: Exploding the Myth of Jewish Passivity in the Face of Nazism* (Rowman & Littlefield, 2013), 56.

67 Joseph W. Bendersky, *The "Jewish Threat": Anti-Semitic Politics of the U.S. Army* (Basic Books, 2000), 360.

68 List of all residents of Seegasse 9 KZ-Rückkehrerheim, October 16, 1947, folder "Diverse," Rückkehrerheime, Seegasse 9, B13, AD, IKG Archiv Wien.

69 Report by Nicholas Lazarowitsch, manager of the Seegasse 9 KZ-Rückkehrerheim.
70 Report by Nicholas Lazarowitsch, manager of the Seegasse 9 KZ-Rückkehrerheim.
71 List of payments in currency and points to camp residents, 1949, folder II, "Punkte [Points] 1948," Rückkehrerheime, Seegasse 9, B13, AD, IKG Archiv Wien.
72 "Kultusgemeinde Korrespondenz," AD, Rückkehrerheime, Seegasse, 1949, B13, IKG Archiv Wien.
73 List of payments in currency and points to camp residents, IKG Archiv Wien.
74 Report by Nicholas Lazarowitsch, manager of the Seegasse 9 KZ-Rückkehrerheim.
75 "Max Hirschmann," Rückkehrerheime, Seegasse 9, B13, AD, IKG Archiv Wien.
76 "Rapporte: Joint, IKG," Rückkehrerheime, Seegasse 9, 1949, B13, AD, IKG Archiv Wien.
77 "Rapport Woche," report of December 13, 1948, Rückkehrerheime, Seegasse 9, 1949, B13, AD, IKG Archiv Wien.
78 "Rapport Woche," report of December 13, 1948, mentioned on various reports from 1948, 1949. Amusingly, American soldiers' accounts tell of residents celebrating Passover, "the Jewish Easter," and Hanukkah, "the Jewish Christmas."
79 "Rapport," report on Seegasse 9 to Mr. Healy, July 1, 1949, Rückkehrerheime, Seegasse 9, 1949, B13, AD, IKG Archiv Wien.
80 Lazarowitsch briefcase (not cataloged), various photos, captioned and dated April 12, 1946, IKG Archiv Wien.
81 1.3.2.119.A41—VEAV—Vermögensentzug-Anmeldungsverordnung, 1947, 9. Bez., C 3, WStLA.
82 Letter from Lazarowitsch to the IKG Amtsdirektion, August 21, 1948, IKG Archiv Wien.
83 "Rapport," report on Seegasse 9 to Mr. Healy, April 7, 1949, Rückkehrerheime, Seegasse 9, 1949, B13, AD, IKG Archiv Wien.
84 *Der Lebensbaum: Der Wiener Israelitischen Kultusgemeine 1960–1964* (Israelitische Kultusgemeinde Wien, Fritz Molden Grossdruckerei und Verlag Gesellschaft m. b. H., 1964), 133.
85 Caro letter, doc. 1339, WHL.

14

JUSTICE FOR ALL?

Restitution and Compensation for Elderly Holocaust Survivors in Hungary

Borbála Klacsmann

A salient characteristic of the Hungarian Holocaust was that while able-bodied Jewish men of military age were drafted to unarmed military labor service, women, children, and the elderly remained at home and were ghettoized and deported in the spring and summer of 1944. The authorities emptied rural Hungary, and only the Jewish community of Budapest remained. As both the Hungarian army and the Nazis singled out healthy and fit young and middle-aged individuals for work, the majority of Jewish children and elderly perished during the Holocaust. Therefore, postwar documentation about elderly survivors is sparse, and this social stratum became quasi-invisible in the postwar years, with at least two generations growing up with the general experience that "I did not have grandparents."[1]

This is reflected in the fact that Hungarian scholarship on the Holocaust—indeed, all scholarship on the Holocaust—has dealt very little with their experiences.[2] There are no comprehensive studies tackling related issues, and only one paper that deals with elderly female Holocaust survivors. Historian Dóra Pataricza reconstructed the postwar circumstances of survivors from the Szeged community, based on their registry cards and requests for various household items and clothing.[3] Another author who has written about the sociological characteristics of Hungarian survivors—including the elderly—is sociologist and historian Viktor Karády. He found that in the rural areas, 78 percent of the Jewish population was annihilated, and the youngest and oldest age groups suffered the highest proportion of losses: in the former, this meant a 12.5 percent survival rate, while among the elderly it was a mere 9 percent.[4]

One way to gain insights into the experiences of the elderly is through compensation files. Research on restitution in rural Hungary has shown that the cases of elderly Jews (sixty years old and above) appear only sporadically in the postwar years, with most reparation cases initiated by young or middle-aged survivors.[5] Still, this is often the only possible source for the researcher to access. Most of the survivors who were middle aged or older during the Holocaust passed away before major institutions, such as the USC Shoah Foundation, began interviewing survivors. Consequently, restitution files can be precious documents providing insights into the life of the elderly. However, they have their own limitations. First, restitution and compensation cases generally contain information only about the applicant, with the fate of the closest family members mentioned but not elaborated on. Second, the survivors had a definite goal when writing restitution letters or applying for compensation: acquiring their lost property or getting compensation. Therefore, they edited their narrative accordingly, which must be taken into consideration when analyzing these sources.

In this study, I rely mostly on the research I conducted at the Hungarian National Archives—Pest County Archives (Magyar Nemzeti Levéltár Pest Vármegyei Levéltára, henceforth referred to as MNL PVL). Through the restitution cases, I review the indemnification, as well as the wartime and postwar experiences of elderly survivors in three time periods: the immediate postwar years, early socialism, and the 1960s–70s.

A Brief History of Reparations in Hungary

A peculiar feature of the Hungarian Holocaust was its velocity: within less than three months, the rural Jewish population—close to 440,000 people—was locked up in ghettos, robbed of their property, and deported. Even though the government aimed to redistribute Jewish wealth centrally, these efforts proved futile. During the hasty process, civil servants, law enforcement, organizations, and civilians alike took part in the plunder. By the end of the war, several valuables changed hands multiple times, were taken either by Wehrmacht soldiers or the Red Army, were destroyed, or their value changed, and therefore it was next to impossible to trace them.

Thus restitution became extremely difficult and was further complicated by a number of other factors, such as the unwillingness of non-Jews to give back Jewish property, and the fact that institutions that participated in "Aryanization"—among them, most importantly, the Financial Directorate (Pénzügyigazgatóság)—were now responsible for restitution.

In the postwar years, approximately two hundred thousand Jewish survivors remained in Hungary.[6] Most of them were impoverished, traumatized, and in poor physical shape. Therefore, they would have needed extensive help from the state in the form of restitution, as well as with social, psychological, and health care. Initially, it seemed that these needs would be tended to when the Provisional National Government withdrew all anti-Jewish laws and decrees in accordance with the ceasefire agreement with the Soviet Union on January 20, 1945.[7] The political elite also agreed to fulfill the prescriptions of the Paris Peace Treaty to return property confiscated after September 1, 1939, or to give compensation instead.[8]

Until the Communist Party came to power in Hungary, a number of laws and decrees regulated property issues and reparations. Among them decree no. 300/1946 was considered a legal breakthrough, as it allowed Holocaust survivors to reclaim their "Aryanized" property.[9] The government also introduced Act 25 of 1946, which reinforced the withdrawal of anti-Jewish laws and acknowledged the survivors' right to restitution. The law also dictated that heirless property be transferred to a fund that would then aid survivors in need.

Despite these laws and decrees, the efforts of survivors to obtain their property were not supported by the state for various reasons. Most importantly, after Hungary's defeat in the war, the Hungarian economy was in ruins, and rebuilding the country was a governmental priority above other urgent social issues. Additionally, politicians wanted to retain their voters, many of whom had benefited from "Aryanization." Plus, the political parties themselves had also received Jewish properties.[10] This went hand in hand with the fear that promoting and facilitating restitution would lead to increased antisemitic sentiment or attacks.[11]

As a result, survivors were left to their own devices. Many of them initiated official or legal cases in the hope that the authorities would aid them. They could turn to the Financial Directorate, the municipal leadership, or the housing offices—civil servants working within the municipality whose responsibility was the distribution of empty or "abandoned" houses.

These cases were complicated by the fact that several houses previously owned by Jews had been given or rented out to poor families or bombed-out individuals. There also was a shortage of intact apartments, so in many cases, two or more families were placed in the same house.

The Hungarian government established the Government Commission for Abandoned Property (Elhagyott Javak Kormánybiztossága) in 1945. Its main task was collecting and taking care of "abandoned" property, looking for the original owners, and returning it to them. However, this institution did not provide restitution; besides, it did not have a centrally allocated budget but had to cover its expenses from the income of renting out "abandoned" houses, equipment, and other valuables. The Jewish community voiced criticism concerning the commission's scope of responsibility, as it handled both the wealth of deported Jews, German-friendly civil servants who had fled to German territory, and later on, that of the "resettled" ethnic Germans.[12]

In accordance with the prescription of the Paris Peace Treaty and Act 25 of 1946, in 1947 the National Jewish Restitution Fund (Országos Zsidó Helyreállítási Alap, henceforth referred to as OZSHA) became responsible for heirless Jewish property. The original vision coordinating the fund's activity was that after its staff revised inheritance cases and acquired heirless real estate, they would sell those properties and, from the income, support survivors in need, Jewish self-help organizations, and the Jewish community in general. However, even during those years when the fund operated actively, numerous problems arose. Several "abandoned" assets that had been owned by Jews were not transferred to the fund from the Government Commission for Abandoned Property, and the fund's functioning was gradually rendered impossible by the socialist government and wide-scale nationalization. Soon they had to cede certain buildings to the government, the staff was reduced, and then in 1954, OZSHA was merged with the State Office for Church Affairs (Állami Egyházügyi Hivatal).[13]

Therefore, in the immediate postwar years and even during early socialism, Hungarian survivors relied entirely on the help of Jewish self-help organizations. The International Red Cross, the American Jewish Joint Distribution Committee (JDC or the Joint), and the World Jewish Congress maintained soup kitchens, health care facilities, and orphanages, and made efforts to reintegrate the survivors into society.[14] The Joint distributed millions of dollars through 1953.[15] Besides the international organizations, the Hungarian Jewish Community also established its own self-help institution, the National Jewish Aid Committee (Országos Zsidó Segítő Bizottság), which was financed by the Joint, and its main goal was to bring home the deported and provide aid to the survivors.

The surviving Jewish community hoped for years to get proper restitution and negotiated constantly with the responsible government officials.[16] They could not, however, reach a breakthrough, and talks about reparations were terminated during the socialist era. The socialist government was not willing to treat Holocaust survivors as a group with special needs: they considered them merely the "victims of fascism," among several other victim groups, denying the totality of the Final Solution.[17] This was combined with glossing over Hungarian collaboration and responsibility, as the victorious Soviet Union emphasized the antifascist struggle in Eastern Bloc countries, and thus restitution was only supported in the form of Western European countries handing back Jewish property that had been taken to their territories.[18]

Ironically, but not surprisingly, ultimately the same socialist government was the one that through diplomatic and political machinations got West German compensation programs extended to Hungary. Both the Bundesentschädigungsgesetz (BEG) and the Bundesrückerstattungsgesetz (BRÜG) Acts' eligibility clauses excluded Hungarian survivors. The first required applicants to have lived on German territory at some point before December 31, 1952, while the latter promised compensation only in case the applicant's home country had diplomatic relations with the Federal Republic of Germany (FRG).[19] At this point, the FRG and Hungary had no such connection.

In 1957, the Hungarian Socialist Workers' Party created the Hungarian National Committee of Persons Persecuted by Nazism (Nácizmus Magyarországi Üldözötteinek Országos Érdekvédelmi Szervezete, henceforth referred to as NÜÉSZ) which, together with financial and economic experts, lobbied for compensation for Hungarian survivors. In their letters sent to the West German Ministry of Finance, they argued that even if compensation sums were not paid, at least decisions should be made in the survivors' cases.[20] At the same time, sixty-two thousand Hungarian survivors submitted their applications. They had to wait for one-and-a-half decades for compensation. Finally, the International Court of Justice decided in Hungary's favor; therefore, in 1966 negotiations started between the two countries.[21]

The first compensation program extended to Hungary in 1960, aimed at aiding the victims of Nazi medical experiments.[22] In its framework, the survivors received 5 million DM.[23] In 1971, an intergovernmental agreement was concluded, according to which the NÜÉSZ received 6.25 million DM and then a lump sum of 100 million DM.[24] In exchange, the FRG asked that its commercial representatives be given the right to operate with the function of a consulate.[25] This was considered a diplomatic success, as officially the FRG and Hungary established diplomatic relations only in 1973.

The compensation procedures were mediated by NÜÉSZ, the International Red Cross, and the Financial Institutions Administration representing the Hungarian state. Most survivors received 6,500–13,000 HUF or occasionally higher sums.[26] These compensation amounts would have been much higher had the government not profited on the currency exchange.[27] Even so, this was the first time in twenty-five to thirty years that survivors received substantial compensation.

The Postwar Years: The Jewish Committee of Újpest

Újpest, a town just outside Budapest (now a district of the city), had a substantial Jewish community of more than twelve thousand individuals.[28] Merely two thousand survived the Holocaust.[29] They reestablished the congregation at the beginning of 1945 and soon started to deal with restitution issues. Contrary to the sporadic and uncoordinated efforts of survivors from small Jewish communities, the Újpest community negotiated with the local government in a united effort from the beginning. The surviving population was still large enough to put considerable pressure on the authorities and enforce the interests of its members, and therefore the municipality kept restitution on its agenda from February 1945.[30] In this section, I investigate the activities of the forming and re-forming Jewish self-representative committees and the role an elderly survivor played in them. The fact that only one such elderly person participated actively in these endeavors is indicative of the low percentage of surviving older Jews. Nevertheless, this man's presence proves that age, experience, and wisdom evoked respect and appreciation.

The first committee facilitating restitution in Újpest was the Jewish Committee, established on February 28, 1945. Apropos was the letter from a member of the National Committee,[31] written two days earlier to Mayor Sándor Szalay, criticizing the process of appointing trustees to "abandoned" Jewish buildings. As he explained, the Alliance of Jewish Military Laborers suggested potential trustees to the Court of Chancery, which in turn accepted the suggestions without investigating whether the trustees were related to the original owners. While the author did not dispute the importance of aiding the survivors, he suggested that the Jewish community should set up a committee that would take "financial and moral responsibility" for handling Jewish property.[32]

Just two days later this committee was established, which proves that the municipality cooperated closely with the Jewish community and accepted their participation in the restitution process. The committee consisted of seven representatives of the Újpest Israelite Congregation and the Alliance of Jewish Military Laborers, all leading, active personalities of the local community, such as János Hartmann, who later became the vice president and then president of the congregation, and lawyer Dr. Imre Ländler, whose family had owned two large stores in the city center.[33] All of them were middle-aged men, except for Miksa Manowill—he was born in 1879 and had been on the board of directors of the Rex leather factory before the war.[34] Manowill survived the war in Budapest, then returned to Újpest and, as an influential and well-known personality, took a role in the community leadership.[35] The composition of the committee indicates that the traditional age distribution in leading positions had shifted; as most of the elderly were murdered during the Holocaust, the reestablishment of the community became the task of younger men. Manowill was one of the few elders and, as such, his expertise and knowledge were utilized. On the other hand, having been a wealthy man, he was probably especially interested in the issue of restitution, and it is therefore not surprising that he wanted to take part in this important endeavor.

On March 6, 1945, the National Committee approved the Jewish Committee as a representative body.[36] On March 8 the mayor held a meeting with attorney general Pál Magyar, Court of Chancery vice chair Henrik Técsőy, and five members of the Jewish Committee—among them Miksa Manowill. According to the minutes, the main topic of the meeting was the nomination of trustees. All participants agreed that if a survivor returned, their property should be returned immediately. If the owner did not return but had living relatives, then they should be appointed as trustees. The

Jewish Committee argued that they would suggest trustworthy nominees and take responsibility for them in the case of heirless property. In exchange for controlling the trustees and in order to cover their own expenses, they required a share of the trustees' fees. Magyar and Técsőy accepted the terms; however, they also wanted the Court of Chancery to have the possibility to nominate trustees themselves. This then caused a dispute among the participants of the meeting.[37] The question was who would benefit from the income of Jewish apartments. A trustee responsible for a certain house handled its finances, and the Jewish community was interested in keeping such positions for the survivors. Since no agreement was reached, another meeting was held on March 13. This time all parties accepted the proposition that the Jewish Committee would propose enough candidates so that one person would handle only one estate.[38]

Only half a month later, the National Committee dissolved the Jewish Committee and formed a new one, chaired by Pál Magyar.[39] According to the attorney general's invitation to the new committee's first meeting, the following organizations delegated members to it: the Újpest Israelite Congregation, the Hungarian Communist Party, the Social Democratic Party, the Independent Smallholders' Party, the National Aid, and the Alliance of Jewish Military Laborers.[40] This was not a unique event but rather a structural feature of the restitution process: political parties as well as other representative bodies all wanted to be in control and thus the Jewish community's will could not prevail. While the Jewish Committee was made up entirely of Holocaust survivors, the community delegated merely two members to the new committee. Thus the government took the issue of the trustees out of the survivors' hands. Another problem emerging as a result of the prolonged bureaucratic process was the time factor: while the government tried to find the best ways for restitution, the survivors had to live day to day without financial means or possessions returned to them.

In the end, the story of early restitution in Újpest was quite similar to that in other towns: despite the community's efforts, the local government and political parties hindered them, due to the reasons enumerated in the previous section of this paper: they feared antisemitism because many non-Jews (and even the parties themselves) received Jewish valuables that they did not want to return. Thus in Újpest the government balanced between seemingly embracing the survivors' cause and still giving representation to non-Jews in restitution matters.

The presence of Miksa Manowill in this process is an interesting feature because very few elderly survivors participated in or initiated restitution cases, even in Újpest, where relatively many survivors returned. The low survival rate of elderly Jews resulted in a missing age group; Manowill could only survive because he escaped to Budapest where there were no mass deportations in the spring and summer of 1944. As a member of the short-lived Jewish Committee, for a brief time he had insight into local restitution and most probably the community leaders depended on the influence of his age and experience. Unfortunately, his name does not turn up in any other documents concerning restitution, which, in turn, shows us how elderly people disappeared from historical records—also from those concerning restitution. Highlighting individuals such as Manowill not only calls attention to the striking absence of other elderly in the restitution process but also facilitates a more thorough understanding of their Holocaust and postwar experiences.

Early Socialism: The Weisz-Guttmann Family's Case

Alfréd Weisz, his wife, Szidónia née Guttmann, and her sister, Matild Guttmann, all lived together in 1944. Their house on Thurzó Street, Pestszenterzsébet, a town on the outskirts of Budapest, was worth 11,200 Pengő.[41] In May 1948, the district jury of Pestszenterzsébet had to make a decision concerning Alfréd Weisz's property: in the absence of a will, either the state or OZSHA was entitled to receive their wealth—depending on the date and cause of the owner's death. The case was further complicated by the claim of Mrs. Henrik Roskies, Matild Guttmann's daughter, who lived in Canada at the time. The fate of the Weisz-Guttmann family—especially that of elderly Matild Guttmann—and their house tells a great deal about restitution, its personal aspects, and attitudes toward elderly survivors. The participants in the inheritance case had various motivations: the fact that Matild Guttmann was a Holocaust survivor who really needed the house was almost forgotten.

During the legal case, OZSHA and Mrs. Roskies's representative, Dezső Goldstein, stated that Alfréd Weisz passed away due to the persecution.[42] At this point, the two parties cooperated to exclude the state treasury from the inheritance. However, as soon as the state disappeared from the picture, the two parties had to continue the litigation—this time against each other. In April 1949, Mrs. Roskies wrote to the court: "Alfréd Weisz's death was not connected to the persecution of the Jews, taking into account that he died half a year after the siege [of Budapest]. He had suffered from a heart condition for decades. [. . .] But he, personally, was not persecuted, nor deported, he stayed in his house and passed away at the age of over 70."[43] Not surprisingly, here Mrs. Roskies stated exactly the opposite of what her representative had said a couple of months earlier. Her motive is clear: to exclude OZSHA from the inheritance. In order to achieve this, she even lied by stating that Weisz had not been persecuted.

According to law, in order to receive the inheritance, Mrs. Roskies had to prove that Mrs. Weisz had inherited it from her parents and therefore she would have the right to lineal succession.[44] In her letter to the court, she claimed that Mrs. Weisz had much more substantial wealth than her husband at the time of their marriage and she had bought the house from the money she had received from her parents. "As it is lineal inheritance, according to law the heirs are first defendant [Matild Guttmann] as the devisor's sister and me as her sister's child."[45] This was the first occasion that Matild Guttmann's name appeared—before that, no one seemed to be concerned about her rights.

The date of the lawsuit between OZSHA and Mrs. Roskies was approaching; therefore, Dezső Goldstein sent a letter to OZSHA in which he asked them to renounce their claim. As he wrote, "in the house in Pestszenterzsébet, first defendant [Matild Guttmann] lives who is a helpless elderly lady and does not let anyone close to her, not even her relatives. If the Fund wins the case, you would be responsible for her eviction and supporting her which would cost more than the estate's worth."[46] Goldstein's letter finally provides a glimpse into reality: the apartment was not abandoned at all. Matild Guttmann still lived in it. The elderly woman had lived there for a long while and if Goldstein's description was correct, she must have been oblivious to the legal case concerning her home. From the previous documents, it seems that in the lawsuit preparations everyone forgot about her existence. However, in light of Matild Guttmann's age and attitude, Mrs. Roskies's struggle to obtain the house seems much more substantiated.

Even so, OZSHA chairman Lajos Stöckler ordered the staff to continue the litigation.[47] According to an internal report, shoemaker Lajos Hoffmann tried to acquire the house to win back the sum he had spent on caring for Matild Guttmann, whereas "Dezső Goldstein, [. . .] Mrs. Roskies' representative does not care for the elderly lady and the latter sees her persecutor in him, stating that Dezső Goldstein wants to dispossess her."[48]

In the October 1949 lawsuit, the court of justice decided that OZSHA would inherit the apartment.[49] Afterward, the fund investigated the house's condition. The resulting internal report states that Lajos Hoffmann had hidden Alfréd Weisz and Matild Guttmann during the Holocaust, while "Arrow Cross members had identity checked and deported Alfréd Weisz's wife on May 1, 1944, when she went to the city [Budapest]. Since then, she has been missing."[50] Ever since Alfréd Weisz's death in September 1945, Hoffmann considered Matild Guttmann the house's owner.[51] According to the report, the older woman received 100 HUF a year in aid from the Joint, and her daughter, Mrs. Roskies, also sent her parcels, but most importantly, Lajos Hoffmann took care of her. From this description, it seems that Hoffmann was a long-term and committed friend of the Weisz family. He stood by them during the Holocaust and did not abandon the elderly woman who, apparently, accepted him as a friend and guardian.

In October 1950, Alfréd Weisz's cousins also filed a claim for the house—it is unclear why they did not do so earlier.[52] OZSHA sent a letter to their representative, lawyer Dr. István Balázs, from which it is clear that the relatives did not want to care for Matild Guttmann, and added that they "could not expect Lajos Hoffmann to continue caring for Matild Guttmann from his own money."[53] In his reply, Balázs mentioned that Lajos Hoffmann proposed to buy the apartment: "he would buy the estate and undertake to care for Matild Guttmann and pay the heirs 5,000 HUF in order to settle the costs of the proceedings."[54]

Eventually, in an April 1951 contract, the house's value was established at 31,500 HUF, of which OZSHA received 3,000, the other heirs 4,000, while they deducted 10,000 HUF for the costs of taking care of Matild Guttmann in the past and an additional 14,000 HUF for providing for her until the end of her life. According to the contract, Lajos Hoffmann and his wife "cared for Alfréd Weisz for 16 months, between May 1, 1944, until August 19, 1945, and have been caring for his sister-in-law who is a helpless elderly lady until today."[55] Finally, on May 23, 1951, the house was officially transferred into Lajos Hoffmann's possession and thus the case was closed.

This case tells a great deal about how elderly survivors were treated during restitution processes. While OZSHA's main task was to obtain heirless apartments and from their sale aid needy survivors, in several cases they found themselves in the impossible situation that the collateral relatives of the victims claimed the same houses—and thus allowing them to take possession would have served OZSHA's original aim. In the case described, an elderly survivor lived in the apartment and even though she was not the owner, humanitarian considerations did not allow for her eviction. Thus flexibility was required from both the fund and the other actors in the course of the legal procedure, and finally the case was resolved in a way that reflected both financial and humanitarian interests.

The sources reveal that Matild Guttmann received a small sum from the Joint but, otherwise, she was entirely dependent on Lajos Hoffmann's benevolence—meaning she did not get any substantial help from the government, either as restitution or in health or social services. This is an authentic picture of the survivors' situation: they could rely only on Jewish self-aid organizations and occasionally on decent non-Jews who decided to help them. Moreover, had it not been for Hoffmann, the institution that had been created to provide compensation to survivors would have dispossessed Matild Guttmann.

The case also contains information about a complex network of actors: relatives of the deceased couple, an elderly survivor, the representatives of a state institution, and a non-Jewish family whose fate intertwined with the original owners. In this respect, two main threads can be distinguished: the legal procedure concerning the house and the story of the Hoffmann and Weisz-Guttmann families. By all appearances, Lajos Hoffmann was an honest and good-hearted man who stood up for his Jewish friends at the time of their persecution and selflessly took care of elderly people even after the war. Eventually, he even bought a house, which neither he himself nor his family members apparently had use for, only to save the elderly Matild Guttmann from eviction.

The Kádár Era: Mrs. Pál Totisz's Case

Mrs. Pál Totisz, née Erzsébet Krausz (b. 1909), applied for compensation from the FRG in September 1957. Her case is typical for survivors who were young or middle-aged at the time of the Holocaust and afterwards, now elderly, never received adequate restitution or compensation. It reveals a characteristic feature of compensation from the FRG: namely, that many times it took years—even decades—until a case was resolved and in the meantime the applicant had passed away. This kind of treatment prolonged the discrimination the survivors experienced.

Before the war Mrs. Totisz lived in Pestszenterzsébet. Upon her return, she gave a testimony to DEGOB, the National Committee for Attending Deportees, in which she described how a policeman had taken her off the tram and arrested her on March 20, 1944.[56] After an identity check, she had been interned at the Kistarcsa internment camp and from there, on April 28, she was deported to Auschwitz.[57] "On the day after our arrival, they took us to work at 2 a.m. We laid down the rail tracks between Auschwitz and Birkenau [. . .]. The work was hard, the working hours terribly long and the treatment very bad. They beat us and rushed us. Whatever weather we had, it did not matter, we had to work in our thin rags which they gave us instead of our clothes; besides, the food was inedible." Later on, Mrs. Totisz was assigned to various work commandos, and eventually she took part in the dismantling of the crematoria. After the evacuation of Auschwitz, she was taken to Bergen-Belsen: "When the British arrived, we did not have any energy left. [. . .] Everyone who was alive, regardless of whether they were ill or healthy, were taken to hospital where we were fed and given the best nursing."[58] Mrs. Totisz arrived home in November 1945.

According to the data provided in Mrs. Totisz's compensation form, when she applied, she lived in Budapest, she was divorced, and she worked in a bakery as a shop assistant. She claimed to have suffered from various types of diseases during her stay at the camps and even afterwards. She enumerated the valuables that had been confiscated from her in Auschwitz, among them precious jewelry. Taking into account the thoroughness of "Aryanization" in Hungary, and the fact that most Jews had to give up their valuables already in the ghettos and transit camps, we may assume that Mrs. Totisz had lost these valuables even earlier. However, in the compensation claims the applicants blamed as much of the robbery as possible on the Nazis in order to justify their claim.[59] Additionally, Mrs. Totisz stated that her husband's workshop and storage space, as well as their home, had been looted in their absence: furniture, clothing, kitchenware, glass- and porcelain ware, and jewelry worth 53,000 HUF were stolen.[60] A report attached to the form contains more details: Sándor and Tibor Totisz, the couple's children, were murdered in Auschwitz. The couple divorced after the war—they did not even keep in touch.[61]

In 1975, the case was concluded successfully and the staff of NÜÉSZ wanted to determine the beneficiaries. From the documents, it turns out that Mrs. Totisz had worked as a cleaner in the late 1960s, and both she and her husband had passed away in 1970. Even so, both of them were entitled to compensation, as Mrs. Totisz had been persecuted and robbed during the Holocaust; additionally, the Nazis murdered their children. Altogether 19,500 HUF was distributed among Mrs. Totisz's relatives and Pál Totisz's second wife, Ilona Juhász: while the former received less than 5,000 HUF per person, Juhász got 6,500 HUF.[62]

This case is characteristic of the Hungarian reparation process from several points of view. First, the timeline provides an overview of how historical events influenced an individual's life. Mrs. Totisz applied in 1957, the first possible instant available to Hungarian survivors, which was already thirteen years after the peak of the persecution in Hungary. For more than a decade nothing happened, and the breakthrough came only in the mid-1970s, when Hungary and the FRG reached an agreement. Thus almost two decades after the applicant had written and handed in the compensation claim, NÜÉSZ could finally transfer the compensation.

Additionally, Mrs. Totisz's example demonstrates how prolonged compensation cases damaged survivors. Several applicants passed away during the long bureaucratic procedures and thus they never received the compensation they deserved.[63] Mrs. Totisz was 61 years old when she died, and no doubt she could have used financial aid at the end of her life, considering that she worked as a cleaner. Instead, her relatives received it. As they were also Holocaust survivors, this seems less of an issue than Ilona Juhász (Pál Totisz's second wife) getting compensation: she was neither Jewish nor related to Mrs. Totisz or her murdered children in any capacity—ironically, though, she received the largest sum. In this case, the question arises whether and how the responsible authorities could ensure the rightful distribution of compensation if an applicant died before a decision was made in his or her case. Since we do not know how the rest of the beneficiaries were related to Mrs. Totisz, we may only guess on which basis the sums were divided: According to inheritance laws? Hungarian or West German? Did every living relative receive money? How were the sums determined? Unfortunately, the sources do not contain any answers; the relatives received only a notification about the outcome of the case.

Last but not least, Mrs. Totisz's compensation also shows that Central and Eastern European history was not particularly merciful toward Holocaust survivors. While young and middle-aged Jews survived the Holocaust in Hungary in greater numbers than the elderly and children, due to the unfavorable circumstances they never received proper restitution or compensation, and by the time the representatives of the FRG decided to extend the compensation programs to Hungary, even those who had been young in the 1940s had become middle-aged or old—and those who had been fifty to sixty years old were eighty to ninety.

Conclusion

Restitution in the postwar years was mostly hampered both by the government and the local municipalities. Efforts by the Jewish community met with reluctance and were usually blocked by leading civil servants. In this period, very few elderly survivors lived outside of Budapest—usually only those remained who had either escaped to Budapest in 1944 or had been hidden by their non-Jewish friends. Since restitution in general was withheld and the success of individual cases usually depended on the survivors' resourcefulness and perseverance and the benevolence of particular local civil servants, at this stage it would be hard to establish any characteristics of restitution for elderly survivors.

The case was somewhat different under early socialism and during the Kádár era, as many middle-aged survivors reached old age by then. They restarted their lives without the help of the state and dependent on self-aid organizations, while a major portion would have needed health care, as well as psychological and financial aid. Elderly survivors were in a vulnerable position—as Matild Guttmann's case demonstrates—not only because of their age but also due to health issues and incapacitation, which often rendered them dependent on caretakers. This limited their involvement in restitution issues, which were often decided above them, with the participation of younger relatives or friends.

Compensation arriving from the FRG had another specific feature vis-à-vis elderly survivors: the procedures took so long due to diplomatic complications that by the time the compensation sums reached the recipients, many of them had become old or had already passed away. While we must emphasize that this was the first time that Hungarian survivors received substantial help, it is also noteworthy that this aid came very late and many who would have been entitled never received it.

Finally, after the fall of the socialist system, a new era opened in the history of compensation. By this time, even those who were children at the time of the Holocaust had grown old, but finally a combination of national and international aid became available for them.

Notes

1 See the proportions of survivors by age group in Randolph L. Braham, *A népirtás politikája—A Holocaust Magyarországon*, vol. 2 (Belvárosi Könyvkiadó, 1997), 1249; and Aaron Hass, *In the Shadow of the Holocaust—The Second Generation* (Cambridge University Press, 2001), 30.

2 Tamás Stark, who has repeatedly written about the statistics related to Holocaust survivors, did not include a sociological analysis: Tamás Stark, *Zsidóság a vészkorszakban és a felszabadulás után (1939–1955)* (MTA, 1995). Gábor Dombi, who wrote about the resettlement of Budapest Jews during the socialist era, quoted György Haraszti, according to whom mostly children and men perished during the Holocaust, therefore the majority of survivors were women and the elderly. Interestingly, however, on the next page Dombi adds, "The majority of the survivors and those who stayed at home were adults and elderly. During the Shoah, vulnerable women, children and the elderly perished in greater proportions while a considerable proportion of the strong Jewish youth emigrated [later]." Gábor Dombi, *Osztályellenségek—Az 1951-es budapesti kitelepítés zsidó áldozatai* (NEB, 2020), 44–45. The latter view coincides with Braham's statistics: from among the men and women living in rural Hungary, those of the age groups twenty to forty and forty to sixty survived in higher proportion than did children and the elderly.

3 Dóra Pataricza, "Resilient Women, Rebuilt Lives: A Study of JDC's Work in Szeged After the Holocaust," *Quest: Issues in Contemporary Jewish History* 24 (2023): 164–88.

4 Viktor Karády, *Túlélők és újrakezdők: Fejezetek a magyar zsidóság szociológiájából 1945 után* (Múlt és jövő, 2002), 70, 74.

5 Borbála Klacsmann, "A holokauszt túlélőinek kárpótlása és jóvátétele Pest megyében, 1945–1989" (PhD diss., University of Szeged, 2021).

6 Stark, *Zsidóság a vészkorszakban*, 76; János Botos, *A magyarországi zsidóság vagyonának sorsa 1938–1949* (Magyar Napló, 2015), 64.

7 "Act V of 1945," Jogtár, accessed October 10, 2023, net.jogtar.hu/ezer-ev-torveny?docid=94500005.TV&searchUrl=/ezer-ev-torvenyei%3Fpagenum%3D42.

8 "Act XVIII of 1947," Jogtár, accessed October 10, 2023, net.jogtar.hu/jogszabaly?docid=94700018.tv.

9 *Magyar Közlöny*, no. 22, January 26, 1946, 2–3.

10 Botos, *A magyarországi zsidóság*, 67, 72. See for instance the Hungarian Communist Party's claim on Sándor Hartmann's house MNL PVL V.1102 Db, 615/1947; the Hungarian Communist Party's claim for Árpád Klein's villa, MNL PVL V1102 Db, 419/1945.

11 This was a realistic fear, as in Hungary, just like in other Central and Eastern European countries, pogroms broke out in the postwar years, some of which were inspired by unsettled property issues. Éva Vörös, "Kunmadaras—Újabb adatok a pogrom történetéhez," *Múlt és jövő* 6, no. 4 (1994): 69–80, and János Varga, "A miskolci népítélet, 1946," *Medvetánc* 6, no. 2–3 (1986): 293–314.

12 Regarding the government commission, see Kálmán Kardos, "Az Elhagyott Javak Kormánybiztossága (1945–1949)," *Levéltári Híradó* 10, no. 2 (1960): 53–64; Borbála Klacsmann, "Neglected Restitution: The Relations of the Government Commission for Abandoned Property and the Hungarian Jews, 1945–1948," *Hungarian Historical Review* 9, no. 3 (2020): 512–29.

13 Gergő Bendegúz Cseh, "Az Országos Zsidó Helyreállítási Alap létrehozásának körülményei és működése (1947–1989)," *Levéltári Közlemények* 65, no. 1–2 (1994): 119–27; Borbála Klacsmann, "Vitatható kárpótlás: az Országos Zsidó Helyreállítási Alap működése esettanulmányok tükrében," in *Tanulmányok a magyarországi zsidóság történetéből*, ed. Csaba Fazekas (Milton Friedman Egyetem, 2019), 204–18.

14 American Jewish Joint Distribution Committee, Hungarian Representation's collection, XXXIII-4-A, unit 46, Hungarian Jewish Archives (Magyar Zsidó Múzeum és Levéltár, henceforth MZsML).

15 In 1945, Hungary received 23 percent of all aid that the Joint distributed in Europe (almost 4 million US dollars). This figure rose to 27 percent in

1948 (amounting to 8.5 million US dollars). Hungarian Jews thus received the largest total amount of funding from the Joint in Europe. See Kinga Frojimovics, "Different Interpretations of Reconstruction: The American Jewish Joint Distribution Committee and the World Jewish Congress in Hungary After the Holocaust," in *The Jews Are Coming Back: The Return of the Jews to Their Countries of Origin After WWII*, ed. David Bankier (Berghahn–Yad Vashem, 2005), 280.

16 See, for instance, Memorandum of the Pest Israelite Congregation, XXXIII-6, unit 26, MZsML.

17 Eszter Bartha and Slávka Otčenášová, "Memory and Politics: 'Totalitarian' and 'Revisionist' Approaches to the Study of the Holocaust in Hungary and Slovakia," *Central European Papers* 7, no. 1 (2019): 14.

18 Cseh, "Az Országos Zsidó Helyreállítási Alap," 125.

19 See paragraph 4, "BEG," accessed October 12, 2023, www.gesetze-im-internet.de/beg/BEG.pdf; paragraph 5a, "BRÜG," accessed October 12, 2023, www.gesetze-im-internet.de/br_g/BR%C3%BCG.pdf.

20 NÜÉSZ's letter to Finance Minister Dr. Heinz Starke, February 18, 1962, B 126, 117174, Bundesarchiv Koblenz.

21 Róbert Győri Szabó, *A kommunizmus és a zsidóság az 1945 utáni Magyarországon* (Gondolat, 2009), 338–39.

22 "Wiedergutmachung—Provisions Relating to Compensation for National Socialist Injustice," 15, accessed October 12, 2023, www.bundesfinanzministerium.de/Content/EN/Standardartikel/Press_Room/Publications/Brochures/2018-08-15-entschaedigung-ns-unrecht-engl.pdf?__blob=publicationFile&v=24.

23 Gábor Kádár and Zoltán Vági, *Self-Financing Genocide: The Gold Train, the Becher Case and the Wealth of Hungarian Jews* (CEU Press, 2001), 148.

24 Stephen J. Roth, "Indemnification of Hungarian Victims of Nazism," in *The Holocaust in Hungary: Fifty Years Later*, ed. Randolph L. Braham and Attila Pók (Rosenthal Institute for Holocaust Studies, 1997), 748; Győri Szabó, *A kommunizmus és a zsidóság*, 339.

25 Andrea Dunai, "Kárpótlás, devizabevétel, diplomácia," *Múlt és jövő* 15, no. 4 (2004): 69–72.

26 In comparison, in the 1960s, the average monthly wage was HUF 800–1,200, while in the 1970s it was HUF 1,600–2,000. Rudolf Andorka and István Harcsa, "A lakosság jövedelme," in *Társadalmi riport 1990*, ed. Rudolf Andorka et al. (Tárki, 1990), 99.

27 Kádár and Vági, *Self-Financing Genocide*, 148.
28 József Kepecs, ed., *A zsidó népesség száma településenként (1840–1941)* (KSH, 1993), 232.
29 Randolph L. Braham, ed., *A magyarországi holokauszt földrajzi enciklopédiája*, vol. 2 (Park, 2007), 887.
30 See an overview in Borbála Klacsmann, "'Óriási erkölcsi szolgálatot tenne a városnak'—Holokauszttúlélők és a kárpótlás Újpesten," part 1, *Újpesti Helytörténeti Értesítő* 27, no. 4 (2020): 12–13, and part 2, *Újpesti Helytörténeti Értesítő* 28, no. 1 (2021): 13–14.
31 After the war, national committees were established in all major cities and towns. They had no defined legal status. They were not supposed to participate in public administration, but still they actively took part in reorganizing local governments and other organizational tasks. Balázs Gábor, "A nemzeti bizottságok működése Pest megyében," accessed October 17, 2023, felsooktatas.oktatolapok.mnl.gov.hu/letoltes/Balazs_Gabor_A_nemzeti_bizottsagok_mukodese_pest_megyeben_1_bevezetes.pdf.
32 Letter to the mayor, February 26, 1945, V.675.C, 4723/1945, Budapest City Archives (Budapest Főváros Levéltára, henceforth referred to as BFL).
33 The congregation's letter to the mayor, February 28, 1945; László Szilágyi-Windt, *Az újpesti zsidóság története* (Lahav, 1975), 224; Elfeledett újpestiek, accessed October 17, 2023, Újpest önkormányzata, ujpest.hu/elfeledett-ujpestiek-up-rendezvenyter/#section-eu-36.
34 István Hegedüs, *Őrségváltás* (István Hegedűs, [1942]), 246.
35 "Miksa Manovill [*sic*]," accessed October 17, 2023, Yad Vashem, collections.yadvashem.org/en/names/11662209.
36 Decision of the National Committee, March 6, 1945, V.675.C, 4723/1945, BFL.
37 Meeting minutes, March 8, 1945, V.675.C, 4723/1945, BFL.
38 Meeting minutes, March 13, 1945, V.675.C, 4723/1945, BFL.
39 Decision of the National Committee, April 7, 1945, V.675.C, 4723/1945, BFL.
40 Pál Magyar's letter, April 13, 1945, V.675.C, 4723/1945, BFL. The National Aid (*Nemzeti Segély*) was established by the Hungarian Communist Party in January 1945. Initially it was controlled by the four major parties that built a national network. The organization's main activity focused on child welfare.
41 One month after the German occupation of Hungary, according to decree no. 1600/1944, every Jewish family was obliged to hand in their

declaration form to the Financial Directorate. The forms contained information about real estate, precious metal items, shops, stocks, pieces of art, and every other asset. The Pest County Archive holds the collection of every declaration form sent in by the Jews living in the county's territory. Alfréd Weisz's declaration form, April 28, 1944, MNL PVL VI.101 C/1/B, 7613/1944.

42 Pro domo report, June 23, 1948, XXXIII-9, 3654/1948, Hungarian National Archives (Magyar Nemzeti Levéltár Országos Levéltára, henceforth referred to as MNL OL).

43 Henrik Roskies' letter, April 26, 1949, XXXIII-9, 3654/1948 MNL OL.

44 According to Hungarian law, lineal succession is applicable exclusively if there are no descendants. Lineal property is inherited by the parents or the grandparents of the deceased—or if they are dead, then more distant ascendants of the deceased person. This inheritance comprises those assets which the deceased person acquired from an ancestor by inheritance or gift.

45 Mrs. Henrik Roskies' letter, April 26, 1949, XXXIII-9, 3654/1948, MNL OL.

46 Dezső Goldstein's letter, June 26, 1949. XXXIII-9, 3654/1948, MNL OL.

47 Lajos Stöckler (1897–1960), industrialist, from July 1944 a leading member of the Jewish Council. Between 1945 and 1950, he was the president of the Pest Israelite Congregation. In 1953, he was arrested and framed for the murder of Raoul Wallenberg. He was released in 1956 and emigrated to Australia, where he died in 1960.

48 Report, May 30, 1949, XXXIII-9, 3654/1948, MNL OL.

49 Judgment, October 1949, XXXIII-9, 3654/1948, MNL OL.

50 Report, February 13, 1950, XXXIII-9, 3654/1948, MNL OL.

51 Report, February 13, 1950, XXXIII-9, 3654/1948, MNL OL. In reality, Mrs. Weisz was captured by Hungarian gendarmes, as the Arrow Cross Party came to power only in October 1944; but after the war, the survivors often attributed anti-Jewish acts and persecution to this party.

52 Pro domo report, October 19, 1950, XXXIII-9, 3654/1948, MNL OL, XXXIII-9, 3654/1948, MNL OL.

53 OZSHA's letter, February 27, 1951, XXXIII-9, 3654/1948, MNL OL.

54 Dr. István Balázs's letter, April 10, 1951, XXXIII-9, 3654/1948, MNL OL.

55 Contract, April 24, 1951, XXXIII-9, 3654/1948, MNL OL.

56 The National Committee for Attending Deportees (Deportáltakat Gondozó Országos Bizottság) was a subcommittee of the National Jewish Aid

Committee. It organized trips to concentration camps at the end of the war to bring home the deported and prepared lists of Hungarian survivors. The subcommittee also collected forty-six hundred testimonies from them, which is one of the major and earliest collections of Hungarian survivor testimonies. The original sources are kept at the Hungarian Jewish Archives. More than thirty-five hundred of them are digitized and available at http://degob.hu/ (accessed October 15, 2023). Rita Horváth, *A magyarországi zsidók Deportáltakat Gondozó Országos Bizottsága (DEGOB) története* (Magyar Zsidó Levéltár, 1997).

57 The internment camp in Kistarcsa was established at the end of the 1920s and after the German occupation, mainly Jews arrested during "Einzelaktionen" were kept there. A group of prominent Jews were also held there as hostages. Braham, *A népirtás politikája*, 849–951, and Braham, *A magyarországi holokauszt*, 861–63.

58 DEGOB protocol no. 3493.

59 On this topic, see Borbála Klacsmann, "After the Storm: The Long-Term Consequences of the Holocaust and Compensations in Hungary," in *Dubnow Institute Yearbook XVIII*, ed. Yfaat Weiss (Vandenhoeck & Ruprecht, 2022), 233–58.

60 Mrs. Pál Totisz's compensation claim, XIX-L-20-o, 20544, MNL OL.

61 Report, May 2, 1962, XIX-L-20-o, 20544, MNL OL.

62 Compensation resolution, July 30 and August 13, 1975, XIX-L-20-o, 20544, MNL OL. Unfortunately, the sources do not reveal how the beneficiaries were related to the Totiszs. However, because Mrs. Totisz's maiden name was Krausz and because the compensation sums for both the murdered children and Mrs. Totisz were divided among them, we may assume that they were her relatives.

63 Yael Danieli, "Massive Trauma and the Healing Role of Reparative Justice," in *Reparations for Victims of Genocide, War Crimes and Crimes Against Humanity*, ed. Carla Ferstman et al. (Martinus Nijhoff, 2009), 57.

CONTRIBUTORS

Elizabeth Anthony is director of Visiting Scholar Programs at the United States Holocaust Memorial Museum's Jack, Joseph and Morton Mandel Center for Advanced Holocaust Studies. Her book, *The Compromise of Return: Viennese Jews After the Holocaust*, was copublished by Wayne State University Press and the US Holocaust Memorial Museum in 2021 and was a commended finalist for the Wiener Holocaust Library's Ernst Fraenkel Prize. Anthony was coeditor of and a contributor to *Freilegungen: Spiegelungen der NS-Verfolgung und ihrer Konsequenzen, Jahrbuch des International Tracing Service* (2015). She also has published chapters in *Lessons and Legacies*, vol. 12 (2017); *The Future of Holocaust Memorialization: Confronting Racism, Antisemitism, and Homophobia Through Memory Work* (2015); and the *Nürnberger Institut für NS-Forschung und jüdische Geschichte des 20. Jahrhunderts Jahrbuch 2010*. Anthony received a PhD in history at Clark University in 2016.

Kierra Crago-Schneider is the campus outreach program officer at the United States Holocaust Memorial Museum's Jack, Joseph and Morton Mandel Center for Advanced Holocaust Studies. Her research focuses on the relationships formed between Holocaust survivors living in Jews-only displaced persons' centers in Germany and American occupiers, international aid workers, and Germans from 1945 to 1957. Her publications include "Years of Survival: JDC in Post-War Germany, 1945–1957," coauthored with Avinoam Patt, in *The Joint Distribution Committee: 100 Years of Jewish History*, edited by Atina Grossmann, Linda Levi, Maud Mandel, and Avinoam Patt (Wayne State University Press, 2019); "A Community of Will: The Resettlement of the Orthodox from Föhrenwald," *Holocaust and Genocide Studies* (2018); "Jewish 'Shtetls' in Postwar Germany: An Analysis of Interactions Among Jewish Displaced Persons, Germans, and Americans Between 1945 and 1957 in Bavaria," *Proquest* (2013); and "Antisemitism or Competing Interests? An Examination of German and American Perceptions of Jewish Displaced Persons Active on the Black Market in Munich's Möhlstraße," *Yad Vashem Studies* (2010).

Maria Ferenc is a research fellow at the University of Wrocław, Poland, and a Claims Conference Saul Kagan Fellow in Advanced Shoah Studies. She is working on a book discussing the biography and memory of Mordechai Anielewicz. Maria has received various fellowships, including at the Jack, Joseph and Morton Mandel Center for Advanced Holocaust Studies at the United States Holocaust Museum in Washington, DC (2022), Fondation Memoire de la Shoah (2020–22), and Yad Vashem (2016). She coordinated the research project "The Encyclopedia of the Warsaw Ghetto" at the Jewish Historical Institute (2018–24) and coedited several volumes of documents from the Ringelblum Archive. Her book, *"Everyone Asks What Will Become of Us": Inhabitants of the Warsaw Ghetto and the News of the War and the Holocaust* (2021) won and was shortlisted for many prizes and is currently being translated into English. Her other publications include articles, among others, in *Radical History Review*, *Zagłada Żydów: Studia i Materiały*, *Annales de démographie historique*, *Media History*, and *Yalkut Moreshet.*

Katharina Friedla is a research fellow and the Taube Family Curator for European Collections at the Hoover Institution Library & Archives at Stanford University. She has pursued history, East European studies, and Jewish studies at the Free University in Berlin and the Hebrew University in Jerusalem, and received her PhD from the Department of History, University of Basel, Switzerland. She has published several books and dozens of articles on nationalism, identity politics, and forced migration, with a special focus on European Jewry. Most recently, she coedited two volumes: with Lidia Zessin-Jurek, the book *The Siberian Odyssey of Polish Jews* (in Polish), and with Markus Nesselrodt, *Polish Jews in the Soviet Union (1939–1959): History and Memory of Deportation, Exile, and Survival.*

Michael Geheran is associate professor of history and deputy director of the Resnick Center for Holocaust and Genocide Studies at the United States Military Academy at West Point. He is the author of *Comrades Betrayed: Jewish World War I Veterans Under Hitler* (2020) and a contributing coeditor of *Beyond Inclusion and Exclusion: Jewish Experiences of the First World War in Central Europe* (2018). He is currently completing a digital history of General Roméo Dallaire's leadership during the Rwandan genocide.

Niamh Hanrahan is a PhD student at the University of Manchester in the United Kingdom, based in the Humanitarian and Conflict Response Institute. Her PhD project examines the migrations undertaken by Jewish refugees from Europe to Japan during WWII. Niamh was the postgraduate representative for the British and Irish Association for Holocaust Studies in the 2022–23 academic year. She has been awarded fellowships to conduct research in the USA, Germany, Japan, and Australia.

Borbála Klacsmann is a Hungarian Holocaust historian. Her areas of expertise include the microhistory of the Hungarian Holocaust and restitution and compensation for Holocaust survivors. She completed her doctoral studies at the Department of History at the University of Szeged in 2021. Previously, she had worked for the Holocaust Memorial Center in Budapest, the Anne Frank House, and the Yad Vashem Archives and was a postdoctoral researcher at the Centre for War Studies, University College Dublin. Currently, she is a Claims Conference Saul Kagan Fellow in Advanced Shoah Studies at Eötvös Loránd University. She is also the editorial assistant of *Eastern European Holocaust Studies* and the owner and editor of the Facebook history blog *Holokauszttörténetek*.

Anat Kutner holds a doctorate in Jewish history from Bar-Ilan University. She is the former director of the JDC Archives in Jerusalem, and a former department director at Yad Vashem Archives. She currently researches the connections between Jewish philanthropy and Jewish communities in Israel and around the world.

Roxy Moore is a doctoral candidate at Royal Holloway, University of London. Her research focuses on Anglo-Jewish humanitarianism, displaced persons, the Roma genocide, and British responses to the Holocaust. Roxy is the author of the educational website *The Holocaust Explained* and curator of the Wiener Holocaust Library's online exhibition *Tarnschriften: Covert Resistance in the Third Reich*. She has forthcoming chapters on Roma genocide consciousness in 1960s Britain (with Professor Becky Taylor) in *Holocaust Memory in the United Kingdom in the 1960s* (2026) and on the correspondence of the Jewish Committee for Relief Abroad in North Africa and Europe in *Letters and the Holocaust: Methodology, Cases, and Reflections* (2026). Outside of academia, Roxy has worked as a researcher and writer for the BBC Radio Four historical comedy show *You're Dead to Me*.

Katarzyna Person is a historian of the Holocaust and director of the Warsaw Ghetto Museum. She has published extensively on the history of Jews in Poland during the Holocaust and in the immediate postwar period. Person is the author of *Assimilated Jews in the Warsaw Ghetto, 1940–1943* (2014); *Warsaw Ghetto Police: The Jewish Order Service During the Nazi Occupation* (2021); *Przemysłowa Concentration Camp: The Camp, the Children, the Trials* (with Johannes-Dieter Steinert, 2023); and *Polnische Juden in der amerikanischen und der britischen Besatzungszone Deutschlands, 1945–1948* (2023), among others. She is the author and coauthor of five volumes of documents from the Ringelblum Archive and she heads the full edition of the Ringelblum Archive publication project at the Jewish Historical Institute in Warsaw.

Christine Schmidt is acting codirector of the Wiener Holocaust Library. Her research has focused on postwar tracing and documentation efforts, the Nazi concentration camp system, and collaboration and resistance in France and Hungary. Her current book project examines gender, migration, and knowledge production in the archive, and the underrecognized roles of Eva Reichmann and other Jewish women who shaped an important initiative to collect survivor accounts in the 1950s and '60s for the Wiener Library. She has a forthcoming chapter in *Holocaust Memory in the United Kingdom in the 1960s* (2026). Schmidt has recently published articles in the *Journal of Transport History*, the *European Review of History*, *American Imago*, *Culture Unbound*, and the *Journal of Holocaust Research*, and is coediting (with Sandra Lipner, Clara Dijkstra, and Charlie Knight) *Holocaust Letters: Methodologies, Cases, and Reflections* (2026) and (with Suzanne Bardgett and Dan Stone) *Survivors of Nazi Persecution: Beyond Camps and Forced Labour* (2024).

Joanna Sliwa is a historian at the Conference on Jewish Material Claims Against Germany (Claims Conference) where she also administers the Saul Kagan Fellowship in Advanced Shoah Studies and the University Partnership in Holocaust Studies. Joanna's research concerns the history of the Claims Conference, compensation for Holocaust survivors, and Jewish property restitution. Joanna's own scholarship focuses on the Holocaust in Poland and on Polish Jewish history. She is the author of *Jewish Childhood in Kraków: A Microhistory of the Holocaust* (2021), which received the 2020 Ernst Fraenkel Prize from the Wiener Holocaust Library, and *The Counterfeit Countess: The Jewish Woman Who Rescued Thousands of Poles During the Holocaust* (with Elizabeth White, 2024).

Dan Stone is professor of modern history and director of the Holocaust Research Institute at Royal Holloway, University of London. He is the author of numerous articles and books, including *Breeding Superman: Nietzsche, Race and Eugenics in Edwardian and Interwar Britain* (2002); *Histories of the Holocaust* (2010); *Goodbye to All That? The Story of Europe Since 1945* (2014); *The Liberation of the Camps: The End of the Holocaust and Its Aftermath* (2015); *Concentration Camps: A Very Short Introduction* (2019); *Fate Unknown: Tracing the Missing After World War II and the Holocaust* (2023); *The Holocaust: An Unfinished History* (2023, 2024); and *Psychoanalysis, Historiography and the Nazi Camps: Accounting for Survival* (2024). He is coeditor, with Mark Roseman, of volume 1 of the *Cambridge History of the Holocaust* (2025) and is currently writing a book on the Holocaust in Romania.

Xin Tong is assistant professor at Shanghai Academy of Global Governance & Area Studies, Shanghai International Studies University. She received her PhD from the Institute of Media and Communications, University of Hamburg. Her dissertation focused on a comparative perspective of the memory cultures of the Holocaust and Jewish exile in contemporary Germany and China. Her major research interests include memory studies, media theories, exile studies and migration studies. Recent publications include *Transmedia Remembering: Eine Fallstudie des Shanghaier Exils in Deutschland und China seit 1990* (2022); "Erinnern als interkulturelles Handeln am Beispiel des Shanghaier Exils," *Interkulturelles Forum der deutsch-chinesische Kommunikation* (2022); "Redeveloping the Heritage of Migration: The Shanghai Jewish Refugees Museum and Urban Transformation," in *Urban Exile: Theories, Methods, Research Practices*, ed. Burcu Dogramaci et al. (2023); and "Exilforschung in der chinesischen Germanistik: Rückblick, Stand und Perspektiven," *Jahrbuch für internationale Germanistik* 2 (2023).

Marek Tuszewicki is assistant professor at the Institute of Jewish Studies, Jagiellonian University in Krakow and the Katz Center for Advanced

Jewish Studies fellow for the 2024–25 fellowship devoted to new research at the intersection of Jewish studies and medicine. He is the author of the book *Frog Under the Tongue: Folk Medicine of Ashkenazi Jews*, trans. J. Taylor-Kucia (2021), as well as numerous articles. Currently he is researching, among others, topics related to the institutional and social aspects of old age and aging.

Lidia Zessin-Jurek is a historian and researcher of memory (Holocaust, Gulag) and refugee movements in the Polish lands. She holds a PhD from the European University Institute in Florence and has held fellowships from Imre Kertész Kolleg Jena, the German Historical Institute, Fordham University, and the New York Public Library. From 2019 to 2024, she worked on the European Research Council project "Unlikely Refuge" at the Masaryk Institute and Archives of the Czech Academy of Sciences in Prague and European Holocaust Research Infrastructure (EHRI). From 2024 to 2026, she was a postdoctoral fellow in the Master of Arts in Holocaust and Genocide Studies at Stockton University in New Jersey. With Katharina Friedla she coedited a volume on the wartime experiences of Polish Jews in the Soviet Union, *Syberiada Żydów polskich: Losy uchodźców z Zagłady* (2020), and she edited Meier Landau's memoir, *A Lost World: The Galician Shtetl and Siberia* (2023).

INDEX